2.

BEYOND FARMER FIRST

BEYOND FARMER FIRST

Rural people's knowledge,
agricultural research and
extension practice

Edited by IAN SCOONES and JOHN THOMPSON,
with a foreword by ROBERT CHAMBERS

INTERMEDIATE TECHNOLOGY PUBLICATIONS 1994

Intermediate Technology Publications Ltd
103–105 Southampton Row, London WC1B 4HH, UK

© International Institute for Environment and Development
1994

ISBN 1 85339 250 2 Paperback
    1 85339 237 5 Hardback

Typeset by Dorwyn Ltd, Rowlands Castle, Hants
Printed by SRP, Exeter

Contents

PART III: TRANSFORMING INSTITUTIONS AND CHANGING POLICIES

Acknowledgements

This book has its origins in a research programme initiated by the Sustainable Agriculture Programme of the International Institute for Environment and Development (IIED) during 1991. The Beyond Farmer First: Rural People's Knowledge, Agricultural Research and Extension Practice programme began with the commissioning of detailed field research by 12 collaborating institutions from Africa, Asia and Latin America. In October 1992, this core group met at the Institute of Development Studies at the University of Sussex, UK, together with almost 50 other researchers and field practitioners from every conceivable disciplinary background and from every corner of the world. The workshop aimed to examine how far agricultural research and extension practice had come since the landmark 1987 *Farmer First* conference and 1989 book. We would like to thank the many people who, in a variety of ways, made the workshop such a success.

This book contains an edited selection of the case studies and discussion papers prepared for the 1992 Beyond Farmer First workshop. It is divided into three main parts, following the pattern of the workshop. After the foreword by Robert Chambers and an introduction, the book starts with Theoretical Reflections on Knowledge, Power and Practice (Part I). This is followed by a detailed discussion of Methodological Innovations, Applications and Challenges (Part II). The book concludes with an examination of processes for Transforming Institutions and Changing Policies (Part III).

The Beyond Farmer First research programme, workshop and book have been made possible by the generous support of the Swedish International Development Authority (SIDA), the Swedish Agency for Research and Cooperation with Developing Countries (SAREC), the UK Overseas Development Administration (ODA), the Technical Centre for Agricultural and Rural Cooperation (CTA), and regional offices of the Ford Foundation and the International Development Research Centre (IDRC) of Canada.

Our editorial endeavours have benefitted enormously from many helpful comments and much needed encouragement from our friends and colleagues. We would especially like to thank Anthony J. Bebbington, Robert Chambers, Andrea Cornwall, Michael Drinkwater, Irene Guijt, Jules N. Pretty, Kathrin Schreckenberg, Parmesh Shah and Lori Ann Thrupp.

We would also like to thank all of the contributors to this book for their patience and tolerance during the editing process. This, at times, meant accepting truly savage reductions in length to their papers and, in some instances, the splitting of papers between different parts of the book.

The production of this book would have been impossible without secretarial and administrative support from Fiona Hinchcliffe, Kate Kirsopp-Reed, Ginni Tym and Deviani Vyas at the Sustainable Agricultural Programme of IIED.

IAN SCOONES and JOHN THOMPSON
Sustainable Agriculture Programme
International Institute for Environment and Development
London
February 1994

Abbreviations

AEA	Agroecosystem Analysis
AFNETA	Alley Farming Network for Tropical Africa
AKRSP	Aga Khan Rural Support Programme
ARPT	Adaptive Research and Planning Team, Zambia
BFF	Beyond Farmer First
CGIAR	Consultative Group on International Agricultural Research
CIAT	Centro Internacional de Agricultura Tropical
CIDE	Center for International Development and Environment (WRI)
CIMMYT	Centre for Maize and Wheat Research
CIP	Centro Internacional de la Papa (International Potato Centre)
EV	Extension Volunteer
FAO	Food and Agriculture Organization of the United Nations
FF	Farmer First
FPR	Farmer Participatory Research
FSR	Farming Systems Research
FSR/E	Farming Systems Research/Extension
GATT	General Agreement on Tariffs and Trade
GIS	Geographic Information Systems
GO	Governmental Organization
GRO	Grassroots Organization
IAK	Indigenous Agricultural Knowledge
IARC	International Agricultural Research Centre
ICLARM	International Centre for Living Aquatic Resources Management
ICRAF	International Centre for Research in Agroforestry
ICRISAT	International Centre for Research in the Semi-Arid Tropics
IDS	Institute of Development Studies, University of Sussex
IIED	International Institute for Environment and Development
IIMI	International Irrigation Management Institute
IITA	International Institute for Tropical Agriculture
ILCA	International Livestock Centre for Africa
ILEIA	Information Centre for Low-External-Input and Sustainable Agriculture
IPM	Integrated Pest Management
IRRI	International Rice Research Institute
ISNAR	International Service for National Agricultural Research
ITK	Indigenous Technical Knowledge
NARS	National Agricultural Research System
NGO	Non-Governmental Organization
ODI	Overseas Development Institute
PAR	Participatory Action Research
PRA	Participatory Rural Appraisal
PTD	Participatory Technology Development
R & D	Research and Development
R & E	Research and Extension

RPK	Rural People's Knowledge
RRA	Rapid Rural Appraisal
SWC	Soil and Water Conservation
T & V	Training and Visit
TAC	Technical Advisory Committee of the CGIAR
TOT	Transfer of Technology
VIDCO	Village Development Committee
WARDA	West African Rice Development Association
WRI	World Resources Institute

Foreword

Robert Chambers

In July 1987, some fifty natural and social scientists met for five days at the Institute of Development Studies at the University of Sussex, UK, for a workshop on Farmers and Agricultural Research: Complementary Methods. The aim was to bring together professionals who had been involving farmers in the research process to share expriences and methods, to take stock and to plan for the future. The focus was on the resource-poor farming systems on which perhaps 1.4 billion people depended for their livelihoods. The papers and discussions were edited to become the book *Farmer First: Farmer Innovation and Agricultural Research* (Chambers, Pacey and Thrupp, 1989).

The *Farmer First* book argues that the approaches and methods of transfer of technology which have served industrial and green revolution agriculture, do not fit the resource-poor farming of the third, complex, diverse and risk-prone agriculture. It contrasts the more traditional, technology-driven agriculture, with its standardizing package of practices, with the complementary farmer-first approach or paradigm, which generates baskets of choices to enable farmers to vary, complicate and diversify their farming systems. It stresses, illustrates and explores the abilities of resource-poor farmers to experiment, adapt and innovate; the importance of giving priority to farmers' agendas and knowledge; a range of practical approaches and methods for farmer participation in research; and the implications for outsiders' roles and for institutions.

Since 1989, when *Farmer First* was published, much has happened. The analysis and thrust of that book have been more and more widely accepted. Growing numbers of professionals have made personal changes and accepted risks by advocating and adopting a farmer-first approach. But many scientists, teachers and extensionists are still trapped in top-down, centre-outwards institutions and transfer of technology (TOT) thinking and action, where 'we' determine priorities, generate technologies and then transfer them to farmers, and where farmers' participation is limited to adoption. All too easily, the farmer-first label and the rhetoric of participation have been adopted without the substance. A huge task remains for the personal, professional and institutional changes needed to enable research and extension adequately to serve resource-poor farm families. The changes advocated in the *Farmer First* book are still nowhere near being realized on the scale or with the commitment needed.

The arguments, cases and recommendations of that book stand, if anything with more force now in 1994 than they did in 1989. Increasingly, they apply not just to complex, diverse, risk-prone agriculture, but also to green revolution and industrial agriculture, especially as subsidies are reduced and farming systems are complicated, diversified and intensified. The number of very poor people in the world has also increased. Those whose livelihoods depend on the third agriculture have risen by some 100 to 200 million, to a total now of over 1.5 billion. Sustainable livelihoods with adequate food and decent incomes from complex, diverse, risk-prone agriculture become an ever higher priority as pressures mount on the environment and on urban life and services through migration. So more than ever it is vital for professionals to struggle to learn how to serve vulnerable and resource-poor farmers better.

Fortunately, the frontiers of professional insights and methods have continued to be explored and opened up. As part of this, the Sustainable Agriculture Programme of the International Institute for Environment and Development conceived a three-year programme of research support and institutional collaboration entitled 'Beyond Farmer First: Rural People's Knowledge, Agricultural Research and Extension Practice'. Collaborators in a dozen countries prepared detailed case studies on the interplay between formal and informal knowledge systems and assessed the wider implications for agricultural research and extension practice. The cases were presented and reviewed, along with a variety of discussion papers prepared by a diverse group of researchers on key theoretical, methodological and institutional issues surrounding knowledge, power and agricultural science, at the Institute of Development Studies, University of Sussex, in October 1992. Together, they provide the basis for this book.

Readers who have been trying to achieve farmer-first objectives may note some new language and critical comments. Both the language and the comments deserve to be taken seriously. Scientists and extensionists who have been struggling in the field to offset biases against women, the poor and the excluded can take heart that they have already moved away from what is described here as 'naive populism'. In a farmer-first mode, more and more people have become sensitive to social inequality and differences, gaining insights and developing practices parallel to those presented and advocated in this book.

It is, though, more than just the language that has changed and moved on. Sometimes new words say old things, but important new things are also being said. Even when some of the major points of *Beyond Farmer First* can be found in earlier work, they are new here in emphasis, elaboration and empirical evidence. Let me summarize how these new emphases appear to me. Three sets of insights stand out.

The first concerns power and the pluralism of knowledge. Systems of knowledge are many. Among these, modern science is only one, though the most powerful and universal. Rural people's knowledge is in contrast 'situated', differing both by locality and by group and individual, and differing in its modes of experimenting and learning: different people know different things in different places, and learn new things in different ways. These differences are reflected in and reinforce power and weakness. Scientific establishments and local élites (male, less poor, 'progressive') link together and monopolize some types of knowledge, while those who are weaker, dispersed and local are marginalized. The terms 'farmer', 'farm family', 'household' and 'community' need to be broken open, and differences of gender, age, social group and capability recognized and acted on.

Nor is knowledge just a stock, but a *process*. The issue is not just 'whose knowledge counts?', but 'who knows "who has access to what knowledge" and who can generate new knowledge, and how?' Especially, the questions are how those who are variously poor, weak, vulnerable, female and excluded can be strengthened in their own observations, experiments and analysis to generate and enhance their own knowledge; how they can better seek, demand, draw down, own and use information; how they can share and spread knowledge among themselves; and how they can influence formal agricultural research priorities.

The second set of insights concerns behaviour, interactions and methods. Farmers, extensionists and scientists are seen as social actors. Power relations are reflected in how they interact. The changes of role entailed in farmer-first approaches – for extensionists, to become not top-down TOT conveyor belts, but convenors, facilitators, catalysts, consultants and searchers and suppliers for farmers – these require changes in attitudes, behaviour and methods. The roles of farmers as observers, analysts, experimenters, monitors and evaluators require strengthening through new approaches and methods. Beyond the farmer-first repertoire of the late 1980s, there are now, as reported in this book, new methods and combinations of methods available, many involving visual analysis by groups. Poor people, whether literate or not, have in the early 1990s, in more than a score of countries, shown a far greater capacity to map, model, diagram, estimate, rank, score, experiment and analyse than outsider professionals have believed. Farmers have shown unexpected capabilities (even surprising themselves) and facilitators have a new and growing repertoire of analytical tools for farmers to use.

The third theme and set of insights concerns institutions. It is even clearer now than it was before that for organizations to facilitate participation requires that their own procedures, style and culture be participatory. Ways forward are presented by networks, alliances, lateral links, interactive learning environments and organizational strategies which permit and promote scaling up and spread. There are examples already and immense future opportunities in government departments, farmers' organizations and international organizations, as well as the more obvious and better documented NGOs. There are implications for authority, communications, personal attitudes and behaviour and relations between organizations. The changes required are reversals, from top-down hierarchies with supply-driven orders, targets and supervision, to bottom-up articulation of needs with demand-drawn search and supply, and lateral sharing.

Reversals imply a new professionalism. This is not a rejection of modern scientific knowledge, of research stations and laboratories, of scientific method. These remain potent, have their own validity and will always have their place. Rather it is a broadening, balancing and up-ending, to give a new primacy to the realities and analyses of poor people themselves. These themes and insights are liberating for agricultural scientists and extensionists, opening up new ranges of experience and ways of working. The comfortable certainties of known normal science are then complemented by the exciting unknowns which follow from facilitating analysis by poor rural people and learning from and with them. Anyone concerned with agricultural research and extension who reads this book can hardly fail to be thrown back to questions basic to the agricultural professions:

● Whose criteria and priorities count?
● Whose knowledge?
● Whose modes of learning and analysis?
● Whose tests, experiments, observations, assessments?
● Whose reality counts?

The logic and realism of this new professionalism deserve promotion now more than ever. Decentralization, diversity and empowerment of the poor become key values to focus effort. Direct and personal facilitation in the field, and learning from, with and by farmers, is invested with professional prestige.

The new professionalism is dynamic. Change accelerates. We, outsider professionals concerned with agricultural research and extension, and more broadly, with rural development, have always to ask: what should we now be doing? The contributions to this book point forward to new issues, new challenges and new opportunities. To address these issues, meet these challenges and seize these opportunities makes demands in different ways on all actors in agricultural policy, research and extension: to question, innovate, take risks, embrace errors, and learn; to create and support new environments for learning and enabling; to develop, adopt and spread new methods and approaches; to form new alliances and associations; to articulate a vision of a new agriculture of equity and participation; and in many ways, in many places, to work to make that vision real, with poor farmers gaining more say and playing more of a part in the processes of agricultural research and extension, the better to serve and sustain their lives and livelihoods.

Introduction

IAN SCOONES and JOHN THOMPSON

Challenging the professions

In the closing paragraph of the preface to *Farmer First: Farmer Innovation and Agricultural Research*, the book's editors, Robert Chambers, Arnold Pacey and Lori Ann Thrupp (1989: xv) declared that it was:

> not a final statement, but a part of a process . . . We hope it will stimulate and encourage readers, of whatever profession or discipline, to learn from farmers' innovations, to put farmers' agendas first, and to support practical participation by farmers. Above all, we hope it will encourage many more to join in pioneering and writing, adding to and sharing experience and methods. For it is through hands-on experience and efforts to communicate that the practical potentials of farmer-first approaches and methods will spread and be realized.

In the intervening five years between *Farmer First* and the publication of this book, there has been a radical rethinking of the role of farmers – and professionals – in agricultural research and extension. Prevailing theories of the social construction of knowledge have been questioned; innovations in the conception and application of participatory methodologies for research and development have occurred faster than the formal literature has been able to document; power-laden relationships between agricultural scientists, extensionists and poor farmers have been challenged; and the bureaucratic organizational structures and rigid operational procedures found in most conventional agricultural research, extension and teaching institutions have been confronted.

While not all of these transformations can be attributed to *Farmer First*, this populist perspective has made a significant contribution to the *process* of change by eloquently and forcefully articulating a vision of 'the third agriculture . . . complex in its farming systems, diverse in its environments, and risk-prone' . . . that gives priority to 'not just sustainable agriculture, but sustainable livelihoods based on agriculture' (Chambers *et al.*, 1989: xvii–xviii). It is a vision shared by growing numbers of agronomists, anthropologists, ecologists, economists, entomologists, extensionists, geographers, planners, sociologists – and farmers.

The need to move beyond *Farmer First*

The thesis underlying *Farmer First* is that much of the problem with conventional agricultural research and extension has been in the processes of generating and transferring technology, and that much of the solution lies

1

in farmers' own capacities and priorities. The interest and support that this populist philosophy has received since the late-1980s has led to a virtual revolution in the agricultural sciences; some have even termed it a 'paradigm shift'. As a result, conventional approaches to agricultural research and extension have come under increasing scrutiny. Moreover, in national and international agricultural research centres, universities, government agencies and NGOs, there is a growing acceptance of the need to involve local people as active partners in all aspects of the research and development process. The focus is on bridging gaps between development professionals and resource-poor farmers, and on finding new ways to understand local knowledge, strengthen local capacities and meet local needs.

While many hail this populist perspective as a step in the right direction, others have argued that such an approach fails to confront the impact of power on relations between different groups within farming communities or between local people and/outside change agents. Further, it does not capture the complex sociocultural and political economic dimensions of knowledge creation, innovation, transmission and application within rural societies and scientific organizations. Because they do not adequately address these fundamental issues of power and knowledge, critics charge that *Farmer First* initiatives often encounter many of the same problems as conventional transfer-of-technology (TOT) strategies.

Background to the book

In 1991, the Sustainable Agriculture Programme of the International Institute for Environment and Development launched a three-year programme of research support and institutional collaboration, entitled Beyond Farmer First: Rural People's Knowledge, Agricultural Research and Extension Practice. Its purpose was to challenge the populist conception of power and knowledge, to analyse questions of 'difference' by asking 'whose knowledge counts?', and to dispel the notion that agricultural transformation is a straightforward process that can be improved simply by the interventions and innovations of sensitive external support agencies.

This collection of papers arose out of that programme. In October 1992, some 60 physical and social scientists from a diverse range of public, private and voluntary national and international institutions on six continents gathered at the Institute of Development Studies (IDS), University of Sussex, in Brighton, UK, for five days to take stock of how far the idea of a 'third agriculture' had progressed, giving due recognition to its achievements and drawing lessons from its shortcomings. The event was divided into three main parts: (1) theory; (2) method; and (3) institutions. These issues were examined in intensive working group sessions, during which the participants shared detailed case studies and discussion papers which examined the interplay between formal and informal knowledge systems and assessed the implications for agricultural research and extension practice. The case study themes ranged from indigenous soil classification in Zambia to potato production in the Andes to integrated pest management in Java. The discussion papers considered crucial theoretical, methodological and institutional issues in agricultural science, drawing on concrete case examples to reinforce their arguments.

The challenge for both the case study and discussion paper authors was to assess how people in different agroecological and sociocultural contexts make sense of and deal with constraining and enabling processes related to agricultural research and extension practice; how they attempt to enlist one another in these various endeavours; and how they use relations of power in their attempts to gain access to and control of vital environmental and sociopolitical resources.

The workshop deliberations led the participants to ask how these contending parties could be brought together to use conflict creatively (i.e., constructively, rather than destructively) and negotiate mutually beneficial outcomes. Working with this 'creative conflict' was seen as a way to move beyond zero-sum, either-or results (where one side 'wins', and, consequently, the other side 'loses') towards creating conditions out of which empowering and enabling research and development activities could arise.

Structure and objective of the book

This book represents a distillation of the more than 700 pages of material prepared for the Beyond Farmer First workshop. Following the structure of that event, the book is divided into three parts, the first on theoretical considerations, the second on methodological challenges, and the third on institutional innovations. Each part begins with a broad introductory overview which sets the stage for the more focused case material and discussion papers that follow.

The authors begin their papers by viewing 'knowledge' as a social process and 'knowledge systems' in terms of a multiplicity of *actors* and *networks* through which certain kinds of technical and social information are communicated and negotiated, and not as single, cohesive structures, stocks or stores. The guiding phrase is *the analysis of difference*, which suggests that knowledge is manifold, discontinuous and dispersed, not singular, cohesive and systematized. From this vantage point, knowledge emerges as a product of the interaction and dialogue between different actors (e.g., 'insiders' (farmers) and 'outsiders' (development agents, extensionists, researchers, etc.) and networks of actors (e.g., resource poor/resource rich, men/women, old/young, junior/senior staff, etc.), often with competing interests, conflicting allegiances and incomplete knowledge.

The principal objective of this book is to not only complement the achievements of *Farmer First*, but supersede it in at least four ways:

(1) By investigating *who knows* through the analysis of differences in knowledge derivation, adaptation, and diffusion by gender, ethnicity, class, age, religion, etc;

(2) By examining *access to and control of resources and processes*, including relationships of power between outsiders and insiders and among different kinds of outsiders and insiders;

3

(3) By presenting and comparing experiences with *new participatory methodologies* for enabling local people to conduct their own analyses and establish their own research and extension priorities;

(4) By outlining what these new perspectives and methods mean for *change in institutions and policy*.

The first two objectives require a more rigorous and sophisticated analysis of the theoretical issues surrounding our understanding of the relationship between knowledge, power, and agricultural science than has been found in most farmer-first literature to date. This analysis will demonstrate that agricultural research and extension, far from being discrete, rational acts, are in fact part of a process of coming to terms with conflicting interests, a process in which choices are made, alliances formed, exclusions effected, and worldviews imposed. By going *beyond Farmer First*, this theoretically-informed perspective accommodates and articulates an image of agricultural development, even at the local level, for what it is: a highly ideological and political process, not a series of carefully planned and rational acts. Theoretical reflections on knowledge, power and practice are the subject of Part I of this book.

The third objective demands more attention to methodological challenges, including a critical assessment of the approaches now being promoted widely for supporting farmer participatory research, extension and experimentation. Issues of quality and ethics, as well as method, need to be addressed. This means asking not only *'who knows?'*, but *'who does not – and why?'* The methodological challenges prompted by these questions are examined by the papers in Part II.

The final objective calls for a systematic appraisal of the changes now taking place within various public, private and voluntary institutions, including their operational procedures and organizational cultures, as well as their agricultural and rural development policies. A variety of institutional innovations are discussed in Part III, where a number of fundamental questions are asked: Can large institutions support discrete, site-specific, local-level, farmer-first activities, and will these activities be viable after the large institutions withdraw their assistance? Can a farmer-first perspective make these institutions more accountable to local people? Can farmer-first initiatives, as promoted by these institutions, contribute to a process of collective self-empowerment and sustainable development?

Understanding complexity

One of the major conclusions of the Farmer First workshop (Chambers *et al.*, 1989) was the need to further refine participatory research and development methodologies that recognize the complex, diverse and risk-prone environments of resource-poor people. A 'sustainable livelihoods' focus was seen to be a central feature of putting farmers' priorities first on the agricultural research and development agenda. Without doubt there have been significant advances in the development of 'farmer-friendly' approaches to understanding the complexity of agricultural and livelihood

4

systems, but certain key areas remain a challenge for research and development practitioners.

It is increasingly recognized that agriculture is a complex social process, not simply a complex, diverse and risky technical activity. This implies new theoretical as well as methodological challenges, many of which we highlight in our introductory overview paper to Part I. Combining social theory with empirical evidence, Michael Drinkwater (Zambia) and Norman Long and Magdalena Villareal (Mexico) then extend these theoretical discussions to assess the importance of multiple, sometimes competing, actors as they engage in the vigorous and rather messy business of knowledge generation, transmission and application. Both contributions demonstrate that we must develop a more adequate analytical approach to understanding the relationships between policy, practice and outcome than a farmer-first perspective has so far provided. David Marsden adds other challenges: the need for management, negotiation and arbitration processes to be linked to research and extension interventions 'from above' and the support of struggles for access and control of resources 'from below'. To reinforce these points, the contrasting interests and contending worldviews of different internal and external actors in development programmes and the potentials for conflict and compromise are highlighted in two detailed case studies by Frank Matose and Billy Mukamuri (Zimbabwe) and Maria Salas (Peru).

A major theme running through many of the contributions to Part I and later sections of this book is the analysis of difference: how to understand how social difference (due to age, gender, status, wealth, political influence and so on) affects perceptions, actions, and access to and control of resources, including ideas and information. James Fairhead and Melissa Leach illustrate this concept with a case study from Guinea in West Africa. They show how the social dimension of local complexity is critical to understanding how rural livelihoods are composed.

This social dimension of difference can be complicated further by an equally complex agroecological dimension which must also be understood, as Patrick Sikana's discussion of indigenous soil classification in Zambia and Johan Pottier's examination of 'family secrets' and agricultural experimentation in Rwanda reveal. As these contributions show, it is not only the *patterns* of difference that are important, it is also the *processes* by which such differences are expressed that play a significant role.

In short, the social, political and ecological nature of agricultural development must be set centre stage if we are to comprehend the dynamic nature of rural livelihoods and develop appropriate methodologies and policies, a point made forcefully by Anthony Bebbington. Basing his argument on experiences in Andean America, he calls for a more holistic 'food systems' perspective as opposed to the narrower 'farming systems' approach for understanding rural people's capacities and constraints.

Of course, these arguments are not entirely new. They draw on long-running debates in social anthropology, rural sociology, political economy, as well as agriculture. What is new is the recognition that a merging of theoretical and methodological traditions, making use of a variety of insights from different sources, offers the way forward in 'learning how to learn'.

Whose knowledge counts? Multiple actors, control and conflict

Farmer First provided a powerful argument that farmers' voices needed to be heard during the process of agricultural development and that the methodological tools used by 'us' (the so-called 'outsiders') had to gain insights from 'them' (the so-called 'insiders'). This argument has been increasingly effective in persuading mainstream research and development to take farmers' views seriously. Understanding farmers' perspectives has been a major influence in the development of participatory research methodologies, such as visualization and diagramming, as illustrated in case studies by Parmesh Shah (India) and Karen Schoonmaker Freudenberger (Senegal).

However, in counterposing 'insiders' and 'outsiders' in a dichotomous contrast, this populist view simplifies the role of the range of actors involved in participatory inquiry and activities, and so excludes important dimensions of such encounters. As a number of papers in Parts I and II reveal, reflection on the role of different actors is critical to the effectiveness of methodologies.

Interactions with farmers occur in very different settings, with radically different implications for the role and influence of external actors. For instance, in a TOT approach, the extension agent or research officer is in the powerful, controlling position, being the purveyor of 'new' knowledge to farmers. In participatory research which attempts to understand different farmers' local knowledges, but remains essentially extractive, the researcher is equally in a dominant position (e.g., Farming Systems Research-Extension (FSR-E), Rapid Rural Appraisal (RRA) and many conventional anthropological studies). By contrast, participatory research and development may focus on empowerment, either through conscientization, activism and confrontation (e.g. the Participatory Action Research (PAR) or Theatre for Development traditions) or through facilitating and catalysing local-level learning, analysis and action (e.g. some of the more recent Participatory Rural Appraisal work). In these settings, the external actor is still present and influential, but the research is so bound up in action that this influence is seen as part of a participatory and empowering process, as described by Andrea Cornwall, Irene Guijt and Alice Welbourn in their introductory overview to Part II.

As a consequence, participatory methodologies mean different things to different people. Interactive, visual tools and techniques, such as mapping and diagramming, may be used in a variety of settings: as part of conventional extension for conveying an externally derived 'message' to farmers; in more extractive research that draws on farmers' knowledge and perceptions; and in action-research work that has a focus on empowerment. All of these approaches have their role in agricultural development. But it is important to be explicit about the expectations and roles of external actors and their relationships with local people. The danger is that 'participation' becomes trivialized by glib generalizations and sloganeering.

There is also a danger that crucial questions about quality, consistency, trustworthiness and ethics are overlooked. These sensitive issues are

6

addressed in provocative papers by Janice Jiggins and Ann Waters-Bayer (Nigeria), in which they focus our attention on quality and ethics in methodological innovation, training and application.

Experimentation by and with farmers

Proponents of a farmer-first approach argue that greater attention needs to be paid to on-farm conditions and that farmers need to play a more active role in agricultural experimentation. They claim that greater participation of farmers in on-farm, adaptive research will result in a technology development process more attuned to local conditions and local priorities. Conventional on-farm research, largely designed and managed by external researchers, was thus transformed into farmer participatory research (FPR), where farmers became the central actors in the research and experimentation process.

FPR has had some significant successes; some of which are reported by Michael Drinkwater, John Farrington and Anthony Bebbington, Sam Fujisaka, Peter Gubbels, and Patrick Sikana in Part III. But some FPR approaches have only offered farmers the chance to participate in the agricultural scientists' research projects, rather than providing the opportunity for true collegial learning. In most cases, the basic terms and conditions, and particularly the experimental methodologies, are still set by the researcher.

That said, there is now an increasing recognition of farmers' own research and experimental investigation. In Part II, three case studies from West Africa, by Arthur Stolzenbach (Mali), David Millar (Ghana), and Paul Richards (Sierra Leone), demonstrate that experimentation is a process of inquiry that runs continuously as part of farmers' own agricultural performances. A central challenge discussed at the Beyond Farmer First workshop and reflected in the papers collected in this book, is for agricultural researchers to appreciate and understand this process of farmer experimentation and to seek ways of articulating on-farm research with farmers' own research projects and modes of inquiry. Three different ways of meeting this challenge are suggested by the papers in Part II.

The first recognizes the comparative advantages of scientific investigation and argues that farmers can be taught improved forms of experimentation using scientific methods, such as controlled plot comparisons or enhanced examination techniques (e.g., microscopes or laboratory analysis). Jeffrey Bentley and Yunita Winarto offer examples from Central America and Indonesia where successful innovations in pest management have arisen from researchers introducing appropriate techniques for manipulating and enhancing predator-prey dynamics which build upon farmers' own knowledge and observational skills.

The second approach argues that some farmers already follow scientific methods of inquiry, such that agricultural innovations result from the progressive accumulation of experimental insights. Richards argues that some farmers in Sierra Leone follow a scientific rice-breeding strategy through progressive selection of land-races. He contends that effective linkages

7

with formal science (in this case crop breeding) is best effected through those farmers who follow such scientific methods of analysis.

The third emphasizes farmers' own experimentation and argues that this should be treated as a form of inquiry in its own right and not be judged by the criteria set by Western science. Trying to force farmers' own methods of inquiry into a straight-jacket provided by researchers' constructs undermines the value and potential of farmers' experimentation. Stolzenbach and Millar provide cases from Mali and Ghana that examine the processes of farmer experimentation and illustrate how, in some important respects, farmers' own methods of inquiry differ from those of conventional science. The challenge is thus to seek ways in which farmers' experiments are shared both with other farmers and with research scientists, on their own terms, in order to encourage learning.

These alternative approaches to FPR are, of course, not mutually exclusive. A combined approach which draws on the strengths and potentials of each is clearly the best option.

Scaling-up: from the micro to the macro

The papers in Part II of this book reflect the important advances that have been made in the development of methodologies for local-level analysis by and with farmers. However, relating such findings to wider issues and scaling up local-level successes remains a major challenge. Discussions at the *Beyond Farmer First* workshop posed three related questions:

- How should the largely qualitative, case-study oriented, participatory methodologies (such as PRA, PTD and related approaches) relate to more formal, quantitative approaches to inquiry? What are the comparative advantages of different approaches? What are the appropriate criteria for trustworthiness for each?
- How can participatory inquiry methodologies be linked with the classic methods of rural development planning, such as conventional appraisal approaches, log-frame planning, indicator-based monitoring and evaluation techniques and economic analysis so as to bring local-level perspectives into the mainstream?
- How can local-level insights derived from participatory investigations articulate with larger-scale policy formulation and planning approaches at regional or even national levels? What methodological approaches are needed to allow the range of interest groups to be heard in the process? What approaches to conflict management and process negotiation are needed to facilitate such planning or policy analysis?

These questions remain a major frontier for methodological development; easy answers are not available. Nevertheless, experience in scaling up local-level analysis and relating participatory inquiry to more conventional forms of analysis is growing. For instance, Lori Ann Thrupp, Bruce Cabarle and Aaron Zazueta (Part II) present examples from Central and South America, where participatory approaches and grassroots initiatives have

8

influenced and shaped higher-level policy and planning in natural resource management.

For participatory approaches to have a wider impact, methodological innovations must take place within a strategic, flexible, open institutional environment. This institutional and policy context is the subject of Part III of this book.

Institutional and policy issues: getting the context right

The backdrop for institutional change in the mid-1990s must take into account major policy shifts in many parts of the world. For instance, structural adjustment policies have resulted in a decreased level of state service provision and the need for NGOs and grassroots organizations to take a more active role in many parts of the world, both north and south. Similarly, decreasing levels of both government and international donor funding has resulted in a contraction of conventional research and extension activities, requiring alternative solutions to be sought. Finally, democratization of political processes, combined with trends towards decentralization, offer hope of greater accountability in agricultural development strategies in some parts of the world.

A shift from the linear, TOT approach to a process of agricultural research and development driven by demands from farmers potentially coincides with many of these broader policy shifts. The TOT mode is reliant on extensive external support for both basic and applied research in order to supply the extension delivery system. A 'top-down' technology development and extension approach, typified by the Training and Visit (T & V) system, is compatible with centralized institutions, able to offer a standardized conveyor-belt supply of packages or messages to farmers.

By contrast, a farmer-first approach envisages a more devolved and decentralized arrangement, focused on farmers' identified needs and led by local demands, rather than external supply. Such a system is arguably more cost-effective and resource efficient, and is reliant on a diversity of different types of organizations, each offering different skills and support. But transforming organizations – and the individuals within them – is by no means an easy task. The TOT approach is firmly entrenched in institutional cultures, and in management and financial procedures, and is continuously reinforced by training in mainstream educational institutions.

The papers in Part III offer insights into some notable experiments in institutional innovation, with cases ranging from Australia to Zambia. The authors argue for the involvement of a diverse range of institutional actors, and, in particular, for the forging of equitable alliances between them. A recognition of institutional comparative advantages in fulfilling agricultural development functions provides opportunities for a variety of organizational linkages and associations. John Farrington and Anthony Bebbington review a range of cases that show the potential benefits of links between national agricultural research systems (NARSs), international agricultural research centres (IARCs) and a variety of NGOs. Drawing on a case from Sri Lanka, Norman Uphoff argues for links between local organizations

9

and state agencies in the management of complex agricultural development, such as large-scale irrigation. Bebbington draws on the experience of federated farmers' organizations in Latin America to make the case for interest group alliances in order to lobby for policy change, funding and other forms of external support. Jorge Uquillas shows how diverse interest groups compete in the agricultural policy arena in the Ecuadorian Amazon, making the important point that the social and political context of institutional change is key.

The future of agricultural research and extension

The dilemmas faced by agricultural research institutions are highlighted by Sam Fujisaka and Kwesi Atta-Krah, who review the experience of the centres of the Consultative Group for International Agricultural Research (CGIAR) and associated regional research networks. While the rhetoric of participation has been embraced and some important experiments in participatory research with farmers have been initiated, the CG Centres remain wedded to the linear, technology transfer mode. This is likely to remain the case, as the Centres are being encouraged to concentrate on so-called strategic or basic research activities. Workshop groups questioned this strategy, arguing that ultimately strategic and basic research must be informed by farmers' priorities lest it runs the risk of being high-quality science with no applied relevance. Further, if the mandate of the CGIAR remains the provision of support to national systems, then one key area of priority research must be the development of participatory methodologies for agricultural research.

Most innovation in this area is the domain of those institutions with good field connections. Papers by Peter Gubbels and Patrick Sikana provide two cases from Africa where institutional innovations have occurred, allowing farmers a greater role in agricultural research. Gubbels reports on an NGO-supported project in Burkina Faso, while Sikana focuses on a government adaptive research team in Zambia. As these cases show, both government organizations and NGOs are capable of successful innovation, as long as the right combination of adventurous, innovative individuals and supportive organizational procedures (including flexible funding) are available to make it happen.

The future role of extension is the subject of the next set of papers in Part III. Niels Röling argues that the new challenges of a farmer-first approach to agricultural development requires a complete rethink of extension services. If extension services are to be transformed from technical delivery conduits to organizations that are client-oriented, supplying a service that is demand-led, then a new profession of extension must emerge. Parmesh Shah's paper offers a glimpse of what a transformed extension system might look like. Run by and paid for by rural communities, village extensionists in Gujarat, India, offer services such as watershed planning which are in high demand. The service organization, in this case an NGO, acts as a low-profile facilitator, providing initial training and capacity building support, seed funding for micro-projects and links with wider networks

10

of technical and research expertise. It is envisaged that some of these roles will ultimately be taken on by a federated body of village organizations.

In a very different setting, Andrew Campbell provides another case of demand-led research and extension support: the Landcare programme in Australia. Here rural people join together in groups to carry out catchment planning and environmental monitoring in their own areas. Simple tools and techniques are used to develop farm and catchment base maps and monitor water quality. Local Landcare group members own the information, are committed to dealing with its implications, and are less intimidated by the technical wizardry of the scientific bureaucracy. As a consequence, a new role for rural research and extension is emerging in Australia. In the search for a sustainable agriculture, land users now need support less in the form of technical packages, but more in the form of facilitation and co-ordination of group processes, assistance with planning and technical support in the compilation and analysis of community-collected data.

Training needs

As these papers make clear, there are a growing number of examples where shifts to a farmer-first approach are occurring. So often, however, the missing link in sustained institutional transformation is in the area of training. With new professional challenges for agricultural research, extension and development workers, the need for fundamental changes in curricula and teaching styles in educational institutions become essential ingredients for success. In addition to the conventional technical understanding of agriculture, agricultural professionals must now learn skills of facilitation, co-ordination and institutional development that previously were never thought part of the agricultural professional's kit-bag. These must be supported by attitudes and behaviours that encourage listening and learning, rather than lecturing and prescribing. Few agricultural training institutions offer this kind of education. One notable exception is Hawkesbury College (the University of Western Sydney) in Australia where students are not 'taught' in the conventional sense, but take an active part in their own learning. In the final paper of Part III, Richard Bawden describes the evolution of a flexible learning organization committed to a people-centred systems approach to agricultural education and development.

Basic conditions

The cases presented in this book, along with a growing number of others, provide us with a new vision of institutional change. Jules Pretty and Robert Chambers describe the core elements in their introductory overview paper to Part III: changes in attitudes and behaviours; shifts in professional reward systems to support change; organizational and management structures that encourage innovation and experimentation; institutional alliances and networks that foster effective learning and training; and professional support to encourage sharing and spread.

Indications are that with an effective combination of the basic elements that encourage a pattern of agricultural development which puts farmers first, returns from agricultural development investment can increase (Shah, Part II). Demonstrating this impact is an important challenge for the coming years. As more institutional innovations are put in place, there is an urgent need to monitor and assess both the successes and the failures. For without such honest and rigorous evaluation, the mainstream approaches will cling tenaciously on and *Farmer First* (and its successors) will be dismissed as 'populist pipedreams' (Gubbels, Part III). Cautionary words written twenty years ago remain well worth heeding today:

> All too often participation claimed from the platform becomes appropriation and privilege when translated into action in the field . . . This should scarcely be surprising, except to those who, for ideological reasons or because they are simple minded, or more commonly for a combination of these causes, reify 'the people' and 'participation' and push them beyond the reach of empirical analysis (Chambers, 1974: 109).

PART I

Theoretical Reflections on Knowledge, Power and Practice

Part 1: Introduction

The papers in Part I offer a variety of theoretical reflections on knowledge, pointing in particular to the implications of power and control for agricultural research and extension practice. While some of the theoretical literature is somewhat daunting, as it is often rendered inaccessible by complex language and obscure concepts, it does offer some important insights relevant to practical field-level concerns. The overview paper by Ian Scoones and John Thompson provides an introduction to this debate by contrasting different representations of rural people's knowledge and emphasizing the shift away from a positivist view of knowledge and a populist ideal for development intervention. In particular, the overview highlights the need to understand the social and political contexts within which different actors – farmers, researchers, extensionists, development workers – operate.

These themes are picked up by other papers in Part I which each illustrate theoretical concerns with practical examples. Michael Drinkwater draws on a case from Zambia which examines how viewing knowledge in context is critical for farming systems research and the development of effective agricultural research programmes. These issues are explored further in a detailed exposition by Norman Long and Magdalena Villareal on the interweaving of knowledge and power in development 'interfaces' and the development of an actor-oriented perspective. They use brief cases from Mexico to highlight the dilemmas posed by participatory approaches to development which make claims of 'empowerment'. In the next paper, David Marsden argues that new forms of 'indigenous management' will be required to meet these challenges; these require the support of an interpretative social science which will help uncover the hidden and ignored agendas of local actors.

The cultural dimension of the knowledge conflict is explored by Maria Salas in a detailed case study from Peru. Salas shows how Western science has dominated agricultural science in Peru, with its concerns with researching and extending the 'scientific potato', and how this has excluded local Andean knowledges. The paper concludes with an assessment of potentials for developing a common language where scientific and local knowledges meet on equal terms. The local political consequences of galvanizing indigenous knowledge for woodland management are discussed by Frank Matose and Billy Mukamuri with a case study from Zimbabwe. Their paper critically analyses the conflicts arising both locally and between local people and outsiders in the context of a natural resource development project.

The ways knowledge is expressed, classified and used in agricultural and environmental management is the subject of the next three papers. James Fairhead and Melissa Leach demonstrate that a 'who knows what?' approach to examining rural people's knowledge may be misleading. Drawing on case material from Guinea in West Africa, they assert that local

15

people have a fairly integrated understanding of agroecological processes, and that, although certain differences in knowledge may be declared publicly, this may reflect power differences rather than any 'real' knowledge differentiation. Patrick Sikana's contribution reveals how local classifications of soil in northern Zambia do not necessarily match those of scientists; instead, farmers' constructions of local reality are a reflection of the dynamic and strategic nature of local knowledge. Conventional positivist science must, Sikana contends, come to terms with this if it is to seek effective partnerships with farmers. The dangers inherent in encouraging such partnerships are further discussed in a case study of urban agriculture in Rwanda by Johan Pottier. Pottier explains why farmers often keep their agricultural knowledge secret, and share it only with close friends or relatives, not strangers. He warns against knowledge appropriation by experts in their quest to understand indigenous knowledge.

The final paper in Part I argues that we must take account of the wider context within which rural people live when designing any research or development activity. Knowledge is neither static nor simply 'local', but is situated within a dynamic setting which goes well beyond the farm gate and the rural household. Anthony Bebbington illustrates this point with case material from the Andes, which shows how rural people's knowledge is embedded within a wider sociocultural and political economic context. In order to comprehend issues of knowledge, power and agricultural practice, we must understand these wider structural conditions and their role in shaping local livelihood strategies.

Knowledge, power and agriculture — towards a theoretical understanding

IAN SCOONES and JOHN THOMPSON

Introduction

In this overview, we assess the populist perspective on agricultural research and extension practice, commonly referred to as the farmer-first perspective (Chambers *et al.*, 1989), in the light of recent research into the complex questions concerning the social construction of knowledge and relations of power. We begin with a synthesis of some of the major themes surrounding the analysis and implications of rural people's knowledge (RPK) systems for agricultural science and community-based development, drawing on a large and diverse body of literature from anthropology, ecology, geography, sociology and other disciplines. Through this analysis, we aim to demonstrate that agricultural research and extension practice, far from being a set of discrete, rational, systematic acts, are in fact part of a dynamic process of coming to terms with conflicting interests, changing alliances and competing worldviews. By moving *beyond* farmer-first, this

16

theoretically informed perspective challenges the populist conception of agricultural science as a series of carefully planned and logical acts, and shows it to be a highly social and political process.

The literature examined generally falls into three broad categories:

- *The nature of knowledge* – anthropological, cultural ecological, ethnographic and phenomenological analyses of rural people's knowledge and formal knowledge systems.
- *The interactions of actors* – sociological examinations of farmer–researcher–extensionist encounters; assessments of the development, adoption, adaptation and diffusion of ideas and innovations.
- *The institutional context* – the political economic and sociological analyses of the organizational culture and management of research and extension services and development planning.

We do not intend this paper to be either an exhaustive review of the literature or a definitive analysis of knowledge, power and agricultural science. However, we do endeavour to highlight different sides of the debate and suggest some key theoretical challenges for the future. We also attempt to establish a preliminary conceptual framework through which a number of common theoretical threads can be interwoven. Our ultimate goal is to explore the linkages between the contending theoretical perspectives and assess the potential for an effective and equitable partnership between RPK and formal knowledge systems through adaptive, people-centred, agricultural research and extension practice.

The following sections expand on this discussion, exploring the contrasting representations of RPK, the consequences of taking a sociopolitically differentiated view of scientific and rural people's knowledges, the methodological challenges inherent in a reevaluation of the theory of knowledge and power and the institutional implications of facilitating reflexive encounters between competing, sometimes conflicting, groups involved in agricultural research and extension. We conclude with some reflections on the opportunities for productive engagement between formal agricultural science and rural people.

Contrasting representations of rural people's knowledge

In the literature, Rural People's Knowledge (RPK), is presented by observers in three contrasting ways:

- RPK is 'primitive', 'unscientific', 'wrong', etc. Formal research and extension must 'educate', 'direct' and 'transform' rural people's production and livelihood strategies in order to 'develop' (i.e. modernize) them.
- RPK is a 'valuable and under-utilized resource' and needs to be intensively and extensively studied, and 'incorporated' into formal research and extension practice in order to make agriculture and rural development strategies more 'sustainable'.
- Neither RPK nor Western science can be regarded as unitary 'bodies' or 'stocks' of knowledge. Instead, they represent contrasting multiple epistemologies produced within particular agroecological, sociocultural

and political economic settings. The interaction of RPK with current research and extension practice must address fundamental issues of power and need in development.

Each of these representations defines the concept of 'development' in a distinct way. In the first instance, development is seen as a modernizing force or process, one which acts to transform traditional practices. This remains·the conventional thinking in many settings of agricultural research and extension. The superiority of 'rational science' is assumed and the pursuit of change (development) is derived almost exclusively from the findings of the research station and transmitted to the farmer through hierarchical, technically oriented extension services. Farmers are seen as either 'adopters' or 'rejectors' of technologies, but not as originators of either technical knowledge or improved practice. This is generally known as the transfer-of-technology (TOT) model or approach (Chambers and Ghildyal, 1985; Sachs, 1992).

Since the late 1970s, the TOT view has been challenged by the advocates of the second perspective. This position sees the starting point of development as an active and equitable partnership between rural people, researchers and extensionists (Howes and Chambers, 1979; Chambers, 1983; Farrington and Martin, 1988; Chambers et al., 1989). Outsiders are viewed primarily as catalysts or facilitators of the open exchange of ideas and information between various interested groups (e.g. farmers, local leaders, researchers, extensionists, etc.). Proponents of this populist approach emphasize the rational nature and sophistication of rural people's knowledge and believe that knowledge can be blended with or incorporated into formal scientific knowledge systems. They argue that if local knowledge and capacities are granted legitimacy within scientific and development communities, existing research and extension services will pay greater attention to the priorities, needs and capacities of rural people and, in the end, achieve more effective and lasting results (Thomas-Slater et al., 1991; Thompson, 1991). Over the past decade, a good deal of the work in farming systems research (Ashby et al., 1989; Collinson, 1982; Lightfoot and Noble, 1992), agroecology (Altieri, 1987), agroecosystem analysis (Conway, 1985), rapid and participatory rural appraisal (Khon Kaen, 1987; Chambers, 1992b; IIED, 1988–present) and other approaches have continued to develop and promote different aspects of this thinking.

The original focus of the populists was on indigenous *technical* knowledge (ITK), an emphasis indicative of a rather narrow interpretation of local people's knowledge and abilities that concentrated attention on their role in agricultural production (IDS, 1979; Biggs and Clay, 1981). In recent years, this perspective has been expanded to consider indigenous knowledge as *cultural* knowledge, producing and reproducing mutual understanding and identity among the members of a farming community, where local technical knowledge, skills and capacities are inextricably linked to non-technical ones (i.e. cultural, ecological and sociological factors: Richards, 1985, 1986; Moock and Rhoades, 1992). In this way, 'ITK' becomes 'RPK'. Although this change is still in the making, it appears that this broader conception of indigenous knowledge is gaining wider currency.

18

This shift has involved the development and/or modification of methodologies for examining and supporting local knowledge, with parallel changes occurring in professional attitudes and behaviour towards local people's capacities, practices and values. These methodological, professional and institutional transformations now under way are seen by some as part of a broader paradigm shift in the direction of greater empowerment of local people, local level adaptive ('bottom-up') planning and low external-input agriculture.

This emerging farmer-first or populist paradigm has had considerable success over the past decade in challenging the predominance of the modernization paradigm, in which RPK has been discredited, ignored or generally undervalued. A number of centres of the Consultative Group for International Agricultural Research (CGIAR) have adopted elements of this approach in their work (although the bulk of their activities remain firmly set within the conventional TOT framework; TAC, 1993). The same applies to some national agricultural research and extension programmes. Non-governmental organizations (NGOs) have been particularly innovative in promoting this approach (Part III).

Challenges to Populism

Critics of the populist perspective argue that the attempt to blend or integrate local knowledge into existing scientific procedures falsely assumes that RPK represents an easily-definable body or stock of knowledge ready for extraction and incorporation. They point out that RPK, like scientific knowledge, is always manifold, discontinuous and dispersed, not singular, cohesive and systematized. It is never fully unified or integrated in terms of a logical system of classification or categorization.

The appreciation of the dynamic interplay of these multiple, diffuse knowledges requires a multidimensional analysis of rural livelihoods and political or ecological change. Such an analysis inevitably calls into question the validity of a unified view of rural people's knowledge and demands that we interpret indigenous knowledge as being constructed through rural people's practices as situated *agents:* 'as *agents*, because they are actively engaged in the generation, acquisition and classification of knowledge; and as *situated* agents because this engagement occurs in cultural, economic, agroecological and sociopolitical contexts that are products of local and non-local processes' (Bebbington, Part I). To remove local knowledge from the web of meaning and influence in which it arose and attempt to fit it into the constrictive framework of western scientific rationality is likely to lead to significant errors in interpretation, assimilation and application.

To highlight how these differences in conceptualization can lead to misinterpretation of local practices, Paul Richards (1989) contrasts the observed 'plan' of complex intercropping systems with the actual sequential 'performance' of farmers' actions. Simple observation of crop layout may be interpreted as a farmer's scientifically rational, carefully planned response to the problems of inter-specific competition, and weed and pest control in the cropping system, whereas the crop layout is in fact a series of

19

contingent responses to unfolding events through the season. In Richards' words (1989: 40):

> The crop mix . . . is not a design but a result, a completed performance. What transpired in that performance and why can only be interpreted by reconstructing the sequence of events in time. Each mixture is an historical record of what happened to a specific farmer on a specific piece of land in a specific year, not an attempt to implement a general theory of inter-species ecological complementarity . . . Researchers are looking for combinatorial logic in intercropping where what matters to the . . . farmer is sequential adjustment to unpredictable conditions. It is important therefore not to confuse spatial with temporal logic – not to conflate plan with performance.

In short, researchers and farmers use different frames of reference when thinking about agriculture. The researchers' thinking is 'out of time'; they have the luxury to run their experiments in controlled environments, even when conducting on-farm trials. By contrast, the farmers' performances can only occur 'in time', where they are embedded in particular agroecological and sociocultural contexts, which give rise to a plethora of changing conditions to which the farmers must make a series of rolling adjustments. For the researcher, then, what counts is replication and comparison. For the farmer, what counts is fitting available resources to changing circumstances well enough to make it through the season.

Attempts to 'scientize' rural knowledge can also act to devalue it. Lori-Ann Thrupp (1989) observes how agroforestry, a practice of rural farmers since agriculture began, has been modified and repackaged by scientists, and transmitted back to farmers through extension systems. The repackaging has occurred to such an extent that extension agents and researchers are often unable to recognize 'traditional' agroforestry practices, since they do not share the same characteristics as the recommended packages.

Actors and interfaces

Institutional analysis of participatory approaches requires a detailed analysis of the roles of different actors and the linkages and divisions between them. The superficial notion of 'participation' as espoused by many farmer-first advocates does not reveal the sociopolitical complexity of settings where farmers interact with researchers, extensionists and development workers. These social 'interfaces', according to Long (1989, 1992), are critical points of interaction between different social (and knowledge) systems where competition over resources and conflicts over social and political agendas are most likely to be found.

Agricultural research and extension involves encounters between individuals or groups representing different interests and supported by different resources. Typically, these interacting parties will be differentiated in terms of relations of power. Analysts of social interfaces attempt to reveal the dynamic and emergent nature of the interactions taking place and to show

how the objectives, perceptions, priorities and relationships of the various actors and their networks are influenced and reshaped as a result of the encounter. In addition, they aim to explore how these interactions affect and are affected by individual perceptions, institutional alliances, local and external market conditions, national and international policies (e.g. structural adjustment) and other forces which lie beyond the interface situation itself. This may be termed the *Beyond Farmer First* perspective.

Farmer first and beyond

This perspective by no means rejects the major tenets of the farmer-first position; a similar agenda of active participation, empowerment and poverty alleviation is in mind. However, it points to where the farmer-first approach lacks a certain analytical depth and presents a more radical programme that incorporates a sociopolitically differentiated view of development – where factors such as gender, ethnicity, class, age and religion are highlighted – with important implications for research and extension practice.

The populist perspective of many farmer-first adherents and the emerging alternative views of those wishing to move the debate *beyond* farmer-first can be compared in terms of their basic assumptions, processes of interaction, the roles assigned to the various actors and their styles of investigation (Table 1). Before beginning this comparison, however, it must be said that these perspectives, or schools of thought, should not be seen as polar opposites, but rather as representations of points on a continuum, and different ways of viewing the world.

First, with regard to their assumptions, farmer-first promoters sometimes present the view that farming communities in complex, diverse, risk-prone environments share common goals, access to resources (including information) and worldviews, and that local knowledge is unitary, systematized and available for assimilation and incorporation with western scientific knowledge. The emphasis is on information or knowledge exchange between the different parties, who are seen as knowledge 'generators', 'disseminators' or 'utilizers.' The beyond farmer-first advocates counter that different types of local and *non*-local people hold many divergent, sometimes conflicting, interests and goals, as well as differential access to vital resources. Knowledge, which is diffuse and fragmentary, emerges as a product of the discontinuous and inequitable interactions between these competing actors. Through their respective 'discursive' networks, different kinds of information and processes are communicated and legitimated. Misunderstanding and apprehension over hidden agendas and manoeuvres for power are the rule, not the exception.

Second, the processes through which different interactions take place are viewed quite differently. For the farmer-first populists, the emphasis has been on finding consensus solutions to identified problems through managed research and/or development activities. Local people may be actively involved in the diagnostic analysis of priority problems, and in planning and implementation of specific projects (e.g. rehabilitation of irrigation structures, formation of marketing co-operatives, etc). By contrast, the guiding concepts for beyond farmer-first work are dispute resolution and negotiated

Table 1   Beyond Farmer First: challenging the populist view

	Populist Approaches: Farmer First	Beyond Farmer First?
Assumptions	Populist ideal of common goals, interests and power among 'farmers' and 'communities'	Differentiated interests and goals, power, access to resources between 'actors' and 'networks'.
	'Stock' of uniform, systematized, local knowledge available for assimilation and incorporation.	Multi-layered, fragmentary, diffuse knowledges with complex, inequitable, discontinuous interactions between (local and external) actors and networks.
Process	'Farmer' or 'community' consensus solutions to identified problems.	Bridging, accommodation, negotiation and conflict mediation between different interest groups.
	Managed intervention, designed solutions and planned outcomes with farmer involvement in planning and implementation.	Process learning and planning with dynamic and adaptive implementation of negotiated outcomes; collaborative work requiring dialogue, negotiation, empowerment.
Role of 'outsider'	Invisible information collector, documenter of RPK; planner of interventions; manager of implementation; more recently: facilitator, initiator, catalyst.	Facilitator, initiator, catalyst, provider of occasions; visible actor in process learning and action.
Role of 'insider'	Reactive respondent; passive participant.	Creative investigator and analyst; *active* participant.
Styles of investigation	Positivist, hard-systems research (FSR, AEA, RRA, some PRA, FPR & PTD).	Post-positivist, soft-systems learning and action research (PAR; increasingly FPR, PRA & PTD).

agreements between different interest groups vying for control of resources and power. This conflict mediation may occur through a process of adaptive learning and planning resulting in dynamic and flexible implementation of negotiated outcomes.

Third, the roles of the 'insider' and 'outsider' are defined in contrasting terms. While the populists have long espoused the role of the researcher or extensionist acting as that of a 'facilitator' or 'initiator' or 'catalyst', and that of the local person as 'partner' or 'analyst', in reality, most farmer-first practitioners have remained information collectors and documenters of RPK, and designers, planners, managers and evaluators of research or development initiatives (in some cases with the active involvement of local people and in others without it). Those wishing to move beyond farmer-first accept these definitions of 'insiders' and 'outsiders' in principle, but believe they will only be fulfilled in practice when all actors consider development as a transaction *process* involving negotiation over divergent goals and struggles over room to manoeuvre.

The final difference between the farmer-first and beyond farmer-first approaches is in their styles of investigation. Despite recent shifts to the contrary, the populists have followed a 'positivist' agenda centred on structure and systematic organization determined by controlling forces. This entails a hard-systems approach focusing on discrete elements and hierarchical patterns. Most farming systems research (FSR), agroecosystem analysis (AEA) and rapid rural appraisal (RRA) fall within this framework. The beyond farmer-first agenda, by contrast, concentrates on the actor. It involves a soft-systems approach centred on networks, relations of power and dynamic 'performances'. Participatory action research (PAR) and increasingly, farmer participatory research (FPR), participatory technology development (PTD), and participatory rural appraisal (PRA) all share elements of this new style of investigation (Cornwall *et al.*, Part II). The promoters of these, and other related approaches, are helping to push the populist agenda beyond farmer-first.

Strategic silences

Many farmer-first promoters acknowledge that they are well aware of the points put forward by their critics, but claim they have chosen to remain silent on them for strategic reasons. They imply that they can achieve crucial goals and changes in the thinking of certain key agricultural agencies and institutions indirectly, and that to be too explicit about cultural contexts and relations of power may in fact inhibit or dissuade the very audience they are trying to influence. For example, while a farmer-first proponent is trying to convince crop scientists of farmers' experimental skills, to be told that actually farmers link their practices to particular cosmologies may take the scientists back to thinking that farmers are 'primitive' and 'unscientific' after all. Hence, they argue that there is a strategy underlying the populist alternative which should be recognized. For these farmer-first advocates, then, the issue is under what conditions is it appropriate to break these strategic silences and under what conditions is it not?

While the logic behind this argument is beyond dispute, the fact that few farmer-first writers have described this strategic thinking in clear terms in any of their writings over the past decade has left them open to charges of superficial analyses and naive populist activism. Moreover, it can be contended that while the populist rhetoric may win over some mainstream supporters, there is still a large degree of 'preaching to the converted' about it.

Recent commentaries and policy statements by some of the most influential thinkers and agencies in the field reveal just how little impact these farmer-first arguments have had on some quarters in conventional agricultural research and extension (TAC, 1993). For example, Norman Borlaug (1992: 2), the Nobel laureate and plant geneticist, writing on the state of agriculture in Africa, has declared:

> Development specialists . . . must stop 'romanticizing' the virtues of traditional agriculture in the Third World. Moreover, leaders in developing countries must not be duped into believing that future food requirements can be met through continuing reliance on . . . the new, complicated and sophisticated 'low-input, low-output' technologies that are impractical for farmers to adopt'.

Would a more theoretically rich and politically sophisticated argument about knowledge, power, research and extension help convince sceptics such as Borlaug that there is no simple 'techno-fix' just as there is no simple 'participation-fix' to the agricultural problems of the world's resource-poor farmers? We believe it would, particularly if it is accompanied by realistic methodological and institutional alternatives.

Power and knowledge: the theoretical setting

How do cultural, economic and political relationships and differences affect the generation, innovation and transmission of knowledge? How do we know what we know?

Every system of knowledge, agricultural science and RPK included, has its own epistemology, its own theory of what constitutes and what counts as knowledge. The shortcomings of positivist, rationalist, western scientific epistemologies have been widely debated and discussed for many years (e.g. Kuhn, 1962; Feyerabend, 1975; Goodman, 1978; Rajchman and West, 1985; Harvey, 1989; Guba, 1990; Sayer 1992).

This critique undermines the assumption of a positivist view of investigation that sees knowledge as a tangible stock or store to be tapped, extracted and documented. It also suggests that the process of knowing should be seen as engaged, value-bound and context determined, rather than detached, value free and independent of context. The human mind is not simply a 'mirror' that accurately reflects a reality 'out there' (Rorty, 1980, 1982, 1989). Interpretation, translation and representation are social acts that cannot be assumed to be neutral and objective. Rather than talking of 'things', we should begin to talk about the way we talk about things (Quine, 1953). While we cannot escape the strictures of our own language (Derrida, 1978) or our own ways of reasoning (Hacking, 1983), we can acknowledge that these provide us with only a partial views of our world and that a multiplicity of other equally valid ones also exist.

It is also essential to ask how power affects knowledge. Michel Foucault observes that 'the criteria of what constitutes knowledge, what is to be excluded and who is designated as qualified to know involves acts of power' (Foucault, 1971). Norman Long and Magdallena Villareal (Part I) point out that 'power differences and struggles over social meaning are central to an understanding of knowledge processes'. Forms of discourse come into being,

24

evolve and survive or decline because they are used by people in a dynamic interplay with one another and with their physical environment. Thus, to borrow and extend Roy Bhaskar's (1979) terminology, knowledge and power are both 'ever-present conditions' and 'continuously reproduced outcomes' of human agency. This approach – seeing pattern in each new action and innovation in the repetition of past patterns – has now been adopted by a generation of social theorists from Foucault (1971, 1973) to Bourdieu (1977) and from Giddens (1979, 1987) to Habermas (1984, 1987, 1992).

To explain the direction of change it is necessary to introduce power into the equation and explore the relationship between the character of domination by certain groups and the evolution of discourse. The purpose of studying knowledge systems in apparent conflict, whether resource-poor farmers and extensionists in the Andes (Salas, Part I), or pastoralists and extensionists in the Horn of Africa (Fre, 1993) or farmers and agronomists in the Himalayas (Jodha and Partap, 1993), is to understand those factors within societies which shape and influence discourse in locally relevant terms, and, at the same time, present a countervailing force against a dominant or potentially disempowering external discourse of formal research or extension.

Analysing the links between relations of power and local people opens up a difficult problem of scale; the extent in time and space of things being studied. Local social forms (the rituals or narratives of a particular place) deserve to be given special weight, yet relations of power can never be understood within narrow local boundaries. No knowledge system can exist in a cultural, economic or political vacuum. Knowledge of any form, like the language systems through which it is transmitted and transformed, must always confront other knowledge systems, whether they are those of development agents or neighbouring societies. It is on these 'battlefields of knowledge' (Long and Long, 1992), through a dynamic process of contestation and assimilation, that innovation and knowledge creation operate. And it is in this dynamic social setting that research and extension is practised.

The social construction of knowledge

A broader view of knowledge, its generation, transmission and application, suggests a range of issues of importance for agricultural research and extension. What is the relationship that people have to their knowledge? How is local agricultural knowledge generated? How is knowledge shared and transmitted? As James Fairhead (1990: 23) asks:

> Do people 'know', 'believe', 'think' or 'suppose' all this [indigenous technical knowledge] and how much disagreement is there? How do farmers come to 'know', and how do they become confident in what they know? Who talks to whom about it?

Knowledge is held, controlled and generated by different people in a society. A differentiated view of knowledge generation is an essential component of understanding RPK. The simplifications inherent in the labelling of 'farmers'' (or indeed 'rural people's') knowledge presents problems. Who is the farmer whose knowledge should be put first? Male or female?

25

Rich or poor? Old or young? Influential or powerless? Since, as we have seen, knowledge is socially and politically constructed, it requires a socially differentiated, politically astute analysis to comprehend.

Understanding the processes of agricultural innovation and experimentation has become an important focus of social scientists involved in agricultural research. Farmer experimentation is promoted as a process to encourage a more participatory partnership between researcher and farmer. But how does local innovation occur? How apparent are farmer's 'experiments'?

Simply asking people, or inferring particular structures of knowledge from observation may be inadequate methods for understanding. Knowledge is bound up with action. But what people do is not necessarily what people consciously 'know.' Moreover, knowledge may be articulated in many ways. In some instances, explanations for practices may be incompletely articulated or idealized; in others, myths or metaphors may be the most significant mode of transmission. For example, Jan van der Ploeg (1989: 148–9) describes how Andean farmers, confronted with a huge variety of different agroecological conditions, observe, interpret, evaluate, cultivate and improve each of their plots using an extensive cluster of bipolar and metaphorical concepts:

> The distinction *fria/caliente* (cold/hot), for instance, is used to characterize certain aspects of what we would call soil fertility. It relates – but not in an exact or unilinear way – to the amount of nutrients and humus in the subsoil. *Dura/suavecita* (hard/soft) is another conceptual pair: it refers to the degree to which the soil has been tilled in previous years. It also communicates another important meaning, i.e. the degree to which the particular plot has been 'cared for' and therefore the degree to which the plot may be considered as 'grateful.' . . . These and other concepts are not unequivocal, nor do they lend themselves to precise quantification. They cannot be built into nomological models of the kind used in applied science, and technology development . . . Yet their inaccurate character does not prevent farmers from establishing fairly exactly the overall condition of specific plots . . . [In fact] it is precisely the vagueness or 'imprecise' character that allows for interpretation and change.

Knowledge is often expressed in the private domain, in terms which outsiders can find difficult to decipher. Farmers often view their agricultural adaptations, procedures and experiments as 'normal' and unsurprising; descriptions in terms of 'creativity' and 'innovation' are misleading (Fairhead, 1990). Farming practices may be expressed (to outsiders especially, but also to other locals) in terms of ideal-type descriptions (e.g., of rotations, cropping patterns, etc.). These can give a false impression, as they may not reflect the wide variety of actual practices which arise not out of a cognitized, rational 'plan', but through a series of contingent responses, a 'performance' (to use Richards' (1989) term), to uncertain agroecological and social circumstances. They may also involve acts of secrecy and reactions to perceived threats, including divination and sorcery, where an individual or group presents false or misleading information in order to protect ideas or innovations from others or from powerful magical forces (Pottier, Part I).

The hidden transcript and the transmission of knowledge

Knowledge is not evenly distributed. Different individuals are recognized as 'specialists' in particular fields and are key in the transmission and interpretation of knowledge within a community or family (Swift, 1979; Feierman, 1990; Go and Go, 1993; Bentley; Winarto, both Part II). The dynamics of this transmission has a clear political dimension: who controls the flow of information and who imposes an interpretational gloss on its transmission?

As Maria Salas (1991; Part I) has pointed out, impressions of local people as passively receiving external knowledge (and ideologies), or at best as reacting to external initiatives, are widely distributed in academic writings. The image of peasant culture as inert is equally common, and very misleading. Peasant farmers are not necessarily trapped by patterns of domination. Those labelled as 'power*less*' or 'subjugated' or 'repressed', within specific circumstances, are not always passive victims and may be involved in various forms of active resistance. Conversely, the 'power*ful*' (e.g. resource-rich farmers, researchers, extensionists, etc.) do not always control all aspects of social life, and the degree to which they themselves are influenced and affected by the actions and agendas of the less powerful should not be underestimated.

James Scott has written eloquently about the role of power in interactions between people of different social groups. In his writings, Scott (1985, 1989, 1990) uses the term 'hidden transcript' to describe how the exercise of power in nearly all public encounters between resource-rich and resource-poor (and between authority and subordinate) almost always drives a portion of the full social transcript – that is, people's opinions, beliefs, ideas and values – underground. The normal tendency will be for the subservient individual or group to reveal only that part of their full transcript to authorities in power-laden situations that is both safe and appropriate to reveal. The greater the disparity in power between two individuals or groups, the greater the proportion that is likely to be concealed.

How many times have social scientists tried to decipher the elusive, enigmatic, often elliptical answers of rural people to probing questions about their livelihoods? How many times have extensionists witnessed the deferential, submissive attitude of peasant farmers as they were presented with the latest technical message? This, in practical terms, is the hidden transcript at work.

It is possible to think of a continuum from the free dialogue between equals that is close to what Jürgen Habermas (1984, 1987) has called the 'ideal speech situation' – by which the rationally motivated attempt to reach agreement is protected from internal and external repression, and all actors have the opportunity to proffer comments and refute statements – all the way to the transcript which is driven underground, leaving only stilted deference born of fear.

The hidden transcript thus represents the whole conversational reply of the subordinate (e.g. the peasant farmer), which, for reasons of repression, fear and suspicion, cannot be spoken openly. What domination achieves, in this context, is the fragmentation of discourses, so that much of what would have been a cohesive and integrated statement of perspective and opinion is sequestered and remains hidden. Thus, as Barrington Moore (1987: 84) reminds us:

> In any stratified society there is a set of limits on what . . . dominant and subordinate groups can do . . . What takes place, however, is a kind of continual probing to find out what they can get away with and discover the limits of obedience and disobedience.

This discursive view of power and knowledge involves human agency and occurs within sociopolitically constituted networks of actors and their institutions (Long and Villareal, Part I; Uphoff, Part III). Such a view takes us beyond the socially-deterministic conceptions of many *dependistas* and political economists, who argue that nothing will change unless the whole system changes. It also takes us well beyond the simplistic diffusion models of knowledge and technology transfer, which categorize groups of people as 'innovators', 'adopters' or 'laggards' (Brown, 1982; Hägerstrand, 1968). In fact, processes of negotiation, compromise and resistance do exist and are important in initiating change, often incrementally, sometimes radically (e.g. Drinkwater; Long and Villareal; Bebbington, Part I). Discourse arises through the discontinuous, diffuse, value-bound interactions of different actors and networks, the 'encounter of horizons' – a process of both interpretation and negotiation (Habermas, 1987, 1992; Long and Long, 1992). In some instances, the actors can co-ordinate 'their individual action plans without reservations on the basis of a communicatively achieved consensus . . . ' (Habermas, 1984: 410). Whether this consensus yields a common or joint action plan, or only the pursuit of divergent goals on the basis of a reciprocal acknowledgement of differences, obviously depends on the actors involved, their respective agendas and the structural context in which they find themselves.

Exploring the transmission and transformation of local knowledge is a key research theme of vital importance to extension practice (Röling and Engel, 1991; Röling, Part III). Constructing historical biographies of particular crops opens up insights into this process (Box, 1987), as does the diagramming of networks of information exchanges. Examining this in relation to the networks of different actors and institutions (farmer experimenters, extension agents, research stations, markets etc.) demonstrates the importance of social context and power relations in patterns of knowledge transmission (Long, 1989; Long and Long, 1992; Long and Villareal, Part I).

In order for agricultural researchers and extensionists to engage in meaningful dialogue with farmers, they must recognise the complexities of socially and politically differentiated knowledge generation, transmission and adaptation, and explore methodologies that take this into account.

Rural people's knowledge and agricultural science: prospects for collaboration

Rural people's knowledge is often characterized as highly specific and context-bound, with knowledge emerging simply from localized, practical experience. This characterization is contrasted with agricultural science which is seen as theoretically based, providing objective, generalizable, propositional knowledge. Following the long-running philosophical bias in favour of theoretical knowledge over practical knowledge, agricultural science is thought to show 'superior' qualities (Hacking, 1983). This characterization has resulted in the domination of science over RPK (Marglin and Marglin, 1990). RPK is thus relegated to a role appropriate for the slow process of local adaptation of technologies, while agricultural science is regarded as superior at technological innovation and dissemination (Farrington and Martin, 1988).

Previous sections of this paper have demonstrated that this simplifying contrast between RPK and agricultural science is inadequate however. Both RPK and agricultural science proceed with context-determined, experiential and theoretical knowledges, reinforced by continuous interactions between theory and practice (Hacking, 1983).

The problem is that rural people's conceptual frameworks are often hidden in studies that divide up knowledge into 'bits' that relate to separate resources, geographical units or social groups. RPK is often seen as a useful source of particular 'facts' or 'classifications' that are subsequently interpreted within a theoretical framework derived from agricultural science (Fre, 1993; Sikana, Part I). But studies that do not compartmentalize RPK in this way show that rural people do theorize about agroecosystem processes and dynamics (Fairhead and Leach, Part I); such theories are locally situated (Van der Ploeg, 1989) and articulated within conceptions of local cosmologies (Salas, Part I; Millar, Part II).

Studies that explore the dynamics of farmer experimentation also show that rural people empirically examine alternatives leading to progressive learning. RPK is thus not only about the relatively static, finely tuned adjustment of historically well-established 'indigenous technologies'. Nor is RPK simply the collection of a vast array of highly particular, socially and environmentally constructed knowledges. RPK, like agricultural science, can be involved in cumulative exploration of alternative practices, employing progressive, adaptive learning through hypothesis formulation and the application of replicable methodologies. In other words, some elements of farmers' science show strong parallels with conventional, positivist, empirically based scientific approaches. A well established, durable process of experimentation exists that offers the potential for articulation with formal agricultural institutions (e.g. Richards, Part II, for rice farming in Sierra Leone; Millar, Part II, for cereal and tuber farming in Ghana).

RPK and western agricultural science are both general *and* specific, theoretical *and* practical. Both are value-laden, context-specific and influenced by social relations of power. The critique of positivist science makes redundant the dichotomy between 'traditional' (inferior) and 'modern' (superior).

Thus, science and RPK are not so different. Elements of each may be incommensurable, but commonalities in processes and outcomes clearly exist. However, for formal research and extension to engage with local knowledge systems it requires a leap of imagination – the need to enter into the world of farmers' ideas, values, representations and performances, and to develop participatory research and extension approaches that allow constructive dialogue between different 'languages'. Salas (1989: 3) comments:

[The extensionist/researcher must] find out the meaningful categories that organise and conceptualise the concrete aspects of life . . . The insights gained . . . can be the foundation of a partnership for an exchange of knowledge and experiences which can mobilise creative forces on both sides . . .

It is in exploring this common ground, and the opportunity for creative exchanges that it offers, that the future beyond farmer-first lies. This implies a number of key methodological challenges for both the practice of agricultural science and the exploration of RPK.

Methodological challenges

If knowledge is socially constructed and continuously negotiated and contested in varying social and ecological settings, then the question of *how* we learn about rural people's agriculture takes on new significance. The theoretical re-evaluation of the nature of knowledge explored in previous sections suggests a number of important methodological challenges. Indeed, the emerging critique of positivist views of knowledge puts methodological concerns centre stage.

In the past, methodologies have concentrated on positivist ways of describing farming systems. The study of farming systems has included the examination of indigenous agricultural practice and technical knowledge, but largely within a conceptual framework specified by scientific analysts. Early FSR formulations saw a more or less linear progression from problem and opportunity diagnosis to technology design, adaptation and verification. These 'hard systems' approaches concentrated on defining *what* farming systems are and *what* emergent properties these systems possess (Conway, 1985; Tripp, 1991). By specifying the boundaries, components and linkages in farming systems, it was assumed that limitations and opportunities for technological development could be found (Collinson, 1987; Biggs, 1989a).

The past ten years have witnessed a virtual revolution in the development of a diverse array of methodological innovations. Yet, until recently, the fundamental question of *how* we come to understand farming systems and farmers' livelihoods have not featured much in methodological debates. Instead, they have concentrated on the elaboration of techniques and tools for the efficient extraction of information. As a result, the methodological repertoire has grown faster than our understanding of how we learn about rural people's knowledges and local constraints and conditions.

Today, however, alternative methodological approaches are emerging from several convergent strands of thinking. For example, 'soft systems'

30

approaches are challenging the hegemony of 'hard systems' analysis (Checkland, 1984; Bawden, 1992a), overturning the assumptions of positivism and opening the way for an alternative, 'naturalistic' approach to scientific inquiry (Lincoln and Guba, 1985; Reason and Heron, 1986; Guba, 1990). There is also an increasing awareness of agency in research encounters (researcher-farmer, researcher-reader, etc.) which highlights the need for reflection on the context of research and extension activities (Long, 1989; Drinkwater; Long and Villareal; Sikana; Bebbington, Part I). Finally, an explosion of methodological experimentation with performative approaches (diagramming and visualization, theatre and song, etc.) has led to a re-examination of whose knowledge counts, who carries out the analysis and whose representation is recorded (Cornwall *et al.*, Part II).

The boundaries between researcher, extensionist and farmer are being broken down by these changes in methodological practice. The researcher is no longer considered to be a detached, invisible investigator while administering questionnaires, conducting on-farm trials or 'participant observing'. With an interactive, dialogical approach, the researcher acts as a catalyst, a facilitator and a provider of occasions, with learning occurring continuously and reflexively. In this dynamic, power-laden process, there are no neutral parties; everyone is engaged.

Such an interpretation of the research encounter forces us to reconsider the role of the researcher/extensionist. How visible is the researcher/ extensionist? Whose knowledge, perceptions, priorities are 'made known' and taken seriously through their involvement? Whose are not? Why? Even if the researcher/extensionist adopts a sympathetic, enquiring mode of investigation, what are the chances of hearing an expression of what a farmer really thinks or expresses to other farmers (i.e. the 'hidden transcript')? It is critical to explore the nature of farmer-researcher-extensionist roles and relationships if we are to develop emancipatory, people-centred research and extension approaches.

Conclusion

From the foregoing discussion, it is clear that a radically new concept of agricultural science is required. Advocacy of simplistic, deterministic models of blueprint research and extension (i.e. transfer of technology), or populist processes of farmer participation (farmer-first) are unable to account for the full range of social and political forces at work in the interaction of contrasting, sometimes conflicting, knowledge systems. A more sophisticated view of this interaction sees the relationships between farmers and the external development agents (be they representatives of the state or an NGO) in terms of the on-going struggles, negotiations and compromises between different actors (Long and Long, 1992).

In this paper, we have not sought to provide a 'totalizing critique' (Bernstein, 1983) that shows no hope of undistorted communication and dialogue between farmers and agricultural scientists. Rather, our argument is that if the knowledges and capacities of rural people and agricultural scientists and extensionists are to have any chance of being articulated productively, then attempting to force RPK into a straight-jacket imposed by the framework of formal science is unlikely to work. Instead, productive engagement is only possible when common ground is found. In some instances, farmers' experimentation may follow a positivist mode of inquiry, involving hypothesis testing through empirical exploration. In such cases, the marriage of RPK and science may be relatively uncomplicated. However, in many other situations, agricultural science must change its investigative approach in order to learn from *and with* farmers' knowledges and not simply assume that farmers must learn 'good science' by being taught the ancient art of split-plot trials and the 'tyranny of averages and norms' (Hacking, 1990).

Where frameworks of local understandings are conditioned by socio-cultural settings, where agricultural experimentation follows a performance rather than a rational plan, and where power, politics and influence affect the expression and application of local knowledges, alternative research and extension approaches must be adopted if real communication and understanding are to be realized. This, in turn, requires significant professional attitudinal and behavioural changes, methodological innovations, transformations of agricultural research and extension policies and institutions, and a more theoretically sophisticated analysis of knowledge, power and agricultural science.

Knowledge, consciousness and prejudice: adaptive agricultural research in Zambia

MICHAEL DRINKWATER

Complementary approaches?

A central question that has arisen with the emergence of the farmer-first approach to agricultural research and extension over the last five years or so, is that of the status of this new approach *vis-a-vis* the conventional transfer-of-technology (TOT) model. On the one hand, the language of 'reversals', turning the TOT model 'on its head', and 'instead of' lends credence to the view that they are dichotomous alternatives.

> Instead of starting with the knowledge, problems, analysis and priorities of scientists, [farmer-first] starts with the knowledge, problems, analysis and priorities of farmers and farm families. Instead of the research station as the main locus of action, it is now the farm. Instead of the scientist as the central experimenter, it is now the farmer, whether woman or man, and other members of the farm family (Chambers *et al.*, 1989: xix).

On the other hand, however, some do not see the two models as alternatives. Paul Richards (1985: 150) stresses the need for 'active complementarities' to be achieved between informal and formal research and development sectors . He sees 'people's science' as being worth pursuing on the grounds that it is good science'. Chambers *et al.* (1989: xx), express the same sentiments:

Farmer-first approaches and methods constitute a complementary paradigm. 'Complementarity' is used since the transfer-of-technology approach, including commodity research, on-station and in-laboratory basic investigations, and so on, will always be needed.

Yet how complementary are the two approaches? After all, Chambers *et al.*, describe farmer-first as a wholly new paradigm, in the sense that the approach consists of a 'mutually supporting pattern of concepts, analysis, methods and behaviour'. Moreover, these characteristics are not the same as those of conventional science. For instance, Richards' (1989) conceptualization of the activities of small-scale farmers as an annual adaptive performance is quite different from seeing agriculture as constituting a set of ideal practices as does the TOT approach. The summary report of the Khon Kaen University conference on rapid rural appraisal (RRA) in 1985 makes this even clearer. In the summary the 'new paradigm' is seen as constituting an altogether different set of ideas about development and change. In this paradigm, 'the world is seen as composed of a highly interactive set of variables rapidly changing and subject to a high degree of uncertainty' (Khon Kaen University 1987: 7). Thus, development is conceived as 'adaptive change' rather than 'progress':

evolution and development are viewed as processes of change driven by the need to solve problems in existing systems (adaptive change) rather than as a series of inventions and discoveries whereby older and intrinsically inferior systems are steadily replaced in a linear fashion by newer and intrinsically better systems (progress) (Khon Kaen University, 1987: 7).

It is because the farmer-first approach sees agriculture as performance that it advocates that, rather than packages of technology, what should be provided to farmers is a menu of options in the form of 'genetic material, principles, practices and methods' for them to test and incorporate as appropriate (Chambers *et al.*, 1989: 185). This contrasts with seeing agricultural development as merely a process of persuading farmers to follow technical recommendations in order that they may move up the rungs of the technical development ladder.

In short, the farmer-first approach is epistemologically different from the transfer-of-technology model, something which the new wave of participatory rural appraisal (PRA) work is making very clear (IIED, 1988–present; Chambers, 1992a–c). The technology transfer approach relies on a conventional view of science, in which science is seen as dealing with universality, deterministic laws of causality, equilibrium conditions and a narrow, ends–means (or positivist) notion of rationality. Thus we have two distinct conceptualizations of reality (Scoones and Thompson, Part I). One is an ahistorical, asocial conceptualization, tied to a positivist view of knowledge, which generally assumes a stable world of order and progress and scientific certainties. In the other view of reality, instead of being 'orderly, stable and equilibrial' the social and natural worlds become 'bubbling with change, disorder and process' (Toffler in Prigogine and Stengers, 1985: xv). This latter view is the world with which the farmer-first paradigm deals – but, significantly, it is also the world which modern science has begun to recognize.

My argument is therefore as follows. If we are to move 'beyond Farmer First', what is required is to transcend the conceptualization of 'farmer first' as a dichotomous alternative to the transfer-of-technology approach to agricultural research and development. The achievement of this, however, requires essentially that people change the way they look at both knowledge and science, and to accept the resulting methodological and institutional implications.

The positivist conception of science and knowledge, which so far has largely bounded the 'farmer first' versus transfer-of-technology debate, is increasingly being attacked not only by social philosophers (whose attack is not new), but also by scientists themselves. In the following section this shall be elaborated in an outline of an alternative conception of knowledge (and how we develop understanding) to the positivist approach and the old objective–subjective dichotomy it draws upon.

I shall illustrate this with reference to the work being carried out by the Adaptive Research Planning Teams (ARPTs) in the Central and Copperbelt Provinces of Zambia, the type of methodologies and concepts which can be used within an alternative theoretical framework (Drinkwater, Part II). These methods do not always generate obvious or easy directions in which to work. Much engagement is required. Institutionally this can be extremely difficult to organize. The final part of this paper consequently raises some of the institutional barriers and concomitant issues that are being encountered in the Zambian situation (Sikana, Part III).

The social contextuation of knowledge

The subject of knowledge is neither a transcendental ego nor an absolute spirit but an embodied, labouring subject whose capacities develop historically in the changing forms of the confrontation with nature that is the perpetual natural necessity of human life (McCarthy, 1984: 54).

This statement, taken from a discussion by Thomas McCarthy of one of the early books of Jurgen Habermas, *Knowledge and Human Interests* (1972), encapsulates much of the argument presented here. One undoubted fact is that the statement is at odds with a positivist view of knowledge – and science – which holds that as long as an objective attitude is maintained (through, for instance, the use of 'scientific method'), the truths and technology produced will have a universal character, recognizable to any objective observer across space and time. In this view, knowledge is a relatively portable commodity. Hence the populist early formulation of a farmer-first approach, in which the key problem to be solved is seen as how to incorporate farmers' knowledge within a conventional agricultural research paradigm – the marriage of a bottom-up with a top-down approach.

Recently, however, scientists have themselves begun to question this conceptualization of their activities. The reason for this is that science has been rediscovering time. For science and theories about method this has three immense implications. The first is that it results in us understanding natural systems as being primarily ones of non-equilibrium. In conditions of non-equilibrium, matter and energy flow; a state which is undeniably more the natural order of things than the timelessness of equilibrium. Indeed, non-equilibrium is a source of order; it brings 'order out of chaos'. But crucially, this order is unpredictable in advance. There are strong resonances here with the view of development as adaptive change, rather than as progress *per se*.

The second implication results from the realization that all science is time and space situated. It is not just that where and when scientists are clearly affects the outcome of their work, but that it is also not possible for us to learn about nature 'from the outside', as if we were only a spectator. Nor is it possible for science to understand a phenomenon fully without taking account of its historical dimensions.

Finally, this historical and turbulent view of nature or society, and the embeddedness of the scientist participant within it, implies that neither nature nor society can be understood independently of the other. Nature can only be fully understood through an awareness of ourselves and our relationship with the world, and similarly society can only be understood through our awareness of nature.

The philosophical implication of this shift in science is highly significant. Theoretically, the social sciences' break with positivism has been heralded for some time (Fay, 1975; Bernstein, 1976). In practice, ingrained habits die hard and the old rigidities are far from being demolished. Who does not make the distinction between 'objectivity' and 'subjectivity'? The assumed distinction between objective science and the more subjective nature of ongoing human action has often drawn upon the Aristotelian distinction between *episteme* and *phronesis*. The importance of *episteme* is that it denotes the sphere of universal, theoretical knowledge about the order and nature of the cosmos. It is assumed to be separated from productive knowledge, or *techne*, the technical skill required to undertake a craft or art. These types of knowledge are distinguished again from the practical knowledge which social actors require to go on in the moral–political sphere of human action; *praxis*. In the muddy, complex world of social reality, *phronesis* is the quality of having 'a prudent understanding' of variable situations with a view of what is to be done (McCarthy, 1984: 2). Today however, this rigid distinction between *episteme*, theoretical knowledge, and *phronesis*, ethical know-how, is unsustainable.

> The more closely we examine the nature of this scientific knowledge, the more we realise that the character of rationality in the sciences, especially in matters of theory-choice, is closer to those features of rationality that have been characteristic of the tradition of practical philosophy than to many of the modern images of what is supposed to be the character of genuine episteme (Bernstein, 1983: 4).

This coincides with the argument that many scientists are themselves presenting (Uphoff, 1992b). Science is not an abstracted activity and since its motivations and truths will always be contingent, there will always be the opportunity for social, as well as empirical, critique. Knowledge is thus socially and politically contextuated, but, for a phenomenon to be known it needs to be understood within its historical and spatial situation. This is why there is now more recognition that farmers' knowledge, even in the form of technical practice, cannot be abstracted quite as easily as the spawning of the acronym 'ITK' might seem to suggest. Examples can be used to demonstrate this.

Knowledge in context: agricultural practice in Central and Copperbelt Provinces, Zambia

The following three case studies are taken from ARPT work being carried out in Central and Copperbelt Provinces. Each case illustrates, in different ways, how understanding knowledge in context assists in the practice of farming systems research and the development of an adaptive research programme.

Beans, compost and mounds

Bean trials during 1992 at Mpongwe in Ndola Rural, Copperbelt Province, showed that beans planted on the flat and ridged up at weeding produced a higher yield than beans established on mounds (even though they were not as healthy). This was because of the higher plant population per unit area on the flat (Copperbelt Province ARPT, 1992). Yet, for farmers in Serenje in Central Province, there are four good reasons for always planting beans on mounds.

- The composting nature of the mound keeps the soil in the mound warm and moist for up to two months beyond the end of the normal growing season;
- Constructing the mounds is a form of 'productive fallowing', to quote one farmer. The fields used are those where maize has been growing for several seasons and where, even with the use of chemical fertilizer, yields are declining;
- The mounds protect the crop against climatic extremes (flooding from heavy rain or dry spells), and because the plant growth is more vigorous than when planted on the flat, there is better resistance to pest attack;
- The beans are intercropped with cassava and sweet potatoes (the latter a growing cash crop).

In Serenje, the predominantly hoe-based farming system is very diversified, and with the use of both wetland and upland mound cultivation techniques, the planting period is spread over seven months. It is a labour-intensive production system, but because the labour load is spread out, there is time to construct and plant the mounds. This contrasts with Ndola Rural where the farming system is maize-based and planting concentrated in a narrow band of six to eight weeks. Members of the farmer research group at

Ibenga, near Mpongwe, agreed that to grow beans on mounds was preferable, but as the time for doing this coincided with maize weeding, most who did plant beans did so only on the flat.

'Beans', as a cropping activity amongst small-scale farmers in Central and Copperbelt Provinces, can thus only be understood in the context of specific production systems. Broad brush recommendations for the crop would be totally irrelevant.

Crop breeding: sorghum for yield or sorghum for livelihood?

Like the activities of farmers, those of crop breeders must also be understood in context. As Latour (1987) shows persuasively, science is a highly social and political activity; peoples' achievements are measured in terms of what others will accept, pay for, and reward. So a crop breeder will almost inevitably push to release the highest yielding varieties of those being screened, because that is what the research departments, donors, seed institutions and other researchers, will fund and acknowledge, and what the scientist's reputation is based upon. It is not always what farmers want, however. In recent years in Zambia there has been a large sorghum and millet breeding programme, a response to the heavy emphasis on the production and spreading of new maize varieties in the early 1980s. By the mid-1980s maize was the dominant cereal crop in just about every farming system in Zambia, frequently to the overall detriment of household food security (Young and Evans, 1989; Sharpe, 1990; Sutherland and Drinkwater, 1990; Drinkwater and McEwan, 1992). The sorghum programme has been focused on the country's dry, valley areas, where maize yields are least resilient. In these areas, an improved sorghum variety, Kuyuma, released in 1992–93, has been initially welcomed by farmers.

Sorghum, however, like finger millet, has traditionally also been grown in many of Zambia's northern high rainfall areas. In these areas, the small grain crops, previously dominant, are now only a supplement to maize. The new sorghum varieties available so far for these areas are mostly hybrids (apart from Kuyuma, which is highly susceptible to bird attack). But sorghum is valued as a cheap, low-input crop, which you can plant and virtually forget about, and yet still have additional grain for food and beer. Consequently, the Copperbelt ARPT has found one improved variety, Serena, which, although by no means the highest yielding of the new varieties, is universally liked by the farmers with whom ARPT has been working. It is reliable, relatively bird resistant (a quality of enormous labour saving significance), does outyield the local varieties, and produces magnificent beer (Copperbelt Province ARPT, 1992). In the 1991–92 season, farmers in Central Province also tried the variety with favourable initial views. Yet the sorghum breeding team has rejected Serena on the basis that its yields are too low.

Wetland cultivation: managing complexity

Research has recently been initiated on wetlands (*dambo*) cultivation practices in Central and Copperbelt Provinces. Similar research elsewhere in

Zambia has shown that these practices are frequently complex and adapted to a range of wetland environments. In the Teta area of Serenje we attempted to differentiate between a range of mound practices: *ifisebe*, where the grass is turfed up, left to dry, burned and then maize, beans and pumpkins planted in the ashes; *imputa* and *imyolo*, the former round and the latter longer; *ifisebe* where after planting the seed (often including sweet or Livingstone potatoes) has been covered with a layer of upturned turf; and *ifibunde*, long unburned mounds, higher up and parallel to the *dambo* slope, on which maize, sweet potatoes and particularly cassava are grown.

These methods are a response to the agronomic problems posed by the *dambo* soils; poor drainage, high acidity and a proneness to micronutrient deficiencies, amongst other factors (Dougnac, 1986; Kokwe, 1991). Although relatively little researched, these are old practices and therefore with a wealth of experience behind them (Peters, 1951; Seur, 1992). But it will take us some time to find out what knowledge lies behind these practices, how good it is and how it can be improved upon. The practice of burning is one issue. In certain types of mounds people burn and in others they do not, but it is not immediately clear why there is the difference and what is the relative efficiency of burning versus composting, since the latter, although slower, produces more nutrients and biomass. In Ibenga, where *dambo* farming has altered its form from the growing of traditional crops to predominantly vegetable production for the Copperbelt markets, burning is more indiscriminate, simply a setting fire to the grass cover, and then some piling of ashes. Farmers in the research group when questioned about this said it was 'good', but their reasons slid away from being convincing; it was merely a habit.

Knowledge about agricultural practices is embedded in the performance of those practices and in the linking of those practices into an overall farming and livelihood system. For this reason, insights into why certain practices occur, and why they vary between different places, may at first be unclear. Not everything can be learnt on a diagnostic survey, neatly documented and written up for the design of future experiments. A close engagement is usually necessary; if farmer knowledge is bound up in their actions, then researchers need to learn through practice too. *Dambo* research trials are now being initiated on a partnership basis, with farmer research group members designing the layout with researchers and then constructing the actual mounds.

Knowledge, contexts and interests: can they be brought together?

How does one bring different knowledge contexts and interests closer together in the field of agricultural research and development, in order to develop a greater commonality of understandings? In providing some theoretical reflections I shall refer to what I have loosely described as critical hermeneutics (Drinkwater, 1992a).

The field of hermeneutics is concerned with the interpretation and understanding of texts or social action. Perhaps the most important principle hermeneutics establishes is that we can only come to understand others through our own experience. If we are concerned to analyse a rural society, the society cannot be understood as a static map, but only as a 'living tradition' (Gadamer, in Bernstein, 1983) or mapping process (Leach, 1992). A living tradition is a complex phenomenon, reflectively appropriated by individuals and thus always only partially grasped and always evolving. As researchers or farmers we are in the same situation, we all have a limited grasp of how our own experience influences our understanding of others and their situations.

Hermeneutics thus focuses on the methodological problem of our understanding being constrained by history. We can, in short, only understand a 'living tradition' through those that live it, but we are also constrained in our ability to understand by the extent to which we are aware of our own tradition. Crucial to understanding, therefore, is the type of prejudices that we bring into an interpretive situation. Prejudices can be blinding or enabling. For instance, a scientist who automatically assumes that a farmer who does not use higher yielding varieties and recommended methods is backward, inefficient and ignorant is not going to learn much about that farmers' situation. On the contrary, a person who sees production activities as the outcome of physical, social, economic, institutional, as well as technological and cultural factors, is more likely to grasp the 'why' of a farmer's actions. By engaging with farmers for long enough, our understanding of them, as well as theirs' of us, will gradually emerge. And so we can come to perceive that understanding, because it is conditioned by individuals' histories and their relative grasp of these, that is, because it is always contextuated, is neither ever purely subjective or arbitrary, nor ever wholly objective (Drinkwater, 1992a).

This to and fro process by which understanding emerges, is one which Clifford Geertz has described as 'dialectical tacking' (1983: 69). This can be seen in terms of a pendulum movement from immersion in the view of others to a reflection on those views in an attempt to grasp them more fully (Drinkwater, 1992a). This process involves essentially delving into the lifeworlds and consciousness of participants, and thence into our own (as juxtaposed and simultaneous events). The lifeworld of an individual is the accretion of her or his personal experience and social inheritance. All individuals share smaller or larger aspects of their lifeworlds with those from common communities. Even with those whom we are not initially familiar we might expect to have overlapping lifeworld elements and some grounds for establishing communication (Seur, 1992).

The key point about the idea of a lifeworld is that it is a largely unthematized entity, yet it is the basis of many of our actions. This is why it is so difficult to penetrate human action, and why we cannot expect farmers to provide simple transparent accounts of their activities (assuming they trust us sufficiently to want to be honest in the first place). For instance, as a researcher who worked recently in Central Province showed, if one wishes to interact with farmers one must bear in mind from the outset that young males learn tasks mostly from working with their fathers and girls from working with their mothers (Rap, 1992). Learning is largely by doing (and sometimes by seeing). This means, in Giddens' terminology, much of what these farmers do lies at the level of practical consciousness, they are aware of what they do, but are not given to reflect upon it discursively:

> Human beings can in some degree – fluctuating according to historically given circumstances – give accounts of the circumstances of their action. But this by no means exhausts what they know about why they act as they do. Many most subtle and dazzlingly intricate forms of knowledge are embedded in, and constitutive of, the actions we carry out. They are done knowledgeably, but without necessarily being available to the discursive awareness of the actor . . . Any analysis of social activity which ignores practical consciousness is massively deficient (Giddens, 1984: 63).

Challenges for participatory research methods

The challenge for participatory research approaches is how to open up to exploration of people's lives, which normally lie beneath the surface. One criticism that is commonly made of farmer-first RRA and PRA methods is that although 'supposedly geared to gaining a fast understanding of peasant level circumstances', they have 'the effect of shielding off planners and scientists from the complexities of rural life' (de Vries, 1992: intro). It is particularly the use of such positivist terms such as 'ITK' which has drawn the fire of academic critics.

Participatory approaches can certainly be devalued very easily. Nowadays, everyone who goes into an area for a day or two and speaks to a few farmers is 'doing an RRA'. On the other hand, there are those who speak of participatory techniques as simply playing games with farmers and therefore of being demeaning and insulting. Clear positions – and methods – are required for tackling these criticisms and misconceptions (Cornwall *et al.*, Part II). Since staff within agricultural research and extension institutions, as also NGOs and other development organizations, do not have the luxury of extended time for social research, it is still preferable to have staff camp out in a rural area for several days than conducting the one-day sortie from a base station which is the usual bureaucratic mode. But this is not a justification in itself of quick and dirty methods of appraisal. There are two questions that have to be addressed:

- Can such methods really allow us to penetrate beneath the surface in an exploration of local production cultures?
- What about the question of empowerment, the emphasis on which is the main reason for the recent advocacy of a switch from RRA to PRA (Chambers, 1992a) – can one really expect government institutions to undertake such a role?

I think both questions can be answered together. No single short-duration exercise – RRA or PRA – can stand by itself. What is required is an ongoing process where methods are linked over time as part of a continuing dialogue. Such dialogue is essential if the social world of farmers is to be opened up and their knowledge to become more accessible. If this can take place, then through an exploration of farmers' practical consciousness, a deepening awareness of both the context in which activities occur and the nature of those activities, will also occur. A central aim of such an ideal process would be the empowerment of both farmers and researchers; for farmers so that even the resource-poor and vulnerable can confidently state what they need (and can do themselves), and for researchers so that they have the confidence to address and promote those needs. Thus, the question turns from whether empowerment can be achieved to whether an ongoing process of engagement can be maintained.

The interweaving of knowledge and power in development interfaces

NORMAN LONG and MAGDALENA VILLAREAL

An actor-oriented perspective

During the late 1970s and early 1980s, a number of social scientists interested in the theorization of uneven development turned towards political economy and institutional models for an explanation. While this gave some new insights and a framework within which they could order their data and experiences, it did not in the end provide much practical help to those in the 'frontline' of planned development who were confronted with the day-to-day dilemmas of implementing policy and of interacting with so-called 'target' and non-target groups. Many of the abstractions used were far removed from the detailed workings of everyday development practice and failed to explain the differential outcomes of change. Hence while 'class struggle' and 'surplus extraction' might characterize some important features of intervention, they were seldom enough to explain the particular situations that emerged. This approach in fact promoted a somewhat pessimistic view of the possibilities of initiating change 'from below', through the actions of local groups themselves or by means of outside-planned interventions aimed at increasing the claim-making capacities of local people.

In the field of development practice, extension science was for many years associated with models of the adoption and diffusion of innovations (Rogers, 1962; Rogers and Shoemaker, 1971; Rogers 1983) and with the Land Grant type of applied rural sociology (Lionberger, 1960). More recently this has given way to a more thorough-going application of communication and systems theory (Beal *et al.*, 1986). This is signalled by the mushrooming of research dealing with farmer knowledge and with the complex set of links between research establishments, extension services and the farming population. Simultaneously these developments have been accompanied by a growing interest in 'farming systems analysis', which is aimed at developing a multi-level, interdisciplinary approach to understanding farming practice, placed within the context of the wider ecological, technical, economic and social constraints and in relation to technological change in agriculture (Hildebrand, 1981; Collinson, 1982; Fresco, 1986).

It is our view that both of these paradigms are essentially inadequate for developing a sound understanding of change processes and fail to come to terms with the complex issues involved. Instead, we aim to elucidate the advantages of adopting an actor-oriented approach. We do this through investigating and theorizing the nature of agricultural knowledge processes. Hence, we concentrate on issues of knowledge generation and transformation and on the organizational and strategic elements involved in rural development interfaces.

Knowledge as an encounter of horizons

Recently researchers have pinpointed certain critical limitations in what Dissanayake (1986: 280) has designated 'the transportational paradigm', for understanding knowledge processes. The paradigm assumes that the process of knowledge dissemination/utilization involves the transfer of a body of knowledge from one individual or social unit to another, rather than adopting a more dynamic view that acknowledges the joint creation of knowledge by both disseminators and users. This latter interpretation depicts knowledge as arising from an encounter of horizons, since the processing and absorption of new items of information and new discursive or cognitive frames can only take place on the basis of already existing networks of knowledge and evaluative modes, which are themselves re-shaped through communication. Moreover, although knowledge creation/dissemination is in essence an interpretative and cognitive process entailing the bridging of the gap between a familiar world and a less familiar (or even alien) set of meanings, knowledge is built upon the accumulated social experience, commitments and culturally-acquired dispositions of the actors involved.

Processes of knowledge dissemination/creation simultaneously imply several interconnected elements: actor strategies and capacities for drawing on existing knowledge repertoires and absorbing new information, validation processes whereby newly introduced information and its sources are judged acceptable and useful or contested, and various transactions involving the exchange of specific material and symbolic benefits. Implicit in all this is the fact that the generation and utilization of knowledge is not merely a matter of instrumentalities, technical efficiencies, or hermeneutics (i.e. the mediation of the understandings of others through the theoretical interpretation of our own), but involves aspects of control, authority and power that are embedded in social relationships. It is for this reason that there are likely to be striking dissonances between the different categories of actors involved in the production, dissemination and utilization of knowledge.

As studies of 'experimenting' farmers show, critical social divisions do not coincide neatly with the distinctions between knowledge 'producers', 'disseminators' and 'users' (e.g. Richards, 1985; Box, 1987; Rhoades and

42

Bebbington, 1988; Millar; Stolzenbach, Part II). A recent study on the use of information technology among Dutch farmers, for example, argues that the category of 'users' must be extended beyond farmers-as-clients to cover also government agencies and farmers' organizations wishing to use the technology to improve their competitiveness *vis-à-vis* other producer groups, to researchers and extension workers who deploy it to promote their own models of farming and to agroindustrial enterprises that seek to tie customers to their business interests (Leeuwis, 1991). Leeuwis' data suggest that conceptualizations of 'information needs' in terms of information technology are often problematic, as they are viewed as 'static', as if they could be 'predicted in advance and relate[d] to formal decision making models'. Dutch cucumber growers, he claims, choose a specific software programme considering all sorts of 'context' situations, such as personal ties and loyalties, group composition and the need to avoid social isolation (Leeuwis and Arkesteyn, 1991).

This case lends support to the argument that so long as we conceptualize the issues of knowledge creation/dissemination simply in terms of linkage or transfer concepts, without giving sufficient attention to human agency and the transformation of meaning at the point of intersection between different actors' lifeworlds, and without analysing the social interactions involved, we will have missed the significance of knowledge itself. Our guiding notions, we suggest, should be discontinuity, not linkage, and transformation, not transfer of meaning. Knowledge emerges as a product of the interaction and dialogue between specific actors. It is also multi-layered (there always exists a multiplicity of possible frames of meaning) and fragmentary and diffuse, rather than unitary and systematized. Not only is it unlikely therefore that different parties (such as farmers, extensionists and researchers) will share the same priorities and parameters of knowledge, but one also expects 'epistemic' communities (i.e. those that share roughly the same sources and modes of knowledge) to be differentiated internally in terms of knowledge repertoires and application. Therefore engineering the creation of the conditions under which a knowledge system (involving mutually-beneficial exchanges and flows of information between the different actors) could emerge seems unattainable; and, if indeed one did succeed, this would be at the expense of innovativeness and adaptability to change, both of which depend on the diversity and fluidity of knowledge, rather than on integration and systematization.

Discontinuities and accommodations at knowledge interfaces

In order to explore these issues in more depth it is necessary to develop an analysis of 'interface situations'. We define a social interface as a critical point of intersection between different social systems, fields or levels of social order where structural discontinuities, based upon differences of normative value and social interest, are most likely to be found (Long, 1989).

Interface studies then are essentially concerned with the analysis of the discontinuities in social life. Such discontinuities are characterized by

43

discrepancies in values, interests, knowledge and power. Interfaces typically occur at points where different, and often conflicting, lifeworlds or social fields intersect. More concretely, they characterize social situations wherein the interactions between actors become oriented around the problem of devising ways of 'bridging', accommodating to, or struggling against each others' different social and cognitive worlds. Interface analysis aims to elucidate the types of social discontinuities present in such situations and to characterize the different kinds of organisational and cultural forms that reproduce or transform them. Although the word 'interface' tends to convey the image of some kind of two-sided articulation or confrontation, interface situations are much more complex and multiple in nature (Long and Long, 1992).

The interactions between government or outside agencies involved in implementing particular development programmes and the so-called recipients of the farming population cannot be adequately understood through the use of generalized conceptions such as 'state-peasant relations' or by resorting to normative concepts such as 'local participation'. These interactions must be analysed as part of the on-going processes of negotiation, adaptation and transfer of meaning that take place between the specific actors concerned. Interface analysis, which concentrates on analysing critical junctures or arenas involving differences of normative value and social interest, entails not only understanding the struggles and power differentials taking place between the parties involved, but also an attempt to reveal the dynamics of cultural accommodation that makes it possible for the various 'world views' to interact.

This is a difficult research topic, but one which is central to understanding the intended and unintended results of planned intervention carried out 'from above' by public authorities or development agencies or initiated 'from below' by diverse local interests. Some of the complexities involved in the interaction of governmental agencies with local groups are explored in the following two cases from Mexico, which illustrate how the understanding of different (and possibly conflicting) forms of knowledge and ideology is central to the analysis of rural development.

Bridging the gap between peasants and bureaucrats

The first case (Arce and Long, 1987) focuses on the dilemmas of Roberto, a *técnico* who tried to bridge the gap between the interests of peasant producers and the administrative structure and its priorities. As a *técnico*, Roberto was the 'frontline' implementor of SAM (Mexican Food System, a national programme which aimed at providing a degree of capitalization to rural producers of basic staples) in direct and regular interaction with his client population. He was expected to follow certain administrative procedures in the implementation of the programme. At the same time, however, he accumulated experience in dealing both with the demands of the administrative system and its routines, and with those of his peasant clients.

The *técnico*'s involvement with these two contrasting, and often conflicting, social worlds produced a body of knowledge drawn from individual experience which led him to devise his own strategies of intervention in both the village and official administrative arenas. Although it might appear that such strategies are highly idiosyncratic, being based upon the chronology of experience of particular individuals, in fact they are shaped by the possibilities for manoeuvre and discourse that already exist and by the dynamics of the structural contexts within which the different parties interact. The case shows how these different parties or social categories develop their own everyday shared understandings or models for action that originate from and acquire their potency and legitimation through social interaction and confrontation with opposing views and forms of organisation. Roberto could not escape these influences and constraints by attempting to ignore their existence, and if he did try to do so, he would lose legitimacy as a *técnico* in the eyes of both peasants and bureaucrats.

He launched a criticism of the shortcomings of SAM and made charges of administrative malpractice. However, the end result was that he was labelled a 'troublemaker' (*un grilloso*) and sent to a special 'trouble-makers unit' (an isolated or 'problematic' zone) for remedial treatment. His lack of success in persuading his administrative superior to accept his approach for mediating between peasant and government interests confirmed and supported the peasants' existing model of government practice and personnel. Hence, their experience with this particular *técnico* reinforced their beliefs in how the state works. The situation also became an important factor in the reproduction of their particular livelihood strategies, which they effectively concealed from government, and in the reproduction of their own diverse configurations of knowledge. The combined effect of these various processes kept the social worlds of peasants and bureaucrats in opposition through the mutual generation of socially constructed systems of ignorance.

Women beekeepers

The interaction and accommodation between world views can be observed among a group of women beekeepers from Mexico (Long and Villareal, 1989; Villareal, 1990). Their case highlights the importance of both muffled and overt power processes, as well as the interweaving of knowledge networks. The beekeepers group was organised as an 'agro-industrial unit for peasant women', a state initiative, following new legal guidelines which called for the creation of peasant women's enterprises. Although each of the women attributed a different meaning to their participation in the beekeeping project and to the benefits they derived from it, their interests were intertwined at certain points, addressing issues relating not only to the project itself, but to household strategies, to relations within their kin networks, etc. Thus, the project comprised shared as well as conflicting definitions by the group members, involving matters such as the size of the enterprise, the relations they assumed with groups and institutions outside the village, and also their self-definition as beekeepers, as women entrepreneurs and as housewives. The women struggled together against male villagers who labelled them lazy and irresponsible towards household chores, redoubling their efforts to care for their children and husbands. They contested the ideas of ministry officers who pressed them to expand their enterprise and enter into the 'men's world of business'. However, during the process of interaction with each other, with their families and other people from the village, as well as with outside intervenors, the boundaries of the project and their roles as women in the face of it were constantly redefined. This redefinition involved not only their aims as beekeepers, but their prospects and projects as women in other fields of their everyday lives.

Knowledge networks and epistemic communities

Consistent with this emphasis on viewing knowledge generation and acquisition in terms of encounters at multiple interfaces is the notion of knowledge networks, through which, as Box (1989: 167) argues, certain types of information are communicated, legitimated, and sometimes segregated. Using the case of cassava production in the Dominican Republic, Box shows how the lifeworlds of researchers, extensionists and farmers are partially sealed off from each other. He concludes that:

> Knowledge networks are highly segmented. They are, like the sierra landscape with its cleavages, holding communities apart. Instead of one knowledge system there are many complex networks, which lack articulation among each other. The lifeworlds of the participants, or their values, norms and interests, differ so greatly that they do not allow for communication and interaction between the parties.

These differences are intrinsic to the everyday life of the actors, and constitute the social conditions for both change and continuity. A key problem for the analysis and management of so-called knowledge systems is, then, precisely the fragile, changeable or non-existent communication channels between the various parties involved, not the permanence and coherence of existing linkages. Moreover, as Box underlines, the knowledge repertoires of sierra migrants – who arrive with certain pre-existing social networks but also quickly create new ones – cannot therefore be detached from the social relationships and exchanges in which such knowledge exists.

There are important differences in the nature and operation of knowledge networks within the same farming populations. Hence, network analysis can help to identify the boundaries of epistemic communities and to characterize the structure and contents of particular communicator networks. As previous studies of communicator networks have shown (e.g. Allen and Cohen, 1969; Long, 1972; Long and Roberts, 1984), certain individuals or groups often become the sociometric stars of a defined network of social ties, as well as the points of articulation with wider fields. That is, they operate as 'gatekeepers' or 'brokers' to structurally more distant networks and social fields. Gatekeepers play a strategic role in both facilitating and blocking the flow of certain types of information and thus are of crucial importance in understanding the functioning of knowledge networks. Related to this issue is the proposition that effective dissemination of ideas and information within a network of individuals depends upon the existence of what Granovetter (1983) calls 'weak ties' 'which bridge divergent network segments that otherwise would be isolated from one another' (Milardo, 1988: 17). Such weak ties have been shown to be particularly significant for obtaining access to diverse fields of information, such as, for example, those associated with seeking employment or housing, or information concerning prices in dispersed market locations. On the other hand, to act on information usually requires that individuals secure some support from others. This entails a minimum of normative consensus and, in some situations, the capacity for making rules and enforcing compliance from members (Moore, 1973). The latter presupposes the existence of a relatively dense social network, which might also, paradoxically, hinder the absorption of new information and the quick adaptation to changed circumstances (Long, 1984: 23,fn.14).

These and similar network findings provide a fertile source for ideas on how different types of social networks and exchange contents within networks affect the flow of information and processes of knowledge dissemination/creation. This is a fruitful but still neglected field of research (Cornwall *et al.*, Part II).

Knowledge heterogeneity and agency in farm practice

As the above examples indicate, farming populations are essentially heterogeneous in terms of the strategies adopted for solving problems. Varying ecological, demographic, market, political, economic and sociocultural conditions combine to generate differential patterns of farm enterprise, leading to differences in farm management styles, cropping patterns and levels of production. Implicit in this process, of course, is the differential use and transformation of knowledge: that is, agricultural knowledge varies and is accorded different social meanings depending on how it is applied in the running of farms. This is readily seen in the use of different technologies (e.g. tractor, plough, hoe or axe), but is also evident in the specific meanings that a particular instrument or factor of production acquires (van der Ploeg, 1986). Hence adopted technology is forever being reworked to fit with the production strategies, resource imperatives and social desires of the farmer or farm family.

Included in this is not only the process by which 'new' technologies or packages are adopted, appropriated or transformed, but also the ongoing processes by which particular farmers combine different social domains based on, for example, the family, community, market, or state institutions. The farmer's task becomes that of selecting and co-ordinating the most appropriate normative and social commitments for organizing the process of farm production and reproduction. The decisions the farmer makes, of course, are based upon value preferences and available knowledge, resources and relationships.

Viewed in this manner, the farmer is seen as an active strategizer who problematizes situations, processes information and brings together the

47

elements necessary for operating the farm. That is, a farmer is involved in constructing her/his own farming world, even if s/he internalizes external modes of rationality.

This line of argument leads us once again to emphasize the importance of an actor-oriented approach to the understanding of knowledge processes. Central to the notion of social actor is the concept of human agency, which attributes to the actor (individual or social group) the capacity to process social experience and to devise ways of coping with life, even under the most extreme conditions of coercion. It is important, however, to stress that 'agency' is not simply an attribute of the individual actor. Agency is composed of social relations and can only become effective through them; it requires organizing capacities. The ability to influence others or to pass on a command (e.g. to get them to accept a particular extension message) rests fundamentally on 'the actions of a chain of agents each of whom 'translates' it in accordance with his/her own projects' . . . and 'power is composed here and now by enrolling many actors in a given political and social scheme' (Latour, 1986: 264). In other words, agency (and power) depend crucially upon the emergence of a network of actors who become partially, though hardly ever completely, enrolled in the 'project' of some other person or persons. Effective agency then requires the strategic generation/manipulation of a network of social relations and the channelling of specific items (such as claims, orders, goods, instruments and information) through certain 'nodal points' of interaction (Clegg, 1989: 199). In order to accomplish this, it becomes essential for actors to win the struggles that take place over the attribution of specific social meanings to particular events, actions and ideas. Particular development intervention models (or ideologies) become strategic weapons in the hands of the agencies charged with promoting them (Long and van der Ploeg, 1989).

This process is illustrated by van der Ploeg's (1989) analysis of how small-scale producers in the Andes succumb to 'scientific' definitions of agricultural development. He shows that, although peasants have devised perfectly good solutions to their own production problems (here he is concerned with potato cultivation), their local knowledge gradually becomes marginalized by the type of scientific knowledge introduced by extensionists. The former becomes superfluous to the model of 'modern' production methods promoted by 'the experts', and development projects become a kind of commodity monopolized and sold by experts who exert 'authority' over their 'subjects'. In this way the rules, limits and procedures governing the negotiation between state agents and farmers and the resources made available are derived (in large part) from external interests and institutions. Hence, although it is possible to depict the relations between Andean peasants and outside experts or state officials in terms of a history of distrust and dependency, science and modern ideologies of development eventually come to command such a major influence on the outcomes of dealings with cultivators that they effectively prevent any exchange of knowledge and experience. This creates what van der Ploeg calls 'a sphere of ignorance' whereby cultivators are labelled 'invisible men' in contrast to the 'experts' who are visible and authoritative (Salas; Muka-muri and Matose, Part I).

Such processes are by no means mechanical impositions from the out-side. They entail negotiation over concepts, meanings and projects which are internalized to varying degrees by the different parties involved. Thus the ability of extensionists to transform the nature of agricultural practice is premised on two elements: their skills in handling interface encounters with farmers; and the ways in which the wider set of power relations (or 'chain of agents') feeds into the context, giving legitimacy to their actions and conceptions, and defining certain critical 'rules of the game'. Counter-balancing this is the fact that cultivators, too, assimilate informa-tion from each other, as well as from 'external' sources, in an attempt to create knowledge that is in tune with the situations they face.

Power and the social construction of knowledge

The foregoing discussion brings out the relationships between power and knowledge processes. Like power, knowledge is not simply something that is possessed, accumulated and unproblematically imposed upon others (Foucault in Gordon, 1980: 78–108). Nor can it be measured precisely in terms of some notion of quantity or quality. It emerges out of processes of social interaction and, as suggested earlier, is essentially a joint product of the encounter of horizons. Knowledge must therefore, like power, be looked at relationally and not treated as a commodity. Someone having power or knowledge does not entail that others are without them. A zero-sum model is thus misplaced. Nevertheless both power and knowledge may become reified in social life: that is, they are thought of as being real material things possessed by agents and regarded as unquestioned 'givens'. This process of reification is, of course, an essential part of the ongoing struggles over meaning and the control of strate-gic relationships and resources that we discussed earlier.

If, therefore, we recognize that we are dealing with 'multiple realities', potentially conflicting social and normative interests, and diverse and frag-mented bodies of knowledge, then we must look closely at the issue of whose interpretations or models (e.g. those of agricultural scientists, politi-cians, farmers, or extensionists) prevail over those of other actors and under what conditions. Knowledge processes are embedded in social pro-cesses that imply aspects of power, authority and legitimation; and they are just as likely to reflect and contribute to the conflict between social groups as they are to lead to the establishment of common perceptions and inter-ests. And, if this is the normal state of affairs, then it becomes unreal to imagine that one can gently 'nudge' knowledge systems towards better modes of integration and co-ordination.

If we now look at knowledge dissemination/creation in this way we are forced to place it fully in its social context, not as a disembodied process made up of 'formal institutions', 'ideal-type conceptions' or 'linkage' mech-anisms, but as involving specific actors and interacting individuals who become inter-related through networks of interest and through the sharing of certain knowledge frames.

The analysis of power processes should not therefore be restricted to an understanding of how social constraints and access to resources shape social action. Nor should it lead to the description of rigid hierarchical categories and hegemonic ideologies that 'oppress passive victims'. Standing back from the tendency to empathize ideologically with these hapless victims, one should, instead, explore the extent to which specific actors perceive themselves capable of manoeuvring within given contexts or networks and develop strategies for doing so. This is not to fail to recognize the often much restricted space for individual initiative, but rather to examine how actors identify and create space for their own interests and for change (Long, 1984).

Making room for manoeuvre implies a degree of consent, a degree of negotiation and a degree of power – not necessarily power stored in some economic or political position, but the possibility of control, of prerogative, of authority and capacity for action, be it front- or backstage, for flickering moments or for long periods (Villareal, 1992). Power, then, is fluid and difficult or unnecessary to measure, but important to describe more precisely. It is not only the *amount* of power that makes a difference, but the possibility of gaining an edge over others and using it to advantage. Power always implies struggle, negotiation and compromise. Even those categorized as 'oppressed' are not utterly passive victims and may become involved in active resistance. Likewise, the 'powerful' are not in complete control of the stage and the extent to which their power is forged by the so-called 'powerless' should not be underestimated. Rather, as Scott (1985) points out, one must speak of resistance, accommodation and strategic compliance. Although resistance is rarely an overt, collective undertaking, individual acts of subtle defiance and the muffled voices of opposition and mobilization nevertheless act to divert the possibly coercive or oppressive strategies of others. In this manner, accommodation and strategic compliance – sometimes shielding acts of defiance – become regular features of everyday social life (Scott, 1985).

All this suggests that power differentials and struggles over social meaning are central to an understanding of knowledge processes. Knowledge is essentially a social construction that results from and is constantly being reshaped by the encounters and discontinuities that emerge at the points of intersection between actors' lifeworlds.

The discourse and dilemma of 'empowerment'

This view sheds light on crucial dilemmas faced by development practitioners. For example, much recent work within development enterprises is oriented towards the aim of 'empowerment' of local groups (Huizer, 1979; Chambers, 1983; Kronenburg, 1986). Although the concept of empowerment forms part of a neo-populist discourse supporting 'participatory' approaches that emphasize 'listening to the people', understanding the 'reasoning behind local knowledge', 'strengthening local organizational capacity' and developing 'alternative development strategies from below', it nevertheless seems to carry with it the connotation of power injected from outside aimed at shifting the balance of forces towards local interests. Hence it implies the idea of empowering people through strategic intervention by 'enlightened experts' who make use of 'people's science' (Richards, 1985) and 'local intermediate organizations' (Esman and Uphoff, 1984; Korten, 1987) to promote development 'from below'. While acknowledging the need to take serious account of local people's solutions to the problems they face, the issues are often presented as involving the substitution of 'blueprint' by 'learning' approaches to the planning and management of projects (Korten, 1987) or in terms of 'new' for 'old' style professionalism aimed at promoting participatory management and participatory research and evaluation methods (Chambers *et al.*, 1989).

Such formulations still do not escape the managerialist and interventionist undertones inherent in development work. That is, they tend to evoke the image of 'more knowledgeable and powerful outsiders' helping 'the powerless and less discerning local folk'. Of course, many field practitioners, who face the everyday problems of project implementation, show an acute awareness of this paradox of participatory strategies. Kronenburg (1986: 163) – himself a practitioner – for example, provides an insightful description of some of the dilemmas of 'empowerment' experienced by implementors of a non-formal education programme in Kenya which was strongly committed to participatory and conscientizing goals. Discussing the interplay between emancipatory and manipulative processes, he explains:

> There was contradiction looming in the thin line between the use of DEP [Development Education Programme] skills to enhance the capacity of communities and their members to decide on their own development priorities or to attain goals the facilitators themselves had set. Often, discussions on the topic of manipulation emerged at national . . . workshops usually at a stage that trust between participants and facilitators had not fully developed. Yet, the possibility was always there that unwittingly participants would be following the path laid out by the facilitators . . .

Closely related to the issue of emancipation versus manipulation is the power of the facilitator to either allow group dialogue to follow its course or to control the discussions by imposing various forms of discipline. By applying time limits on topics judged irrelevant or by emphasising topics familiar or foreseen for discussion, the facilitator could influence the direction of the discussion. This is a dilemma facilitators, applying a nondirective methodology, are faced with continuously. To forestall manipulation, DEP workers attempted consciously to develop sensitivity to group needs and feelings. To do this optimally facilitators always operated in teams to provide counterweight to the undesired tendencies inherent to their work (Kronenburg, 1986).

Kronenberg's account exposes the multi-faceted nature of power inherent in the relations between development practitioners and their local 'partners' in participatory projects. It also shows how external social commitments intrude into this arena and shape the outcomes of participatory activities. Hence his study adds weight to the earlier argument that social processes (and especially so-called 'planned' interventions) are highly complex and cannot easily be manipulated through the injection of external sources of power and authority. The issue he mentions of conflicting loyalties and ideologies, likewise, brings us back to the earlier discussion of negotiations over 'truth' claims, battles over images and contesting interests which are implicit in the interlocking of lifeworlds and actors' 'projects'.

The Kenyan project illustrates the central importance of strategic agency in the ways in which people (i.e. development practitioners, as well as local participants) deal with and manipulate certain constraining and enabling elements in their endeavours to enrol each other in their individual or group 'projects'. The case also suggests the significance of social networks for gathering information, forming opinions, legitimizing one's standpoint, and thus for generating differential power relations. The idea that designing participatory strategies based upon the effective use of local knowledge and organization would enable one to avoid, what Marglin (1990) calls 'the dominating knowledge' of science and western 'scientific' management is clearly untenable (Marsden, Part I). The question of empowerment, then, brings us back the central issue of the encounter between actors and their knowledge repertoires.

Conclusion

The foregoing discussion provides a profile of current theoretical concerns essential for developing an actor-oriented analysis of agricultural knowledge processes and development intervention. The agenda is extensive and the theoretical issues daunting. But it is our view that we have made important headway towards developing a revitalized sociological perspective that challenges systems models and interventionist thinking. Such an approach enables us to build a better bridge between theoretical understanding and social practice. It does this by providing a set of sensitizing analytical concepts based on an actor and interface perspective and a field methodology geared to developing theory 'from below'. This framework necessitates a thorough reassessment of issues of intervention, knowledge and power. Yet let us not be intimidated by the enormity of the tasks before us. Though arduous, the path ahead is likely to be exhilarating and much more in tune with the needs and dilemmas of frontline practitioners in search of a better understanding of intervention processes and their roles in them.

Indigenous management and the management of indigenous knowledge

DAVID MARSDEN

Local strategies

The idea of 'indigenous management' is seen as a possible way forward in the task of strengthening and sustaining local institutions and capacities. To reveal some of the complexities that lie behind this notion, many threads of analysis must be pulled together, each with its own interpretation of reality and conception of the task of development.

The current discourse of development is dominated by the supposedly neutral vocabulary of management. This has replaced, or is rapidly replacing, the lexicon of economics. Efforts are directed at increasing efficiency, economy, effectiveness and providing opportunities for the encouragement of private entrepreneurial activity. A radical reassessment of the roles and responsibilities of the state is taking place. Policies for privatization aim at sectors that have traditionally been defined as part of the public domain. This is not, of course, peculiar to the Third World. It is based on the presumed superiority of a particular world view that is dominant in the liberal democracies of the West. A new realism, not governed by dogmatic adherence to hegemonic convictions, emerges as the West questions the viability of large public corporations and ushers in the 'post-Fordist' era. Nowhere is this more evident than in former socialist countries as they struggle to loosen the chains of state control and create more opportunities for individual initiative.

A renegotiation of the limits of individual freedom in the West has meant an attack on those institutions that are perceived to hinder expressions of individual entrepreneurial activity. This has resulted in the unleashing of what some see as the rapacious and avaricious pursuit of profit and self-interest. A similar renegotiation in the socialist bloc has resulted in attacks on the monopolistic control of the state, calls for regional autonomy, and the radical restructuring of entrenched and ossified political systems. These transformations run parallel to fundamental changes taking place throughout the Third World. In those countries, failures of top-down, externally-conceived, development projects and programmes have led to the elaboration of locally-based, indigenous strategies and the adoption of more flexible management approaches.

As efforts are made to get government off the backs of people, more attention is paid to the development of local institutions that are small enough to command authority and promote participation. The complexities of micro-level intervention move centre stage and analyses of local cultures gain greater importance. The assumption is that people will be more responsive if they are central to the design and implementation of programmes that affect their lives and livelihoods, and if they make some personal investment or commitment to them. A recognition that there is more to development than just economic productivity leads to a focus on *processes* as well as products, on the strengthening of local institutional capacities and on the fostering of constructive dialogue.

In pursuit of these aims, the appeal of indigenous management is self-evident: the mobilization of local strategies by local people for the control and use of their own resources in the struggle for self-reliant development. However, a major conceptual problem immediately arises when we reflect on what the terms 'indigenous' and 'management' mean, both of which are key expressions in current development discourse. The different ways in which they are used and the meanings attached to them need to be

53

examined before we can assess the appropriateness of advocating indigenous management further.

An analysis of the terms takes us back to the essential nature of the
development task and to basic problems of interpretation currently at the
centre of discussions within the social sciences. How are we to understand
other cultures? If management is no longer the application of explicit sets
of techniques (if it was ever), what is it? In development strategies that
emphasize indigenous creativity, what is the role of the 'outsider'?

The Oxford English Dictionary defines 'indigenous' as: 'born or produced naturally in a land or region; of, pertaining to, or intended for the
natives.' This definition raises more questions than it answers. What is
meant by 'natives'? What does 'naturally' mean? Is the term equivalent to
'traditional'? An additional meaning is also implied. This refers to 'authen-
ticity' and local 'legitimacy', derived from claims for originality, not so
much in terms of uniqueness as in connections with an unbroken historical
association with a place. As Illich (1982: 108) has pointed out in his analysis
of vernacular culture: 'Each village does its own dance to the tune of its
own regional music.'

Conservation and preservation

A dominant theme in the development debate is that of 'conservation'
of resources, both natural and intellectual, in the interests of 'preserving' heterogeneity. The monolithic forces that apparently guide
modern development strategies and lead to the homogenization of cultures are responsible for the destruction of our environment and the dis-
appearance of worlds of understanding. This 'declining base' reduces
opportunities for expansion and for cultural and natural adaptation in the
future.

Yet strategies for 'conservation' and 'preservation' are informed by a
world view which assumes that the earth offers a finite number of opportunities. This belief influences many attitudes to education and the acquisition of knowledge generally. It ignores the ways in which knowledge is
created and the dynamism and imminence of culture and resources.

Techniques, technologies and cultural forms (organizations and institutions) do not stand alone. They are tools that can be used in a variety of
ways. It is important to understand how they are employed and why they
are applied, and to discover who uses them and under what conditions.
Knowledge, like technology, is never neutral. It can never be completely
packaged. Its history and its content must be uncovered if we are to approach its meaning and not be mystified by its current form. This is the
essence of the 'process' approach to development which seeks not to impose a preconceived understanding of the most efficient, effective and
economic ways forward, but to build, through increased trust and mutu-
ality, sustainable strategies that create room for manoeuvre by concentrating on where people are, instead of where we would like them to be.

54

Multiple actors, multiple knowledges

Despite these shifts, the development project remains only partially articulated with the realities of everyday life. Indigenous management is an attempt to further this articulation. This process can be viewed from two competing theoretical perspectives. Both perspectives agree that the issue of control is central to the managerial task. As Reed (1989: 34) has observed, for those who perceive management as a neutral activity 'the process of control is broken down into an interrelated set of mechanisms or procedures through which [it] can restructure . . . to meet more effectively the demands and threats posed by its environment.' The issue is finding the mechanisms that can produce a neater fit between those doing the managing and those being managed. For those who perceive management in more Machiavellian terms, the problem of control is 'one of simultaneously securing and mystifying the exploitative relationship between a dominant and a subordinate class whose interests are placed in a position of structured antagonism because of the conflicting priorities embedded in such a relationship' (Reed, 1989: 34). The instruments of control are enshrined in 'good faith' relationships that disguise the actual ways in which unequal relationships are maintained and through which surplus value is extracted (Bourdieu, 1977).

There are many ways of experiencing, perceiving, understanding and defining reality. In addition to conflicting interpretations generated within the western scientific tradition, there are contending interpretations within local groups – the knowledge of elites is different from that of peasants; the knowledge of women is different from that of men, and so on. If indigenous management is about utilizing local, folk, or vernacular knowledge and organizational methods in the service of more appropriate development strategies, then it is important to investigate how that knowledge is gained and interpreted, what the knowledge is and how it might be most effectively used. Knowledge is a key asset in securing control and thus any discussions about it must necessarily recognize the political dimensions of its use (Drinkwater; Long and Villareal; Matose and Mukamuri; Sikana, Part I).

How is knowledge produced? What are the differences between indigenous knowledge and exogenous knowledge? Who creates the distinction between these forms of knowledge, bearing in mind that many of the scientific underpinnings of Western knowledge are derived from non-Western (indigenous?) sources? What sorts of knowledge count and who decides when they count? To answer such questions it is necessary to analyse the ways in which knowledge is generated, exchanged, transformed, consolidated, stored, retrieved, disseminated and utilized (Scoones and Thompson, Part I).

A commonly asserted dichotomy distinguishes between the written and the oral tradition. 'Indigenous' is associated with 'oral' – information is not written down and thus remains outside recorded history. One temptation is to consign this oral knowledge to a position of inferiority. The old divisions between 'traditional' and 'modern' are thereby resurrected in a new way. Another temptation is to romanticize and idealize local knowledge in a new reverence, and imply thereby a functional separation between two sorts of knowledge validated by different sets of criteria. The superiority of one form of knowledge is proclaimed by one and the essential separation or incommensurability of disparate knowledge bases, blocking comparisons, by the other.

When conceptualizing indigenous knowledge systems we are often thinking of 'other cultures' and the technical and non-technical features of such cultures. Such knowledge is supposed to be based on unique epistemologies, philosophies, institutions and principles which are seen often as tied to mystical or religious beliefs (Millar, Part II; Salas, Part I). All knowledge is culture bound whether it is classified as indigenous or scientific, oral or written. The danger is that we perceive cultures as discrete, bounded systems (undynamic and unchanging). Current research in the production of ethnographies cautions against such a view and forcibly proposes a much more sensitive approach to modes of cultural representation. The activity of cross-cultural representation is distinctly problematic. As Clifford (1988: 23) has pointed out: 'An ambiguous multi-vocal world makes it increasingly hard to conceive of human diversity as inscribed in bounded, independent cultures.'

Specialists and generalists

Can we recast the distinction between indigenous knowledge and exogenous knowledge, then, in terms of distinctions between 'specialists' or 'professionals' and 'generalists', or 'amateurs'? Those employed as 'experts' in development projects bring specialist knowledge to the task as distinct from the layperson who brings practical knowledge of everyday existence. Until recently, local, practically based knowledges have largely been ignored in development; professional, specialist knowledges have dominated. But what new thinking about management and organization suggests is that effective pursuit of the complex tasks of sustainable development requires both specialists and generalists.

Traditional knowledge and decision making shares many of the attributes that modern management theory is trying to promote – flexibility, fluidity, responsiveness. Modern management principles, as with local agricultural practice, conflate the roles of specialists and generalists. The image of order, precision and regularity is almost always clouded by informal considerations and processes. Referring to changes in industrial enterprises, Reed (1989: 117–8; 155) has commented:

> Managers' interest in participation strategies springs directly from [the] problem of consent and coordination that is at the heart of the 'management' job . . . The search for flexibility has become something of a catch-all concept for everything and anything employers find desirable to increase operational efficiency and company profitability.

This thinking has shifted emphasis away from management as a science, towards the norms, conventions and belief systems in 'an organisation that can lead to excellent performances' (Davies et al., 1989: 3).

So the trend in modern management is towards increased generalization within a professional context that attempts to secure control over more and more areas of knowledge. It is interesting to note that in current discussions of NGOs, they are being advised to move in the opposite direction by casting off their amateur second-generation image and developing 'third' and 'fourth' generation characteristics of increased professionalism (Pretty and Chambers; Uphoff, Part III).

The development of more effective managerial systems requires increasing amounts of general, informal, indigenous information, a strong partnership between specialist consultants and generalist practitioners and a commitment to new forms of organization that allow many voices to be heard. An interpretative social science, committed to uncovering the hidden, excluded, or ignored agenda of social action provides the prerequisites for an examination of these sorts of indigenous knowledge, currently at the centre of the debate about indigenous management.

'The technicians only believe in science and cannot read the sky': the cultural dimension of the knowledge conflict in the Andes

MARIA A. SALAS

Reading the sky

The purpose of this case study is to analyse the knowledge conflict experienced by contemporary Andean peasants when they express 'we are losing our ancestral knowledge because the technicians only believe in modern science and cannot read the sky'. This message conveys the problem of the interactions between science, technology, development and history and the nature of the interplay between two world views which are closely intertwined in Peruvian society.

This paper focuses on three main issues. The first concerns the power dimension of knowledge: who benefits from the knowledge interaction? Too often there is a detrimental impact of modern science on ancestral, indigenous knowledge. The second issue suggests the question: can Western science understand Andean knowledge? Since knowledge is inextricably linked to cultural interpretation and knowledge is interpretation of interpretations, is western science capable of getting inside the system of meaning of Andean knowledge without distorting it? The third issue is: whose limitations are causing the conflict? Is Andean knowledge limited by its cultural setting? Or is it that Western, modern knowledge has its own epistemological limitations? Or, is it that both knowledge systems are embedded in totally different and incompatible world views?

The focus of this case study is the potato crop. It provides an excellent example of the differences of orientation between international and national scientific interests and those of peasant society. On the one hand I will follow the institutional efforts of producing and disseminating knowledge which solves a set of problems defined by agronomists. On the other hand I will show how peasants create, recreate and apply their knowledge according to another set of problems and priorities. Finally, I will examine the role of extension as part of modern, western knowledge and propose an opportunity for interaction with the Andean knowledge system.

Western science and technology in Peru

Peruvian science has historically been determined by influences from abroad from the European conquest of the 16th century to the present. The imported science responds to Western social logic and not to the requirements, demands, potentials and limitations of Peruvian society. Furthermore, the dominant scientific style insists that only Western science can offer solutions. Knowledge systems that do not fit scientific modes of thinking have been systematically neglected. The possibility of developing a solid base of our own, within the cognitive structures of rural society, has been systematically denied. The logic of technological development, especially in the agricultural field, has hindered the development of peasant technology and knowledge.

The following agricultural achievements form the central core of Andean scientific excellence (Ravines, 1978; Cabieses, 1982; Murra, 1983; Earls, 1991).

- The articulation of regularities of the celestial bodies with the rhythms of social life;
- The construction of irrigation systems which use hydraulic principles to carry water up hill;
- The development of a terracing system for the protection and careful use of slopes;
- The use of guano, the natural dung from the coastal islands as a main source of fertility of soils;
- The combination of complementary crops in on-going sequences that permit a garden form of production;
- The use of the foot plough, a tool that allows the cultivation and preservation of the fragile soils in the highland slopes;
- The use of a great diversity of plants for foodstuffs (160 species, according to some authors);
- The transformation of foodstuffs for storage purposes, e.g. *chuño*, dehydrated and frozen potatoes under natural weather conditions;
- The welfare of six to ten million inhabitants on the basis of agricultural production.

The International Potato Centre: international solutions for local problems?

The International Potato Centre's (CIP) orientation can be traced back to the 1960s, when, with the ideas of the Green Revolution and with the financial aid of the Rockefeller Foundation, the international agricultural centres were first established. CIP, founded in 1971 and situated in Peru, is part of the system of International Agricultural Research Centres (IARCs) sponsored by the Consultative Group of International Agricultural Research (CGIAR). The CGIAR, including CIP, was established with the goal to improve agricultural technology, increase food production and improve the welfare of poor people in the Third World (Fujisaka, Part III).

Derived from the principles on which the IARC model is based (CIP, 1984: 29), I identify the following values guiding the generation of knowledge:

- The International Centres act as Western knowledge enclaves. Although they produce knowledge within the sociopolitical structures of the Third World, their responsibilities are independent from their host countries;
- The Centres are located in the Third World, but the knowledge produced has no national character. It is called 'universal', and therefore the solutions to agricultural problems are disseminated worldwide, beyond the specific locations, regions or countries from where knowledge is originating. Knowledge is no longer owned by local society and culture;
- The knowledge required to increase food production and welfare of the population of the Third World can only be achieved by qualified senior scientists. Therefore the CGIAR employs an elite of nearly 600 top subject-matter specialists.

The reasons that explain the establishment of CIP in Peru are:

- Potatoes are the most important food crop in Peruvian agriculture. Potatoes are grown on 204,000 hectares, about 90% in the highlands at 2000 meters or more above sea level;
- The Andean region has an enormous diversity of potato varieties. From the 13,733 varieties in the world collection, 82% come from the Peruvian Andes.

The 'scientific potato': what kind of knowledge for whom?

The mandate of CIP is to collect genetic resources of the potato and experiment with it. CIP does not get involved with extension or rural development; these two aspects are the exclusive responsibility of the national organizations.

Despite well-recognised innovations in the social science field (Rhoades, 1982, 1984), CIP, by and large, strives to create the 'ideal potato'. The ideal potato is free of nematodes, insects, fungi, bacteria and viruses; resistance to environmental stresses such as frost, heat, hail or drought; and adapted to the lowland tropics. This 'ideal potato' can be created only in the laboratory, under artificial conditions and through the control of senior scientists. Peasants, who are expected to produce potatoes under field conditions, call this ideal 'the scientific potato'.

59

Local knowledge: the old and the new – what was will be

Local knowledge is practically invisible in the official history of Peru. I consider that it is necessary to make this history visible, along with the social and cultural conditions of the knowledge system. In what follows, I will try to use peasants' own words and graphical representations as much as possible since they contain cognitive categories of their cultural framework. The collective memory of the rural population has evolved a mythology which can be found in many contemporary peasant communities of the Andes. It is very clearly presented in many oral versions or in the form of popular theatre, dances or other manifestations of the Andean culture.

The voices of the peasant are constantly creating and recreating their reality. The following oral tradition, collected in 1985 in the Mantaro Valley (Salas, 1987) and registered in a carved gourd, gives us great insight into Andean life, especially the character of the culture centred around agricultural activities:

> *Mamapacha* (mother earth) and God the Father created the mountains, the glaciers, the mountain chains and the birds. What else can we create in this world? asked God. *Mamapacha* answered, 'a woman that can bear a child'. The woman lived in the mountain range together with the birds. They took care of her, warmed her. Suddenly she was ready to give birth, under an immense rock, she had her baby with the help of the birds.
>
> One day, the woman went to wash in the river and left her child in charge of the birds. The baby slept and the birds were happy that he was so quiet, until he noticed that his mother was gone. The birds caressed the baby but he began to cry and cry. The birds got impatient and asked him to stop crying and continued to caress him with their wings and their beaks. Suddenly they realised the baby was quiet and dead.
>
> 'Now what shall we do?' asked the birds among themselves. 'We will leave no trace of his existence' was the agreement. The oldest bird distributed to the rest all the parts of the child and warned them to hide them very well. Each bird took a part of the child and buried it: from the nails sprouted the Lima beans, from the eyes the peas, from the teeth maize, from the testicle *olluco* and *ocas*, from the bones cassava, from the hair wheat, from the kidneys fruits, from the penis the potato, from the blood, passion fruit and watermelon and from the bladder the water sources . . .
>
> When the mother returned she did not find her child and began to cry. Her tears dropped to the ground and she found herself in a *chacra* surrounded by all these foodstuffs. Since then, we harvest all these fruits from the *Mamapacha* . . .

Nature is a living being

As we can see from these verses, nature (*Mamapacha*) is perceived as a source of life and at the same time like a person with wishes and a will. She is capable of communication and her behaviour the result of agreements with other persons of equal status. This image of equality in the dialogue between *Mamapacha* and God the Father shapes many aspects of Andean culture. For instance, it reflects the perception that nature and society are equal, symbolically bound in the endless cycle of life. Nature is not a dominating figure nor is she dominated by the community of humans. There is an interdependency of both, descending from the cosmological order, so that the relationship between nature and society is not only of equality, but also assumes religious character. Nothing is profane or just utilitarian in the Andean culture. Activities like sewing, harvesting and irrigating are highly ritualised to reflect the relationship and communication between society and nature (van den Berg, 1989; Grillo *et al.*, 1991).

The mountains (*apus*), the water (*yacumama*), the sun (*inti*), the moon (*quilla*) and the stars (*chaska*), coexist in the form of a community. They behave and express themselves as persons. This must be decodified, as in the human process of communication. For example, each *apu* is a principle of order, the administrator of the resources of a limited region. The *apu* defines which zones are of agricultural use or for pastures, which zones have to be preserved as woods and which should be free of use. *Apus* communicate among themselves, 'they talk to each other' about the matters which are under their responsibilities, mainly the security and the welfare of the human community.

The cultural dimension of knowledge

In the Andes, agricultural activities, like sowing, harvesting, ploughing, weather forecasting and so on, are not mere technical procedures. Each one, and the whole agricultural process, is attached to a set of ideas deriving from the perception of reality (a theory) and put into action in social reality – praxis. Both, theory and praxis are not only a product of cultural context, they are so intimately interrelated that they become one constituent, inseparable element of social reality (Salas, 1991).

Theory and praxis are not independent of social relationships. For example, in a peasant community, work is organized according to the principle of reciprocity; this means people help each other with tasks. This working together, mutual help, reciprocity are inseparable notions related to agricultural knowledge. Peasants summarize it very clearly: 'without the help of the family we are lost, we cannot survive'. That means that the mutual help is not just an ideal, it is their social arrangement to act upon reality.

The cultural dimension of knowledge thus implies an understanding of the interrelationship between theory, praxis and social relationships.

Farming performance

Experienced farmers use all their intuitive skills to transform their observations into an agricultural strategy which accounts for the variety of risks and dangers. Older farmers thus determine appropriate crops and crop varieties and dates for sowing for each of their multiple plots. It is after this determination, which is never totally strict, that the family members engage in activities like preparing the seeds, carrying guano to the fields or looking for the help of neighbours and friends. The planning is not strict for several reasons: agricultural inputs are not available in time, or a peasant might acquire new seeds and he will always experiment, even if the signs may have changed.

Experimental observations also have different time horizons. Some apply their predictions to the whole cycle of agricultural production; some apply them only to one crop's yield. Others will announce, half a year in advance, the amount and time of rains during the growing season of winter. Prediction is important, since in dry years beans, lupine and quinua will produce well on normal plots; in wet years potatoes will putrefy, but will give excellent production in dry years. Other indicators and principles help short-term decisions. The moon phase is one basis for fixing the sowing date. But other factors include: whether the rains have given enough moisture to the soil of any plot; whether the oxen are available to yoke; or whether labour is available for fertilizing or for planting.

Crop growing thus involves not only normal agricultural tasks, but also the observation of the sky and moon. By this people know if rain will continue or if hail is threatening. If hail is identified, one specialist is obliged to throw a charge of dynamite so that the clouds will change their route. In this case the prediction has to be done in a short time of hours or minutes. If the specialist fails the community will fine him.

These performances, relating material agricultural practice to cosmological factors, are local and specific. It is therefore impossible to establish a pattern for the whole Andean region. This knowledge is as diverse as the ecological conditions, which vary from village to village, from hill to hill. This knowledge thus survives in the experience and the practices of peasant families. It is embedded in local culture and society and moulded with symbolic and material actions and attitudes towards nature.

The peasant potato

'Our custom is to grow potatoes . . .' is the peasants' answer when they are asked to talk about agriculture. This crop has reportedly existed for nine thousand years. More than four hundred selected, domesticated and improved varieties exist. In order to emphasize the continuity and recreation of the Andean culture in the process of knowledge generation I have selected a cultural form, carved gourds, which is the first crop and the first form of aesthetic expression of the pre-hispanic Peruvian civilization.

Today, the carved gourds are crafts produced by peasant families in communities of the central Andean highlands and can be considered as a system of collective representation, although they are individually performed. Since 'reading' a gourd is a difficult task for non-Andean peasants, the following text is an attempt to introduce us to the terms and categories of the messages that, for me, contain basic elements of Andean agricultural knowledge. The explanations of the graphic codes were given by the artisan during a workshop. The brief description under each of the five figures which follow is a literal translation of the meaning which the artist attributes to the scenes, in her own words. The engraved gourds and

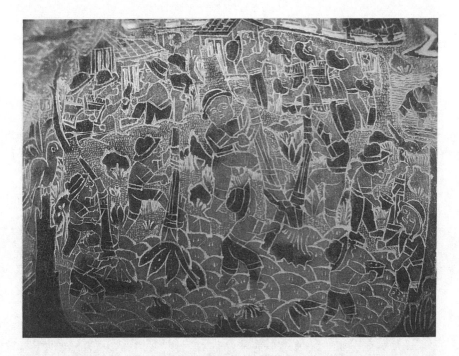

This is 'chakmeo', *removing the earth of the fields 'down below' with* 'chaquitaclla'. *It takes place in February or March during carnival, when the rainy season has started. We do it two or three times before we sow potatoes in July and August, this way we avoid the use of chemical fertilizers.* Chakmeo *is different from* 'tikpa', *minimal or zero tillage, that we practise in the best lands,* 'pulun', *'up there' where nothing has been cultivated for a couple of years.*

engraved gourds and textual explanations demonstrate a number of facets of Andean agricultural knowledge:

- In the Andean agricultural system the technical and cultural aspects build up a coherent internal logic, where the categories of time and space follow a particular way of perceiving reality and acting upon it;
- Agricultural and ritual cycles are mutually embedded in each other;
- Knowledge production is essentially a social process, maintained, reproduced and transformed by the community rather than by the individual;
- Agricultural knowledge is contained in stories, myths and other genres of oral tradition and is integrated into religious practices and worship;
- Agricultural knowledge is intertwined with symbolic meanings which can be understood according to the logic of the peasant world view;
- Agricultural knowledge systems are not fixed and unchanging. They are actively constructed and react dynamically to conflicts with mechanisms of creative resistance.

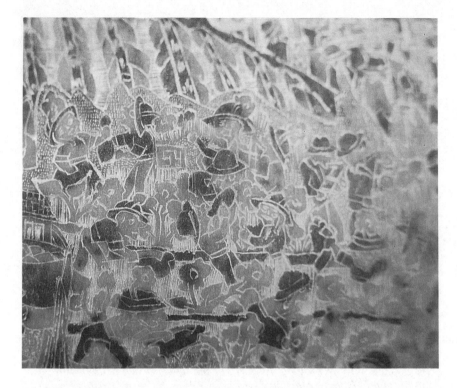

Here we see how we communicate during the work of recultivation of potatoes, when the plants are flowering. We do it in 'minka' *(collective work for the community) or in* 'uyay' *(reciprocity among relatives) but always with joy. Specially the* 'wamblas', *(young unmarried women). They start to play with single men and celebrate the* 'tinkunakuy waylash', *a dance which symbolizes the convergence of the good spirits to call for fertility of the potato fields.*

Knowledges in conflict

I have traced some central aspects of the conflict between two fundamentally different knowledges in Peruvian society. One, from which extension is an instrument for transmitting knowledge of scientific influences; the other Andean, rural knowledge which is embedded in local livelihoods and world views.

Western science has not significantly improved life in the Andes. On the contrary, it has exacerbated the major problems of society and threatens to erase one of the most valuable resources: the original solutions derived from local knowledge.

Western science deals with a perception of the Andean reality, narrowed down by the perspectives of scientific agronomy, in which the development of new plant species, like the 'scientific potato', can help to solve the

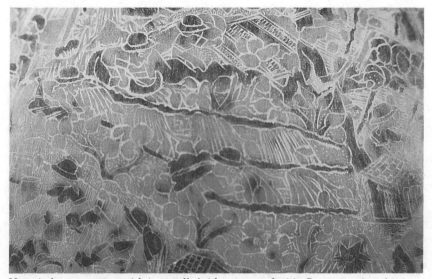

Here is how we sow with 'ampullo' *(the potato fruit). Some 'curious' peasants leave the potatoes plants in flower, along the borders of the plot. They wait until the seeds want to germinate. Others cut the* 'ampullo', *extract the seeds, clean them with ashes and let them dry inside newspaper sheets. After that they help the seeds to germinate. The trials might continue for two or five years until the experience says that we have arrived to a new potato varieties which has better qualities than the mother plant. The 'curious' peasant is always in contact with all of us, he asks us what our preferences are, what kind of potatoes do we want, in colour, size, taste, for what kind of fields, up there or down below . . . like Don Manuel Poma from Cochas Grande.*

problems of food shortages. By doing this, the potential of local knowledge is overlooked. Western agronomy in Peru underestimates the real contribution of peasant knowledge to the existing food system. Peasants, with one tenth of the agricultural land, are capable of producing more than half of the nation's food, despite poor market conditions etc. This performance is not due to ignorance or accident; it is a result of peasants' conscious and careful strategies.

Peasants' observations are guided by a rich and refined intuition and contemplative attitude. Productive activities are highly ritualized in the Andes; knowledge comes from an oral society in which the ritual helps to recreate particular steps. In spite of the advancement of literacy, knowledge remains codified in rituals, ceremonies and in metaphor (van der Ploeg, 1987). Due to this character of knowledge expression, it is necessary to pay more attention to the *process* of interpretation. For example, the use of a metaphor in the classification of potatoes might be seen as an ambiguity if it is interpreted from the repertoire of scientific categories, while in terms of Andean categories it has real meaning.

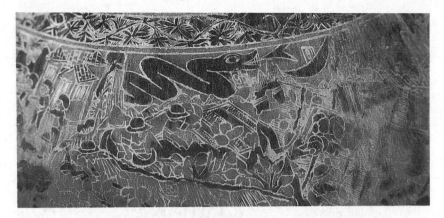

Here you see also the moon. We all believe in the moon. The full moon is a good sign to sow potatoes. If the moon is green (crescent) it won't work. When we sow during 'lullo killa' (new moon) the potato plant only develops leafage. But each community has a different set of beliefs about the moon, in some communities they don't believe anymore. I have been told that since the Americans landed in the moon, she has been spoiled, she doesn't inform us correctly.

The political and institutional characteristics of the knowledge conflict have been highlighted earlier. The main reason why the externally desired knowledges prevail is because they are supported by the powerful political and economic structures which dominate the world. Local knowledge survives as the main form of resistance of Andean culture and society.

The knowledge systems emerging from these different institutional settings appear to be incompatible. Western knowledge forms its view of the world from research praxis conditioned by a particular set of social interests and value systems. Whereas, the Andean knowledge projects a different vision of nature with contrasting values and interests.

Technical-agronomic solutions do not arrive at a point of common interest between science and peasant cultivators. The 'scientific potato' monopolizes genetic resources, ignores the ecological diversity, privileges the lowlands, concentrates on mechanisation and high inputs and minimises the role of social and cultural knowledge systems. For instance, there is very limited research into the bitter potato varieties, which grow above 4000 metres. They are a major concern of peasants since the high, ecological zones offer them the best conditions for production without chemicals, using foot ploughs, natural manure etc. They are able to transform the potato into potato-starch which is the best form of storage.

Alternatives for extension and research

The basic question is to ask if extension, as part of an external intervention, can develop the capability to meet the goals and interests of the local

*In this representation are the community elders and the younger
generations together. The young one says: 'Grandpas, how do you still
believe in all this nonsense. You should grow potatoes using chemical
fertilizers. Until when will you be harvesting these tiny potatoes? Now that
science has advanced you could do much better'. The elders answer, 'Sons,
you are real fools, the scientific potato only brings more diseases, the high-
yielding varieties are poisonous for mother earth and for you. Look at us,
we are old but healthy because we don't eat the improved varieties which
are treated with chemicals'.*

peasants and overcome the conflict? The following conditions seem most
relevant:

Reinforcement of peasant autonomy

Reinforcement of peasant autonomy needs to be encouraged through the
empowerment of self-determination mechanisms of peasant communities,
their collective strategies, their livelihoods and cultural resistance (DSE/
INP, 1989). Since the community is the most meaningful social structure
and serves as a socio-cultural framework for Andean knowledge, one main
concern for extension should be to build a link, rooted in the dynamics of
the peasant community (Bebbington; Uquillas, Part III).

Reorientation of education, training and research

A reorientation of the education, training and research in universities and
agricultural centres is urgently needed (Bawden, Part III). Such centres
should consider peasant knowledge as a main focus of interest. Andean
science should be a source of research and a basis for the development of a
national science.

Rural knowledge can be 'interesting' and 'useful' for western science,
and can be inventoried and disseminated in the rural areas, but it is not
accepted as an original and different scientific form. A reorientation of the
main institutions in Peru towards the construction of an indigenous system
of Andean science could open unexpected and surprising perspectives for

the solution of agricultural problems. A concrete effort of the University of Ayacucho and an NGO can give us an idea of the potentials of this reversal (PRATEC/UNSCH, 1990).

Researchers and technicians are trained to be able to develop in their own institutions a coherent position in favour of Andean knowledge. They learn how to perceive reality in Andean categories and to generate a theoretical understanding about Andean agriculture within the categories of peasant classificatory systems.

Developing a common language

Peasant knowledge needs to be approached from its own cultural categories and achievements, instead of from the technical problems identified through methods and procedures that are intrinsically biased by external imposition. Such methods stress artificial differences and deficiencies instead of helping to arrive at a common language allowing intercultural communication (Salas, 1991).

To start fruitful communication we have to stop looking at the problem as identified under a scientific prism. This is the case of the communication experience of the peasant magazine *Minka* from Huancayo, Peru. After some failed trials to speak for the peasants and extend technical knowledge, it evolved into a periodical where the peasants created their own forum for communication of knowledge. The success of the magazine lies in having assumed the Andean discourse in both its contents and its form and to have focused on the culturally meaningful categories of peasant society (Salas, 1988).

Other fora can also facilitate open, constructive dialogue between local people and scientists. In a recent workshop in which I took part, each peasant delegate described the 'customs' known about growing potatoes. Their contributions were written in the form of family diaries about potato production. Others collected different varieties grown in their communities and explained in a detailed way, the different names of each variety, where they come from, where they grow, when they are sown, different cultivation procedures, when they are harvested, what further transformations can be done with them and other special characteristics. Farmers brought between 14 and 35 identified varieties. With their potato collection they explained the conditions of actual production, distribution and consumption – always accompanied by myths, rites and humour. As a result of a comfortable atmosphere of exchange among peasant specialists, the structure of their knowledge was expressed in an explicit manner.

After this process, they shared their achievements with a group of potato specialists from the national and international potato centres. At the beginning, it was difficult to arrive at a common language, but after two days of intense efforts to learn from each other and becoming aware of cultural distances, the groups coincided on several aspects. Peasants proposed that the scientists support them to construct and reconstruct terraces, to continue to grow their different potato varieties, to stop the use of harmful chemical products, to reconstruct the old canal system and so on.

Agronomists agreed that they need to change some of their far-from-the-field research and extension activities and to continue with these methods of exchange and communication.

Epilogue

The final words of a peasant specialist still sound in my ears:

> We need that you learn more about the influence of the stars in our Quechua language. That you help us to maintain and strengthen our customs and that of our ancestors. If we can engage scientists, we will influence the Agrarian Policy and make it democratic in favour of the community. And so we will understand each other better.

Rural people's knowledge and extension practice: trees, people and communities in Zimbabwe's communal lands

FRANK MATOSE and BILLY MUKAMURI

Official knowledge and extension practice

Official knowledge on forestry has been extended to the Zimbabwean rural poor without any serious attempt at understanding what farmers already know. The history of extension practice cannot be divorced from the politics of domination, modernization and development of the poor under colonialism. Under colonial rule, the poor were seen as backward, uncivilized and consequently unknowledgeable.

Extension practices, therefore, have a long history of being developed elsewhere and passed on to farmers without any attempt at connecting with their practices. As early as the 1920s, a need for tree planting in communal areas was identified. This need arose out of the heavy cutting of the indigenous woodlands, especially by commercial mining concessions. Planting trees was also seen as modern part of the civilizing project of colonialism. The Imperial Forestry Institute in Oxford was the centre in which most Rhodesian foresters were trained and from which official knowledge emanated and was extended to the rural poor across Africa and Asia. The failure to recognize local knowledge can be illustrated by a statement from R.S. Troup (quoted by McGregor, 1991), director of the Institute from 1924 to 1939:

> If educated Europeans fail to realise the necessity for maintaining forests, it is expecting too much of the African willingly to conserve forests on hillsides and in catchment-areas in the interests of generations to come. His whole tendency in the past has been to destroy forests, and he cannot understand the reason for laws framed to preserve them.

In fact, the local people had, and still have, various ways of preserving and managing their forests (e.g. Bradley and Dewees, 1993).

The traditional management of indigenous resources: social and political dimensions

In this paper, we will draw on case studies from southern Zimbabwe to provide a deeper understanding of local resource management practice in a complex political and social context. The consequences of external intervention into this complex local setting are explored through the examination of an NGO project. The discussion focuses on woodland and tree resources, but offers broader insights into the social and political dimensions of knowledge construction and application.

The way knowledge is articulated is directly linked to the positions individuals or groups occupy in the social strata. Shona society in the communal lands is socially and politically organized whereby different groups of people – individuals, men, women, children, immigrants, clans, lineages and chiefdoms – have different degrees of control over, access to and ownership of resources. Decision making is thus highly differentiated. For example, women have less rights than men when land allocation is considered. Some immigrants (e.g. people who arrived after the 1930s) have less access rights than ruling lineage members. This results in the inequitable distribution of wealth and helps shape relationships between people and resources. Interventions aimed at changing environmental resource management therefore relate to issues of control, access and ownership.

Decision making is affected by the nature of local political leadership. Different forms are found in rural Zimbabwe, ranging from the traditional lineage leaders to more recent elected village chairpersons or councillors. Sometimes the two structures become fused, in other cases conflict arises. In many instances lineage leaders lack legitimacy from the state and from local people themselves, but their ability to control their subjects varies from one area to the other. Decision making is either through 'consensus' (usually of male elders) or through injunctions made by the most powerful individuals in the community. The effect of a decision is subject to many factors, for example the degree of recognition of the particular individual and sometimes his or her wealth. Lineages are not politically united groups, but rather comprise various factions which are always at each other's throats. The ruling clan is thus at an advantage when it comes to resource allocation.

Local knowledge about trees and woodland resources is framed within this setting. Since rural societies are not homogenous in terms of material resources under their command, attitudes toward tree resources are different. In Zvishavane and Chivi districts the relatively rich have a negative attitude towards the planting of trees. Their understanding of trees is remarkably limited and issues of management are focused on the private planting of exotics. The poorer members of the community show a greater concern for the environment and explain that its destruction leads to the spirits being angry with them which results in droughts and increased poverty. This argument does not appeal to the rich, presumably because they

70

have other sources of income not dependent on natural resources; for example, husbands are employed in urban areas (Mukamuri, 1992).

Knowledge about particular resources is common to people who occupy a certain niche (ecological, sociological, economic or political) in society. For instance, knowledge about the effects of certain tree species on crops is best explained by people in nutrient-deficient sandy soil areas. By contrast, people in nutrient-rich, heavy-soil areas have less interest in tree humus and quickly accept the destumping of all trees from their fields. Local knowledge about trees is therefore not universal or consistent, but rather localized to suit environmental constraints.

Cultural beliefs

Cultural beliefs also shape people's perceptions and knowledge. Some people protect trees because they believe that they bring rainfall by stopping clouds, as mountains do when causing orographic rainfall. Religious associations are also common; for example, some people believe that big trees should be conserved because the cuckoo bird (*hwaya*) sings for rain and it likes to rest in such trees. Ancestral spirits (*midzimu*), also come and rest in these trees when they attend rain making ceremonies. People also protect trees for fear of retribution. For example, if they cut down trees they can be punished by the high god (*Zame*) who does it by stopping rains.

To understand the way the idioms of conservation are framed as they are, one has to look carefully at the patterns of resource distribution and what happens to conserved areas. As in the wider domain of the struggle over knowledge and the control of resources, at the local level the political and cultural set-up results in dependencies and peripheries in terms of resource access and control. The elites benefit by being powerful, by being seen to be providing and by manipulating the discourses of religion, conservation and development. Power is reinforced through the control of the most important resources – water, and in particular rainfall, soil and trees. The management of resources is at the same time political, religious and economic, played out in a complex and highly differentiated rural society.

Local knowledge and farmer management of indigenous resources are set within a complex local social and political framework. Conservation should be understood in the context of the political monopoly over resource access and control by the ruling elites. It should not be understood solely within a framework of simple economic rationality. The history of resource conservation and management in the communal areas thus must be seen within the context of conflicts associated with resource distribution. Political power, together with 'conservation' and 'ecological' arguments, is used to enhance the economic and political status of rural elites. Political-religious power, framed in arguments about resource management, are thus being used to keep out the politically weak (for example, immigrants).

Community management of woodlands: the Chivi and Zvishavane Project

The Chivi-Zvishavane Project is a research-action project based in the dryland communal areas in the central south of Zimbabwe and supported

71

by a Harare-based NGO, ENDA-Zimbabwe. The project is based on a participatory approach to community planning at village level. The planning process established through the project has to take account of the political, cultural and economic contexts of resource management in the communal lands decribed earlier. The project has shown how establishing a 'participatory' process is no easy task.

In any village a wide range of people are interviewed by the ENDA community worker (CW) in order to avoid bias and get a range of views from the rich and the poor, men and women, young and old. These interviews and workshops attempt to explore the multiple interests of local farmers. Following research in a village, the CW calls a discussion and planning workshop. Here, the CW feeds back the results of her or his findings and a list is constructed of the trees farmers say they would like to plant in their fields, homes, gardens and grazing areas. The list is then used to form the menu for the nursery contents, which are managed by the CWs and their nursery attendants. The seedlings are raised and issued to the communities at the beginning of the rainy season. The CWs rely heavily on farmer knowledge to propagate indigenous trees; the farmers have observed how the trees grow and from which parts of trees they can best be propagated. The meetings also function to site the village woodlots, to determine which species are to be planted in them and to plan who is to be involved in the planting and management of communal trees.

The project has highlighted that dialogue with villagers in an open-ended, unthreatening way reveals a range of priorities for tree planting that was not catered for in the single-species, eucalyptus woodlot approach previously advocated. However, it is in the context of communal woodland management and enrichment planting that the project has faced most difficulties. This involves, in particular, the contestations within local communities, and between local groups and outsiders who bring projects and interventions.

Institutional politics and development

The project experience provides a good example of how political definitions of society are being appropriated by the development strategy of NGOs and development agents. The village development committee (VIDCO) is the basic unit of development in Zimbabwe. The history of the VIDCOs goes back to 1984 when they were imposed on the people by the government. Very few people in the project area know about their functions and mandate. They have surfaced as a counter to the traditional lineage heads (*sabhuku*), some of whom are regarded as legitimate leaders in the project area. The VIDCO boundaries often do not have any relevance to the socioeconomic dimensions of the communities and so bear little relation to resource management terrains. In most cases the VIDCO boundaries have ignored the cultural and social boundaries, splitting families and ignoring traditional grazing areas. Yet most government and NGO workers have been forced to work within the structures set by the state. Operating at VIDCO level is another example of how society has

72

been abstracted by the authorities, leaving, in many instances, a local institution unable to effect resource management. The effects of demarcating areas and imposing institutions on people have contributed to some of the problems faced by the project.

Most of the woodlots planted by the VIDCOs have not been successful. In part, this has been because of the recurrent droughts in the area and their impact on tree survival and growth. Perhaps more importantly it has been an issue of ownership: who owns the trees? Who has the legitimacy to control and manage development in the area? Local power struggles have been played out in the project setting, with VIDCOs competing with traditional leaders.

There has been one addition to this set of actors – ENDA and the project team. Perceived as an external, Harare-based organization with all the trappings of development aid (short visits by senior staff in land cruisers, etc.), the role of ENDA has sometimes been key. In some cases, local disputes have been such that people comment that it is simply 'ENDA's project' or 'the woodlot belongs to the government'; a reflection of the long history of state imposition of development projects in the communal areas, from the colonial era to the present. One comment by a farmer is typical of such situations: 'They wanted to come and plant trees in government plots simply to show us that we are their people. After planting, rules and rules will come and in the end termites will eat all the trees.'

In other areas some aspects of the project were completely rejected. In the case of Madzoke VIDCO the local leadership refused to plant any trees on their land, as there were plenty of remaining indigenous trees. The people relied on their knowledge of their area and refused any imposition. A number of fruit trees and exotics were, however, planted. In one way, this can be viewed as a success from the project's point of view: participation entails the right of farmers to say no!

In other cases, however, community workers have been able to negotiate their way through local conflict and the project has become 'owned' by local groups, with a diversity of woodland management and tree planting activities being carried out. The importance of mediation and brokerage by local extension workers in the context of highly contested, politically charged and disputed resource management options is highlighted by his experience.

Rural peoples' knowledge and extension institutions

The strategies employed by the project envisage a new dimension to the planning of resource use and conservation. What is central to this approach is the realization that local people need to be consulted when planning resource use. The experience shows that there is a need to rely on local people's knowledge and perceptions, and to recognize that this knowledge is situated within a political, social and religious context. Intervention thus must exist as part of an ongoing negotiation with local people.

Locally based extension teams are key to the success of this negotiation. In the Chivi-Zvishavane project, the local extension team was made up of farmers who shared the same problems, experiences, knowledge and hardships with the other members of the communities in which they worked. They never had the chance to be regarded as top bosses (*mashefu*). Conflicts were largely resolved amicably, using the local channels of power and authority and processes of mediation and arbitration.

Open communication and dialogue is vital to success; especially the 'lateral' communication that occurs between the community and the local extension worker. In the ENDA project, the collection of lists of preferred species, raising them in the nurseries and taking them back to farmers has had a double function:

- It demonstrated to farmers that the knowledge they have is valuable;
- It demonstrated that the poorly regarded indigenous trees can be propagated just as well as exotic ones.

Awareness and confidence have grown – both are critical ingredients of a participatory process. Discussion fora and regular feedback interviews carried out by the community workers encouraged a level of local-level dialogue that moved the project beyond a static approach, to a process of continuous communication and interaction.

However, there have been problems. One important one was the conflict between the administrative division of VIDCOs and resource management centred on woodlots, mentioned above. Other problems centred on the interface between project staff and local farmers. As already noted, extension workers were already members of their community. This had major benefits for engendering dialogue and negotiating conflicts arising from the project process. However, the very existence of a 'project', an outside-funded intervention, introduced certain dilemmas. This fact clearly changed the status of community workers: they were now at the same time community members and project workers. Their insider status became blurred and confused by their employment in the project. Their consequent boost in income and their access to transport (as well as the range of assumed, but often non-existent, benefits) sometimes prejudiced their role. This was exacerbated by a centrally directed management structure and a sometimes arrogant approach of Harare-based staff.

Conclusion

The rhetoric of 'people's participation' may be seductive to donors and appealing to NGOs and government agencies based in the capital city, but if promoted by a hierarchically structured and centrally managed organization, effective devolution, local empowerment and village-level resource management may well be elusive. Since local resource management decisions are made in the context of local political and institutional structures, recognizing this dimension of RPK is key.

This view suggests a new role for extensionists. They must become managers of encounters, resolvers of conflicts, consultants on 'formal' knowledges. This requires new settings for extension work and new forms of training, emphasizing interactive communication and negotiation and

74

conflict-resolution skills, rather than simply the imparting of technical knowledge. Above all, the style of intervention must shift from one prescribing blueprints (even if 'participatory' in rhetorical design) to one of open learning (Korten, 1980). This will inevitably require new institutional procedures and new professional norms (Pretty and Chambers, Part III).

Declarations of difference

JAMES FAIRHEAD and MELISSA LEACH

Introduction

The determination of 'who knows' – the declaration of differences in knowledge by gender, ethnicity, age etc. – is integral to the sociopolitical processes conditioning access to and control over resources. This applies equally to the relationships between farmers and researchers as to the relationships between farmers themselves.

This paper investigates certain parallels between the analytical isolation of bits of knowledge (for example of particular micro-environments, of the use of particular tree species, or of how to perform a certain task) and the analytical isolation of 'bits of society'. Analysis often links such knowledge and social bits in a 'who knows what' approach, reading a knowledge difference into different people's involvement with different micro-environments, species, activities and so on and identifying certain social groups as proprietors of certain types of knowledge. This focus risks overlooking both broadly held understandings of agroecological processes and the sociopolitical processes which define and maintain differences of practice. It also risks isolating social groups at the expense of understanding social relations. Thus, when targeted R&E (Research and Extension) strategies derived from a 'who knows what' approach attempt to interlock with these understandings and processes in rural communities they will often miss. Examples from our research in Guinea's forest region show that isolating local knowledges may well support the reinforcement or renegotiation of patterns of resource access and control to the benefit or detriment of certain people.

Isolating knowledges

Analyses following a 'who knows what' approach differentiate the 'what' – the knowledge – along a variety of axes. Firstly, local knowledge is often examined in relation to scientific disciplinary distinctions and preoccupations, producing a mirrored set of ethno-disciplines: ethno-botany, ethno-veterinary medicine, indigenous agroforestry and so on. These construct certain aspects of RPK as relevant and important, whilst excluding others as irrelevant, according to the selective concerns of their mirrored sciences, rather than the concerns of farmers.

75

Secondly, knowledge is frequently differentiated in geographical terms, isolating area-specific knowledges at different scales. These may include, for example, knowledge of uplands and lowlands, of wetlands and drylands, of rainfed and irrigated cultivation, of geographically differentiated rice farming systems, of gardens and fields, of micro-environments, gathering grounds and opportunity niches such as water-harvesting sites.

Thirdly, knowledge is differentiated in relation to particular practices, whether in the agricultural cycle (cultivation, soil mounding, weeding etc.), tree management (planting, pruning etc.), pastoral care, or hunting and gathering. A fourth form of division is by crop, species or use, focusing for example on knowledge of grains and root crops, of cassava or peanut varieties, of leguminous trees or of wild foods. Whatever axis is used, the tendency is to isolate discrete bits of knowledge from understandings of broader agro-ecological processes and agricultural strategies (Schoonmaker Freudenberger, Part II).

Yet as Richards (1987: 2) argues, a distinctive feature of local knowledge is that it comprehends the 'processes and continuities within diverse landscape and vegetation communities' and enables these processes and continuities to be manipulated in production. African farming, herding and forest management involve 'a series of variations upon themes and processes observed within nature' as rural people understand them (*ibid*). Knowledge of ecological processes gives resource users the flexibility to direct agro-ecological processes to their own advantage.

Tree management by Kouranko farmers

Tree management by Kouranko farmers in Guinea's Kissidougou prefecture exemplifies this point. It includes:

- Selectively preserving certain species and individuals in clearing and cultivation (e.g., *Mitragyna stipulosa* to maintain water levels in swamps, certain shade and fruit trees in coffee plantations and oil palms and certain leguminous trees in upland fields);
- Protecting useful wildlings and coppices;
- Regulating hunting to protect animals which disperse useful tree seeds (e.g. palm rats);
- Nursing and transplanting seeds and wildlings;
- Encouraging tree growth through fire managment, such as targeted gathering, grazing of grasses and cultivation to create fire breaks, brushing fire breaks, planting fire tolerant species to protect others, early burning and regulating fallow cycles to keep tree size and species composition agriculturally desirable and manageable.

In short, tree management is an integral part of the management of fire, crops, water and vegetation succession, and the ecological and socio-economic possibilities which condition these. Development agencies have often overlooked this, focusing their tree-related extension efforts narrowly on tree planting from nurseries and on purpose-built firebreaks. The tendency to isolate discrete bits of knowledge is thus inscribed in extension

76

practices and in the choices offered by R&E to farmers, failing to build on farmers' process and multi-dimensioned tree-related knowledge.

Watercourse adaptation by Kouranko farmers

A second example shows a similar contrast between R&E agency and farmers' approaches. Following long standing national policy, agricultural development agencies in Kissidougou have promoted swamp rice development packages involving earth (and sometimes cement-reinforced) canalization and new varieties adapted to multi-seasonal cropping, with the aim of carving out homogeneous swamp rice farming systems. This contrasts with existing swamp management which is more integrated ecologically with surrounding uplands, and involves a wide variety of techniques to enhance and maintain swamp productivity.

Farmers in a Kouranko village have been making sequential adaptations to watercourses, gradually broadening the inundated area to take in the surrounding footslopes, reducing weed problems there. In association with barrage banks of earth, weeds and crop residues, which trap silt either from river floods or upland run-off, farmers have, for at least a century, enlarged, levelled and enriched their swamps. Farmers selectively encourage certain trees and weeds which maintain water levels, and they alter crop and varietal choice according to micro-variations in soil, water and weed characteristics, as well as a range of socio-economic and contingent concerns. Our observations here only add to the now large literature documenting the sophistication of West African rice cultivation and the way it harnesses multiple ecological processes (e.g. Richards, 1986; Carney, 1991).

Given such integration of farming practices within broader agro-ecological processes and knowledge of these, it is, to our eyes, extremely difficult to identify particular agroecological knowledges which might be highly socially differentiated between members of 'a community'.

Declaring social differences

Within a 'who knows what' approach, certain knowledges are associated with certain people; with social difference. The axes of social differentiation are often identified *a priori*, as in the selection of apparently self-evident categories such as gender, age, ethnicity and class. Otherwise axes of social differentiation relative to knowledge are identified in relation either to different people's activities, to their 'agricultural systems', to their soils (e.g. Sikana, Part I), their crops, their tasks or to their roles or livelihood responsibilities. Can the identification of certain people as proprietors of certain knowledges in this way be used to assist the targeting of participatory R&E and the ascription of roles within the R&E process? The farmer-first debate has long distinguished 'scientists and their knowledge' from 'rural people and their knowledge', encouraging them to come together in complementary partnerships. Can 'the partnership' be perfected by 'plugging into knowledge differences' within rural communities?

Given, as we would argue, that rural people frequently work with a fairly integrated understanding of agroecological processes, where might the social divisions in such understanding lie? Different people are involved with different aspects of common processes of which it would be hard to imagine and harder still to show their ignorance. Also livelihood patterns and divisions of crops, tasks and responsibilities are largely socially and economically determined, often in a highly dynamic way whether over time or lifecycle stage (e.g. in childhood, marriage etc.). It can therefore be a major error to deduce 'who knows what' from 'who does what', or *vice versa*. The extent to which people are ignorant of activities they are not directly involved in at the present time requires to be shown, not assumed. This in turn raises tremendous problems of method and evidence.

Furthermore, other people's agroecological experiences, fortunes and misfortunes are potent issues for local discussion, albeit not with all and sundry (Pottier, Part I). This is not to say that there is only one idiom of explanation, or that everyone is in every context free openly to express their interpretations and opinions. But even if the capacity to express ecological knowledge is socially bounded, the knowledge itself might not be, or at least not along the same lines. Most Kouranko women know a great deal more about their husband's hunting techniques and animal ecology that they can admit in front of men. In sum, the importance of social differences of agroecological knowledge can be overstressed as a basis for assessing people's differential capabilities, adaptability and flexibility in agriculture.

Declarations of socially differentiated knowledge are, nevertheless, frequently made, as much in rural life as in the relationship between farmers and R&E agencies. Such declarations are important to agriculture, primarily in the ways that they justify and condition particular patterns of resource access and control. The origins of their credibility (and vested interests in their credence) need have little to do with 'real' knowledge differentiation. For example, Kissi people often bring to bear the argument that 'women do not know how (*cee le*) to clear undergrowth' when justifying men's inheritance of control over coffee plantations. Equally in public life, we have often heard it said by Kouranko men that women 'don't know how' (*ma kosan*) to farm rice for themselves; instead they perform certain tasks in the production of rice controlled by their husbands. When saying 'I don't know' in these languages, there is the same ambiguity as in English between ignorance and incapability for other reasons. This ambiguity conceals a range of tenurial and labour access issues which seem, to us, more important in restricting many women from these activities. The instances in which certain women, by overcoming these restrictions, have in fact acquired control over coffee plantations and rice fields of their own would tend to prove our point.

In this region of West Africa declarations of differential knowledge by gender, age and ethnicity are formalized in the men's and women's closed associations (*'forêts sacrées'* or 'secret societies'). These, in local parlance, are schools for learning natural science. Children (at initiation), youth and adults pass through stages of these schools (and universities) and are said gradually to acquire secret social and ecological knowledge from the elders, who control it. But the extent to which the schools impart new practical agroecological knowledge to its pupils is questionable. What is clear is that the formalized secrecy is central to patterns of resource access and control, whether in limiting strangers' access to community resources, in maintaining elders' authority over the young, or in defining gender roles, rights and responsibilities (Bellman, 1984; Bledsoe, 1984).

The power implications of declared knowledge differences apply equally when rural people encounter R&E agencies. Swamp rice development in Kissidougou, for example, has been targeted at men. Canalization is generally a male task and in Kouranko areas at least, it is said to be men who 'know how' to farm rice. The only men who do the 'developed' mud banking are young, well-educated members of large landholding families. They concentrate their efforts exclusively on swamp farming. Drawing on the image of new and scientific agriculture they present themselves as 'improvers' (*aménagistes*), constructing a difference between themselves and other members of the community. Fundamentally, this distinction offers them different forms of resource control. As *aménagistes*, they assert long-term claims to parental land which would otherwise be more ambiguous; they more easily justify opting out of the village-coordinated family upland rice farming, with its calls on their and their wives' labour, and they can construct the 'improved' swamp as a household enterprise on which their wives must work, whereas swamps managed according to local techniques are almost invariably individual enterprises which women and men undertake as an independent source of cash. In this case declarations of a science-RPK difference are important to the social relations of production. Strikingly, the 'improved' swamps as used by the *aménagistes* are scarcely any different, in technical or agro-ecological terms, from those managed according to local techniques. Firstly, the permanent mud bank squares merely replace the annually-made plant debris banks used by farmers in this area and have the same effect of raising and regulating water levels. Secondly, the scientific package (new varieties, timing etc.) has been unpacked and adapted to suit the *aménagistes'* own integrated and processes, understandings and priorities.

In this case, agencies and those they work with have constructed what they do as different from RPK. Inevitably, this has had resource control implications, resulting from the ways that declarations of difference have been incorporated into local social and political processes. Would the project be less disruptive (and more generally acceptable) if agents positively tried to deconstruct the difference between what they know and do and what the farmers already know; to play down the difference? We think so. As for social differences within rural communities, targeting social groups because of their supposed knowledge differences may be less advantageous for (or relevant to) technical change than is often assumed. But such targeting is clearly important to the way the R&E process affects intracommunity resource control.

79

Indigenous soil characterization in northern Zambia

PATRICK SIKANA

Farming systems research in Northern Province

During community studies in the Northern Province of Zambia, the rural sociology section of the Adaptive Research Planning Team (ARPT) realised that farmers have their own way of identifying local soils and land types for agricultural uses. When this was reported to other scientists, it was felt that, if local soil categories could be related to scientific classification, it would be easier for researchers and extensionists to communicate with farmers. So social and natural scientists joined to make a more in-depth study.

Five study areas were chosen to represent major languages (Bemba, Mambwe and Namwanga) and major land regions where soil surveys had already been made. A social science student from the University of Zambia and a soil science student from the Agricultural University of Norway resided in each study area for two weeks. In group interviews, the farmers were asked to name all the soils they use, plus other nearby soils. Afterwards, individual farmers who were reportedly familiar with particular soil types were interviewed in depth about the nature and uses of that soil. Soil samples were taken, and texture, colour, location, micro-relief features (e.g. termite mounds), drainage and vegetation were recorded.

Farmers' soil categories

The farmers identified 27 soil groups with 71 sub-categories. Their categories were not mutually exclusive. The soil types more important for farming generally had more sub-categories. Farmers agreed remarkably well on the features of different soil types. For example, out of 15 farmers in one study area who described a particular soil type, 13 said the top layer is hard when dry, 14 said the soil is slippery when wet and 12 said it tends to stick to the hoe when cultivating.

The main criteria used by the farmers to classify soils were colour of the top layer, texture, consistency and organic matter content. Crops are chosen to suit soil type. For instance, black *Wa fita*, soil rich in organic matter, is often found in the vegetable gardens on the *dambo* (wetland) fringes.

Mismatches with 'science'

There was little correlation between local soil type and Zambian technical soil series, because farmers and scientists use different criteria to categorize soils. Farmers are most interested in features of the topsoil, as these influence important management decisions. Soil scientists base their categories on elaborate chemical and physical analysis of the sub-soil. They are less interested in the topsoil because they seek consistency and reliability. They argue that the topsoil varies constantly on account of numerous factors such as previous management practices, erosion and burning, whereas the sub-soil maintains the characteristics intrinsic to that particular soil type. As the farmers have to deal with the numerous factors which influence features of the topsoil, their perception of soil is more dynamic and their categories are less rigid.

Looking at the topsoil, farmers can recognize numerous local soils in an area where the technical system indicates only one soil type based on features of the sub-soil. Conversely, soils with different sub-soils may have similar topsoil properties, so farmers see these two distinct technical types as similar.

Farmers and scientists not only apply different criteria; they arrive at soil categories in different ways. The scientific system starts with a detailed description of the various chemical and physical properties, and sums these up into a single unit called a soil type. Farmers start the other way round. They arrive at a soil type first by observing a single most notable feature (be it colour, structure or consistency) and then give a more detailed description of the characteristics of that particular soil.

Thirsty soils, greedy crops

The farmers' system of categorizing soils is orientated towards practice, whereas science aims at constructing universal models. The difference is reflected in the way soil fertility is assessed. Scientists use a standardized model involving measurement of the inherent chemical properties of the soil, while farmers use a wider range of criteria. In our study, this included limiting factors such as hardness to cultivate, so the heavy clayey soils were rated as less fertile than the lighter clayey types.

Furthermore, farmers assess fertility levels in a particular soil in terms of observed crop performance, which is affected by several factors other than the soil properties measured by scientists. Therefore, the farmers' perception of the fertility status of a particular soil changes constantly, taking into consideration the factors which favour or impede crop performance, such as plot age, location and previous use, weed infestation and pest build-up.

Farmers often used complex and metaphorical concepts to make sense of soils. The soil is 'thirsty' if well drained and 'weak' if not fertile. The soil can also get 'tired' or 'go mad' if it is cultivated continuously without fallowing. The soil may 'cry' because it is so coarse that it makes a squeaking sound when walked on. Taken together, such concepts form a network of meaning, but they are not fixed in space and time. They do not describe the permanent condition of a soil type, but are used in relation to specific circumstances. For example, because cassava, a 'greedy' crop, can make the soil 'tired', a plot of land on which cassava was previously grown must be managed in a particular way.

Practical knowledge

The local soil classification system reveals much about the nature of indigenous agricultural knowledge. It is relative and site-specific rather than absolute and universal. Each observed soil type is compared to other soils in the area. Thus, a soil type may be described as *we bamba no muchanga panomo* (clay soil with a bit of sand) because it is being compared with another clayey type with less sand. Farmers' classification is contextual. A soil may be identified according to the environment where it is found, for instance, one soil in our study was named after the grass that grows on it, and another after an insect found in it.

Indigenous knowledge about soils is not possessed in a complete and encyclopedic fashion. In our study, a farmer was familiar on average with only three different soils, usually found on the land actually being farmed. Most farmers knew more names but could seldom give detailed descriptions of the soils beyond their fields. Different individuals possess different elements of local knowledge, based on their different practical experiences.

Categories hanging in the air

When the results of this study were presented in Zambia, some scientists criticized that, if a local soil type *x* cannot be related to a technical soil series *y*, then the indigenous categories are hanging in the air, with no practical reference point to make them applicable on the ground. But, it would seem that it is the technical categories which are hanging in the air, judging by the limited applicability of research recommendations based on them. The present technical classification system communicates information about soils to scientists, but not to farmers.

To dismiss indigenous categories because they do not relate to previous soil research is to ignore an important resource that has the potential to advance the productivity frontier. Since farmers' soil characterization often involves detailed descriptions of soil properties in terms of advantages and limiting factors, such information could be systematized into relatively flexible general principles, on which research and extension could be based. The output will then be more meaningful, because the language and concepts used will be familiar to the farmers.

Need to 'peasantize' science

Indigenous soil categories have practical validity in themselves, without having to 'scientize' them by forcing them into the technical framework used by soil surveyors. Instead, they can be entry points for future scientific work. Science should attempt to enter the peasants' world of concepts and representations, in order to establish a sound base for a partnership with indigenous knowledge (Salas, Part I). Synthesis is possible where new elements from outside are transformed by the farmers to become part of their own knowledge system, for instance, farmers incorporate scientific insights into soil acidity and aluminum toxicity into their local soil management strategies.

Partnership between science and indigenous knowledge presents a challenge to conventional positivist science, given the dynamic and strategic nature of farmers' knowledge and practices. But science must come to terms with this dynamism, because this is what farmers' reality is all about.

Agricultural discourses: farmer experimentation and agricultural extension

JOHAN POTTIER

Knowledge ownership in urban Rwanda

Moving beyond the debate on knowledge distribution, researchers have begun to develop an interest in knowledge diversity and dispute. In this paper I present thoughts on the socio political meaning of agricultural experimentation in urban Rwanda, with reference to bean cropping and highlight the issue of 'knowledge ownership'. Two aspects of 'knowledge ownership' receive special attention: first, the social basis of knowledge generation; second, the ethical problem surrounding knowledge extraction by outsiders.

Food producers and extensionists

When I researched livelihood strategies in Butare, Rwanda (1985–86), the agricultural research community had just begun to appreciate the importance of varietal mixtures in bean cropping. Suddenly, mixtures were regarded as the strength of the poor. The notion of resilience-through-diversity was based on the understanding that mixtures reduce risk, that some components will always grow well in the face of climatic irregularities. Whether farmers are having to cope with 'too much sunshine' or 'too much rain', or with sun and rain that is too little, too early or too late, a balanced mix will still yield something.

But the new appreciation that farmers *knew* how to reduce risk and optimize yields through connecting seed types with soil types and drainage patterns, indicative of the farmer-first attitude, found less favour with government officials who wished to promote food security throughout the country. The emphasis on germplasm diversity went against their own perception of national food security which, in the case of beans, required the 'rational' expansion of a bean market led by 'improved', mono-coloured varieties that could be grown nationally (Pottier, 1993). The emerging 'rational farmer' who wisely used varietal mixtures to adapt to the complex conditions of her/his land stood in the way of such a national campaign. The farmer's strength and rationality was the national planner's weakness.

In this conflict of rationalities, agricultural researchers in Rwanda sided with the farmers; they chose to investigate, and soon defended, the view that farmers made rational choices and that planners needed to understand and accept the importance of varietal mixtures (Voss, 1992). But farmer-first enthusiasm resulted in a particular view on extension practice: extension services needed to access and disseminate adaptive farming techniques. Leading a multidisciplinary research programme on bean cropping, storage and consumption, Dunkel (1985: 65; emphasis added) described the challenge:

Because farming techniques are often *family secrets* or because extension systems are undeveloped and national meetings of e.g., bean or sorghum growers do not exist, such successful techniques frequently do not become widely adopted in a country or even in a similar region of the country. Often it is not until a national survey is conducted by persons interested in indigenous farming systems that such techniques surface and become disseminated.

In Dunkel's view, the family (*rugo*) locus restricts experimentation because it limits the flow of genetic materials and management techniques. Extension workers therefore need to extract knowledge (about bean trials) from family farms across the various agroecological regions and make it available to speed up an already existing process of agricultural experimentation at the *rugo* level.

I want to reflect on this particular view of the challenge for extension. I shall argue that it is misleading to see the importance of varietal selection and agricultural experimentation and experiments simply in terms of 'family secrets'; a phrase which implies 'conservatism'. Although sharing Dunkel's view that successful techniques must be promoted, I shall express reservation about asking extensionists to take on the task of accessing and disseminating 'family secrets'.

'Family secrets' in context

Improved, mono-coloured bean varieties (especially *ntabeza* and *mutiki*) have become popular in Butare; they now dominate the varietal mixtures. Rarely though are they grown as pure crops, except in the case of small experiments. Whenever Rwandan farmers are interested in growing new materials they will assess their performance, as is now well understood, either by trying them out on a small area of the farm or by incorporating them at a low percentage into existing mixtures.

In the bean mixtures they grow, women farmers often include both 'improved' and 'traditional' varieties, and take a risk-reducing strategy by including in the latter sun-resistant as well as rain-resistant varieties. Besides the dominant 'modern' varieties (*indobanure*), one finds in many mixtures a whole range of other types (often up to a dozen or more), all of which may be taken out for a 'pure' trial. These trials give rise to 'family secrets'. Popular with the experimenters are large-seeded, precocious, 'traditional' types (*ibinyarwanda*, the ancestors' seeds), such as *nsigarushonje* (greenish colour) and *muhondo* (yellow).

Pride and secrecy accrue to such experiments. Indeed, knowledge about the variety grown as an experiment is shared only with close kin and one or two neighbours with whom the farmer gets on really well. Neighbours not on particularly close terms will not know about each other's experiments. Only after the harvest, especially when successful, does the experiment become public knowledge. In the urban setting of Butare, new varieties are continually brought in through family networks, often from other regions, before being passed on to close neighbours or friends.

The following cases, based on observation, convey something of the full social context of these 'family' trials.

Box 1: Family trials

After a successful trial with *nyiranzobe*, grown pure, Geneviève gave some seed to Alima, her Zairian neighbour and close friend. On returning from a market trip during which she bought a mixture containing a fair percentage of the same variety, Alima added to the given seed and prepared for planting (*Nyiranzobe* occurred infrequently in mixtures). This happened just before the new planting season. Geneviève's gift was one in a series of small food presents that reciprocated for a one-year lease of land (from Alima's husband to Geneviève's) in the preceding year.

After her dry season bean harvest had failed, Jeanne (married, teenager, poor, and not a farming expert) took her neighbour's advice and, with the rainy season in sight, dropped her entire bean mixture in favour of a new one based on *muteja*, a large black traditional variety, which the neighbour 'knew' grew well in poor soils. Too poor to buy a *muteja*-based mix in town, Jeanne obtained the mixture from her neighbour in return for child-minding she promised to do. There was another reason why Jeanne could not rely on the market for her new seed mixture, since marketeers often trade old, damaged stock, which is often alright to eat but not to plant. Reliance on trusted friends or relatives is preferred over reliance on the market.

Extension workers should develop sensitivity and respect for the total social context within which 'family' trials are conducted and results shared. Experiments with new varieties should not be labelled as just a matter of 'family secrecy' and, by implication, an expression of farmer conservatism. Rather, the 'family secrets' should be put in a wider context of sharing and judged against the backdrop of Rwanda's current socioeconomic transformation from being a society based on gift exchange and logic to one governed by commodity exchange and logic (Taylor, 1992).

Agricultural experimentation then is more than a means through which knowledge about production can be tested, it is also an important, frequent means by which small but precious gifts (of seed and knowledge) can be exchanged and society reproduced in the process. Bean trials on household farms are immensely varied, and necessary for technical as well as social reasons. From a technical point of view, the family trials aim to find the best seed for the garden, and encourage the flow of genetic materials and knowledge throughout the country and across its borders. From a social perspective, the sharing of knowledge between close kin (who regularly live in different agroecological zones) and/or neighbours is all that remains of the gift economy. In my view, this gives rise to an important issue. Viewing family farming in the context of a broad sociopolitical transition, one must question whether it is right for (western-trained) extensionists to want to appropriate 'family secrets' in the name of 'development'. Would accessing such 'secrets' serve anyone other than the agricultural research institutions and the bureaucrats?

Agricultural discourses

Rwandan farming concepts (as opposed to those introduced by extension workers) remain close to the integrated and holistic conceptual universe which marked the pre-colonial era. This implies a strong association between notions of plant fertility and human fertility. Unlike concepts from agronomy, indigenous Rwandan concepts touch simultaneously on a variety of spheres. A simple example can make this clear. Scientific research on bean damage which occurs during storage, uses descriptive terms such as 'dented' (French: *creux*), 'shrivelled and small' (*mince*), 'discoloured' (*décoloré*) and 'wrinkled' (*froissé*) (MINAGRI, 1985: 7). While these terms (whether in English or French) do not evoke strong associations with problems in human health, the Kinyarwanda equivalents do. Beans that become 'shrivelled and small' are referred to as *ibinanutse*, a term also used for thin, undernourished people; while 'wrinkled' beans are referred to as *ibyahinyaraye ku ruhu,* an expression denoting sick people with badly wrinkled skin.

In Rwanda, an interplay of fertility and antifertility principles characterized both the royal rituals (before independence) and many practices related to the body. Although several of these practices have disappeared, their underlying logic continues to influence behaviour, particularly in popular medicine and its symbolism (Taylor, 1992). The integration of agroecological knowledge and field management with the domain of human health and reproduction is highlighted by Fairhead (1992: 16):

> Ecological concepts link crop and human reproductive health . . . Thus both human and crop reproduction necessitate the coming together of fluids under warm conditions; of softened earth and rain in crop production and of vaginal secretions and sperm in human reproduction – a dry infertile woman and a dry soil are called by the same name. The coming together of fluids is not just important during the sexual act or at sowing, but must occur throughout the reproductive cycle. Thus during pregnancy, frequent sexual intercourse is necessary as the combined secretions of warmth and love-making constitute the child. At both sowing and weeding, fire used to be taken to the field from the house to warm and soften the field. Crops were improved both by maintaining the household fire and by frequent sex.

The fusion of conceptual fields such as crop health and human health is also evident in the way Rwandan farmers perceive food qualities such as 'taste' and 'cookability'. For scientists, who refrain from integrating multiple meanings, 'good taste' and 'fast cooking time' are linked to the product itself, i.e., associated with large seed size (Lamb, 1985). For the Rwandan cultivators I knew, 'fast cooking time' in beans was a quality associated with soil conditions rather than with seed size. Although seed size was acknowledged, the stress would be put primarily on soil conditions (and possibly implying 'care'). Thus beans grown in:

- *Ubutake bworoshye* (soft/humid soil) → fast cooking, but poor swelling
- *Urunombe* (solid, reddish, sticky soil) → slow cooking

- *Ibumba* (marshland) → slow cooking
- *Umusenyi* (sandy soil) → slow cooking, but good swelling

The Rwandan farmer's ability to integrate levels of thought is in stark contrast with the country's official discourse on farming, which for the majority of Rwandans comes in the shape of the extensionist's (*vulgarisateur*'s) instructions, that is, as 'dos and don'ts' that represent mono-rationality and commodity exchange and logic. Extensionists were always men and their discourse, which borrows from textbook knowledge and French terminology, is conceptually impoverished when compared with that used by the farmers themselves (Pottier, 1989b). The extensionists with whom I was in close contact would tour the area and instruct, for instance, that sorghum was prohibited in 'model' gardens or that a distance of ten metres had to be observed between coffee plantation and banana grove. When dialogue was attempted, the extensionist would use French terminology (*les oxygènes*; *les associations*; *la parcelle moderne*) and ignore the existence of local farming methods based on notions that suggested 'companionship' or 'struggle' between plants, or between plants and people (Pottier, 1989b; Fairhead, 1990; Taylor, 1992).

Whenever extensionists referred to 'good' practice, they meant textbook practice. In contrast, when used by farmers, 'good' often had several referents. For example, for extensionists, a 'good' bean was an improved, large-grained, high-yielding bean; for farmers, too, 'good' referred to size and yield, but equally to the lushness of the plant, the bean's propensity to do well in soft/humid soils, its colour or its being a good companion to other varieties. I recall hearing the bean *igisabo* praised because it has the colour (and name) of the butterchurn gourd and therefore evokes a strong link with human fertility as conceptualized in traditional imagery. I also recall the companionship farmers said existed between certain pairs of beans, e.g., *ntabeza* and *kamembe*, the former being improved and rain-resistant, the latter able to cope with 'too much sunshine'. The companionship of complementary types is widely acknowledged. Against the farmer's multifaceted approach stands the extensionist's clinical language, which refers to one reality only (scientific processes). Small wonder then that Butare farmers sometimes commented that too much of his advice might result in 'a harvest of words'.

The extension workers' challenge is problematic for two reasons. First, there seems to be no need to access (capture and then standardise) household-level farming experiments: people are already doing it and they are doing it in such a way that varieties and technical knowledge do cross agroecological frontiers. However, I am not entirely convinced that the speed with which varietal materials and knowledge travel is beyond improvement. Second, and more important perhaps, the appropriation of agricultural 'family secrets' would be regarded by farmers as a bureaucratic attempt to do away with the last remnants of gift economy and logic; a political act of violence for which no justification can exist. And I think that both women farmers and men would take this view.

Conclusion

Researchers and planners should recognize they face a dilemma. On the one hand, it cannot be right to want to access knowledge about small farming experiments and deliver a final blow to Rwanda's exchange economy; on the other hand, household relations are still governed by thought processes that favour serious gender inequality and that lag behind the overall pace of the transformation which Rwandan society has accepted. In the light of this dilemma I suggest that Rwanda's agricultural co-operatives, being arenas of struggle where language is used creatively to build a more equitable world, should be considered suitable, legitimate places for farmer-first reflection on the performance and future research agendas of the nation's extension service. A move in that direction would then increase the chances of a dialogue about 'family secrets', as opposed to the current threat of knowledge appropriation by experts.

Composing rural livelihoods: from farming systems to food systems

ANTHONY J. BEBBINGTON

Introduction

Rural peoples' knowledge (RPK) is doubly constructed: by those who talk about it, and by those who possess it. Those who possess it, the rural poor, have to continue reworking, updating and changing their knowledge in the often prejudicial environments in which they compose their own livelihoods. This paper suggests that this dynamism (of context and of rural people) makes RPK very different from a more static traditional knowledge; and that much of the populist farmer-first literature has not taken full cognizance of the implications of this difficult and dynamic context in which rural people live.

Constructing knowledge about knowledge: backwards into the future?

The first sense in which RPK is constructed is as a concept in the farmer-first literature. The process of construction has many elements. Simply by naming something called 'RPK' or 'ITK', this literature creates the sense that such a body of knowledge exists in a coherent form. Then, by discussing it with a particular purpose in mind, namely to promote participatory agricultural research and extension strategies that build on farmers' agronomic knowledge, this literature has emphasized the agricultural dimensions of rural life, and the agricultural expertize of the rural poor. In doing so it has helped create the image that rural people are farmers, that agricultural technology is central to solving rural poverty and that pre-modernized techniques hold keys to this solution.

Of course there have been many reasons for arguing this case that go beyond the purely technological. Authors have also been motivated by concerns that are political (to promote participation and social equity and to challenge prevailing 'taken-for-granted' power relationships); and theoretical (to relativize modernist rationality, to challenge political economic approaches and to suggest the validity of the 'native's point of view'). This has achieved a great deal. It has helped change attitudes to farmer expertize and indigenous peoples' knowledge; and it has undoubtedly helped put rural peoples' agency back into the picture, softening the pessimistic determinisms of political economy (Long and Villareal, Part I).

However, I will suggest there are also several limitations to the approach taken in the farmer-first literature:

- The emphasis on the 'knower' and on the knower's capability to invent and create has tended to take agency out of structure, and replace voluntarism for determinism (Giddens, 1979; Long and van der Ploeg, 1991);
- The emphasis on what knowers know about technology and ecology has diverted attention from the myriad things they do not know about markets, politics and the machinations of a world beyond the farm gate, that has long since pushed that gate open and irrecoverably influenced the farm's future;
- The emphasis on revalidating past practices has understated the changes in the present and the implications they have had for rural people.

Constructing knowledge for livelihoods: forward into modernity

Given these observations, I want to argue for the importance of pursuing an image of rural livelihoods that questions the validity of a unified concept of RPK. This approach would interpret RPK as being constructed through farmers' practices as situated agents. As 'agents', because they are actively engaged in the generation, acquisition and classification of knowledge; and as 'situated' agents because this engagement occurs in cultural, economic, agroecological and socio-political contexts that are products of local and non-local processes. These processes have had a socially differentiated influence: different rural people have different livelihood strategies, different identities and different goals. They also have different capabilities to address what they perceive as problems. Finally, this social history is ongoing – people have to continue acting in a changing context, much of whose change is beyond their control. In contemporary times recognising this social construction draws particular attention to the facts that:

- Pressures on and challenges to agriculturally-based livelihoods are intensifying and undermining the relevance of some earlier agricultural practices;
- Rural people are far from being traditional, have many 'modern' goals and ideas, and are constantly presented with new challenges for which locally-generated knowledge may not hold much guidance;

- It is increasingly the case that agriculture is neither the only nor the main problem or income source for many rural people, and that different people have quite different needs.

Let us take a closer look at some dimensions of this changing context within which the rural poor compose their livelihoods. At this point my attention focuses on Latin America and particularly the Andean countries. However, the themes discussed echo changes ongoing in other parts of the world.

A changing context for rural producers

The 'New Technological Agenda': transforming traditional and Green Revolution agriculture

Entering the 1990s in Andean America a series of 'new' realities and 'new' challenges to campesino agriculture have become apparent: some of them genuinely reflect *new* changes, others, I suspect, are not so new for the people who live them, but are 'new' because analysts and policy makers have begun to recognise them. Either way, they have come together to set what Kaimowitz (1991) has termed the 'new technological agenda': a set of technological challenges to a changing world to which the Green Revolution package *per se* is unable to respond, and to which it has, in several regards, contributed. The main changes forcing the new agenda have been (Kaimowitz, 1991):

- The crisis of the 1980s, with reduced investment in research and extension, leading to an ever weaker support system for the rural poor;
- The rounds of currency devaluations which have led to rapid price increases in fossil-fuel based agrochemical inputs, making the Green Revolution less cost effective;
- Trade liberalization and the creation of regional trading blocks, leading to the removal of tariff and other barriers, and thus opening agriculture up to many more competitive pressures;
- The institutional recognition of environment and sustainable development.

The second and third of these place much more pressure on small farmer production to increase productivity to lower its costs, increase its competitiveness and use all inputs much more efficiently, in both technical and economic terms. If it does not, rural livelihoods and knowledge will be progressively undermined.

Rural peoples' knowledge of their land and crops will have important contributions to make to any technical responses to this challenge, particularly in the identification of low external-input options that do not have noxious environmental impacts. Nonetheless the sort of economic efficiency that is demanded will require capacities for numeracy, economic abstraction, market research (e.g. to identify niche markets) and identification of cost-controlling, productivity-enhancing genetic material that the rural poor do not have (Byerlee, 1987). Indeed, a research project in the

1980s identified the positive effects of formal education on productivity in rural areas, precisely because it helped develop skills of abstraction and numeracy required to handle markets (Figueroa and Bolliger, 1985; Cotlear, 1989). Byerlee (1987) has similarly argued that formal education and human capital formation are essential if the momentum of the Green Revolution in Asia is to be maintained. The rural poor are, like it or not, firmly integrated into the market. Their well-being and survival depends on how well they can handle and negotiate this integration.

This has implications for Research and Extension (R&E) practices. Firstly, R&E will have to focus on management, formal skill formation and local institutional development, and not only on technologies. Secondly, the fall in investment in public sector R&E institutions means that this support will have to come in many cases from the private sector. Rarely will the commercial private sector respond to this, and consequently much of the task will fall to NGOs and farmer organizations (Pretty and Chambers; Farrington and Bebbington; Uphoff, Part III).

Regional development for rural areas: linkages, surplus retention and labour markets

A further, albeit intimately related, set of processes and changes to which a reorganised R&E practice, and a relevant concept of RPK must respond are related to patterns of development and underdevelopment in the regions in which the rural poor piece together their livelihood strategies. Even if the political economic literature erred too far in its dependency perspectives, it was at least correct to stress that rural livelihoods depend as much on agrarian structure, land tenure and the relations of unequal exchange that lead to the transfer of surplus to urban and wealthier social sectors, as they do on agricultural technology. Enhancing the rural poor's capacity to negotiate in the market is equally a question of increasing their ability to negotiate these social relationships.

The 'situated' nature of rural livelihoods demands that we look more carefully at this regional context of the rural economy. If we do so, we find that increasingly rural livelihoods depend on many non-agricultural, often non-rural income sources (Barsky, 1990; Klein, 1992). This work is spatially and temporally combined with farm work.

In many areas and for many people, then, agriculture is neither the only, nor main, source of income: people therefore need assistance with these other activities as much as they do with their agriculture. And of course, very many farmers also migrate seasonally to supplement their incomes: most of them would sooner not (Chambers, 1988; Bebbington, 1992).

In this sense, then, agriculture needs to be placed in a wider context. Strengthening other employment sources in rural areas can help take pressure off land, and thus perhaps address issues of land degradation. Also, if much of rural consumption depends on non-agrarian incomes and entitlements, to concentrate on neat, photogenic soil conserving technologies and farmer-to-farmer extension can miss the point. It runs the risk of suggesting 'success' when terraces and soil contours spring up across the landscape,

91

but in fact the unnoticed nutritional status of the families involved becomes yet more chronic as a consequence of other changes in the rural economy.

On the basis of such observations, de Janvry and Sadoulet (1988) have argued that a strategy to alleviate rural poverty should aim in part to promote rurally-based non-agrarian incomes. Such a strategy should do this, they say, primarily by finding ways of increasing agriculturally-derived incomes, in order to create a demand for non-agrarian products and services that could be provided locally (Klein, 1992). The essence of this strategy would be to find mechanisms facilitating the retention of surplus within a region. Such mechanisms might include new marketing arrangements and the incorporation of a processing stage to develop new forward and backward linkages within the regional food system. Aside from a direct creation of employment in processing, the resulting positive impact on farmer income would, de Janvry and Sadoulet (1988) suggest, create a derived demand for services and goods which could be generated locally. Identifying and supporting institutional arrangements for such a strategy, and helping develop the markets for the products being processed, should be a central thrust of reorganized R&E – R&E for a food systems approach cognizant of the realities of the regional economy.

Some of these observations are hardly new. We can turn to sourcebooks on agricultural development like Eicher and Staatz (1984) and find that neo-classically minded and marxian economists were concerned about vertical linkages, surplus extraction (and retention) and social service provision (especially education) 20 or more years ago. The point is that for all our interest in technology and farmer expertiz in resource management we cannot pretend the regional economy is not there. It is, with a vengeance.

Rural aspirations: the new and the old

This integration of rural economies into a far wider economy is constitutive of a whole series of life-style changes that have occurred in the Andean countryside, particularly since periods of agrarian reform in the 1960s. The modern has come, not only in the form of fertilizers, but in radios, new textiles, bicycles, vans, school notebooks, school uniforms. It has also come in the form of the clothes and cars in which extension agents, non-governmental and governmental, turn up in rural communities. With these and other changes come new aspirations, access to many of which requires an increased income. Farmers look for technologies that serve this end. The provenance of the technology (old or new, traditional or modern) matters far less than its effectiveness.

This is a very blunt assertion requiring two immediate caveats. On the one hand, when it leads to rapid abandonment of traditional practices, this technological pragmatism can lead to detrimental effects with which we are all familiar. Observing these effects, many have argued for a recovery of those practices, to allow a more ecologically-benign resource management, and to reassert traditional cultural identities (Salas, Part I).

Also, the opposition between traditional and modern is not an either/or for the rural poor. Indeed, much of the traditional continues in the Andes.

92

The point, however, is that rural people have their own good reasons for doing what they do. They therefore have good reasons for using the modern as well as for using the 'traditional'. Some of those reasons have less to do with the traditions that some NGO personnel and others suggest rural people ought to be interested in, and more to do with a desire for the modern facilities that NGOs themselves enjoy.

A reflection

From these observations, several points about RPK can be made that have implications for R&E:

- RPK is not only technical. It also includes the range of aspirations, values and preferences that rural people have;
- RPK is not static. It is constructed through the socioeconomic and cultural histories of the regions within which people live – histories composed by 'situated' rural actors whose actions contribute to change in those conditions;
- RPK is never enough. Rural people may know a lot, but they would like to know a lot more in order to be more powerful in their negotiations with political, economic and social forces that have long contributed more to their poverty than has bad technology;
- RPK is embedded within a wider policy context and political economy. The advantage that rural people can gain from the locally generated and introduced knowledge they possess depends on 'contextual' factors in the regional political economy (land distribution, marketing relations, vertical linkages, etc.). Improving livelihoods will therefore depend greatly on interventions to influence these 'contextual' factors. Similarly R&E support will be most effective when it integrates knowledge of these contexts with the conventional technical support given to farmers.

PART II

Methodological Innovations, Applications and Challenges

Part II: Introduction

The papers in Part II set out a range of methodological challenges for participatory research and extension with farmers. Andrea Cornwall, Irene Guijt and Alice Welbourn provide an introduction to the the debates with an analysis of key participatory approaches now being developed and applied across a wide range of contexts, including Farming Systems Research-Extension, Farmer Participatory Research, Participatory Action Research, Rapid and Participatory Rural Appraisal, Development Education and Leadership Teams in Action and Theatre for Development. They point to the importance of analysing difference in order to understand competing interests, conflicting alliances and social networks, and point the way towards more strategic, flexible and people-centred approaches to learning, analysis and development.

The overview is followed by papers which offer different perspectives on the strengths and weaknesses of rapid and participatory appraisal methods for agricultural research and extension. There has been an explosion of interest in participatory methodologies over the last five years, with applications ranging from village-level planning in India (Parmesh Shah), to policy-oriented analysis in Senegal (Karen Schoonmaker Freudenberger) to on-farm research with farmers in Zambia (Michael Drinkwater). The methodological tool-box available to fieldworkers has been dramatically transformed. For example, significant advances have been made in the development of visualization techniques (mapping, diagramming, etc.) as tools for joint analysis by farmers and development workers. Participatory, rapid (and relaxed) rural appraisal has become a familiar approach in many parts of the world.

With this methodological experimentation and spread of innovation, important questions about quality, consistency, trustworthiness and ethics inevitably arise. These are addressed in contributions by Janice Jiggins and Ann Waters-Bayer (Nigeria), in which they challenge us to confront the sensitive issues of quality and ethics in methodological development, training and application.

Contributions by Jeffrey Bentley (Honduras), Yunita Winarto (Indonesia), Arthur Stolzenbach (Mali), David Millar (Ghana) and Paul Richards (Sierra Leone) shift the focus to the problems and possibilities of farmer participatory research, placing particular emphasis on the merits and limitations of farmer experimentation. Part II closes with a paper by Lori Ann Thrupp, Bruce Cabarle and Aaron Zazueta who reflect on the methodological challenges of scaling-up local-level inquiry for wider-scale policy and planning in Central and South America.

Acknowledging process: methodological challenges for agricultural research and extension

ANDREA CORNWALL, IRENE GUIJT and ALICE WELBOURN

Changing theory, changing methodology?

Over the last decades, pragmatic and ethical concerns about the inadequacies of conventional approaches to agricultural research and extension in Asia, Africa and Latin America have fuelled the development of alternative, more participatory methodologies. Yet there is continued neglect of the social processes that take place during and following the use of these methodologies, and of the experiential, practical and political elements.

New practices have challenged the theory of agricultural development, and in turn have been challenged by theoretical shifts (Scoones and Thompson, Part I). Farmers, researchers and extensionists must be recognized as social actors within the social practice of agricultural production.

After clarifying the role of methodology in agricultural research and extension, we review challenges to mainstream thinking in agricultural development. Through a critical examination of alternative participatory methodologies, drawing on experiences from community development, we explore ways in which new practices can enrich agricultural research and extension.

Methods and methodologies

Method and methodology are often, erroneously, used as synonyms. Methods are the nuts and bolts, or mechanics, of data collection and information exchange; methodologies shape and inform the processes of research and extension. Methodologies provide the user with a framework for selecting the means to find out about, analyse, order and exchange information about an issue. They define *what* can be known or exchanged, *how* that should be represented and by and for *whom* this is done.

The ways in which we conceptualize research problems define potential outcomes, and how we choose to reach these. The process of research or extension often focuses only on these outcomes: the production or transfer of 'facts'. Methodologies are seen as a neutral means to that end. Yet methodological strategies involve more than selecting appropriate methods. Experiments, surveys, diagramming techniques or interviews can be used differently by each actor, which may result in divergent and sometimes conflicting information. Only part of these differences can be explained from the kinds of information the methods generate. The choices which are made during the application of the methodologies stem from personal experiences, beliefs and assumptions. These aspects often go unquestioned and unacknowledged, yet influence both the procedures and outcomes of research or extension.

Traditionally, science sets certain parameters within which interpretation takes place and favours the use of particular methodologies for specific purposes. The choice of a methodology is, however, not determined solely by its perceived scientific relevance. Institutional concerns include time or financial constraints, or conditionality of donors. More personal criteria also play a role, such as habit, fear of not being respected and imposition by superiors. The choice of a methodology is, as Hesse (1978) suggests, a decision which is both personal and political. Recognizing this enables us to look more closely at the consequences of the conscious or unconscious methodological choices we make.

Challenging constraining conventions

Conventional approaches to agricultural research and extension are based on several common assumptions, which limit their ability to deal with complex and changing realities. The linear sequence of events assumes stability, and neglects local experiences of nature and previous interventions. Those in the higher ranks define what is worth knowing and use others to transfer this to those who lack it. The generation of knowledge is separated from its use in decision making and implementation (Korten, 1980).

Conventional experimental design reduces the complex dynamics of farming to technical procedures. Within surveys, used to determine socioeconomic production constraints, the views of some farmers are solicited and assumed to represent everyone. Information is aggregated and analysed using variables determined to be relevant by researchers. Recommendations are passed to planners who set objectives which are insensitive to the contexts in which they are to be realised.

While conventional research and extension can contribute substantially to agricultural development, even the most well-intentioned scientists and extension workers, using the best conventional methods available, may still produce and pass on totally inappropriate recommendations (Moris, 1991). Many of the limitations of these approaches result from their perspective of agriculture as a technical activity rather than as social praxis.

Over the last decades, some of the fundamental assumptions made by agricultural researchers and extension workers working in Africa, Asia and Latin America have been shaken. Farmers have been proven to be knowledgeable about their farming systems and capable of conducting trials and experiments (e.g. Millar; Richards; Stolzenbach; Winarto, Part II). Research has shown that:

- Farmers continuously conduct their own trials, partially adopt and adapt technologies to their specific circumstances and spread innovations through their networks;
- There are significant differences between the procedures of farmers' and research station experiments and their criteria for assessment;
- Farmer experimentation is quicker and more able to accommodate changing circumstances and diversity than those of research scientists;
- Farmers' own analysis of farming systems offers important insights, different from that of scientists.

Most methodologies do not explore fully the *processes* of knowing about and doing farming. Erroneous parallels between farming practice and scientific procedure continue to be drawn. Van der Ploeg notes that 'local methods fall outside the scope of scientific design', and therefore so do farmers 'as active and knowledgeable actors, capable of improving their own conditions' (1989: 157).

Conceptualizing agriculture as a largely technical activity obscures the social, cultural, personal and political dimensions both of rural farming practice and western agricultural science. Agricultural production is determined not only by environmental conditions and technological inputs, but also by the opportunities available to different actors. In a single situation, these may be distinctly different for female and male farmers of different ages and social groups. Yet social complexity is masked by a focus on simplistic units of analysis such as 'the household' and distinctions drawn between, for example, 'progressive' and 'conservative' farmers.

Each actor in agricultural development operates within relations of power which determine her/his ability to respond to and initiate agricultural change. Long and van der Ploeg (1989: 228) argue that:

. . . conceptualizing intervention as a discrete and clearly localized activity (i.e., as a 'project') obscures the theoretically important point that intervention is never a 'project' with sharp boundaries in space and time . . . Interventions are always part of the chain or flow of events located within the broader framework of the activities of the state and the activities of different interest groups operative in civil society.

Methodological issues

Conventional agricultural research and extension is based on the production and exchange of knowledge. It is carried out for a particular purpose by people who make methodological choices and define knowledge and its use. To understand how these considerations affect the process and outcome of agricultural research and extension, certain questions must be addressed. What form is knowledge allowed to take – and who decides? Who interacts in agricultural development? Whose knowledge counts? Knowledge for what? And knowledge for whom?

Knowledge is often treated methodologically as if it could be amassed or distributed, found, built on or lost. Yet knowledge is not some*thing* which can be discovered – it is produced through the interactions of people in particular situations, and methodologies provide the means to produce it. Interpretation of these processes into 'data' or 'recommendations' always involve changes – from observations or dialogues into numbers or monologues, from terms lodged in one conceptual framework into another. 'Findings' appear neutral and authoritative, and are cut loose from contexts and interactions. The claim of western scientific objectivity implies that the researcher or extension worker simple conveys, rather than interprets, information. By trying to control 'unwanted' variation or minimize the 'outsider effect', the part people play in constructing versions of reality is denied. People interpret, rather than just describe, these interactions and their outcomes according to their own assumptions and priorities (Uphoff, 1992).

Most methodologies can only deal with knowledge which takes the form of statements. Conventional interviewing techniques require that people convey what they know verbally to the questioner who has set the frame of reference for the answer. Statements are often translated literally, assuming equivalence between the concepts used and masking the use of metaphor (Pottier; Salas, Part I). Farmers' observations may seem to make no sense at all (van der Ploeg, 1989), as they do not fit the world described by researchers and extension workers. Only recognisable elements are included and reshaped. Others are discarded. Yet much of what is known simply cannot be stated: 'they can be represented – and made present – only through action, enactment and performance' (Fabian, 1990: 6).

Methodologies include decisions about who asks questions or delivers recommendations at the 'interface' (Long, 1989). Statements are not made in a vacuum, they are made to people. What is said depends on how the question is phrased, how it is asked and by whom. Sometimes rural people respond with idealized versions or repeat what they have heard from extension workers. They may provide information that they feel is expected, reveal what least damages their interests, or respond to what they think external organizations may have on offer. How rural people react is also influenced by 'collective and individual memories' (Long and van der Ploeg, 1989) of interventions. As their 'hidden transcripts' (Scott, 1990) may vary considerably from the official versions they communicate, they can easily be interpreted as conservative or ignorant by researchers and extension workers.

The question 'whose knowledge counts?' reveals how certain kinds of knowledge turn others into ignorance (Vitebsky, 1993). Conventional research and extension aims to produce and convey recommendations to remedy the absence of knowledge about certain processes, and therefore makes assumptions about whose knowledge is important. The process assumes that farmers are ignorant about certain elements of their practice and, therefore, renders their knowledge invisible. For example, defining rural people's knowledge as 'indigenous *technical* knowledge' obscures its social and cultural dimensions. Researchers seek those who are presumed to know *most*, so-called 'key informants', thereby choosing their versions over others. The contributions of others – often women or children – are often not solicited. That they may have *different* rather than *less* knowledge is rarely acknowledged.

With local agricultural knowledge increasingly in the spotlight, simplistic assumptions are made about what counts as 'local'. Yet, many sources of rural people's knowledge stem from outside their immediate environment. The social networks to which they belong interact in many domains, creating complex 'knowledge chains' (Box, 1987) about issues and innovations. Labelling teachers, extension workers, visitors from town, and relatives from elsewhere as 'insiders' or 'outsiders' simplifies a more complex relationship between them. People may be 'outsiders' *and/or* 'insiders' according to their activity or purpose. The difference between them may be one of degree, rather than kind.

Asking 'knowledge for what?', raises questions about the kind of knowledge which is needed and by whom. Do researchers actually need to know all that they seek? Why? Should only researchers be given the responsibility for producing knowledge or recommendations? What goal is the transfer of knowledge aiming to reach? As Korten (1980) notes, conventional agricultural development assumes that knowledge can be generated independently of the organizational capacity needed for it to be put into practice. What counts as knowledge within research may be entirely inappropriate for action. Knowledge is not necessarily generated in line with the needs of the different constituencies of farmers; organizations have their own agendas which set the terms for interventions. These personal, professional and institutional interests cannot be separated from the choices of methodology which are made.

Finally, the question 'knowledge for whom?' places the quest for understanding firmly in the political and personal arena. Conventional approaches generally regard local people as passive recipients, whose 'needs' are defined for them, according to the agendas of their developers. Chambers (1992a) contends:

> 'Outsiders' have been conditioned to believe and assume that villagers are ignorant and have either lectured at them, holding sticks and waving fingers, or have interviewed them, asking rapid questions, interrupting and not listening beyond immediate replies . . . The apparent ignorance of rural people is then an artificial product of 'outsiders' ignorance of how to enable them to express, share and extend their knowledge. The attitudes and behaviour needed for rapport are missing.

Working with people or facilitating them to work with each other requires a shift in perspective. The methodological challenge is not necessarily that of how researchers can produce more or better knowledge, and how extension workers can transfer it to local people. Chambers (1992b) argues:

> The idea is not to improve our analysis, or even our learning, but their [local people's] analysis and their learning . . . it has been revealed again and again that they can do what only we thought we could do, and often that they can do it better.

The emphasis in methodological development must shift from expanding the repertoire of methods to acknowledging the political aspects of methodological choices and the learning experience that those involved in agricultural research and extension undergo. Participatory approaches try to overcome some of the limitations of mainstream agricultural research and extension, by addressing some of these concerns.

'Participation': rhetoric or revolution?

'Participation' has become a familiar part of the rhetoric of institutions ranging from the smallest NGO to the World Bank. The adoption of participation as a guiding concept has been driven by both ideology and pragmatism (Farrington and Bebbington, Part III). Many institutions with explicit aims to reach the 'poorest of the poor' focus on methodologies consistent with their ideology, involving the intended beneficiaries in the process. Participation has also been recognized to contribute to more effective and sustainable impact of the work done. As a result there has been an immense surge in the conditionality of participation attached to much agricultural research and extension. Appearances may deceive, as Cernea (1991) warns:

> We hear sudden declaration of fashionable support for participatory approaches . . . social scientists should not confuse these statements with actual participatory planning, because under the cloud of cosmetic rhetoric, technocratic planning continues to rule.

'Participation' is easily woven mechanistically into the process of linear development. Although the style of interaction might change, the principles upon which much participatory research and extension are based remain unchanged. Often the actors involved are neither convinced by the pragmatic arguments, nor politically committed to devolving power to local people.

There are myriad interpretations of participation. It has been differentiated according to distinct stages of agricultural research and extension (Farrington and Martin, 1988), while others classify the kind of interactions which take place. Biggs (1989a) distinguishes four types of farmer participation: contractual, consultative, collaborative, and collegiate. Farrington, *et al.* (1993) expand on Biggs' typology which they identify as 'depth of interaction' running from shallow to deep, by discerning scope of interaction, which ranges from narrow to wide. They highlight organizational issues, arguing that deeper levels of participation tend to rely more on group than individual approaches.

The methodologies listed in Box 1 contain the germs of a revolution in agricultural development. Despite the rhetoric of some approaches, they have brought significant innovations and challenges to the mainstream. Often heralded as 'new' directions, these approaches have a half-forgotten history in community development initiatives spanning the last four decades (Holdcroft, 1978, cited in Korten, 1980). Many draw on methods developed in community development for empowerment, yet only a few acknowledge or respond to the challenges of a 'deep and wide' participatory process.

In many of these approaches, rural people's participation is limited to providing information to researchers, who do the analysis and generate solutions for farmers. In several (e.g. BA, FSR, D&D, AEA, RRA) external agents remain in control of which form information takes. Others (e.g. PAR, PRA, DELTA, Theatre for Development) aim to enable rural people to explore their own visions and solutions, through forms they themselves generate. These 'new methodologies' have important contributions to make to agricultural research and extension, yet raise a number of institutional challenges and dilemmas (Farrington and Bebbington; Pretty and Chambers, Part III).

In the following sections, we review the innovations and shortcomings of six approaches: FSR/E, FPR, PRA, PAR, DELTA and Theatre for Development. Each approach allocates specific roles to extension workers

Box 1: Some participatory approaches of the 1980s–90s (in alphabetical order)

AEA	Agroecosystem Analysis
BA	Beneficiary Assessment
DELTA	Development Education Leadership Teams
D&D	Diagnosis and Design
DRP	Diagnostico Rural Participativo
FPR	Farmer Participatory Research
FSR/E	Farming Systems Research/Extension
GRAAP	Groupe de recherche et d'appui pour l'auto-promotion paysanne
MARP	Méthode Accéléré de Recherche Participative
PALM	Participatory Analysis and Learning Methods
PAR	Participatory Action Research
PD	Process Documentation
PRA	Participatory Rural Appraisal
PRAP	Participatory Rural Appraisal and Planning
PRM	Participatory Research Methods
PTD	Participatory Technology Development
RA	Rapid Appraisal
RAAKS	Rapid Assessment of Agricultural Knowledge Systems
RAP	Rapid Assessment Procedures
RAT	Rapid Assessment Techniques
RCA	Rapid Catchment Analysis
REA	Rapid Ethnographic Assessment
RFSA	Rapid Food Security Assessment
RMA	Rapid Multi-perspective Appraisal
ROA	Rapid Organizational Assessment
RRA	Rapid Rural Appraisal
SB	Samuhik Brahman (Joint trek)
TFD	Theatre for Development
TFT	Training for Transformation

and/or researchers. The challenge for the future is to draw from this array of innovation to create new syntheses.

Farming systems research-extension

Farming Systems Research-Extension (FSR/E) emerged in the late 1970s in reaction to the prevailing transfer-of-technology model. It recognised that constraints at the farm level limited the adoption of new technologies coming from outside the system (Gartner, 1990). Advocates of the FSR/E approach, initially mainly agricultural economists, argued that research should be determined by explicitly identified farmers' needs, rather than according to the preconceptions of researchers. Accordingly, applied agricultural research was relocated from the stations to the farm (Gilbert *et al.*, 1980; Collinson 1981; Shaner *et al.*, 1982). Researchers and extensionists were encouraged to work with farmers to design, test and modify improved agricultural technologies to suit local conditions.

Although FSR/E has developed in many different directions, making generalization difficult, there are three common key principles:

- Joint effort by researchers, extensionists and farmers to design, test and modify improved agricultural technologies appropriate for local conditions;
- Agriculture is seen as an holistic system in which all important interactions that affect its performance should be considered;
- A multi-disciplinary perspective to problem analysis, technology design, trial implementation and evaluation.

In practice, FSR/E activities include basic (laboratory) research, research station trials, on-farm trials and extension and production programmes. Most work is done through on-farm and multi-location trials, under farm conditions, to learn about farmers' constraints. The results are then communicated to experiment stations, usually by researchers or extension workers.

FSR/E's contribution is most obvious in an historical perspective as it signified a move away from a crop-only fixation (although this remains a favourite focus of activities) towards an appreciation of the complexity of agricultural systems and decision-making. FSR/E provided the means for making decisions about cost-effective on-farm and on-station measures.

However, it is based on assumptions derived from a positivist approach to agricultural systems, aiming to optimise them through interventions by the 'expert technologist' or 'management consultant' (Bawden, 1992b). Most FSR/E scientists continue to investigate for or sometimes even on their farmer 'clients', rather than with them. Reliant on conventional natural and social scientific research methods, FSR/E remains largely insensitive to farmers' knowledge, and the flow of knowledge is generally in the researcher-back-to-researcher mode.

Farmer participatory research

Farmer Participatory Research (FPR) developed in the 1980s to involve farmers more closely in on-farm research, moving beyond FSR/E's contracting or consulting farmers. It views the context of agricultural production as interactions between on- and off-farm resource management strategies. Recognition of what came to be termed 'indigenous technical knowledge' (ITK) led to a focus on the farmer as innovator and as experimenter, and more interest in 'collaborative' and 'collegiate' relations between researchers and farmers (Biggs, 1980; Richards, 1985; Farrington, 1988; Farrington and Martin, 1988; Amanor, 1990; Hiemstra *et al.*, 1992). Advocates of this shift called the new approach farmer-first (Chambers *et al.*, 1989), and pronouncing the farmer as 'rational' and 'right' (Gupta, 1989).

Despite these innovations, FPR researchers explored the concepts and procedures used by farmers in their experiments, usually applying the positivist assumptions of technical science to ITK and disregarding its social and cultural aspects. A single rationality, modelled on that of western logic, was presupposed and other 'ways of reasoning' (Hacking, 1983) were not considered. Issues of diversity and difference among farmers were virtually disregarded. Recent agricultural anthropological work on farmers' knowledge (Fairhead, 1990, 1993; van der Ploeg 1993; Salas, Part I) has raised three key methodological challenges.

First, do farmers and research scientists share the same notion of what constitutes an experiment or an innovation? Van der Ploeg (1989) argues that they do not. If, as Richards (1989) suggests, agricultural production resembles a 'performance' of complex, situation-specific adjustments, rather than a planned sequence of events, the boundary between 'experiment' and 'normal procedures' becomes blurred. This raises the question of whether farmers regard changes in practice as 'innovations' at all (Fairhead, 1990).

A second set of difficulties arises when considering the basis for such a partnership. Fairhead (1993) anticipates the problems which might be faced in establishing a basis for collegiate dialogue either between researchers and farmers, or between farmers themselves:

> The catch is that local knowledge is good precisely because it is hypothetical and relatively unformulated, and yet precisely for this reason it is almost impossible to access.

If, as van der Ploeg (1989) contends, farmer's understandings of agricultural processes are a complex of personal, metaphorical and contextual knowledge which becomes almost impenetrable when subjected to scientific scrutiny, then reaching a common understanding may be extremely difficult. This draws attention to intimate linkages between cosmological beliefs and processes of agricultural experimentation and innovation (Salas, Part I). Such associations create difficulties for collegiate relationships with rationalist scientists and extension workers.

A third challenge for research and extension which is based on facilitating dialogue and mutual learning is the issue of power and control over knowledge. Fairhead (1990) observes that in Kivu, Zaire, it may be precisely those innovations that are most new and exciting that are least likely to be shared outside the private domain. Farmers' knowledge cannot simply be aggregated as if it were the 'property' of farmers in general: *making* an innovation common property has social and political consequences (Pottier, Part I).

These methodological challenges reveal the paradox of productive collaboration. While each party needs to develop an understanding and appreciation of the others' methodological approach (Millar, Part II; Salas, Part I), this may in itself preclude the possibility of certain kinds of collaboration. What, then, are the prospects for collaboration? Three kinds of approach can be identified.

In the first, conventional agricultural science remains central, either by disseminating simple experimental techniques to farmers (Bunch, 1985, 1987; Lightfoot, *et al*, 1988; Gubbels, 1990) or making on-farm trials more amenable to statistical analysis, thus enhancing research station replicability (Box, 1987). The emphasis is on changing methods of work, rather than methodologies.

Richards (Part II) suggests a second option: to identify those farmers who work along positivist lines and to work with them to enhance their capacity. This makes explicit that which is implicit in much of FPR work, but the implications of such an approach remain problematic. Among them is the prospect that only those farmers conducting experiments in ways compatible with western science would be research partners.

The third approach aims to change the roles of and relationships between researchers, extensionists and farmers towards a process of collaboration based on mutual learning as colleagues with different contributions to make (Chambers, 1993). It gives farmers an array of choices, allows them to suggest criteria for technological development and select elements of packages to adapt and adopt (Rhoades, 1983; Bunch, 1989), and facilitate processes through which they can analyse and implement their own solutions.

The second and third approaches partially overlap. Both provide radical alternatives to conventional research and extension. They place farmers at the centre of activities, focusing on facilitating exchange between farmers and enhancing their organizational capacity to diagnose and solve problems themselves. Over the last few years, several possible strategies have developed, including:

- Farmer-back-to-farmer (Rhoades and Booth, 1982; Rhoades, 1983);
- Village research groups (Drinkwater, Part II; Sikana, Part III);
- Farmer experimenter networks (Box, 1987);
- Farmer groups (Norman et al., 1989; Ashby et al., 1989).

Questions may arise where groups need to be formed, requiring a sensitivity to local political and social dynamics which is often lacking. Without the skills to facilitate these encounters, the divisions and conflicts of interest which support the status quo may merely be reinforced. It may also restrict the participation to those farmers who present themselves as suitable candidates: female farmers may well be excluded from such initiatives. Finally, it raises questions about what agricultural science could hope to contribute to such an independent process.

FPR will need to seek ways to channel institutional and scientific resources more effectively in directions the farmers themselves take part in determining (Pretty and Chambers, Part III). Without an appreciation of contextual issues, however, such initiatives may flounder. It is particularly important that issues of difference, power and control in rural communities are better understood before research and extension is conducted. This can help to view the 'farmer' as a social actor who interacts in many spheres, rather than someone whose life revolves solely around agricultural production.

Rapid rural appraisal and participatory rural appraisal

While FSRE and FPR retain agriculture as pivotal, another approach developed which located agriculture as one among other elements of people's livelihoods. Growing dissatisfaction with two common approaches to development research, 'rural development tourism' and 'survey slavery' (Chambers, 1983), led to the emergence of Rapid Rural Appraisal (RRA) in the late 1970s (Carruthers and Chambers, 1981; Khon Kaen University, 1987).

RRA stresses cost-effective trade-offs between the quantity, accuracy, relevance and timeliness of information. It combines a range of methods for rapid and cumulative data collection. Other key features include: multidisciplinarity, a semi-structured and flexible sequence that is regularly reviewed and refined, and exploring local categories, classifications and perceptions. Initially, RRA teams of researchers and planners gathered, represented and analysed the information. Farmers generated data and discussed the researchers' findings, but were excluded from any analysis.

By the late 1980s, users of RRA had been inspired by agroecosystem analysis (Gypmantasiri et al., 1980; Conway, 1985, 1987), applied anthropology (Brokensha et al., 1980; Rhoades, 1982, 1990), participatory action research (Rahman, 1984; Gaventa and Lewis, 1991) and FSR/FPR (Ashby, 1990). The focus shifted from the rapid collection of data by researchers and planners to facilitating farmers to generate, represent and analyse their own data (IIED, 1988–1994; Mascarenhas et al., 1991).

This implied a reversal of roles for farmers and development workers, and methods developed to help change the behaviour and attitudes of 'outsiders'. A new label emerged: *Participatory* Rural Appraisal. Advocates of this approach argue that the production of knowledge and the generation of potential solutions should be carried out by those whose livelihood strategies formed the subject for research. PRA combines research with action, offering opportunities for mobilizing local people for joint action (Devavaram et al., 1991; Mascarenhas et al., 1991).

RRA and PRA make use of a rich menu of visualization, interviewing and group work methods (Box 2), of which visualization has proven particularly innovative within agricultural development. Rather than answering a stream of questions directed by the values of the researcher, local people represent their ideas in a form they can discuss, modify and extend. They become creative analysts and performers, rather than reactive respondents (Chambers, 1992a). Seasonal calendars help to understand the many dimensions of seasonal welfare (Chambers, 1993), and highlight the dynamics of rural livelihoods. Ranking and scoring exercises draw out some of the complexities involved in decision-making, which are rarely accessible through formal surveys and which enable researchers to appreciate farmers' differing needs and preferences. Methods such as crop biographies, network and pathway diagramming (FARM-Africa/IIED, 1991) and systems diagramming (Guijt and Pretty, 1992; Lightfoot et al., 1992) have developed.

However, visualization is not a neutral medium and retains translation problems. Visual versions are presented to and interpreted by the viewer. They facilitate further discussion, but do not replace dialogue. The paradox of participation becomes clear where large groups form to create diagrams. While ostensibly encouraging a wider participation, the size of the group

Box 2:	Methods used in Participatory Rural Appraisal	
Visualized Analyses	Interviewing	Group and Team Dynamics
• Participatory mapping and modelling • Aerial photograph analyses • Seasonal calendars • Daily and activity profiles • Historical profiles and trend analyses • Timelines and chronologies • Matrix scoring • Preference ranking • Venn and network diagramming • Systems and flow diagrams • Pie diagrams	• Semi-structured interviewing • Transect and group walks • Wealth ranking • Focus group interviews • Key informant interviews • Ethnohistories • Futures possible	• Team contracts • Buzz sessions and reviews • Rapid report writing • Do-it-yourself (taking part in local activities) • Villager and shared presentations • Self-corrected notes and diaries

influences the process. As with verbal communication, local people filter what they choose to present, including their expectations of what the agricultural development worker can offer (Jonfa *et al.*, 1992).

The apparent ease with which information can be gathered using P/RRA methods belies the more complex political and social context in which such interactions take place. There is sometimes a naive assumption that if the external agent behaves appropriately and hands over control, then they will not bias the information. External agents are often, and rightly, assumed to have access to resources of some kind or even to represent threats (Mosse, 1992). In turn, external agents often regard farmers as willing discussion partners who provide the truth. They have their own agendas, and encounters are set within relations of power. Only few cases have addressed local power dynamics and conflict (Conway *et al.*, 1989; Poffenberger *et al.*, 1992).

RRA and PRA offer a creative approach to information sharing and a challenge to prevailing biases and preconceptions about rural people's knowledge. PRA further recognizes that, besides producing timely and relevant knowledge, rural people should have control over its use. However, the methods can easily be applied mechanistically within any framework and for any agenda, and PRA is rapidly becoming a fashionable label for short-cut research. Adopting PRA is, as Chambers (1992a) urges, not only about facilitating 'participation', but also about changing the approach of development agencies at their core, which has been one step too far for many.

Participatory action research (PAR)

Participatory Action Research developed during the 1970s and draws together both the personal and the political. It recognizes the marginalization caused by 'universal science' and its creation of ignorance, and challenges relations of inequality by restoring oppressed people's self-respect and voice. Its aims are, therefore, explicitly political, as PAR focuses on the experiences of poor and exploited groups. PAR seeks to disrupt the hegemony of western science and official histories in which the contribution of ordinary people plays no part. The versions of knowledge they create, 'people's science', are used to confront forces of domination.

'Participation' in PAR means breaking out of relations of dependency to restore to people their ability to transform their worlds (Freire, 1972). Local people are involved at all stages in research. Rather than being the objects of research, they produce and own their own information. In theory, in this process the initial agents of change 'become redundant . . . the transformation process continues without the physical presence of external agents, animators and cadres' (Fals-Borda and Rahman, 1991).

Practitioners of PAR stress the importance of recovering people's own histories in the process of collective confidence-building. The methods used in PAR include:

- Collective research – meetings, socio-dramas, public assemblies;
- Recovery of history – through collective memory, interviews, witness accounts, family coffers;
- Valuing and applying 'folk culture' – through the arts, sports and other forms of expression;
- Production and diffusion of new knowledges through written, oral and visual forms.

The principles of PAR have inspired recent developments within PRA. Yet in its direct concern with the politics of inequality it is often perceived as deeply threatening to established interests: both those within communities and of the development agencies. Its goal of societal transformation is a long-term 'project' for which the personal and political commitment of the external agents is vital. It requires the researchers or extension workers acting as agents of change to be above all skilful communicators and leaders, willing and able to hand over total control of the change process.

DELTA (Development Education and Leadership Teams in Action)

DELTA developed in the mid-1970s in Kenya and is much used in grassroots community work in East Africa. It offers dynamic, process-oriented ways of identifying and responding to local concerns by emphasising long-term commitment and building confidence and trust.

The approach brings together Freire's (1972) work on critical awareness and conscientisation, human relations training in group work (Hope *et al.*, 1984), organizational development, social analysis, and ideas from Liberation Theology. These sources are depicted as flowing together into a river of DELTA training that, in turn, forms a delta of sectorally-divided issues (literacy, agriculture, health, management, family and social problems). Facilitators conduct 'listening surveys' in communities and prepare 'codes', such as pictures or songs, which reflect local problems. Each code is then discussed and processed in an open meeting. An 'action plan' forms the follow-up, which aims to address the causes of the problem.

The DELTA approach places people's experiences of their problems at the core of research and extension. Rather than prescribe or project solutions, DELTA agents facilitate local level reflection and action. By building confidence and providing an opportunity for the participation of marginalized groups, DELTA brings more people into the process of local self-development.

However, DELTA agents determine the process they initiate, as they provide the codes for discussions. The facilitator becomes the lynch pin whose own agenda can define the process. Resting, as it does, on a notion of 'the community' and on reaching a consensus, this approach may fail to confront the relations of power which establish hierarchies of interests and agendas within the community. This is particularly problematic where the Christian message of DELTA may marginalize or exclude those who do not share these beliefs.

Theatre for development

Performance arts, such as theatre, song, dance and puppetry are used in extension in many parts of the world. In some places, performance provides a means to convey prescriptive messages within a top-down approach to extension. Harding (1987) clearly distinguishes theatre *in* development from theatre *for* development. The former is created and performed by external agents to offer their recommendations and solutions. The latter 'aims to make the processes of drama-building accessible to people who can in turn use it as part of their access to development' (Harding, 1987: 332).

Augusto Boal, whose work forms one of the major influences on Theatre for Development, contends: 'Theatre is a weapon and it is the people who should wield it' (1979: 22). By inviting people to intervene in dramatized scenarios of their everyday lives, Boal's method encourages them to create their own solutions. Acting out becomes a rehearsal for action.

In common with DELTA agents, Theatre for Development practitioners use the 'listening survey' and 'codes', in the form of open-ended problem-posing sketches. As they perform in public places, spectators are drawn into the performance to act out their versions and experiment with possible solutions. In contrast with DELTA, creative conflict, rather than consensus guides, the process of action and reflection. Practitioners recognize the inherently conflictual nature of community relations, seeking to build the awareness to confront or expose the relations of power which sustain inequalities (Abah and Okwerri, pers. comm.).

Theatre for Development techniques have been used in several development settings to raise awareness and mobilize, as well as to monitor and evaluate projects (Cornwall *et al.*, 1989; Mavro, 1991). The principal

111

strength of this technique lies in its emphasis on a performative approach to research and extension, and on the power of theatre as a mobilizing and enabling force for change. As such, Theatre for Development offers complementary methodological strategies to discussion and diagramming.

Creating new directions for agricultural research and extension

Due to its orientation towards technical and economic problem-solving, conventional agricultural research and extension often reduces situations and masks the complexities of rural life. The participatory approaches reviewed above aim, in different ways, to restore some of these complexities. By recognising that 'participation' involves more than consultation, rural people are increasingly becoming actors, rather than instruments in the development process. This is reflected in changing roles for extension workers and researchers.

While striving to improve mainstream approaches and theorizing about the ideal, it is essential to recognize and accept certain constraints. Communication, on which agricultural research and extension hinges, is far from straightforward. We can never step outside our own ways of reasoning or the confines of our language (Hacking, 1983). Communicating what is known and showing what is done involves interpreting others' intentions using our own. Other methods, such as performances or visualizations, will not lay bare what people know, but do provide further opportunities for interpretation.

There is a danger, too, of drowning in pluralities. If many different versions of knowledge are produced, then no single version can provide one truth. Yet a choice is always made. If truths are relative, then choosing a version becomes a matter of appropriateness or applicability (Goodman, 1978), and less objective and neutral than conventional science would let us believe (Quine, 1953). Choices then are made on the basis of political and personal beliefs. Being explicit about such choices would already be an enormous step forward in understanding agricultural research and extension.

If agriculture is to be treated as the social process it is, then several key aspects of context will need to be considered. Agricultural development needs to be set in time, as a longer-term process rather than a series of defined projects, and needs to consider people's historical experiences. Diversity within rural communities and among external agents need to be addressed, by recognizing that different actors hold different versions of knowledge. Issues of power, control and conflict will need to be considered (Scoones and Thompson, Part I). Changing conventional approaches also involves challenging the nature of interactions between rural people, and researchers or extension workers. The importance of training to recognise the political and personal dimensions of agricultural development will also need to be addressed.

Time

Change takes place over time, and it takes time. Crop varieties, like people, have their own biographies, which are often intimately entwined with those who cultivate them (Box, 1987). 'New' crops can be woven into 'old' systems of practice, or stand alone as products of modernity with only a market value. Cropping patterns, land preparation techniques, ownership and innovation are always located within a complex of historical processes. Without understanding these dynamic processes, agricultural research and extension may obstruct, rather than facilitate, positive change. There is no such thing as a timeless, perfect variety or technique that stands outside wider processes of change. Some of the most interesting challenges for research and extension lie in understanding how people bridge different ways of knowing, adapt extension recommendations and tips from contacts from outside the 'local' area and integrate the 'new' into 'traditional' practices.

Understanding the dynamic nature of agricultural processes requires an appreciation of local histories. Yet histories, like any form of knowledge, are neither singular nor necessarily consensual. As Cross and Barker (1991) show, accounts of history as told by local people are retold and reshaped to reflect current concerns and contingencies. They present personal reactions to and experiences of events, and are therefore necessary to understand local perceptions of innovations and interventions.

Participatory approaches increasingly draw on oral history to explain the past, to make sense of the present and to plan for the future. Both FSR/E and FPR are still weak in this respect. PAR offers important experiences for agricultural methodology, while PRA is increasingly incorporating dynamic, historical perspectives in its approach (Schoonmaker Freudenberger, Part II).

One implication is the need to move away from quick-fix solutions, a fallacy which remains largely unchallenged. Whilst dwindling financial resources make ever-increasing demands for short-term solutions to problems, experience has repeatedly shown that these interventions are either ineffective, unsustainable or counterproductive. Cost-cutting does not equal cost-effectiveness, no matter how desirable this might be. Making long-term commitments is crucial, yet depends on the willingness and capacity of those within agricultural institutions to make the appropriate decisions.

Location

Agricultural interventions need to address issues of location within the community, between disciplines and sectors and between organizational levels. If we acknowledge that each person has her/his own valid version of events, then methodological change will be needed to address issues of difference, such as gender, age and ethnicity, more systematically (Welbourn, 1991). Gender analysis has been partially incorporated into some methodologies, such as FSR/E and PRA, and differences in economic status guide most approaches, although not always thoroughly.

It is critical that *locally*-perceived axes of difference form the basis for research and extension activities, rather than differences considered relevant and imposed by outsiders. There is no reason to assume that 'our' notions of gender or wealth are shared by others. Axes of difference are not rigid, universal categories that hold for all aspects of people's lives, but are often cross-cutting, defined and context-specific. In certain activities women's age may be more important than their femaleness. In others it may be their wealth, ethnicity or religion, or a combination of all of these differences. These complexities present crucial methodological challenges.

Differences between the disciplines and approaches used in research and extension also need to be considered. Multi-disciplinary teams have been stressed especially in FSR and RRA. Rarely, however, are the methodological challenges of such teamwork fully addressed. Specialists often continue to impose their own fragmented concerns, rather than explore the challenges of *inter*disciplinarity (Rhoades *et al.*, 1987; Rhoades, 1990). Rural people have much to offer specialists in their own analyses of their complex and interdependent livelihoods (Chambers, 1992a). Methodologies are needed which focus more on both team-building and on linking disciplines and sectors, for which PRA can provide much inspiration.

Interventions take place within the multi-level linkages of institutions and organizations of agricultural development. Inevitably, the idea of working at multiple levels is fraught with practical as well as conceptual difficulties. Yet for agricultural research and extension methodologies, it is important, at the very least, to consider the politics and implications of how these different levels interact, and how this might influence the process of agricultural change. Locating interventions in the political arena is only considered systematically in PAR.

Whose knowledge counts? Control and conflict

Participatory approaches for empowerment which explicitly aim, at least in theory, to give control of the development process to rural people include PAR, DELTA, Theatre for Development and PRA. Protagonists of such approaches may stress that it is the knowledge and solutions of rural people which count, yet rarely consider what implications this has for their own roles, expectations and influence.

The different people who comprise the 'local community', and who are urged to control their own research and solutions, have relative positions of power. Each position offers differential access to the support of others and to resources. As different interest groups or individuals are consulted, so competing, contested and changing versions of 'community needs' emerge. Their different versions stem from different agendas and means for enacting some solutions or blocking others.

These considerations raise several key questions. Can all the, potentially conflicting, versions and solutions be considered? If not, then whose side will be taken and how will this be decided? Who will benefit or lose in the long-term from interventions which might initially be aimed at marginal groups? Such political questions are as relevant for crop breeding as for community development, as they will determine the final impact. Even if they are not explicitly addressed, implicit choices will always be made.

The main question is: who calls the shots? Insensitive intervention by development workers can undermine the strategies used by marginalized

114

people to resist domination, disarming them of their 'weapons' (Scott, 1985). Some women, for example, may not wish to have their interests represented where it involves exposing their strategies for dealing with present constraints. The temporary presence of resource-bearing agents may temporarily force concessions or gloss over deep-rooted conflicts, but might not generate structural change. By ignoring, rather than exploring, conflict, they may make matters worse and effectively silence marginal voices. In general, existing methodologies are weak at recognizing and dealing with situations of inherent or emergent conflict.

Not all conflict is negative, nor should it necessarily be stifled. Provoking creative conflict can have a positive impact. In situations where overt conflict is *lacking*, creative conflict may stimulate constructive change. Here external agents contribute more as catalysts than as listener and learner. Rather than a limitation, the power of external agents, or 'outsider effect', can have its advantages (Messerschmidt, 1991, 1992). One methodological area worth exploring is how to reveal and deal with creative conflict. The methodological challenge lies in enabling both external agents and local people to cope with creative conflict and conflict resolution. Such skills or increased awareness can be used by local people to conduct their own struggles following their own priorities.

FSR/E and FPR neither recognize nor deal with conflict or political choices. PRA has been used for conflict resolution (Conway *et al.*, 1989), but it does not approach this systematically. DELTA tends to obscure conflict by dealing with 'the community'. Both PAR and Theatre for Development are based on the assumption that conflict exists and must be addressed, from which agricultural research and extension can learn much.

Interaction

Agricultural research and extension is based on interactions between external agents and farmers. While all the approaches discussed here highlight the importance of good rapport, the effect that external agents can have on the processes of knowledge production is only partially recognized and rarely are communication skills stressed sufficiently.

PRA highlights the importance of being aware of – and suspending – biases, although in practice this generally falls short of the ideal. PRA, along with DELTA and Theatre for Development, appears to offer a strategy where the initiator of a discussion or exercise plays no further part in determining what is represented. In practice, this often leads to the mistaken belief that they do not influence the production of information. Each external agent carries with her/him an identity which affects how the interaction develops.

Important lessons can be learned from PAR which situates research in a process of mutual learning between people with different experiences, knowledges and skills. The conventional subject/object relations between researcher and researched, and the power relations this implies, are rejected and a common goal is sought. Such collegiate relations, in which external agents have an explicitly proactive role, are only possible where

115

such common goals can be identified. This poses considerable methodological and institutional challenges, as the value systems embodied in agricultural institutions are generally not those of rural people.

Opening up research and extension institutions and enabling rural people to understand the workings of western science in practice is as important as urging external agents to appreciate local knowledge. Rather than teaching the farmers 'basic science', it may be more constructive to allow them to ask their own questions about western scientific experimentation and extension. This may reveal to scientists the many, often conflicting, dimensions of their own knowledge.

The most important question for conventional agricultural scientists and extension workers is how they can deal with their changing roles. When farmers analyse and experiment, external agents will serve as advisers, catalysts and convenors. When farmers choose specific changes, external agents will help to search for and supply them with it (Chambers, 1993). This is no mean feat and will require extraordinary efforts of the individuals and institutions involved.

Towards experiential learning

If agricultural researchers and extension workers are to deal with dialogue, through which ideas are shared and learning occurs, then they will require fundamentally different training. New approaches to continuous learning need to be developed within and outside agricultural institutions. This type of learning differs radically from the formal training setting 'where the trainee becomes the object of training and a depository of knowledge delivered by a trainer' (Tilakaratna, in Fals-Borda and Rahman, 1991: 138). Shifting from a teaching to a learning style has many implications, such as increasing the focus on *how* we learn, rather than what we learn, and focusing on personal exploration and experience.

Bawden (1988) distinguishes three facets of the learning process, arguing that only two of these – *scientia* (learning that) and *techne* (learning how) – form part of standard curricula for agricultural students. The third, which he calls *praxis*, concerns the experiential aspect which is often ignored. Bawden urges a recognition of the central importance of personal development in learning. This involves addressing the experiences through which students develop their understanding, and acknowledging the limited role that technical training plays in becoming an effective agricultural worker.

Future challenges

The challenges laid out here will require serious attention and a concerted effort if they are to increase the effectiveness of agricultural research and extension. Addressing the issues of time and of location requires a fundamentally different approach to the scope and dimensions of research and extension. While some argue that this process would become too expensive, the past has shown that avoiding these issues will not lead to

116

sustained and positive changes. Acknowledging the political dimensions of agriculture through the issues of interaction, control and conflict reveals the wider implications of the choice of methodology and of the role that different actors play in the process. Incorporating experiential learning in developing new methodologies that embrace these challenges is a highly personal and political process.

For such changes to spread and be sustained will require the mutual reinforcement of participatory methods and new approaches to learning and institutional support (Pretty and Chambers, Part III). Many methodological limitations to date stem from paying insufficient attention to the institutional contexts in which they take place. This is where many of the new challenges lie (Part III). Learning to acknowledge the value and specificity of our own experience, while seeking ways to appreciate other perspectives inevitably entails making 'mistakes'. Institutions will need to support self-critical awareness to benefit fully from these valuable opportunities for reflection and change.

Participatory watershed management in India: the experience of the Aga Khan Rural Support Programme

PARMESH SHAH

Alternatives to conventional soil and water conservation

Conventional soil and water conservation (SWC) programmes have been remarkable failures. Huge amounts of resources have been spent in the name of conservation and environmental protection, encouraging, often coercing farmers to adopt SWC. Few farmers benefit, structures are rarely maintained and inadequate implementation by outside technical teams often causes more erosion than it prevents (Pretty and Shah, 1992). Consequently, many rural communities have become disillusioned with conventional SWC programmes and have resisted efforts to implement them.

New evidence suggests that there are a growing number of mostly small-scale projects that are sufficiently successful to warrant their application on a much wider scale. These include both government and non-government initiatives in India. These have adopted flexible and long-term approaches that build upon local knowledge and skills, reinforce local village organizations, involve villagers in technology generation and employ village facilitators for appraisal, planning, implementation and monitoring. The external institutions act as support organizations playing a catalytic role of facilitation and networking. The result of working closely with farmers at all stages has significantly increased crop and livestock productivity; the measures and practices have persisted beyond the life of the projects; attitudes of both the professionals and the local people have changed; and the communities have received wider economic benefits.

The Aga Khan Rural Support Programme

The work of the Aga Khan Rural Support Programme (AKRSP) offers a useful example of one such participatory SWC programme. AKRSP is a non-government organization established in 1985 to promote and catalyse community participation in natural resources management through village institutions for increased income generation and productivity for rural communities (see also Shah, Part III).

AKRSP's experience demonstrates that a participatory approach to watershed management that involves the external support organization as a facilitator, draws on local knowledge and capacities and opens social and political space in which local groups can debate issues, challenge authority and set priorities, can be extremely effective. At the start of the process, AKRSP spends a considerable amount of time enabling local communities to participate in appraisal and planning, technology generation, adaptation and diffusion. It then acts as a catalyst to revitalize existing institutions and form new ones capable of assuming the responsibilities for productively upgrading their watersheds.

AKRSP has supported participatory watershed management in Gujarat through the:

- Application of Participatory Rural Appraisal and Planning (PRAP) for development of natural resources in the village;
- Formation of village institutions for implementation of a Village Natural Resources Management Plan (VNRMP) prepared by the villagers;
- Implementation of the activities identified in the VNRMP through local institutions;
- Establishment of regular technical and financial training and management support to village institutions for implementing the VNRMP by their own team of village extension volunteers, village institution office bearers, AKRSP professional support team and external support agencies. The emphasis is on first identifying the local source of expertize and facilitating its access, then seeking external support when required;
- Development of local-level federated support institutions for managing the development process;
- Execution of participatory impact monitoring and evaluation by the villagers and the local institutions;
- Incorporation of the VNRMPs into the development plans of the government. Local people raise resources for funding their plans from government, banks and other development agencies; and village institutions perform most support functions without external support;
- Promotion of participatory approaches among government agencies and NGOs involved in the development process and advocation of policies supporting the development of such approaches.

Participatory appraisal of natural resources in the village

Participatory appraisal of natural resources involves preparing an inventory of all natural resources in the village, and studying indigenous and adapted practices, local institutions and existing management systems of the village. It is important that the village and not the watershed is used as a unit for interaction and appraisal with the community. Since people are more familiar with conditions directly in and around their village, this focus enables them to analyse their resources and assess their development potential. This process involves using a sequence of participatory methods in a joint appraisal exercise involving the external team and local people. This collaborative analysis ensures that the analytical capacity, knowledge and innovations of the watershed inhabitants are used as a basis for planning the watershed programme (Shah, 1993).

The appraisal process involves nine basic steps used sequentially and concurrently. This leads to the preparation of community resource management proposals and presentations to external agencies.

(1) *Base maps*. Base maps are prepared on the ground or paper using various locally available materials (seeds, twigs, leaves, flowers, lime, thorns etc.). They show the location of major natural resources, landmarks, boundaries and divisions, drainage points, settlements and so on (see Figure 1). They can also highlight changing land-use patterns, local land use and soil classifications, the status of community assets or infrastructure (such as the condition of ponds, drinking-water wells and irrigation tanks), and tenure and resource management issues.

(2) *Transect walks*. Transect walks mainly focus on observation of physical characteristics and conditions, such as the level of soil erosion, waterlogging, soil depth and moisture retention. Normally, transects are done while walking along a pre-determined route (identified on the base map) with local people, to appraise different resources like private and public lands, forests, grazing areas, rivulets, *nullas*, gullies and so on. They involve semi-structured interviews with the local inhabitants about their perceptions of key resource issues.

(3) *Thematic maps*. Thematic maps are prepared by individual or small groups of village experts who have specialized knowledge of water resources, local land-use classifications, cropping-patterns, aquifers and so on. These maps lead to questions about problems and constraints faced in effective utilization of resources and help focus attention on possible solutions. People are encouraged to suggest solutions which they have tried out earlier, both those that worked and those that did not. People are also asked the reasons for their not trying out some solutions that they have identified.

(4) *Opportunity identification matrices*. Opportunity identification matrices are diagrams produced during the transect showing local land-use classifications, the existing state of resources, constraints to effective management of those resources, solutions tried and options identified by local

119

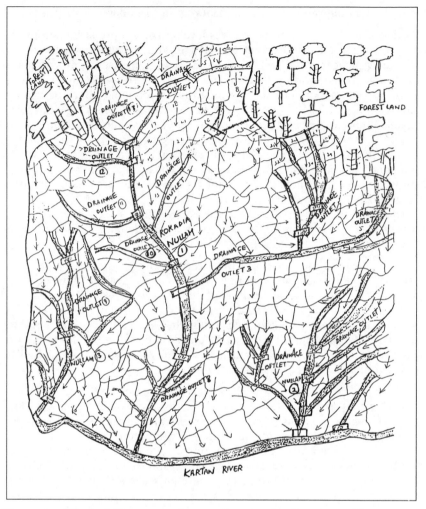

Figure 1:   *Watershed status and treatment map for Pangham village,*
Bharuch District, prepared by Extension Volunteers and
aggregated from outlet maps.

people for solving the problems and development of each resource). The matrix is used as a facilitating input to other methods used subsequently.

(5) *Equity appraisal and well-being ranking.* The next phase of the approach looks at equity aspects in the village. To ensure that wider consultation is carried out and that poorer and less articulate sections of the village community are involved, a simple well-being ranking exercise is conducted to identify the various social groups in the village community. The most important aspect of this exercise is learning the criteria used by the local people to stratify or differentiate themselves. This helps in identifying

120

those groups who have not been represented in the mapping or transect exercises. It also helps in identifying focus groups for further discussions.

(6) *Focus group discussions.* Based on the outputs and the process started through the mapping, transects and ranking, semi-structured interviews are conducted with different groups separately. These groups could include:

- Resource owners;
- Resource users;
- Resource non-owners and users;
- Resource non-owners and non-users;
- Groups facing a common problem related with a resource;
- Women;
- Socially disadvantaged communities;
- Groups left out of the initial appraisal process.

A focus group discussion builds upon the information collected on maps and during transects, and each problem identified is discussed in depth. New problems and possible solutions are analysed. People also indicate the likely conflicts that might arise in implementing proposed solutions, point out inconsistencies, discuss their past experiences, identify areas of agreement and begin to set priorities.

Seasonality and livelihood analysis involving variables like rainfall, fuelwood and fodder availability and employment are carried out to identify major constraints to adoption of certain priorities. Even in a small group, considerable discussion goes on before any consensus is arrived at. AKRSP's experience also shows that a larger community meeting is more participatory and effective when preceded by smaller group discussions.

(7) *Organization of village meeting and presentation by focus groups.* Since focus group discussions indicate priorities of particular social groups or networks within a village who share a common problem or agenda and sometimes an agreed set of solutions, it is important that these sometimes overlapping, sometimes conflicting visions are expressed publicly. Hence, the next step is to organize a village meeting where most people can attend. Each group nominates a representative who presents their problems and priorities. Outputs produced earlier are used to explain various solutions identified by each group.

During this village presentation, the inter-group dynamics become more clear. If there is a strong resistance by a group towards a priority identified by another, then there is a need to explore further the relationship between the groups and the resource at issue in order to understand the underlying reasons behind the competing visions. This could be done in the meeting itself or subsequently, in smaller groups over a number of interactions. AKRSP's experience has been that most villages will have an intensive meeting on their resource management concerns and come to an agreement on most conflicting issues. This is aided by the realization that they can put their plans into action in the way in which they themselves have proposed. However, in highly-stratified communities more interaction is required before arriving at a consensus.

121

(8) *Prioritization of options and appraisal.* At this stage, discussions are initiated with the community in order to identify priority options under the resource management plan. This leads to conducting shorter, but intensive topical appraisal exercises which include transect walks with the focus groups. These concentrate on the local solutions identified by the people. The aspects considered during the appraisal exercise include: the technical feasibility of the solution, financial viability, the extent of benefits and the impact on the poor, resource investment and contribution by the community, the institutional framework and training inputs required.

This process takes place at varying speed in different villages. In some villages, the participatory appraisal and planning process takes less than a month. In others, it can take up to half a year by which time the community has gone through a number of intensive discussions.

(9) *Preparation of proposals and presentations to the external agencies.* Depending on the activities identified by the community, a simple proposal is generated by the community. This proposal is then shared with the external agencies which want to fund the implementation of the plan (e.g. AKRSP, government, banks). This village natural resource management plan also becomes a future reference for monitoring and evaluation.

Investment in watershed management: programme impacts

After the initial phase of appraisal, planning and training, the extension volunteers' (EV) capacity to handle the programme improved considerably, and AKRSP is now in a position to triple the expenditure and investment in the watersheds. It should be noted that this increase in investment has been accompanied by corresponding increases in local contributions. The concept of building a local stake has been retained with higher investments in the programme and lower unit costs. The costs of watershed treatment in the programme work out to roughly Rs 1340 per hectare, compared with the Rs 3000–7000 per hectare incurred by various government-administered watershed management programmes. This is significant, since all major government programmes in the area give a 100 per cent subsidy for similar programmes. This reinforces the argument that local communities invest more of their internal resources in a programme if they are supported by a facilitating institution once their local capacities are strengthened.

The performance of the programme has been analysed for economic performance indicators. Table 1 demonstrates the impact on income in the watersheds in which AKRSP is working. It shows a significant increase in the profitability of the investments made. The impact of long-term flows from common property resources has not been taken into account in these computations. These data are in essence no different from those of any other watershed management project. They have been presented to show that enabling institutions supporting participatory watershed management can also effect significant increases in productivity and income generation over a relatively short time-frame.

The data show the high profitability and low start-up costs for the technologies developed, managed and administered by the local institutions.

Table 1: Performance indicators of the AKRSP-supported watershed development programme in Gujarat, India

Performance indicators	1988–9	1989–90	1990–91
Number of villages covered (cumulative)	3	29	36
Area developed each year (ha)	240	852	2,146
Investment made (Rs)	78,515	663,603	2,862,560
Contribution by community (Rs)	36,732	321,395	1,445,046
Overheads as a percentage of the total programme cost	29	14	5
Cost of preparing treatment plan per acre (in Rs)	325	113	25
Cost for arranging community ploughing per acre (in Rs)	125	75	13
Area of watershed covered per professional (ha)	40	150	220
Net income increase affected by each professional (in Rs)	44,000	165,000	242,000
Number of extension volunteers trained	38	83	77

These initiatives have proved to be viable and the communities have been increasing their contribution every year. The communities are also involved in monitoring and evaluating the impact of the programmes.

Additional benefits due to the strengthening and support of the village institutions multiply the productivity and sustainability of the watershed activities. Village institutions have achieved significant results in mobilizing local savings, initiating short- and long-term group credit and marketing farm produce. This process not only improves the sustainability of watershed management as an activity, but also helps to improve the viability of the village institutions, as they are able to build a capital base. This capital enables the village institutions and their members to take risks that they might not otherwise have taken.

The investments made by farmers on their private lands have increased by more than 50 per cent since the initiation of the watershed management programme. The village community has also taken up a number of community operations such as ploughing, plant protection and use of implements and post-harvest equipment, coupled with credit and pooled marketing of the agricultural produce. This shows that the village institution is becoming a conduit for higher economic investment and diversification. This is also reflected in the confidence of financial organizations to advance credit to those institutions with a large membership of small farmers with rainfed holdings. These were earlier considered high-risk groups by the bankers.

In the past, the watersheds in which AKRSP operates had a high level of out-migration before the village institutions initiated participatory watershed-management activities. A dramatic drop in the migration rate has led to sustained livelihoods for many in the community. This has resulted in higher school enrolment and improved nutrition and health standards. Finally, the development of local institutions with a cadre of professionals and village volunteers and their federations will ensure that the development process continues.

AKRSP's experience in Gujarat shows that if an external support institution takes the role of a facilitator and spends enough time on the participatory process, the programmes are cost-effective, more efficient in their use of the resources, can be scaled up by the local institutions without high overheads and lead to village institutions taking up activities with multiplier effects like credit and savings.

Challenges in the collection and use of information on livelihood strategies and natural resource management

KAREN SCHOONMAKER FREUDENBERGER

The failure to understand local livelihoods

Our failure to understand and adequately appreciate local knowledge systems has contributed to the failure of many development projects and policies. 'Indigenous' knowledge comprises not just a catalogue of technical skills in agriculture, forestry, health and so on, but also the strategies that permit people to maintain their livelihoods in the face of adverse conditions and to cope in times of extreme stress (Fairhead and Leach, Part I). These include economic strategies at the household level, political strategies that determine the allocation of resources at the community level and various social strategies such as those that redistribute wealth in the community or provide a 'safety net' for those in urgent need. By failing to understand these strategies, we have in many cases undermined them, increasing the vulnerability of local populations.

To the extent that ignorance is at least partly responsible for 'development' actions that end up jeopardizing local populations, the ability to collect information is part of the solution. It is also essential, however, that this information be used and that programmes and perspectives be altered in response to what we learn. This offers a particular challenge since in many cases the methods to generate information on local knowledge systems have evolved faster than our collective willingness to change our perspectives in response to that information. In this paper, I will reflect on problems that arise both in collecting information with participatory research methodologies and in using that information to devise programmes that reinforce the capacity of local populations to improve their own well-being.

Collecting information on local resource management strategies

Participatory research methodologies have proved to be powerful approaches for focusing on local realities and understanding the complexities of such issues as resource management, livelihood strategies and household and community coping mechanisms. Certain characteristics of RRA, PRA, and related approaches enhance their effectiveness in generating this kind of information (Chambers, 1992a and b; Cornwall *et al.*; Shah, Part II). Among the strengths of these approaches (which I will refer to collectively as 'PRA') are the combination of research structure and flexibility, the diversity of methods used to collect information and the direct interaction with local populations.

Any good research needs a systematic approach to collecting information. In studying local knowledge systems, it is also important, however, that researchers are permitted to exercise their curiosity and to pursue surprising leads. Because local knowledge systems, almost by definition, arise from unfamiliar experiences and situations, we can only understand them by opening ourselves to very different ways of thinking. The more research is bound by closed-ended questions and closed-ended expectations, the less likely it will produce insights about the multiple constructions of local knowledge and the more likely it will generate data to fit into our old, familiar patterns of thinking. Participatory research demands that investigators be exploratory and open-minded if we are to understand these multiple knowledges and perspectives.

The diversity of methods used to gather information in the PRA approach is also a considerable asset in trying to understand local knowledge and capacities. By 'handing over the stick' and the beans or by walking with the farmer-experts through their territory and making ourselves the learners in the process, we give local people the chance not only to show us their activities, but also to explain the rationale behind what they do. Methods such as historical matrices let local people analyse changes in their lives over time and offer their reflections on why they reacted as they did to various phenomena. This helps to get away from the more standard patterns where outsiders discern certain changes and ascribe their own explanations using, of course, their own systems of understanding. The researcher or extension worker can launch an exercise – such as a matrix, calendar, or map – and then stand back to let it unfold according to the logic of the local analysts. The less the outsider intervenes, be it to pose a series of predetermined questions or to guide the preparation of a diagram, the more likely the information collected at the end will reflect elements of local perceptions and priorities rather than ours (Figures 1 and 2).

Another critical element of PRA is the direct interaction between the outsiders (who, ideally, are the researchers, extensionists or development workers who will have some responsibility for using the information) and local people. Only the most obtuse sceptics of indigenous knowledge systems can spend time in a village, seriously discussing issues with rural

PERIOD	Until the end of swamp rice >25 years ago	Until the Chinese rice project 15-25 years ago	Period of Chinese rice project 12-15 years ago	3-12 years ago	PRESENT
MILLET	12	19	7	22	30
GROUNDNUT	8	19	5	24	40
RICE	15	6	19	5	10
MAIZE	8	17	8	20	32
FINDOO GRAINS	4	4	4	4	5
GARDENING	14	18	5	20	40
TREE PRODUCTS	20	20	20	20	20
CATTLE	18	20	20	20	20
SHEEP AND GOATS	17	20	20	20	20
MONEY FROM RELATIVES	5	5	10	25	30
FISHING	8	8	10	8	10
PUMPKIN	7	7	10	10	20

Figure 1: *Historical livelihood matrix. This livelihood matrix was prepared by a large group of village men and women in Gillangel, the Gambia. It shows how people have adopted their portfolio of activities over time. Rich discussions took place as the matrix was completed which illuminated the factors affecting people's decisions.*

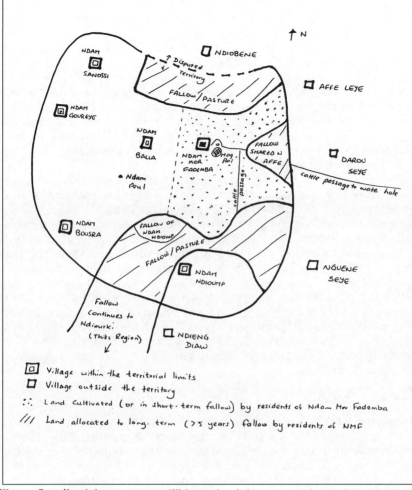

Figure 2:   *Participatory map. This territorial map was drawn by a group of men in Ndam Mor Fademba, Senegal. It shows how six villages identify with a single territory. Discussions highlighted the local people's strategies for managing how land is allocated between communal grazing areas and individually-cultivated fields (Source: Freudenberger and Schoonmaker Freudenberger, 1993)*

populations, and not have their appreciation for farmers' knowledge and strategies radically enhanced. This is a critical step in convincing policy-makers that local knowledge has real value, thereby increasing the chance that information gathered in the field will be taken seriously and have an impact. PRAs create the context for structured, systematic and probing interactions with local people.

127

Collecting information on local knowledge

The strengths of participatory approaches may lead us to a certain dangerous complacency if we begin to think that good information comes automatically or easily. This is anything but the case: tuning into strategies used by local communities challenges researchers to the utmost. It requires a certain humility to abandon our preconceptions and, at the same time, considerable perceptiveness to capture the invisible structure that weaves activities into *strategies*. Because it is considerably easier, PRA studies have had a tendency to stop at describing the activities and physical surroundings of a community without probing more deeply. Moreover, in many places studies have not gone beyond a snapshot view to explore how strategies have evolved over time.

It is one thing to know that people cultivate mostly groundnuts, with some pumpkins and watermelons. It is an altogether different level of understanding to discern why they do so and how their cultivation patterns have changed over time (e.g. to learn that they are consciously diminishing the emphasis they place on groundnuts and seeking to diversify into crops that, while perhaps less profitable, provide income throughout the year, require less initial investment, etc.). Furthermore, the policy recommendations that come out of the two kinds of information are likely to be very different. The first may suggest projects to improve the productivity of groundnuts (which appear to be a local priority), while the second may suggest ways to facilitate farmers' diversification into other activities or to manage groundnut revenues throughout the year. Recognizing the need to probe more deeply, rather than merely surveying local practices, is perhaps the greatest challenge.

Beyond the biases

There are several more pitfalls to avoid. The PRA approach warns researchers to be aware of biases that may distort the results of the study. In addition to the usual biases (e.g. gender, spatial and seasonal biases) which the research team must consider with great care (Chambers, 1983, 1993), there are several other biases which are potentially a problem.

The definition of the community to study at the outset is often an unconscious reflection of our own knowledge and experience. In participatory research, the unit of study is frequently the village. This may not be the relevant management unit for local resource planning purposes, however. In some cases decisions are made at the 'territorial' level, where a group of villages have some shared interest in a physical space and the resources it contains (e.g. a catchment area). In other cases, there are dominant and satellite villages which have a major effect on where and how decisions are made. Focusing on a single village may generate incomplete and biased information in such situations.

Similarly, certain user groups may not be permanent residents of the community studied, particularly in the case of local resource management systems where there are complex and overlapping rights of access depending on product, season and so on. Because PRA teams typically spend relatively short periods in the area and talk to those who are present, there is a danger of overlooking the interests of absent users. This tends to introduce a systematic bias against, for example, transhumant pastoralists. While there is nothing in PRA that precludes studying a territory rather than a village or searching out seasonal users of resources, this rarely happens.

Since natural resource management almost always involves a combination of state rules and local rules/practices, it is essential to understand how each of these work in the community and the interaction between them. Biases on the part of researchers frequently make it difficult for them to understand the full range of rules and administrative arrangements that affect resource management in a given community. Government officials often find it difficult to accept that there are systems at work other than those promulgated and condoned by the state. The opposite bias is equally dangerous. Some researchers may glorify the effectiveness of indigenous practices and see them as entirely self-sufficient when, in all likelihood, they interact considerably with state provisions, whether the result is defiance or conformity.

While the biases noted above relate to where, how, and from whom the researcher seeks information, another potential bias relates to how the community presents information. Who participates and who decides who will participate in the PRA exercise? Natural resource management, tenure and the distribution of rights of access are inherently political issues and, therefore, so is the process of studying them. Depending on how contentious an issue the management of resources is in a community, there may be active attempts to manipulate the flow of information by various interests. A powerful person may attach him/herself to the team and intimidate others from giving information inimical to his/her interests, or the team may be guided to people who have a single point of view in a conflict. Once again, this is not a problem unique to PRA but, precisely because the approach is billed as participatory, investigators may not be as vigilant as they otherwise would in questioning the meaning of that participation.

Bias in collecting information is something to which any good PRA team is very sensitive. The methodology puts a high premium on collecting accurate information. It provides guidance on how to do this by triangulating the researchers' perspectives, the methods used to gather information and diverse views of informants. The kinds of biases outlined here can never be entirely avoided. But good researchers will have their antennae out for just this type of problem and will act quickly to neutralize the offending bias, whether by seeking out minority opinions or enlarging the scope of the study to include other sites or perspectives in the territory. What happens, however, once we succeed in gathering quality information on local knowledge systems? This brings us to the critical issue of how – and even whether – this information is used.

Using information on local resource management strategies

The question of using information is one on which neither PRA, nor any other methodology, provides much guidance and yet it is where some of the thorniest issues arise where local knowledge systems are concerned. To make matters worse, it is often the very best studies that cause the greatest difficulties when it comes time to use the information. These are the studies that uncover complexities and subtleties – the pastel shadings that are extremely difficult to fit into the broad brushstrokes of government planning perspectives and project activities. A good study will illuminate divergent perspectives, whether within communities, between communities, or with outside development agencies, but is unlikely to provide answers for how the contradictions can be resolved. This may cause a build up of frustrations and even produce a certain nostalgia for the simpler days when 'we were not aware of [and didn't have to deal with] all these complexities'.

This gap between the collection of information and its use seems so obvious that it would hardly be worth discussing except that the expectations for PRA seem to go far beyond information collection. We seem almost to take for granted that once the information is obtained, it will be used in a productive manner, consistent with values of participation and local empowerment. My own experience belies this expectation. It suggests instead that vast amounts of fascinating information collected using participatory techniques, while *potentially* of immense value in planning and programming, continue to go largely unused. The organizations doing the studies have in some cases made minor, marginal changes in symbolic salute to participation, but more fundamental reorientations have yet to occur.

More often than not, there is never an explicit decision *not* to use information. Instead, time passes, attention moves to other things, the PRA report may be held up as a commendable model of the agency's participatory activities, but nothing changes. In any given case, if someone bothers to ask, there is likely to be a superficially adequate explanation for why a report or its recommendations were never acted upon. One has to look harder to see the *pattern* of information neglect percolating through the excuses and forgotten documents. It is this pattern that should concern those of us who have up until now put our energies into gathering information, attempting to fill the gap between local realities and our knowledge of those realities. Collection of good information is vitally important; the fact that we have arrived at a stage where good information exists, but is not being used, is a credit to the progress that has been made in developing and using participatory research methodologies. However, evidence of systematic information neglect suggests that we now must begin to direct more of our energies toward the next challenge: understanding why this information is not being used to respond to local needs and closing the gap between improved knowledge and the effective use of that knowledge.

Using information from the field

There are several common problems that arise when teams come back from the field, proud and excited by the richness of information they have collected on local practices and knowledge systems, and confront the realities of integrating this knowledge into donor or government programmes. Four areas where contradictions frequently arise are: differences in values, time frames, activity focus and local practice versus state policy (though in practice they rarely fit into such neat classifications).

Differences in values

Some of the most intransigent issues arise when disharmony between the objectives of the outsiders and the values underlying local practices are uncovered in the course of the research. Whereas *practices* may be relatively easy to adapt on both sides, the fundamental values or objectives behind them may be considerably less malleable.

- Many donors have put a heavy premium on 'sustainable' management systems in recent years. Policies to promote sustainability often imply excluding users from common property areas, such as community forests or pastures, for a certain amount of time. This kind of restriction may clash with local imperatives, such as maintaining systems of reciprocity with neighbouring communities or guaranteeing access to communal reserves to those who are in need. While sustainability may be an important value for local people as well, the term may be defined very differently by the two parties. Sustainability for the village, for example, may imply the ensemble of strategies needed to maintain livelihoods, while the outsider may be focusing simply on the productivity of the biomass;
- Another quite common example of clashing values comes when the outsiders put a premium on serving the poorest of the poor and favour interventions on behalf of the most disadvantaged members of the community. Research may reveal local systems of management that are highly effective, but far from equitable. Similar conflicts arise when outsiders seek to promote the position of women in ways that are inconsistent with dominant local value systems.

Differences in time-frame

While this is commonly portrayed as a problem where projects have to deal with villagers' short planning perspectives, in my experience the opposite is as common.

- The situation sometimes arises where villagers have a need to maintain current economic benefits – even if they are modest – and are unable or unwilling to forego those benefits, even if larger returns would become available in the future;
- In other cases, villagers may have very long-term planning horizons that enable them to react to unforeseeable situations well into the future. Flexible systems of resource management which permit land-use patterns to adapt to changing economic and environmental conditions are an example of this. For their part, donors and governments often seek visible results in a finite period of time defined by project evaluation periods, elections, etc.

Differences in activity focus

The more research is participatory, the more villagers' priority concerns will be illuminated. This can be extremely frustrating when the funding agency or government department has another agenda. The researcher is often caught in the middle.

- At times these divergences can be vast if, for example, the community is facing a severe health problem or severe drought and the team is supposed to be studying post-harvest technology or community woodlots;
- Often, however, the divergence is rather more subtle and may require considerable understanding of local livelihood strategies. In one recent example an agency with an interest in regenerative agriculture wanted to work with local populations to improve the productivity of the land. The PRA study revealed that, while the community was indeed concerned about issues of decreasing soil fertility and were well aware of the decreasing productivity of agriculture, their response was to diversify their livelihood strategies and to move into a whole range of activities including emigration, animal raising, commerce, etc. Since seasonal emigration made investing in improvements on the land during the dry season impossible, the villagers' diversification strategy conflicted with donor plans to increase the productivity of a single element of the livelihood portfolio.

Differences in local practice and state policy

A particularly troublesome dilemma arises when the field study discovers local practices, some of which may be extremely innovative or effective, that do not conform to state policies or rules. Often these practices exist with impunity only as long as they are 'invisible' to the authorities and thus do not pose any significant threat to more formal legal and administrative structures. This may include such local practices as pruning trees (illegal under some forest codes) to provide forage and stimulate regeneration, or local land use patterns which contravene national land laws. The simple act of describing the practice in the PRA report may alert the authorities and endanger its continuation. Projects that go further and attempt to build on successful local practices based on years of experience may find themselves in the difficult position of flouting state regulations with whatever consequences that may entail.

In principle, it should be possible to use the information gathered in each of these cases productively. While highlighting differences may involve some rather perplexing dilemmas, it is better to confront the issues frankly and search for solutions than to proceed as if the differences did not exist. It should be possible to discuss the various positions, assess their relative merits and eventually design more nuanced programmes that reflect the complexities uncovered by a PRA exercise. Even in the best of cases this is not an easy process. However, information neglect occurs because it is much easier to ignore differences than to address the institutional issues needed to confront and reconcile them.

Those of us concerned that local knowledge be not only documented, but also reinvested in programmes to reinforce and enhance livelihood strategies must devote more of our attention to ensuring that this second step actually happens. It means putting more emphasis on ways of using information from participatory research in planning and policy formulation. It means more systematically including decision makers who have the influence needed to make administrative and policy level changes in field studies. And it means continuing to insist that information be collected and analysed in a way that makes it immediately accessible to local people themselves. Constant vigilance and critical self-assessment will be needed to ensure that studies of local knowledge do not end up adding yet another burden on rural populations, but instead make a real contribution to their well-being.

Developing interaction and understanding: RRA and farmer research groups in Zambia

MICHAEL DRINKWATER

Farmer research groups

The Adaptive Research and Planning Teams (ARPT) of Central and Copperbelt Provinces in Zambia have begun experimenting methodologically with two new types of practice. The first is on-farm trial work with farmer research groups, and the second is the carrying out of rapid rural appraisal (RRA) exercises with farmers to explore issues of food security. In each case, our aim is to establish informal, collaborative relationships.

Farmer research groups have committees elected by the members (the only proviso being that there must be a women's representative) and a membership which consists of those people which register with the committee for a particular season's activities. Interaction with researchers revolves around planning meetings (which often use a participatory exercise such as a food or labour calendar as a basis), field visits during the growing season, and final evaluation meetings (again during which a range of participatory techniques may be used). Groups are now being encouraged to undertake off-shoot activities, such as the multiplication of crop varieties which farmers have preferred in trials, but which are not widely available.

There have been multiple benefits from working with the farmer research groups. The first is that one builds up a relationship with a community of farmers – the type of 'relaxed rapport' Chambers states as being vital for uninhibited communication (1992: 14-15) – and which occurred minimally when we worked with individual farmers. The membership of the research groups is not fixed. People flow in and out of them, although a core of members will always provide continuity from one season to the next. The groups, however, have a collective memory which individuals, unaggregated, do not have. Groups can be demanding. They may want to know how information from a previous participatory exercise – a social

133

map or food availability calendar – is being used. Thus collective activities help quicken the adaptive research process. At the end of season evaluation meeting, consensual agreement – or disagreement – from farmers is sought. Crop varieties can be clearly accepted or rejected, and simple technical issues such as planting methods, plant spacings and fertilization practices, adjudicated upon. But the real challenge is whether we will be able to move with the research groups into the more complex issues of improving food security, improving returns to labour without necessarily having to capitalize farming systems and to develop more low-input and sustainable forms of agriculture.

Another attribute fostered by the groups is individual learning. Through their own adaptive experimentation, farmers can learn from just working in their own fields. But there are obviously greater opportunities in learning from others. Within local communities, however, it is rare to find a tradition of visiting the fields of others. At root is the fear of being accused of *ukungula*, the theft of part of a crop's yield by witchcraft. Usually the visiting of fields of others is limited to that of close relatives. Sometimes if people wish to learn a new technique they will consequently either hire in labour or hire themselves out to the farmer concerned for piecework purposes (Rap, 1992; see also Winarto, Millar, Part II, for other examples). The research group legitimizes the concept of visiting the trials of others, at least in a normative sense.

Additional interaction with farmers in research group areas was carried out as part of the second type of methodological experiment. This was the conduct of a series of R/PRA field research exercises in interdisciplinary and interinstitutional teams. The aim of these exercises has been threefold. First, the development of a dynamic understanding of farming systems, including the human relationships involved, through the use of a series of strongly 'processual' concepts. This then allows, second, key issues, conflicts and constraints to be identified and elaborated, and then, third, possible future programme activities. The RRAs have consisted of three iterations: analysis, validation and elaboration and (problem and) programme identification and ranking.

These RRAs, together with the other ongoing work with the research groups, is forming part of a general reorientation within ARPT as a whole. Other provincial teams are also changing what they are doing and how they are doing it. The exploratory RRAs conducted so far have been anchored by three principal concepts. These proved of tremendous value and are worth detailing. They are:

- A 'livelihood and food security model' which has been used to map the production system as a process;
- The idea of a 'cluster' and hence of 'cluster types', as a means of understanding human and material resource relationships;
- The dual notions of system and cooperative conflicts, the former being used to denote a key dilemma faced in maintaining the production system of the cluster as a whole, and the latter a dilemma faced in interpersonal relationships within the cluster.

134

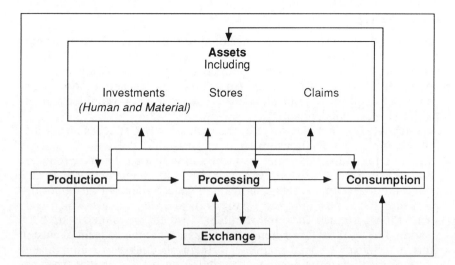

Figure 1: *A model for the analysis of livelihoods (adapted from Swift, 1989)*

Livelihood and food security model

In the field exercises undertaken so far we have found the model (Figure 1) to have three major attributes. First, it is a model which can be used to look at the entire agricultural production and livelihood system. It provides a good checklist or guide for semi-structured interviewing and a basis for analysing the information that is collected. The model helps guide an interview, but also allows one to pursue and explore different themes.

Second, through a focus on the links between components (the arrows), it is a good model to use for an analytical emphasis on resource flows over time, rather than just a single season production map. The idea of trying to understand the principles which lie behind resource-use decisions has helped here. An example is whether a particular category of farmers see credit as something essential to their production system, and therefore to be secured at all cost, or whether it is used opportunistically, a bonus if you obtain it, but not a particular problem if one fails to repay.

Third, the model has also proved a valuable basis for integrating an analysis of household food security with an analysis of farmer production systems. We have been developing an entitlements based approach (Sen, 1983 and Dreze and Sen, 1989), in order to incorporate a food security perspective into the work of provincial teams, within an overall livelihoods framework. The model can be used to focus on how an endowment bundle (assets) is transformed through production, processing and exchange into entitlements, and hence to a commodity bundle. This also enables the interaction between on-farm and off-farm production activities to be appreciated, and hence enables a conceptualization of how household food security can be considered within a sustainable livelihoods framework.

Cluster concept

It has long been an issue as to what should be the social and economic unit of analysis at the local level. The unit most commonly used is that of the household, but, as is frequently pointed out, this is far from being an undifferentiated entity. Not only gender, but age, kinship, economic circumstances and social political status all affect the opportunities and activities of specific individuals.

Gatter (1989) discusses some of the problems ARPT faces in not differentiating social relationships. He suggests that the unit of analysis should be the individual male producer and individual female producer. But this is unsatisfactory too. As Leach (1991: 50) points out, women and men cannot be seen merely as 'individuals' since, 'they work from locally particular social positions and relations of interdependence which construct their activities and opportunities'. Instead, we should start by a focus on the resource flows themselves. This is what the concept of cluster aims to achieve: a social mapping through an analysis of human and material resource relationships. The definition of cluster that we have been using is:

> A group of producers between which there are multiple resource exchanges usually based on the factors of kinship, labour and food exchange and/or common access to draught power (Drinkwater, 1992b).

Using the cluster as a unit of analysis has yielded more benefits than initially anticipated. The concept allows extremely complex social relationships and networks to be illustrated quite clearly in discussions with farmers during a village social mapping exercise. The essence of intracluster resource relationships is that they are informal, compared with the more formalized exchanges which generally characterize external relationships. Within the cluster we have used a series of categories to indicate different types of producers. These are: primary producer, secondary producer, client producer, wives and single males or females.

The use of the cluster as a unit of analysis in the intensive RRA exercises has shown that it does enable a remarkably quick understanding to be developed of the social relationships involved in production between people of different gender, generation, marital and economic statuses and ethnicity. It also allows one to perceive clearly why in one area, for instance, where less than a quarter of 'households' own livestock there is no hiring (as was the case in the Mobe area of Kapiri Mposhi District), whilst in another area where there are similar ownership levels there may be hiring (St Anthony's, Ndola Rural and Muswishi, Kabwe Rural). Even where resource links are more tenuous, as in the predominantly hand hoe system of Teta, Serenje, or where production systems have become more individualized, the cluster concept will illustrate these processes. Another benefit of the concept is that by using an interview to map a cluster, thirty or so interviews is usually sufficient to provide information on well over 100 households. Triangulating with one or two other members of a cluster allows this information to be verified and supplemented.

136

Similar clusters can be aggregated as 'cluster types'. During five RRA exercises conducted in Central and Copperbelt Provinces in 1992, a rough ordering of types according to scale emerged.

- Small-scale commercial – Primary producer: 12+ or 15+ ha of maize, cattle owning;
- Successful small-scale – Primary producer: 5–10 ha or 7–12 ha of maize, cattle owning;
- Vulnerable – Primary producer: 2–5 ha staple crops, sometimes draught-power owning or hiring;
- Resource poor – All producers: 2< ha staple crops, rarely draught power owning, hire undertaking and/or hoe cultivation.

It would be misleading though to reduce the distinctions to solely ones of scale. In fact in Ibenga, the 'small-scale commercial' often had tractors rusting in their backyards, having switched from growing over 10 ha of maize to 2 ha of intensive vegetable production during the rainy season (when vegetables are scare and therefore highly profitable). All facets of the farming system are integrated in the description of the cluster type and must be considered together.

One very important implication for agricultural research and extension which our analysis of cluster distinctions indicates, is that more commercialized cluster types do not serve as models for less commercialized clusters, because the types are culturally and socially distinct. Agricultural recommendations thus must be socially and culturally relevant. They cannot just be pulled 'off the shelf' and extended. Understanding the differentiated nature of rural societies is the key, and the RRA methods employed have certainly increased our understanding significantly. Why this is important is illustrated simply by a case from Kapiri Mposhi district.

In Mobe there was one Swaka producer, Roy Katandala, who was trying to model himself after the patrilineal Tonga. It was proving disastrous. He was obtaining huge loans and planting an area of 12 ha or so, but simply could not assemble the labour he required (his three wives, unlike the well-marshalled Tonga wives were relatively indifferent to his endeavours). Consequently much of his crop was usually planted late, remained unweeded and his yields were poor. So his debts were mounting. In contrast his chief model amongst the Tonga, Maxwell Chibi was moving from one ambition to another. He settled in the area in 1985, with one ox of his own. In his first season he was loaned another by his father, cultivated just 1 hectare of maize, from which he sold 17 (x 90 kg) bags. Each year since his output has escalated. From the 1990–91 season, Chibi marketed 780 bags and purchased both a second-hand pick-up truck and the driving licence to go with it. After the 1991–92 drought year it was a second-hand tractor he procured. In short, this case illustrates both why farmers' activities cannot be understood without a contextuating analysis, and why 'recommendations' cannot be simply lifted out of one system and advocated for another.

The cluster analysis has therefore allowed us to understand individuals as themselves, as part of larger social aggregates and as part of representative groups. This allows us to bring into view agency and structure simultaneously (Drinkwater; Long and Villareal, Part I). This is important for ARPT as a national agency, since we are trying to achieve both a depth of understanding into the diverse nature of farming systems within an area, as well as to spread the benefits of this understanding to achieve broader coverage.

System and co-operative conflicts

Relations between households within a cluster and between individuals within households are constituted by elements of both co-operation and conflict. This means that outcomes of co-operative conflict, like those of production activities in general, are unlikely to benefit participants equally. Co-operative conflicts are thus those that occur between individuals or producer households within a cluster. They can be contrasted with system conflicts, which are those which affect the cluster and its (implicit) objectives and activities as a whole (cf. Sen, 1984; Sen and Dreze, 1989).

Examples of both types of conflict can be provided from the Tonga farmers in Mobe. Their production activities are cash crop oriented – maize and cotton – with the result that although the clusters are nearly always staple secure, foodstuffs for 'relish' purposes may be short. Malnutrition was a problem, especially amongst children. Men and women identified causes as lack of hygiene with respect to food preparation, lack of relish varieties, lack of time for food preparation, and polygamous marriage practices which produced too many mouths to feed. Men emphasized lack of hygiene as the primary factor, but women saw this more as an outcome of their having inadequate time for preparation because of their being too busy in the fields.

In this instance a system conflict is connected with a co-operative conflict, the allocation of wives labour time. When it was asked, 'Why do men not give women enough time to work in their own fields?', the following short exchange ensued:

> *Mweene* (Primary producer): If you make the mistake of allowing a woman to work on her field you have lost. Because the next time you want them to work on your field they will refuse and say why have you changed your mind?
>
> *Mrs Soko* (Wife): That is not true because if he gives me two days to work in my fields, I will also want to help him and I won't say no.

Here it is the conflict between men and women with the impact on diet and nutrition that is the greatest problem. Amongst poor farmers, more deeply-entrenched system conflicts can be much harder to address. Amongst Swaka farmers in Mobe it is the maize-vegetable syndrome; difficulties in marketing vegetables have led to declining returns, which means less income to invest in maize, which leads to poorer yields and so on. In St Anthony's, a major system conflict amongst the resource-poor cluster type was slightly different. The dilemma these farmers face with regard to food staples is whether to concentrate on sorghum or maize. Sorghum is the safety-first option as production is reasonably resilient and so one can nearly always produce enough food for the year. But it requires much labour – the bird-scaring whilst the grain is ripening – and there is no surplus and limited market. So if one wishes to try and accumulate, it is maize, 'the business crop', which has to be given the larger acreage. But the maize tends to be planted late (waiting to hire oxen), and in the drought 1991–92 season those farmers concentrating on maize harvested almost nothing.

Conclusion

The RRA participatory research exercises, conducted in the areas of farmer research groups, form part of the ongoing interaction with these groups. As a result of the exercises we are trying to deepen ongoing inter-action with the research groups. This includes developing different relationships with different types of farmers – 'collegial' with slightly larger farmers (+5 ha maize) and 'collaborative' with smaller farmers (Biggs, 1989). The substance of these relationships is slowly evolving too, after the first meetings with farmer research groups in 1990 when we obtained only a list of people's crop priorities for research. We are now understanding more about what impact an intervention will have on a society – who will benefit (or lose), and how differentiation within that society will be affected.

There remain areas where we as researchers perceive things differently from farmers. It is a gap across which knowledge cannot always be conveyed as a portable commodity. One of our major challenges therefore is to remove the gap: through engagement (the use of participatory methods and an active farmer role in on-farm testing), we seek to achieve a mutual broadening of horizons in order to provide a common basis for understanding.

Quality control, method transfer and training

JANICE JIGGINS

Validation through experience

The issue of quality in rural development methodologies is not often raised. Contextual forces appear to be more powerful than method in determining outcomes. But unless the question is addressed, the current wave of participatory enthusiasm could falter.

Participatory approaches and methods are validated experientially, by their efficacy in reality. The methods meet the practical quality test of 'fitness for function' in the sense of providing accurate information and measurements (e.g. Gill on rainfall, 1991), in both biophysical and human domains, in forms readily usable by individuals, communities and outsiders.

As long as the methodologies are taken up by those purposively looking for such approaches and skills, it is probable that peer review among practitioners (and here I include farmers and other community members as practitioners), has helped to maintain quality and a culture of open learning in which mistakes can be admitted and corrected. But with the rapid spread of participatory approaches in agricultural development, is quality under threat?

Quality under threat?

Participatory methodologies are beginning to be adopted by large, often bureaucratic institutions (Pretty and Chambers, Part III). Anil Gupta at the Indian Institute of Management (IIM) in Ahmedabad, frequently has warned that methodologies cannot be expected to instil participatory values in the hands of individuals unable or unwilling to go through the necessary 'reversals'. Participatory research and development approaches such as RRA, PRA and PTD may prove as expert-driven, top-down, and extractive as the methods of the dominant paradigms. Chambers (1992c) worries with respect to PRA:

> The label will be used or claimed for activities where behaviour and attitudes are not participatory; that these activities will be done badly; and that good PRA will be discredited. There is a danger too that the demand for training in PRA will so outstrip good supply that some will claim to be PRA trainers when they have no direct personal experience of good PRA.

Different kinds of quality loss

There are various kinds of quality loss:

- Spurious 'hardening' of qualitative methods occurs by enfolding them in an unwarranted statistical sampling framework;
- Hierarchical modes of learning return even within 'participatory' exercises in which farmers are supposed to be the 'experts' and service personnel the 'learners';
- Gender bias leads to the exclusion of women. Even though the participatory methodologies themselves may be used effectively, the quality of the inquiry is diminished;
- Normal professionalism prevails when people are uncertain or unconfident;
- A method, as an end in itself, is emphasized, rather than methods as effective ways of exploring particular questions.

How method use might fail tests of quality

There are three ways in which method use might fail to meet tests of quality. Firstly, method use might fail to meet the test of *efficacy*, that is, an inappropriate tool is chosen for a given task.

Second, method use might fail the test of *efficiency*, that is, the minimum or constrained resource is not used. Here, participatory methods appear to score rather well. Specialist scientific and technical personnel are desperately thin on the ground in an increasing number of the poorest developing countries. The linkage of farmer experimental capacities and specialist researcher capacities is, in this sense, efficient.

Third, method use might fail to meet the test of *effectiveness*, that is, using participatory approaches might not be the right thing to be doing. In contrast to the narrow confines of what is normally regarded as 'good science', participatory methodologies are effective at understanding the complexities of diverse, risk-prone farming systems.

The challenge of effectiveness: 'good' science and participatory methods

What constitutes 'good' agricultural science has come to be defined narrowly, with problems reduced to their smallest possible components, investigated through a relatively small range of observable variables. Factors that do not fit into a clear chain of cause and effect are not considered significant. Activity which establishes a high degree of control over the system being studied has become equated with acceptable practice. The basic methods, models and their related assumptions establish the criteria by which claims about what constitutes 'good science' are assessed.

However, these criteria tend to exclude the very things that need to be studied in order to operationalize the concept of sustainability: that is, complex, indirect and multiple interactions among composite variables; the possibility of other end-effects than those of linear causal chains; and debate about what constitutes the parameters and terms of the system studied. Participatory approaches are peculiarly well suited for capturing these kinds of effects, and for eliciting debate about the nature, boundaries and performance of complex systems.

Another contrast can be made. 'Good science', in the narrow sense, generates reliable knowledge about the world (i.e. a goodness of fit between ideas about how the world works and observable phenomena) through experimentation. The reliability of the experimental method in the narrow definition of good science depends in part on the understanding that there is a knowable mechanism linking cause and effect, and on replicability, which reduces the significance of the experimenter's identity in the result.

Interpretation of the results, rather than the experiment itself, is where the problems and disputes arise. Often, interpretation draws on the very theory that is being tested. Further, the experiment itself does not necessarily change theory; theories change as people assign different meanings to experimental work. Just as in any other domain of human activity, the construction of meaning in science depends in part on beliefs about an experimenter's honesty, competence and skill. Acceptance of a particular meaning or interpretation emerges through bargaining, debating, compromising and alliances; a peer review process which is not, and cannot be, divorced from wider world views and power relations (Scoones and Thompson, Part I).

141

Indigenous knowledge and local experimentation turn these attributes into strengths. Distributed knowledge and experimental capacity (as opposed to elite knowledge and centralized scientific capacity) enriches the meanings given to experimentation and the interpretation of results. At the same time, idiosyncracy is controlled by peer review and assessment of the experimenter's identity, in as rigorous a fashion as it could be: a household's or community's survival may depend on it.

In much 'normal' science, uncertainty is largely technical, arising from questions of quantitative inexactitude: the tools used ('scientific method') are not considered problematic and are understood to be the source of the guarantee that conclusions are valid.

In the domain of participatory approaches, we are dealing with settings where random variation is small relative to other uncertainties. The rate of system change is high, the sources of uncertainty complex, the number of actors involved potentially huge, and decisions may have enormous consequences. Statistical tools, computer modelling and laboratory research are thus inadequate and inappropriate formalisms.

Uncertainty in participatory method is largely epistemological and ethical. The 'art of the soluble' (the puzzle-solving, 'knowing that' of science), and the 'art of the do-able' (the situation-improving, 'knowing how' of professional activity), must be combined with the 'art of usable ignorance' (the evaluation and creation of future states which are unknown and unknowable, in which 'who knows' counts) (Funtowicz and Ravetz, 1990). Practitioners compromise quality if questions of quality are treated solely as practical concerns and not also as epistemological and ethical issues (Waters-Bayer, Part II).

Participatory methods make explicit contrasting meanings and interpretations, and the different values given to key attributes of sustainability, such as hazard and risk, thresholds, flexibility, adaptability and complexity, differences which are often subsumed or assumed. So, in terms of the effectiveness test of quality, participatory methods, it might be argued, better approximate good practice than normal professionalism.

Transfer of methodology

Quality-conscious transfer of methodology requires systematic documentation, formalisation of methods and of the parameters within which they are efficacious and efficient, effective and clear expression of the underlying concepts and research disciplines from which they have been elaborated.

Documentation. A number of centres, in both the North and South, are providing documentation services. However, communication and diffusion research suggests there is a numerical limit to effective quality control by this means alone: one centre can service something in the range of 500–800 individuals. The way to expand the effect is to increase the number of centres with whom new practitioners might link up; this, in fact, is happening. There are at least eight centres in India, for example, now documenting and circulating practitioners' experiences with participatory methodologies; many of them now also offer field training.

Formalization. The formalization of methodologies might ensure rigour as they spread more widely among institutions which do not formally espouse participatory values. It might ensure also the extinction of creativity and the introduction of mechanistic application. Somewhere between these two potentials there is a need for more guides for practitioners and trainers which stress the 'non-negotiable' principles and values.

Elaboration of underlying concepts. Few practitioners or trainers are aware of the research and concepts which underlie the methods they are using. It is evidently not the case that good quality is dependent on such an awareness. Yet an appreciation of the intellectual and research foundations of practice would strengthen participatory professionalism.

The foundations are grounded in an unusually large range of 'hard' and 'soft' disciplines. If practitioners want to know why it is necessary to iterate methods across populations or within stratified communities, anthropological and sociological research and statistics might provide some answers. If they want to be assured that villagers' mapping is theoretically legitimate, they would need to turn at least to semiotics. A bibliography of key studies for each of the most common participatory methods would assist those who want to, or need to look up the foundation research.

Training and normal professionalism

At the heart of the problem lies the challenge not merely to replicate experiences and methods, but to engage in a process of reproduction as creative evolution. In my view the process must include colleges and universities. Catch-up training relatively late in professional life will not bring about the scale impacts which seem to be needed. Many believe that training in participatory research and development approaches can be done *only* where there are opportunities to learn and try out methods in the field. Others simply believe that field-based training is better.

I believe that, given a participatory training mode, participatory methods and processes can be learned in an academic context. Success requires the weaving together of three basic elements: substantive information, experience, concepts and skills; the 'real time' experience of group dynamics and method practice; and on-going critical review of the participatory process and facilitation techniques.

The key to success is to establish an atmosphere in which participants feel safe to experiment and to criticize one another (and the facilitator), a style of facilitation which encourages participants to take responsibility for planning, evaluating and running the course, and the encouragement of recursive, experiential learning.

The ethics of documenting rural people's knowledge: investigating milk marketing among Fulani women in Nigeria

ANN WATERS-BAYER

Ethics and RPK

Discussions of rural people's knowledge (RPK) tend to focus on production. Much less attention has been given to the processing and marketing of farm products, an important source of income for small-scale farmers and herds people, particularly women. The methods that rural people have developed to process and market foods are based upon their knowledge of local resources and of the local economy. This is very often women's knowledge.

A study of traditional marketing of milk products by Fulani women in central Nigeria might have held important implications for local technical and institutional development in milk processing and marketing based on RPK, but did not (Waters-Bayer, 1988a). This is because the study was conducted as *extractive research*, designed to provide information for development planners. In contrast, an *enriching research* activity conducted by the women themselves would have increased their knowledge, making them better able to cope with external influences on their dairying activities. In comparing these two modes of research, a question of ethics arises: for whose empowerment is RPK being investigated and documented?

Studying dairy women's knowledge

Although millions of dollars have been invested in ventures to develop a modern dairy industry in Nigeria, about 90 per cent of the milk produced in the country is still handled by several hundred thousand Fulani women in the informal sector. These women process milk into products which suit the local climate, human physiology and local tastes. The major product is fermented skimmed milk, *nono* (in Hausa, the market language), mixed with *fura*, spicy balls of cooked millet. This highly nutritious food is commonly consumed as a midday meal in northern and central Nigeria. As milk is easier to sell and brings a higher price when sold with *fura*, the women regard *fura*-making as an integral part of their dairy business. In the dry season, the women compensate for the lower milk supply by mixing the *nono* with a local refreshment made of *kuka* (pith of baobab pods) and water.

The women sell mainly to regular customers in the neighbourhood and at various places in town. Favoured selling sites include road junctions, taxi stops, meeting places, mosques, churches, schools and marketplaces. Although the women are aware that milk prices are higher in larger towns than in the nearby farmsteads and villages, they prefer to sell directly to their regular customers, as this brings other socioeconomic benefits, including occasional gifts. Trusted farm women take care of the goats in which some Fulani women invest part of their dairy earnings. Farm families who loan the Fulani land for dwelling or cropping are regularly supplied with milk. The milk marketing link is part of a web of relations between the manuring and stubble-grazing arrangements. Milk marketing also gives the Fulani women opportunities for communication with their customers and among themselves.

The Fulani women have responded to changing opportunities. For instance, they have adopted plastic and metal containers for transporting milk in vehicles. Some women shifted to new products, such as *wara* (soft cheese), when immigrants offered new markets. They have also found ways to increase profits; for example, when subsidised powered milk from Europe became available, some women experimented with mixing milk powder, local milk and *kuka* to produce a fermented product acceptable to their customers. However, the women do not understand where or how decisions related to modern milk marketing are made, and feel powerless to influence them. They can only choose between taking advantage of favourable opportunities, such as temporary availability of cheap milk powder, or refusing to co-operate with government schemes which bring them no advantage.

Extractive versus enriching research

This study helped explain to planners why innovations meant to increase milk supply to urban processing plants had not worked. The planners had assumed that Fulani men would buy inputs such as feeds on credit, to be repaid when milk was delivered to collection centres. It had not been realized that the men buy inputs but do not earn from milk sales, which are fully controlled by the women. The Fulani rejected the scheme not only because of the gender-related division of responsibilities in the household. Delivering fresh milk to the centres also offered the women less flexibility in choosing when and where to sell and less opportunity to maintain important socioeconomic links. Moreover, the women could gain added income from processing *fura* to sell with the milk.

Before detailed research was made into traditional dairying, planners knew so little about this that their interventions had no positive – but also no negative – impact. Now government officials, armed with more knowledge about the indigenous systems and under pressure from private large-scale entrepreneurs, will be in a stronger position to intervene in the local milk trade. Good documentation of how the informal sector operates could reveal possibilities for bringing it under government control, thus curtailing the dairy women's independence. Much the same process occurred in Europe, where women were pushed out of the small-scale dairying business by government regulation (e.g. in connection with milk hygiene).

In the case of Nigeria, as the difficulties of 'modernizing' Fulani dairying became more apparent, planners shifted focus to non-Fulani cattle-keepers in peri-urban areas. The Fulani women were left to their own devices to develop their knowledge and skills in marketing – a process which could be enhanced if an *enriching research* programme was initiated. This would involve the women themselves in assessing the strengths and weaknesses of their marketing system, identifying what they have already accomplished in innovation and following up on these initiatives. Such an approach could enrich their present marketing knowledge and help them defend their interests.

Ethics and the documentation of rural people's knowledge

To some extent, *extractive research* into RPK, such as the case study of Fulani dairying, can benefit the people whose livelihoods are being examined. Documentation of the findings can make governments more sensitive to the importance of creating conditions that permit indigenous development. In milk marketing, this would mean not imposing price regulations and health standards, but rather improving transport infrastructure to increase the choices for sellers and buyers, providing water in villages to permit more hygienic milk handling, strengthening women's capacity to use credit and helping them obtain information about new technology and adapting it to their needs.

But what of the case of documenting *enriching research* into rural people's knowledge? Does it help or hinder rural people, if the results of their own research are made more widely known? The findings are likely to be more reliable than those of extractive research by outsiders, as the researcher and the 'researched' often know and trust each other. But this better-quality information about RPK could strengthen the position of urban-biased macro-planners and large-scale entrepreneurs in an extractive economic system, allowing them to better manipulate market conditions.

For the purposes of the local people involved in research aimed at enriching their own knowledge, what forms of 'documentation' are most useful? Copies of publications coming out of the study into Fulani dairying were sent to English-speaking relatives of the women, but even those active in adult education found the publications too difficult to read. A booklet in simple Hausa or Fulfulde would have been more useful for schools and adult education, to raise local self-esteem and to serve as a basis for discussion. More visual or oral ways of documenting and sharing knowledge are needed, such as collections of photographs or drawings, slides, video, songs, theatre, dance – praising not only traditional knowledge, but also indigenous innovation. To date, these media are used to convey messages by external agents, rather than express the achievements of local people, for their own enrichment and for exchanging with people in similar situations.

Documentation of the results of both extractive and enriching research can heighten public awareness of the wealth of indigenous knowledge and innovation, and the potential that would be squandered if this was ignored. Nevertheless, it will always be difficult to find a balance between documenting indigenous accomplishments and making valuable know-

146

ledge available to others who might misuse it. Detailed accounts of indigenous techniques invite expropriation. For example, after publication of a small piece about how Nigerian women has developed techniques of making the widely-popular 'local *maggi*' (*daddawa* – fermented soybean), several West African businessmen requested details of the procedure (Waters-Bayer, 1988b). A lengthy description of their fermentation process, which could have allowed urban businessmen to capitalize on the women's innovations and undermine their livelihoods, was deliberately not published.

The question remains: will documenting RPK break down the barriers of defence around indigenous and informal systems or will it strengthen and support them?

Regional centres for investigating and documenting indigenous knowledge are being established in various parts of the world (Warren, 1991). It is important that these centres do not become 'banks' to which only the better educated and economically powerful have access – leaving out the illiterate and particularly the women. To make a real contribution to rural people's development, these centres must develop and promote *approaches* to increase rural people's awareness of the wealth they possess and help them enrich it further.

Stimulating peasant farmer experiments in non-chemical pest control in Central America

JEFFREY W. BENTLEY

Farmer-scientist collaboration

Starting with the hypothesis that farmers and scientists can collaborate to develop better technologies than either group could invent alone, my colleagues at the Escuela Agricole Panamericana, El Zamorano, in Honduras, and I have been attempting to stimulate the work of innovative peasant farmers. We do this by teaching a short course on non-chemical pest control to small groups of *campesinos*, most of whom work for NGOs as extension agents, which offers them new techniques and scientific concepts, and aims to fill key gaps in their knowledge.

Since 1991, we have taught over 300 *campesinos*, many of whom have gone on to teach hundreds and possibly thousands of others. Our hope is that some of these *campesinos* will be real innovators who will go on to develop new, appropriate technologies or devise effective modifications of existing practices.

Farmers know some things that scientists know, some things that scientists do not know, and, also, farmers do not know some things that scientists do know. There are, in addition, a lot of things that neither group knows (Chambers, 1991). Knowledge overlaps, but is different. Much of this epistemological difference can be attributed to different styles of observation, to what I call 'the importance of importance', and to the ease of observation. These concepts are discussed briefly below, before returning to a description of the short course.

Understanding who knows what and why

Styles of observation

Despite the flashes of insight that may come while taking a bath, scientists are supposed to design hypotheses, then test them by formalized experimental observations. Peasant farmers rarely do this (although examples do exist; e.g. Stolzenbach, Millar, Part II). They perceive the natural environment through cultural filters as they modify it through work. Sometimes the difference in observation style is not very important. For example, scientists learn that ear rots cause maize ears to lose weight by weighing a random sample of damaged and healthy ears; but farmers learn the same thing by hefting ears while harvesting. In other cases, different styles of observation lead to radically different conclusions about how the world is made up. Farmers have no way of perceiving chronic toxicity in agrochemicals, and believe that the smell has something to do with toxic strength. They generally apply pesticides with no protective gear, often eating and smoking, cleaning stopped-up nozzles with their mouths and allowing pesticide from the backpack sprayer to drip down their backs. Farmers think that because they do not get ill as they spray, they must be building up a resistance to the agrochemicals. Only recently have Honduran farmers started to notice that years of pesticide use is making them sick, lame and sterile.

The importance of importance

People (including scientists and peasant farmers) pay more attention to things that are culturally and economically important. Entomologists have identified virtually all agricultural insect pests, and many of their natural enemies, while innocuous forest arthropods are poorly documented. In the same way, farmers understand weeds better than many harmless plants.

The ease of observation

People perceive more about things that are easy to observe. All things being equal, people are more likely to name and know large, brightly coloured, diurnal, social animals than small, cryptic, nocturnal, solitary ones. Britain is easier for most scientists to get to and observe than are the rain forests, so entomologists have documented 90 per cent of the insects of Britain (LaSalle and Gauld, 1991), while the tropical rain forests are being destroyed before we have even begun to learn what is in them (Wilson, 1988). Equally, Honduran peasant farmers have many words to describe social wasps, but do not know that solitary, parasitic wasps exist.

148

A short course on non-chemical pest control

Our short course for *campesinos* on natural pest control incorporates the notion that farmers' knowledge is profound, but that the gaps in their knowledge are consistent with topics that are not culturally important or are difficult to observe. The course has five main sections: (1) insect reproduction; (2) entomopathogens; (3) parasitoids; (4) predators; and (5) manipulation of natural enemies.

Insect reproduction is important and difficult to observe. Because insect pest populations are important to farmers, the farmers pay attention to them, but many insects spend parts of their life cycle underground, or are active only at night, or in some other way it is difficult for the farmer to see the whole metamorphosis from egg to larva, pupa and adult. Farmers often think that insect pests (especially caterpillars) are generated by the crops themselves, or increasingly, from the agrochemicals that farmers apply. Insect reproduction is difficult to teach to farmers, because we must contradict farmers' deeply believed perceptions of the world, while maintaining respect for them and their ideas. We challenge the farmers to rethink their belief that insect pests are spontaneously generated by collecting insects and watching them pupate and emerge as adults, and by asking farmers to tell us about the reproduction of bees – which they understand well – and encouraging them to draw analogies from bees to other insects.

Parasitoids and entomopathogens are not (culturally) important and are difficult to observe. Parasitoids are a vast complex of insects, mostly tiny, solitary wasps and flies that spend their larval stages living inside other insect species, eating them to death one organ at a time. Agriculture would be impossible without parasitoids playing the grim reaper on phytophagous insect species, yet I found Honduran *campesinos* (like most people) are unaware that parasitoids exist. Entomopathogens – also unknown to *campesinos* – are the fungal, bacterial and viral diseases that infect and kill insects. Farmers are fascinated by both topics, which we teach using slide shows and by collecting insects in the field and watching parasitoids emerge from them. The topics are relatively easy to teach because farmers have few conflicting, preconceived notions about them.

Predators are not (culturally) important, but are easy to observe. Because predators are generally larger than their prey and are equipped with death-dealing appendages, Honduran *campesinos* often know them, have names for many and are familiar with many of their habits, without understanding that these insects eat others. While it is arguably not as easy to see wasps killing insects as it is to see wasps sipping flower nectar, not knowing about insect predators is consistent with a cultural preconception that all insects (with the possible exception of bees) are bad. To show farmers that social wasps and ants, which farmers know well, are predators of insect pests, we capture *Polybia* spp. (Vespid) wasps returning to the nest with prey, and release the wasp to show the prey item to the farmers. Soon the farmers learn to recognize wasps coming in with the luckless caterpillars, and watch as the wasps eat them on the nest envelope. We place caterpillars on maize plants and ask the farmers to watch them. Within minutes ants begin carrying them off.

Manipulation of natural enemies is important and easy to observe. Once farmers know about predators, they become important and easy to observe. We have learned a lot from farmers who taught themselves to move wasp nests onto their fields, after learning that wasps are predators (Bentley, 1992). We teach manipulation of natural enemies in a seminar-style discussion, asking farmers to tell us how they think they could go about it. Many farmers suggest ways of protecting wasp nests, and other ways of increasing natural enemy populations. Natural enemies of crop pests can be manipulated using traditional practices like intercropping, avoiding herbicides and growing flowers, all of which raise the number of flowering plants – and hence provide supplemental food to many beneficial insects.

While there is much to admire about traditional agriculture, there is no reason to assume that cultural evolution leads to an optimum adaptation any more that biological evolution does (Burnham, 1973). Small-scale farming has room to improve, especially in light of the demands of rising populations and deteriorating natural environments (Cleveland, 1990). Farmers have always experimented, and may be doing so even faster now, in the face of a rapidly changing environment and the availability of new biological and chemical products (Goldman, 1991). The challenge for us is to learn from farmers, and help guide the stream of spontaneous farmer experiments by teaching farmers what they do not know, in a way that is consistent with what they already do know.

Encouraging knowledge exchange: integrated pest management in Indonesia

YUNITA T. WINARTO

The Field School

A government-supported programme of integrated pest management (IPM) in Indonesia has been encouraging farmer involvement in pest control in rice fields in Java, North Sumatra and South Sulawesi. Central to this programme is the IPM Field School. In West Java, this is held over three to four hours over ten consecutive weeks. The Field School sessions are run by the local pest observer and extension worker. The main sessions are based around practical exercises on IPM plots that compare the IPM approach with the rice-management packages. Farmers are encouraged to observe the plants' growing conditions, the pest and natural enemy populations and to control rice pests using selective pesticides.

The trainers try to avoid one-way communication and the imposition of external frameworks of analysis. After providing explanations about the training curriculum, they stimulate the farmers to make their own observations; to carry out insect collection and identification during field observation; to make their own analysis, argumentation and consensus in an agroecosystem analysis and to raise questions. With these observations of local agroecological conditions, the farmers are able to extend their own knowledge. For example, discussion and analysis of their findings take place in relation to farmer knowledge of local agroecological conditions and the characteristics of pest infestation. In having farmers make their own decisions, the IPM approach avoids the 'top-down' transfer of externally-designed 'packages' to them.

In the agroecosystem analysis, the trainers guide the farmers on how to identify, draw and count the average number of pests and predators, to relate the counting results to an 'economic threshold' of each pest, and to reach conclusions on whether there is a need to use chemical pesticides or natural enemies. The drawing and counting, rather than the comprehensive agroecosystem analysis, tends to be emphasized, as this is usually the farmers' primary concern. Moreover, the conclusions of their discussions usually dwell on whether they needed to spray pesticides or not. Whether the discussions achieve the expected aims of the farmers or the field school depends critically on how well the trainers are able to help the farmers build upon their existing knowledge of agricultural pests and diseases and employ a holistic, agroecosystem perspective in their analysis and discussions. With the diversity of local agroecological conditions in West Java and the emergence of a wide array of pests and diseases, the problems raised by the farmers in each new Field School vary.

The IPM training provides the opportunity for farmers to deal with particular local ecological problems, specifically White Rice Stem Borer (WRB, *Scircophaga innotata*) and disease infestations (Bacterial Red Stripe). In one village, Ciasem Tengah (C. Tengah), this led to a mass mobilisation of local resources for WRB control. In another village, Ciasem Baru (C. Baru), farmers planted diverse rice varieties after experiencing a severe WRB attack the previous season in order to reduce the risk of another attack. Farmers later discussed these experiences in their informal talks before training and during field activities.

During discussions, the Field School trainers provide room for farmers' own concepts and idioms and avoid using technical names which are unfamiliar to local people. The entire training activity is, in fact, a process through which local concepts and theories are used as the foundation upon which a new, scientifically sophisticated understanding of the ecology of agricultural pests and diseases is erected. One set of externally developed concepts that are easily understood by farmers is: *musuh alami* ('natural enemy') and *teman petani* ('farmers' friend'). Many other scientific concepts are introduced over the course of the training. Most of these are familiar to the young participants, who are educated in agriculture at high school, but not to the older farmers. Typical of these are: *ekosistem* (ecosystem); *ambang ekonomi* (economic threshold); *siklus hidup* (life-cycle); *populasi* (population); *jaring makanan* (food-chain); and *parasit* (parasites).

There are important differences in the nature of this new approach to IPM knowledge exchange from the previous Green Revolution rice technology transfer strategy. In the latter, farmers were able to observe the results of trying out the new components (varieties, inputs) on the growth and yields of rice. With IPM, the reduction of pesticide spraying or the observation of prey-predator dynamics requires more detailed explanations. Farmers are not easily convinced of the results of these activities on the growth and yields of rice, however. It is only after they have carried out their own experiments and observations that they gain confidence in the IPM strategy.

Farmer observation and experimentation

The Field School training has stimulated farmers' curiosity to make more detailed observations of pests and diseases in their fields. The IPM participants in C. Baru collected unknown insects using their own initiative. They discussed their findings when they met in adjacent rice fields or brought them into training to ask for explanations from the trainers. Several participants who regularly made observations and discussed their findings with others became known locally as 'farmer-scientists' (*pakar petani*). Among some participants, however, observations in their fields did not alter, unless particular phenomena attracted them to go into the field and make a more detailed inspection.

The implementation of new ideas on pest management varied. Experimenting on how to avoid pesticide spraying where pest infestation was absent was done by many participants. Others who did not have confidence in such a strategy, however, were still applying pesticides, and regularly using the banned substances. When there was an outbreak of WRB in the rainy seasons of 1990–91 and 1991–92, farmers' responses were based on the explanation received in IPM training as well as their own conceptual models. Hence, their strategies varied greatly from using mechanical control, such as handpicking and light-traps, to combining mechanical and pesticide control, to employing pesticides alone. Since the farmers brought their collections of WRB eggs home and conducted their experiments there, their relatives and other farmers, both males and females, young and old, were able to observe and to obtain some information. In this way, the form of eggs and larvae that caused the previous harvest failure became known widely.

By continuous observation during daily farming practice, farmers accumulate experience and knowledge year on year. From farmers' experiences in controlling WRB, they acquired knowledge of the different size of the moths and the period from the laying of eggs to incubation. In the following year, additional knowledge of this pest was gained. For instance, in C. Baru, farmers learned about the form and process of *S. innotata* pupae formation; the emerging moth from the pupa; the short life cycle of *S. innotata*; and the place where the pupae bored the rice stalk at the preflowering stage.

152

Outside the Field School, the new IPM knowledge acquired by the farmers is transferred to other farmers through informal conversations in fields and villages. In conversations with neighbours during leisure time and on social and religious occasions, their relatives and others, including owner-non-operators and wage labourers, listen to and participate in the discussions about pest management. Nevertheless, given the rather rigid social hiearchy that exists in West Java, the transmission of IPM knowledge is often restricted to those persons who regularly share such conversations through work or social networks. These tend to be male owner-operators. Variation thus prevails in the extent to which the IPM concepts and knowledge are exchanged and transmitted through communities.

The social context of farmer-to-farmer knowledge exchange

Power, status and knowledge

In villages in West Java, religious leaders and rich owners have high status. However, the 'experts' in agriculture are those who have rich experience and 'good strategies' in farming practices. Farmers with this status gain respect for their agricultural knowledge from others. An example is the farmer-leader in C. Tengah, a *haji* (a Muslim who made the pilgrimage to Mecca) who was previously a hamlet leader. He is considered a very skilled farmer, as well as a good and honest leader. Hence, his ideas and recommendations on farming practices are accepted willingly by other farmers. Others who are considered to be 'experts' in agriculture, however, may not attain high status in religion or social position. Although some participants attending the IPM field school were rich owners and religious leaders, many were chosen solely for their agricultural expertise and did not belong to any powerful social groups. They often faced constraints when trying to share their IPM knowledge with those of higher social standing, as did the younger participants.

Knowledge transfer from younger IPM participants to their parents and older relatives depended on local norms and on the kinds of relationships parents and children had. Not all parents challenged their children, nor did they invite or accept their children's opinions, since many considered themselves to have more mature judgment and farming experience. In these cases, only when successful experiments were made by their children, resulting in good rice growth and high yields, did elders recognize their children's knowledge.

Economic, social and labour relations

Cultivators who are perceived as local leaders or key decision makers, have a predominant role in the knowledge exchange process. Labourers can also act as vital transmitters of information. They often have access to different farming practices on various farms and, sometimes, in various villages. Furthermore, carrying out off-farm jobs, as traders and motorcycle drivers, provides opportunities for farmers, both rich and poor, to gain knowledge from well beyond their local farming areas. Finally, knowledge can be transmitted from observations and conversations when farmers make visits to their relatives outside their hamlets.

Farmers' labour routines also affect the time available for knowledge exchange. Farmers in C. Tengah typically spend their days involved in rice and secondary crop farming, as well a variety of non-farm activities. Hence, they have little time to engage in conversations, except on religious and social occasions or during peak seasons in the fields. Although farmers in C. Baru cultivate more than one rice field, they spend most of their time rice farming. Consequently, they have more leisure time to engage in more intensive discussions about their own agricultural experiments.

Economic assets play a major role in farmers' abilities to experiment. The landless in C. Baru and the small land owners in C. Tengah have fewer resources and, as a result, tend to take fewer risks than their wealthier counterparts. Previous harvest yields and financial commitments (i.e. debts) also determine what farmers can afford for future planting seasons. For instance, harvest failure of soybeans, as experienced by farmers in C. Tengah in the late 1980s, prevented many from experimenting with the pesticide *carbofuran*. The possibility of obtaining credit (either from private or public sources) in order to purchase agricultural inputs provided opportunities for some farmers in various occupational roles to experiment, for instance, in trying new types of pesticide.

Farmers' financial calculations also influence their choice between using labour or pesticides in controlling pests. Some farmers in C. Baru who cultivate a large number of rice fields (either as owner-operators or as cultivators) have been able to calculate the expenses they would incur if they were to buy pesticides as compared to the cost of wages for labour for mechanical control, and make their decisions accordingly.

Knowledge exchange as a social process

Knowledge exchange is thus a social process. Understanding how new knowledge spreads must be situated within a comprehension of the social dynamics and networks of different kinds of farmers – rich and poor, socially powerful and powerless, men and women, and so on. In C. Baru and C. Tengah, knowledge is largely exchanged through casual discussions in informal settings and between networks of friends and relatives. Practical observation and experimentation are central to this action-learning process and play a significant role in knowledge accumulation, adaptation and development.

The exchange of IPM concepts with other farmers and the extent to which these are incorporated into their own knowledges is thus limited to those ideas that are frequently brought into discussion and become their point of reference in their own experiments. Practice through observation and discussion become the main mechanism for transferring and adapting the new knowledge they received through formal IPM training at the Field School.

Learning by improvization: farmer experimentation in Mali

ARTHUR STOLZENBACH

The adaptive rationality of farmer experimentation

The management of a farm requires the ability to handle a multitude of biological, technical, economic and social factors in a changing and largely unpredictable environment. Such 'co-ordination-skills' are not so much based on the formal rationality employed by scientists as on 'adaptive rationality', where adaptive rationality is seen as a 'continuous interaction among visions, experiences and experimentation' (Nitsch, 1991: 101). These coordination skills and adaptive rationality are made up of 'tacit knowledge': knowledge that cannot be reduced to facts and rules and thus cannot be formalized. It is a combination of experience, intuition and practical know-how that can only be learned in the context in which it is applied (Van der Ploeg and Bolhuis, 1985; Nitsch, 1991).

Experimenting is a western concept associated with scientific research. How far can this western concept be applied to small-holders' practice? The practice of farmers is distinct from the practice of scientists: scientists are employed to look for explicit generalizable statements and rules, but the first responsibility of a farmer is agricultural production.

Schön (1983) distinguishes three kinds of experimentation; each kind with its own logic and criteria for success and failure.

- *Exploratory experiment.* When action is undertaken just to see what the results will be, it is the probing, playful activity by which we get a feel for things. It succeeds when it leads to the discovery of something of use.
- *Hypothesis-testing experiment.* There are already expectations about the results of the experiment. The purpose is not to change the environment itself, but to test the assumptions. The experiment succeeds when a competing hypothesis that tries to explain a phenomenon is proved inferior.
- *Move-testing experiment.* The purpose of a move-testing experiment is a certain desired change in the environment itself. The experiment is successful if the results are considered positive, even though the underlying hypothesis and assumptions may be incorrect and unexpected outcomes may have arisen.

The way practitioners gain tacit knowledge is through what Schön calls 'reflection-in-action', where, unlike formal rationality, practice and theory are not separated. Seen from this point of view the management of a farm can be seen as continuous series of experiments, by which, through the labour itself, the agricultural performance improves. It therefore becomes difficult to talk of an 'experiment' as a special action, separated from daily activities. What we can do is to concentrate on 'experimenting' as a continuous and innovative element of the craft of farming.

The importance of flexibility

The agriculture of Sanando in the semi-arid area of Mali is characterized by high variability and unpredictability. Consequently the farmer has to take decisions without being able to gain a complete insight into the situation. As soon as the first rains start the soil is tilled. When the rains appear to be holding, seeding starts. If it stops raining a few days after germination it may be necessary to sow the fields again. Maybe the farmer will now choose another variety or maybe s/he does not have any seed left. This is the way farming goes: a chain of doing, judging and adjusting; improvizing on a repertoire of different and intertwining themes.

In the scientific model of problem solving, learning and decision making are split. First, formal analysis must gain insight into the situation, then the best alternative can be executed. To the farmer this approach is often far too rigid and, besides, it only can begin when complex reality is reduced to a clearly defined problem; a reduction that in the context of farmers' practice is impossible. To farmers it is not relevant to explain how production changes as a result of separate factors. The farmers' interest is to understand the production process as a whole in its full complexity.

Farming is not a matter of doing everything correctly: 'It is not a matter of optimising the parts, it is a matter of making a totality run in a satisfactory way' (Nitsch, 1991: 102). The art of farming is thus to adapt the posing of the problem to the changing situation and act accordingly. This pattern of continuous observation and adjustment – farming performance – is central to experimenting by farmers.

The logic of farmers' experiments

Farmers' experiments (*shifleli*) may be explorative, hypothesis-testing and move-testing experiments at the same time. I will illustrate this with two cases (Box 1).

When Solo Keta started his groundnut experiment he took a step to change the management of his farm. But soon he reconsiders the effect of his action and intervenes. This *move-testing experiment* is completed when he decides not to continue with this idea.

The farmer from Koyan does his move-testing experiment to be able to harvest earlier in response to climatic change. After having harvested, prepared and eaten the new millet variety he affirms his move. Now he changes the problem statement by decreasing the distance between the plants and continues experimenting.

The moves of Solo and the farmer from Koyan also can be explained as *exploratory experiments*. Their actions cause them to appreciate things that go beyond their initial perception of the problem. Solo had not realized that the gynophore might not be able to reach the soil. Equally, the farmer from Koyan decided to explore the impact of planting distance on the variety.

In their statement of the problem, the farmers (implicitly) state an hypothesis. The results of the experiment can confirm or refute the hypothesis.

156

Box 1:   Experimental learning

Fertility management. Solo Keta had sown two plots with groundnut. The plots only differed in the application of fertilizer: one plot had not received any manure at all, the other had received mineral fertilizer. In the fertilized plot the vegetative growth of the groundnut was stimulated, as he had expected from what he had seen before with cereals. But in this particular case he became anxious that after the flowering, the gynophore (containing the growing seed) could not reach the soil and thus would not produce seeds. He intervened by earthing up the plants of the fertilized plot.

After the harvest Solo was very satisfied with the yield increase on the fertilized field. However, the bad taste did not please him. This would not be problematic if he sold his produce, but for him the market for cotton was more interesting than that for groundnuts. In the end, he decided not to continue applying fertilizer, because it was not worth the cost of the fertilizer and the extra labour of earthing up.

Variety introduction. The first time a farmer of Koyan had seen *sunan* was in a village far away from home. He was told that this short variety of millet can be harvested early and yields well. Since the length of the rainy season had been decreasing over the last few years, he was very interested and he received a handful of seed to try out. Back home he decided to sow at the shortest distance the people of his village used when sowing millet (four hand-widths). The new variety produced well, as the other farmer had said, although 'the taste is not so good and the colour is a little bit black when it is prepared'.

Probably the yield could increase by decreasing the plant density and so he reduced the sowing distance the next year. This time he was sowing it on large plots and each year he reduced the distance a little bit, until one year the distance had become too short. At the end, the optimum on his fields proved to be more or less two hand-widths.

In this way the experiments also become *hypothesis-testing experiments.* Solo's hypothesis that fertilization of groundnuts can increase the yield is confirmed. The assumption that fertilized groundnuts can be cultivated in the same way as non-fertilized groundnuts is not. In the case of the millet variety, the assumption that the sowing-distance of four hands gives best results is rejected and leads to a new hypothesis.

In farmers' experiments, reflection and action overlap. There is no neat distinction between theorizing or hypothesis formulation and testing; they are continuous in both time and space. This process of reflection-in-action (Schön, 1983) suggests a need to change the conventional mode of on-farm experimentation by scientists if there is to be a better articulation between the learning processes of scientists and of farmers. This in turn suggests new ways of evaluating experimental success and the recognition of the performative nature of agricultural experimentation.

Criteria for success of experiments

By earthing up Solo Keta 'proves' his hypothesis that fertilized ground-nuts yield more. However, this approach contrasts radically with the scientific way of hypothesis-testing through trying to formally refute the hypothesis.

In order to understand the different approaches to agricultural experimentation, we have to consider the very different praxis of the farmer and scientist. The farmer has a direct interest in improving the situation according to his/her wishes. This still does not mean that s/he is creating self-fulfilling prophecies, because the environment resists total manipulation and gives feedback. The farmer thus understands the situation by trying to change it and reflect on the results. This reflection is subjective because it is deeply rooted in the lifeworld of the farmer; it is also objective because it is continuously tested.

When farmers test a technique on small plots for the first time, this gives them enough information to reject the technique or try it out the next year on larger plots, possibly under slightly different circumstances. They will look for explanations when the new technique does not work out to their satisfaction.

To explain effects, farmers make use of the variation in the results. For instance, if the average yield of a plot is unsatisfactory, but there are spots where the plants do grow and yield well, it can be concluded that not the rain, but the soil fertility has been the most limiting factor. If the production in the whole field is low, the rain has probably been the limiting factor. To farmers, spontaneous variation is a source for interpretation. This is unlike conventional scientific experimentation where variability is screened out (through level fields, standardized treatments) and results are averaged and aggregated in order to be tractable by normal statistics.

A strong point of farmers' experimentation is the frequent observation of their crops during the whole season. Retrospectively they can determine a multitude of factors that could have influenced the yield. For example, the changes of the colour of the leaves can tell something about the soil fertility. Keen observation, comparison and deduction are critical skills for farmer experimentation. These are so often missing on conventional agronomic trials where the scientists may only be present at the field site for a few occasions during the season.

Experimenting as performance

These cases of *shifleli* could be easily identified as such, because they were somehow isolated from the principal production in place and/or time. For a time, it seemed that I saw more *shifleli* than did the farmers, for instance, in Adama Diarra's yard (Box 2).

Where does an experiment start and where does it end? Maybe it never ends, and it is arbitrary to set a limit. Especially in regions like Sanando,

Box 2:   Experiment or experience?

In a corner of his yard Adama had sown beans of a new variety. At the other side he had sown last year's beans at double spacing between rows. One month later, in between these rows, he had sown another of his varieties of beans. He told me that this year he did *shifleli* in the corner of the yard. But although he had never at the same time mixed two varieties of beans and sown them in between each other, he did not consider that *shifleli*, because he 'already knew the varieties of last year'. This year he 'just tried to spread the time of harvest'. Accidentally he had had two varieties at his disposal and found it 'interesting to mix them'. After a discussion he agreed with me that 'indeed you can call it *shifleli* if you want to'. Farmers do not classify this latter case as *shifleli*, because it is completely integrated in the production process and more driven by intuition than by an explicit desire to learn. Nevertheless, to me, it comes close to an experiment, although it may be more similar to 'just' experience.

farming is characterized by variability and unpredictability. In this situation, it is more important to be able to reframe the problem to the changing situation and act according to it than to test a specific hypothesis or design a definite plan.

Experimenting as a learning process

One good aspect of an experiment is that it is easy to talk about it when it is laid down in the field. As such, it is an interesting instrument for learning and demonstration. But also without clearly defined experiments, there are so many spontaneous situations when one can learn by discussion or mere observation that the importance of explicit experimenting for learning may be overrated. For example, it often happens that two different farmers on adjacent fields are cultivating the same crop, each one in a different manner. Also different people working on the same field can cause different 'treatments'. For instance, children may sow at shorter distance because they have short legs, or 'because they have not understood the instructions properly'. An open attitude to such situations may lead to new insight without being planned. One farmer made it clear to me how differently experimenting may be appraised:

Once, simply because of lack of manure, I could only fertilize about half of the field. The manured part produced twice as much as the non-manured part. A few years later, World Neighbours came and proposed to do the same type of test. At that moment I remembered I already had done the test just by accident!

Experimenting farmers in northern Ghana

DAVID MILLAR

Small farmer research with tubers and cereals

In northern Ghana, there is no farmer who is not in some way experimenting. However, in the Tamale region, experiments vary in terms of their diversity, depth and innovativeness. Discussions with farmers reveal four different types of experiments. These are: (1) curiosity experiments; (2) problem-solving experiments; (3) adaptive experiments; and (4) peer-pressure experiments. Each of these is described briefly, using examples of experiments by local farmers.

Curiosity experiments

An example of this type of experimentation was identified in the tuber-growing area (Box 1). The driving force for this type of experimentation is the farmer's own curiosity and quest for additional knowledge.

Box 1:   Cocoyam and a curiosity experiment by Farmer Dachil

Cassava was introduced ten years ago to Yachido in Tatale area from the southern part of Ghana by Farmer Dachil. He said, 'Last year I returned to the South and noticed that cassava was grown in combination with other crops that were not familiar in the North. One of them was the cocoyam (*Xanthosoma sagittifolia*). I wanted to find out if this crop would be as successful as the cassava, so I brought samples along with me. I decided to set up a small 'laboratory' in the middle of my yard. I developed the environment in the south by planting the cocoyam under a mango tree to provide shade which otherwise would have been provided by cocoa trees or other forest trees. I also combined the cocoyam with cassava, ginger and palm plants which are all living with the cocoyam. You know, the cocoyam grows under trees in combination with these crops and I want them in the middle of my compound so that I can regularly and easily attend to them, protect them from damage or animal attack and also be able to observe their performance. If the results are good, my next step will be to set up a small garden on my farm to try it out further before integrating the cocoyam into my whole farm. The garden will help me to multiply the seed. How long this will all take, I do not know, but I am just curious to find out everything I can about the crop.'

Problem-solving experiments

Farmers design experiments to address problems of farming practice, such as weed control (Box 2). Problem-solving also includes responses to external changes such as increasing population pressure, labour shortages through rural-urban migration and climatic change and/or variability.

Box 2: Weed control and a problem-solving experiment by Farmer Nafa

Gill *(Striga hermontheca)* is a notorious weed in northern Ghana which reduces cereal yields significantly. It is becoming predominant in most fields, and research is attributing its presence to declines in soil fertility. As a result, fertilizer, pesticide and sorghum/cereal trials are being conducted to resolve this situation. Farmer Nafa in Tuna has this to say, 'I encountered the problem and have adopted crop rotation to find out which rotation best fights *gill*. With my brothers, I found out that a continuous cultivation of millet on the field for three or more successive years kills *gill*. With other farmers, we are trying to see how long it would take *gill* to come back if other crops are grown after millet.'

Adaptive experiments

This is the most common area of experimentation carried out by farmers in northern Ghana (Box 3). No matter the form or source of an idea, farmers, if left on their own, always modify ideas and technologies. Besides modifications, reinvention is part of farmers' adaptive research. During the conscious process of adaptation, they sometimes rediscover ideas or practices that once were widespread, but which have died out due to lack of use.

Box 3: Cassava and an adaptive experiment by Farmer Mukie

Since cassava *(Manihot esculenta)* is relatively new in the area, government researchers have introduced a new variety which they believe suits local agroecological conditions. The recommended procedure is to plant cuttings vertically, with their aerial portions pointed upwards. In an interview, Farmer Mukie told me that, 'In addition to this, we farmers were advised to reduce the young sprouts to the one or two most healthy. But we men do not do the planting of the cuttings ourselves. The planting is done by the women and children; they also do the thinning. For the women and children it is difficult to identify the aerial portions of the cuttings; and even when they do, it takes them too long. As a result of this, reverse planting is very common, which leads to large portions of non-germination. Also, fewer shoots develop with this method of planting. For these reasons, we have adapted the planting from vertical to horizontal. This modification gives us a lot more shoots, which are then thinned to the two strongest plants per stand.'

Peer pressure experiments

A fourth category, referred to here as social or peer pressure experimentation, is linked to broader social conventions, rituals and cosmovisions (Box

4). It is important that *all* farmers carry out these 'experiments', even if they do not lead to any direct increase in productivity. Their purpose has much more to do with strengthening social cohesion and reinforcing local norms than they do with improving agricultural practices *per se*.

Box 4:   Yams and a peer pressure experiment by Farmer Dozea

In some parts of northern Ghana, yams have been cultivated for over a century. Farmers identify over fifteen varieties which have gone through various stages of experimentation. However, some varieties are planted differently each year and harvested in various ways. Farmer Dozea described his recent experiments with yams this way, 'My son! Varieties like *Ntakar, Barchiga, Naakpan* and *Kpajul*, which are used for sacrifices and for fetish and harvest festivals, have to be grown by every yam farmer. They are planted at the edge of the farm so that other members of the community can ensure that they are grown differently each year, for this is what the ancestors prescribe and the gods endorse. If this is not obeyed, the farmer and, later, the whole village will be punished with a poor harvest or a disease in the yams.' 'What do you mean by 'grown differently'?', I asked. He answered, 'We either stake or do not stake, mulch or do not mulch, weed or not weed, or combine the varieties in a special way or plant them separately. The gods stipulate what is to be done at the beginning of each season and the growth of those varieties helps 'protect' the other common varieties or else they would 'fly away' and yields would be poor and it is possible for this situation to spread to the other crops on the farm.'

In this case, agronomic factor experimentation is combined with socio-cultural, religious and spiritual factors of crop production. It also combines elements of the other forms of experimentation discussed earlier.

Execution, analysis and the use of results

The execution of experiments is an activity that is conducted with the entire household and it is perceived as part of everyday farm operations. However, with the introduction of a new variety, like in the example with cocoyam (Box 1), the farmer follows a conscious and identifiable execution phase which has a built-in stepwise function, because of the close monitoring needed and the evaluative processes required. In the example of yam (Box 4), where experimentation has stabilized over a century of varietal testing, an execution phase is less identifiable, yet experimentation carries on. This type of knowledge generation process is commonly encountered by the outsider and so often the mistaken notion is formed that small farmer experimentation is 'only' trial and error; non-systematic and chaotic.

Analysis and use of results are simultaneous processes that start very early in experimentation; unlike in formal science where they follow data collection. Variables are analysed once identified during design, and the results are utilized while the experiments are even in their rudimentary phases. This aspect accounts for the high degree of flexibility exhibited by farmer experimentation. The four brief accounts reveal that, while experimentation is going on, farmers either ask for and use results immediately or simply observe that which their neighbour is doing and decide whether or not to use aspects of it.

Not withstanding this, end-of-season analysis of outcomes is still an essential aspect of farmer experiments. In northern Ghana, it is often done at different levels and in different forms:

- With close family members (especially wife) and later with the household;
- With neighbours or friends who have agreed to participate in the experiment;
- With other members of the village in conversation after the season is over.

Execution, analysis and use of results are thus overlapping phases, depending on whether they occur in curiosity, adaptive or problem-solving experimentation (when they are more distinct) or occur as a result of social pressure in a form of continuous experimentation (where they are less distinct in character). Farmers, therefore, rely on empirical observations and experiences derived from experiments to take vital and timely decisions with a high degree of precision, but usually without technical instruments. Farmer experimentation relies on intuition, careful observation, skills acquired over time (i.e., experience), common sense and practical knowledge.

Local specialist support to farmer experimentation

Local specialists provide support to farmers' experiments. For instance, in Tatale, a soothsayer with special powers performs functions similar to the role of a seed certification and a plant quarantine unit. The introduction of new varieties requires purification of a particular type by the soothsayer before cultivation. The same soothsayer is also called on when there is an incidence of crop disease.

For purification, the soothsayer is confronted with the new variety and he performs the sacrifices to the gods by asking for permission to cultivate the variety. It is only when this permission is granted that the seed may be cultivated and even then only on a very small scale. After harvesting, some of the harvest is sent to the soothsayer for him to offer to the gods. This offers an opportunity to put restrictions on the type of crops or seeds that are introduced into the village and also to regulate the quality of the produce, because when the variety is 'unsafe', the gods reject the offering and nobody is allowed to grow it. When this occurs, the soothsayer has to supervise the burning of the entire yield.

It is also obligatory that disease incidence in any crop is reported to him to enable him to sacrifice to the gods for a treatment. When he receives a message of treatment from the gods, he goes into the bush for the relevant herbs to prepare a concoction which he sprinkles over the affected crops. During this process, women are not supposed to enter the field for if they do so while menstruating, the entire crop would be destroyed. The position of the soothsayer gives him access to knowledge that makes him a specialist. It is from this position that a good soothsayer is considered more knowledgeable than an ordinary farmer within the same community.

New roles for agricultural extension

Integrating people's knowledge with formal science has to begin with a process of dialogue. This leads to confidence building amongst actors so that extensionists, researchers and farmers see themselves as partners; jointly responsible for a common process and product. Confidence that is built from this type of interaction over time serves as a solid basis for future development. This has been the experience of NGO projects working in the Tamale region of northern Ghana.

Extension staff are being reoriented towards participatory processes. This means learning how to participate in farmers' own programmes and how to give recognition to farmers' different perspectives in the technology development process. This training should be incorporated into traditional forms of teaching and learning such as the use of songs, drama, poems and puppetry. Moreover, traditional forms of documentation, such as the use of maps, diagrams and pictures, could be identified, developed and used.

Using experimenting farmers as resource persons for other farmers and for researchers and extensionists can enhance this shift in extension practice. Such interactions encourage researchers and extensionists to understand the processes of farmers' own experimentation. Equally, in order to enable farmers to understand the processes and contents of formal science better, the rationale behind experimental lay-outs, sequencing and impact assessment needs to be explained. Experiences resulting from excursions, field days, demonstrations, games, exercises and exhibitions help to reinforce farmer confidence.

The process of dialogue envisages first identifying key experimenting farmers through extended village-level interaction. The key farmers identified can serve as resource persons for workshops based on farmer-to-farmer interactions and discussions. Such workshops are intended to identify common knowledge, information and experiences, verified and validated by a group of farmers. The role of 'outsiders' is to facilitate the process and synthesize valuable outcomes. 'Outsiders' can also act to ensure that sharing of experiences with other farmers takes place. Farmer-led analysis recognizes traditional forms of explanation which exist in the community. This is encouraged by field visits to practical situations in order to reinforce the exchanges and discussions.

The experiences and products of initial discussions provides an opportunity for more in-depth analysis by all actors involved. Here, the farmers are intended to be the resource persons and the development agents the participants. This gives farmers the opportunity to talk about their own work. The agents ask them for clarifications and details. This discussion process includes detailed small group discussions of relevant issues and plenary presentations. This allows more interaction between development professionals and farmers and the cross-fertilization of ideas.

Farmer-led analysis as part of an on-going dialogical process, demands a fundamental shift in approach to the research and extension linkage. This requires a change from top-down training to an effective combination of top-down and bottom-up processes, starting with farmers themselves. With farmers training farmers, farmers training researchers and researchers and extensionists training farmers, important changes in relationships become possible. Such interactive training helps research in the (re)formulation and provision of relevant research and extension support. Since these interactive processes are taking place in the farmers' own environments, there is a strong influence of farmers' knowledge, resource requirements – and even their cosmovisions.

From this perspective, farms are viewed as *learning systems*, where knowledge is generated and transformed and where actors (farmers and professionals) interact as partners. Such shifts also help to reinforce the informal networks among farmers and between farmers and development workers. The knowledge so generated then becomes joint property because of the shared responsibility for its production. From my experience in northern Ghana, such decentralized and locally identified programmes are less threatening and more acceptable to small-scale farmers.

Local knowledge formation and validation: the case of rice in central Sierra Leone

PAUL RICHARDS

Redefining local knowledge

The term 'local knowledge' means different things to different people. To some, it is cultural particularity – localized beliefs, attitudes and understandings to be celebrated as part of life's rich panoply. To others, it is 'indigenous technical knowledge' – practical skills adapted to peculiarities of the local environment.

Neither concept of 'local knowledge', I argue, has much relevance to rural development. Rural development has an object, an output. Social anthropology is replete with examples of beautiful, rich, intriguing, ennobling, inspiring beliefs (or their opposites). It is one thing to celebrate these beliefs as exhibits in a display of human understanding and quite another to assert that they have more than transient relevance to the shaping of the material world. 'Indigenous technical knowledge', by contrast, is perfectly at home in the material world. This is the guarantee of its irrelevance to development theory. If it works then there is no need to change it, nor will it be changed, except through the dynamics of local change.

This paper argues for a third concept of 'local knowledge' of importance for rural development: knowledge that is in conformity with general scientific principles, but which, because it embodies place-specific experience, allows better assessments of risk factors in production decisions. One such example would be where farmers reject or modify standard extension recommendations concerning fertilizer or pesticide use because they have detailed knowledge of the way in which crops and soils, or crops and pests, interact, under a variety of local climatic conditions. This kind of knowledge arises where local people undertake their own experimentation, or where they are able to draw inferences from experience and natural experiments (Millar; Stolzenbach, Part II).

For local knowledge to be valuable in development there must be some way to judge its quality, and the quality of inferences drawn therefrom. This requirement for validation is no different from the normal criteria applied to test and judge any other scientific knowledge: replicability, peer critique, etc. This paper describes examples of local knowledge formation and validation procedures deriving from the experience of rice cultivation among Mende farmers in Mogbuama village, Sierra Leone.

Rice in Mende country

Mende-speaking communities are distributed in an arc around the northwestern margin of the Upper Guinean forest block in West Africa, in southern and eastern Sierra Leone and northwestern Liberia. Rural Mende are primarily rice farmers, though many now also have small tree crop plantations. Most Mende farm households plant one or more rices in each of three main farmland categories: wetter, lower slope plots; upper slope plots and hill crest plots; and valley floor swamps. A typical catenary farm will thus contain 4–6 distinct rice types. But many farmers are capable of distinguishing and naming up to 40–50 distinct rice types, and frequently change their selections to match soil and vegetation type, as they rotate their farms through a shifting cultivation cycle, or according to taste and chance. Preferred types set aside for re-planting are sometimes lost, but in most cases farmers can recover material by begging, borrowing or exchanging planting materials with kin and friends. Mende farmers have explicit ideas about the performance of specific types in sandier or heavier soils, in areas of long or short fallow and the impact of weeds, pests and diseases. Farmers will seek, through seed exchange, to secure an optimum set of types for the land they intend to clear and farm in any given year. They are also constantly on the look-out for any interesting new material to augment their repertoire of planting choices.

Some new rice varieties in Sierra Leone have been introduced by extension services working for development projects; about 20 per cent of all rice farm land in Sierra Leone is now planted to improved varieties. Mogbuama, however, is a relatively isolated village beyond the reach of most rural development projects. Few, if any, of the new varieties adopted by Mogbuama farmers during the mid-1980s were research station releases. Most adoptions were indigenous varieties spreading along informal channels, or locally selected spontaneous crosses. In assessing innovations, Mogbuama farmers are keenest to augment the range of short-duration types suitable for early planting on the lower slopes, to alleviate food shortages in the hungry season.

Is Mende knowledge of rice germplasm progressive?

Mende farmers assign rice types to one of three main categories according to duration. This in turn determines where on the soil catena any particular rice will be used. By itself, however, this framework is not enough to qualify for the designation 'local knowledge system' in the third of the senses outlined earlier. It will be necessary, in addition, to show that Mende farmers have the means to discover more about the adaptation between particular types and particular site conditions when both types and conditions are subject to change. Only then can it be said that local knowledge is progressive, and so possesses development potential.

The sections below try to demonstrate three main points: first, that Mende rice farmers have rational well-grounded expectations concerning the appearance of beneficial novelties in the rice germplasm available to them; second, that when screening these novelties they draw upon an explicit methodology capable of yielding objective knowledge concerning crop-environment interactions; third, that this process of discovery is long-established and durable. This persistence is a pointer to the potential continuing effectiveness of local knowledge of rice germplasm as a complement to formal plant improvement initiatives.

The expectation of novelty

Mende farmers point to two sources of novelty in their rice germplasm. First, unfamiliar types may be introduced by birds, animals and humans. Second, it is said to be in the nature of rice to change over time. Farmers seek out and attempt to control and exploit both forms of novelty.

One rice cultivated by Mogbuama farmers is called *tokpoehun*, literally 'in the palm tree'. It was first discovered by a palm-wine tapper, as a single plant growing on the crown of a palm. The tapper carefully conserved the grains, planted and multiplied them. Later, finding the unfamiliar rice to be high-yielding, the tapper adopted it as one of his main upland selections, and gave it to friends. Other farmers found the case remarkable but not mysterious: when asked to comment each person was clear that the seed must have been carried there by a bird.

Another Mogbuama rice type is called *helekpoi* – 'elephant dung'. In settling the forest, the Mende have had to rely on skilled hunters to drive off elephants. Undigested husk rice from the gut of slaughtered elephants is carefully washed and preserved. At times used as a famine food, such rice was also a fine source of germplasm novelties.

People also are agents for the introduction of novelties – intentionally or by accident. A handful of unfamiliar and interesting rice seeds is an acceptable token from stranger to host, or among visiting affines and kin.

Novelties may also travel long distances unintentionally in clothes or packing materials. A rice type (or set of types) called 'OAU' is said to derive from a few isolated unmilled grains found in sacks of white rice imported for the conference of the Organisation of African Unity in Freetown in 1980. This rice is now planted quite widely by Mende farmers.

Rice is largely self-pollinated, but some natural out-crossing takes place at the margins of plots. As a result, spontaneous intra-specific crosses are encountered from time to time. Mende farmers have a number of opinions as to the cause of variation in their planting materials. To some it is simply in the nature of rice to change from time to time. Others have some practical understanding of hybridization. Edge-reaped seed is known to contain a higher proportion of mixed types due both to mechanical mixing of seeds and to outcrossing of adjacent varieties. This tendency was explained to me by a Lalehun villager from Gola Forest, in terms of a human analogy – seed rice from the centre of the field was likened to a 'mother' surrounded by her 'children'. Rice from the centre of the plot is expected to resemble 'mother', whereas phenotypically similar seed from the farm edge harbours some of the variation one might normally expect to find among her numerous offspring.

On some occasions farmers are anxious to keep their seed pure. A field of Asian rice (*Oryza sativa*) heavily infested with adventitious African rice (*O. glaberrima*) is sometimes considered a mild social disgrace. It is a sign that the farmer ran short of rice and had to borrow seed at planting time. In other cases, however, farmers view off-types in a more positive light. Off-types isolated from edge-reaped material may be carefully conserved and planted in small trial plots to assess their potential. Promising material may then be planted more extensively, and subject to mass selection. Over time, this process of experimentation and selection will tend to reduce heterozygosity in the planting stock, and lead to the stabilization of new types approximating to true varieties. Although we have yet to discover how widespread is this process of experimentation and selection, and how frequently it leads Mende farmers to secure new rice types, there is little doubt that the possibility is recognized.

The methodology of experimentation

When Mende rice farmers identify an interesting novelty they will try it out in a portion of the farm reserved for experiments. Often this will be a plot of fertile soil close to the farm hut. At times the spot chosen will be on a junction between soil types on the catena. A trial will be referred to as *hugo* ('to look inside') or *saini* ('a test'). The main purpose is to provide basic information on the rice type: how long it takes to mature, how tall it grows, the main characteristics of the panicle and grain type. Some farmers choose to probe more deeply, however, by planting the novelty alongside a familiar type for comparison. Sometimes, such an experiment will be conducted as an input-output trial. The seed will be carefully measured out in a tin can or calabash before planting, and the same vessel used to measure the grain harvested.

Not all experiments are, however, intentional. What matters is to recognize the circumstances in which experience provides systematic information, or clues, about the way nature works. One farmer in Kogbotuma, southern Moyamba District, asked to gloss the word *hugo*, pointed, by way of illustration, to a natural experiment that had changed his varietal preferences. He found himself with insufficient seed of the preferred (*O. sativa*) type to complete planting his upland farm. For want of something better, he accepted the loan of an unfamiliar *O. glaberrima* type recently introduced by a stranger from northern Sierra Leone. The women of the household were disturbed in their plans to weed this composite plot by a bereavement. Half the *O. sativa* plot and all the *O. glaberrima* plot remained without weeding. The unweeded section of *O. sativa* yielded nothing, but the unweeded portion of *O. glaberrima* seemed to have been affected much less by the weed competition. From this unintentional experiment the farmer derived the information that the *O. glaberrima* type, although low yielding, was tolerant of neglect. He was determined to plant more the following year in order to ease a chronic shortage of labour supply within the household.

The ownership and control of knowledge

Knowledge about rice is dependent on long established and durable social structures and cultural norms. Ownership and control of knowledge of rice is socially differentiated. There is, for example, a well-documented association between women and long-duration, flood-tolerant rice types in the West African rice region (Watts and Carney, 1990). It is common to find, in addition to the large household rice farm, an associated set of smaller private rice plots cultivated by household dependants, especially older women.

In Mende, the name for such long-duration flood-tolerant rice types is *yaka*. Perhaps in support of the suggestion that such rices have their origin in gleanings on the family farm, the word itself is said to carry the implication of 'alms' or 'charity'. There is a definite prejudice against consuming *yaka* rice. Mende villagers reckon them flavourless and lacking in nourishment, even though some recently introduced types are in fact of high quality. Coming last in the harvest sequence, these rices contribute little to household subsistence, and so have a correspondingly low status. In effect they are the rices that women can afford to sell. They have 'little flavour' and at times are suspected of causing sickness, because they do little to nourish the community and its social values.

Acquisition of short-duration seed types, and sharing them among family and friends are, by contrast, activities that assume central significance in repairing social fabric damaged by climatic irregularity and other misfortunes (Richards, 1986; 1990). Farmers search for suitable short-duration types capable of ripening in advance of the main harvest as a durable answer to the social evil of indebtedness caused by pre-harvest hunger. Such material is segregated, carefully conserved and regularly tested in small trial plots.

169

Mende knowledge of rice germplasm is thus based on a sound empirical methodology; one that leads to progressive learning and valid, adaptive lessons. Evidence suggests that Mende rice knowledge system is deeply acculturated, but also adaptive and progressive. One appropriate 'test' of the value of this kind of local knowledge would be to make a representative collection of farmer's germplasm to ascertain whether or not the selections therein perform up to some standard (better than average for 'mixed' seed, equal to or better than research station varieties in local conditions and under local management). This would serve to confirm the likelihood that local types are indeed the result of deliberate selection decisions and not just the outcome of haphazard or undirected reservation of seed.

Participatory methods and political processes: linking grassroots actions to policy-making for sustainable development in Latin America

LORI ANN THRUPP, BRUCE CABARLE, and AARON ZAZUETA

Lessons from innovative participatory processes linked to planning and policy

Innovative participatory approaches to sustainable development are being developed to overcome some of the constraints of previous approaches and to incorporate new dimensions linked with policy issues. Various groups, North and South, are working on such progressive adaptations. While these efforts retain many of the important principles and features of previous participatory methods, they also entail significant changes such as widening the sphere of influence of participatory activities, linking the efforts with policy-making processes, and replicating the successful ideas and actions of local people in broader institutional and political arenas. Examples of these new approaches are found in Costa Rica, Guatemala, Ecuador, Mexico and other parts of Latin America (Box 1), among groups working on natural resource management in collaboration with the Center for International Development and Environment of the World Resources Institute (WRI).

Towards a process orientation in participatory initiatives

Innovative dimensions: scaling-up and evolution into planning

In recent initiatives, participation is developed as a process to fit the rhythms of local communities and within a time frame long enough to ensure continuity, rather merely using a 'project' orientation. The specific kinds of participatory activities vary, and need to be adapted to local conditions, but they generally evolve over time, tying into planning, capacity-building and social development. These new approaches avoid some of the limitations of typical projects, like inflexible targets, termination dates and prescribed rules. Instead, the processes often allow for considerable innovation and 'learning by doing.'

In these experiences, the process generally begins from the 'ground up,' using variants of PRA for community-level analysis and planning, to determine major natural resource management problems and priorities. Representatives of diverse interest groups within a community or a micro-region jointly gather information, discuss, analyse and develop plans. Then, the efforts are 'scaled-up,' by repeating similar PRA workshops in neighbouring

---

Box 1: Widening the impact of participatory resource management planning in Ecuador

In the Andean region of Ecuador, participatory planning and management experiences began with meetings in 1988 between representatives of indigenous peoples' federations, technical people and decision-makers from the Ministry of Agriculture and Livestock (MAG), and facilitators from a local NGO (called COMUNIDEC) and the World Resources Institute. Together, these groups developed ideas and plans, with local people taking a key role in decision-making. The local groups, with the facilitators, then employed participatory planning methods adjusted to local needs. Participants were involved in assessing their own resources, analysing problems and opportunities and developing resource plans. Additional workshops were then held in other communities, over the course of three years. Over 200 Andean communities in the provinces of Chimborazo and Bolivar were involved.

The Andean adaptation of PRA, called Planeamiento Andino Comunitario (PAC) puts more emphasis on oral expression, condenses each exercise into a shorter time, incorporates musical interpretation and short skits and uses village festivals as the main forum such activities. Through the PAC process, the participants reached agreement that soil erosion and declining soil fertility were among priority concerns, and they proposed specific practices, policies and actions to address these problems.

Subsequently, representatives of several federations met to develop a wider plan, based on a sharing of community plans, which was relevant for the entire area. This part of the process also included dialogue with representatives of MAG and a foreign donor (the Dutch Development Agency), who agreed to provide funds to implement the plans developed by the local people. Furthermore, the PAC process had a profound impact on the FAO's Participatory Forestry Development Programme in the Andes, which was significantly modified to incorporate not only the communal plans developed under PAC, but also village institutions as implementing agencies of forest management initiatives.

171

communities, bridging different areas. An effective means to diffuse PRA is through training local people to become facilitators, who then serve as *'multiplicadores'*. Each community generates concrete products (e.g. documents of local resources, problems, options and planned priorities) and then shares them with neighbouring groups. The process evolves into regional participatory meetings to discuss the results and to build a consensus on goals, plans and actions. This involves integrating rural peoples' knowledge and needs into a broader dialogue. Alliances are formed among interest groups, as part of a wider process for regional natural resource management in the long run. This process presents new opportunities for democratic decision-making. Sometimes, the local groups have become political entities capable of negotiating effectively with government bodies or with competing interest groups.

Extending participatory approaches in such ways widens their sphere of influence. It usually requires more time, labour and resources; but the investment pays off and helps build peoples' interests in resolving regional problems.

Methodological innovation and flexibility

These initiatives explicitly avoid using standardized methods and 'recipes' for developing participatory tools and exercises. Facilitators often use basic principles of participatory planning, but have found that blueprint prescriptions are limited or inappropriate. Instead, local people are encouraged to adapt methods and innovate, adjusting approaches to local conditions and interests, so that they will develop understanding and 'ownership' of the methods they develop and will continue to use them. For example, in Ecuador, COMUNIDEC and five federations of indigenous peoples combines some PRA principles with vernacular planning practices to develop Andean Community Planning (PAC), an approach that is compatible with Andean perceptions of nature, causality and time (Box 1).

Cross-fertilization between different groups and participatory approaches is also fruitful. No particular tools are *a priori* considered 'superior' to any others. This kind of methodological flexibility and innovation does not mean that rigour declines. An emphasis on inductive reasoning, triangulation (i.e. posing the same question in different ways to different people), diagrams to aid data collection and analysis and systematic facilitation techniques are some of the ways in which rigour is incorporated into these methods, without falling into rigidity.

Forging links with social organizations and policy fora

Another important characteristic of these efforts is that they are based on ties to effective local organizations that address social/environmental issues. Similarly, collaboration is established in such efforts when the groups are committed to develop participatory processes over time. Both local interest groups and external support organizations must be dedicated to follow up the plans together. It is also essential to reach agreements on the objectives – which must be clear and realistic given available resources – and on the roles of insider groups and external support organizations.

These initiatives have been particularly effective when linked to specific policy decisions. In such cases, timing of activities is very important. For example, in the Ecuadorian case, indigenous federations, along with COM-UNIDEC and the Ministry of Agriculture began developing the Andean Community Planning (PAC) process at the same time that the government began to form a National Forestry Action Plan. PAC was therefore a part of a wider policy change, supported by the government and donor agencies, to address forest management issues and land degradation – a relationship that contributed to its success. Sometimes, this kind of integration into a government plan or policy forum is not possible at the outset, but such opportunities can usually be found if local groups and external supporters search for them.

Appropriate pacing and rhythms

Unlike some rapid assessment approaches, these new participatory efforts do not put a premium on speed. Experiences have shown that these participatory processes are more effective if their pace is matched to the rhythms of rural life and are sensitive to the particular social dynamics and cultural values of the area. Activities need to be timed carefully to avoid disruption of local peoples' work and rituals. For example, harvest time generally requires all of labour and attention of peasant households – a fact that must be respected in planning activities.

The process of extending the efforts into other areas, and scaling up into policy dialogue, may require many weeks and months or even years. However, each individual workshop or group activity must be relatively short, to avoid overburdening participants. Busy people cannot afford to spend a great deal of time in meetings, discussions and the like, because it cuts into the valuable time for productive work. The methods should be iterative, allowing time for the group's reflection, discussions and analyses. Working in step with the communities' pace helps to establish rapport between local people and external actors, and facilitates systematic research and planning. Extending the time of participatory activities can raise costs, especially in terms of labour costs, but it can also increase the returns.

Actors and alliances

Who participates, decides and benefits?

In participatory processes, representatives from many interest groups, classes, ages and both genders are involved and benefit from the activities. Facilitators avoid relying solely on village leaders or 'key informants.' Usually the participants include not only local people and NGOs, but also representatives of public institutions and/or the private sector who are stakeholders in the main issues under consideration. Expanding diversity can make participatory activities more effective and contribute to the aims of resource management, partly because more interest groups are involved in deciding, analysing and taking actions. Certain biases may be desired for some activities. For example, if an initiative's focus is on the needs of marginalized peoples, it may make sense to involve mostly indigenous peoples or poor farmers to help to address previous inequities or exclusionary approaches.

Measures have been developed to bridge the gaps between external and local participants. Establishing genuine partnerships often requires external support organizations to make longer-term commitments and to gain in-depth understanding of the local people and their culture and environment. When possible, it is useful for local people to share central responsibilities at all stages – from early decision-making to documentation and follow-up activities. They also should take a lead role in analysis of the methods and the information gathered in this process and in assessing the participatory activities from their perspectives. This sharing of responsibilities improves the sense of mutual dedication and equity among all involved. It also helps build capacities and facilitates progress.

Local people's ideas and capacities are just as important as the outsiders' ideas. Yet, communication between the two groups can sometimes be difficult, given cultural differences. To facilitate communication, successful participatory planning ensures that all participants are on the same footing. This is accomplished by clearly defining the norms and the premises used in discussions among different interest groups, by agreeing on common terminology for key concepts, and by using diagrams, incorporating local terms and concepts, to record and carry out group analysis. Moreover, outsiders avoid an 'extractive' mode of exploiting local knowledge. Instead, local ideas and alternative epistemologies are valued for their own intrinsic worth and for their vital importance for group decision-making.

Shifting the leadership to local people also can be fruitful in these participatory efforts, and helps to prevent local peoples' dependency on external support. In some cases, however, it is difficult to shift leadership in this way at the beginning, partly because local people may have little experience leading such initiatives. In these situations, locals may develop increasing leadership over time, after they gain familiarity and capacities in participatory processes. At the same time, the outsiders' roles in the field diminish, and the relation between the two groups often matures into a partnership. For example, during project implementation in Ecuador, Indian Federations and communities have a direct role in managing funds, while the NGO collaborator (COMUNIDEC) manages parallel funds to provide technical assistance to the Federations, but does not control the Federations' decisions. Unlike conventional projects, these initiatives hold that one criterion of 'success' is when outsiders can greatly reduce direct support and involvement, and the local people take the lead in promoting and developing participatory approaches.

Roles of policy-makers and policy issues: opening political space

Policies and government representatives can be addressed in various ways. In some cases in Latin America, government representatives participate in the discussion of plans and ideas from communities and become involvedin identifying priorities. They also provide information regarding the

174

means for implementing plans, constraints, or other policy issues affecting environmental and social conditions. Government entities have helped in follow-up activities by providing technical services in response to the peoples' needs (e.g. soil conservation advice), or by co-operating in proposals to donors to request funds for sustainable development initiatives at a regional level. In the case of Coto Brus in Costa Rica, following participatory workshops and consensus-building among local groups, the municipal government responded immediately to requests to complete water piping services and provide access to a communal garden – urgent needs that had been neglected at previous times. These collaborative arrangements help to legitimize 'bottom-up' ways to address policy issues and can facilitate political empowerment.

Considerable negotiation may be needed in order to reach agreements among the different interests involved; and in some cases, disagreements or conflicts emerge. Consensus may not always be possible, but effective facilitators or mediators can help reduce conflict and encourage constructive interaction. For example, in the case of Andean Community Planning, when indigenous groups wanted to have control over funding and decision-making for follow-up, the Ministry and donors opposed this idea, considering it too risky. Eventually, however, after tense debate, all parties agreed a control-sharing arrangement whereby the local organizations would manage funds under the supervision of a third party (FAO).

Building capacities through participatory processes

The processes described above contribute to the stengthening of the capacities of the local people and institutions involved. In particular, the experiences build:

- Capacities in information gathering, analysis and documentation, including the effective use of information;
- Competence in planning, management, leadership and preparing proposals;
- Skills for facilitation and negotiation between different interest groups;
- Commitments and dedication to spread and use the methods in innovative ways.

The processes also may build capacities of formal institutions, including Northern ones, by expanding their experience with participatory processes, providing lessons and critical insights from grassroots groups and formulating activities and policies that better meet local needs.

Remaining challenges

These recent initiatives show how participatory approaches are evolving (Table 1). They involve learning-by-doing and innovation. They are not 'better' than other approaches and methods, but can have a wider and more visible influence. Although experiences with these approaches have usually been directed towards natural resource management, they also could potentially be useful for such other objectives as addressing health problems and increasing agricultural production. Many challenges must be met before these kinds of efforts can fulfil their potential. One key challenge is gaining sufficient funding and political commitment to support such efforts. Such novel measures as pooling funds are being tried and some donors are showing more interest in supporting these kinds of activities. Another critical challenge is ensuring that the plans and policies resulting from these efforts are actually implemented in a timely manner and with sufficient financial backing. Although implementation has begun in some Latin American countries, there are often long delays between completion of plans and concrete field-based actions. Such time-lags need to be avoided to prevent disillusionment among local groups.

Additional issues deserving attention include: overcoming policies that work against participatory efforts for sustainable development; supporting these efforts in the face of oppressive governments; and changing formal institutions (e.g. structures, reward systems, and goals) to ensure that the participatory methods become integrated and legitimized (Pretty and Chambers, Part III).

These kinds of challenges are slowly being addressed in Latin America, partly as a result of innovative collaboration among NGOs, people's

Table 1: Shifting emphasis in participatory approaches: evolving opportunities towards policy linkages

From	To
• Small-scale (grassroots groups)	• Expanded scale (larger areas, more people)
• Community level (isolated, singular)	• Multiple communities and broader regional level
• Participation of few 'key informants' (focus on 'innovators' and leaders)	• Equitable participation of diverse groups (especially marginalized people)
• Avoidance of policy/politics	• Policy linkages and opening of political space
• Analysis by external actors	• Analysis by all actors, especially local people
• Management by external actors	• Management/control by local people
• Rapid pace	• Relaxed, reflective pace
• Ignore policy/political impediments	• Address policy/political constraints
• Lack of funding	• Innovative funding/pooling efforts
• Lack of political commitment from above	• Gaining political commitment and interest
• Blockage by institutional rigidities	• Integrating with institutions
• Hindered by 'top-down' professionals	• Legitimizing alternative interdisciplinary approaches

federations and a variety of international and government agencies. Good examples include the Grupo de Estudios Ambientales (Environmental Studies Group) with the Tropical Forest Action Programme in Mexico, the Organization of Tropical Studies with municipal governments in Costa Rica, COMUNIDEC and the Ministry of Agriculture in Ecuador and the International Potato Center (CIP) and local NGOs in Peru. Yet much more work is needed to realize the strong potential from innovative convergences of approaches, institutions and policies.

PART III

Transforming Institutions and Changing Policies

Part III: Introduction

Since the *Farmer First* workshop in 1987, there has been a variety of institutional innovations in both government and non-government settings in all parts of the world. A picture is now emerging of the conditions and requirements for the transformation of agricultural development institutions for research, extension and education. The papers in Part III of this book present examples of some of these experiments, pointing to both the potentials and the pitfalls.

In their overview paper, Jules Pretty and Robert Chambers identify the principal challenges for translating a farmer-first approach into mainstream practice. This involves the effective combination of professional and institutional elements, including a deeper understanding of the linkages between knowledge, power, research and extension; the adept use of participatory methodologies; the embracing of new attitudes, behaviours and professional norms; and the creation of enabling institutional structures and flexible organizational procedures.

Drawing on a wealth of empirical evidence from Africa, Asia and South America, John Farrington and Anthony Bebbington assess the prospects for building effective alliances between NGOs and public sector research and extension services. Norman Uphoff uses a detailed institutional case study of the Gal Oya irrigation scheme in Sri Lanka to examine effective means for strengthening local organization for agricultural development. Shifting to Latin America, Bebbington charts the experiences of farmers' federations in the Andes to suggest a range of lessons regarding local organizations, agricultural research and extension, while Jorge Uquillas demonstrates how diverse interest groups in the Ecuadorian Amazon compete in the agricultural policy arena, pointing to the complexities of affecting institutional change from the ground up.

The past experiences and future prospects of farmer participatory research in the International Agricultural Research Centres are charted by two 'insiders', Sam Fujisaka and Kwesi Atta-Krah. After reviewing the erratic and ambiguous history of farmer participatory research in the centres of the Consultative Group for International Agricultural Research (CGIAR), Fujisaka concludes that fundamental institutional changes must occur before its survival can be assured. Atta-Krah points to a positive example of institutional change in the form of the Alley Farming Network for Tropical Africa, an effective collaborative between three CG centres and numerous National Agricultural Research Systems, where farmer participatory research is being implemented within a framework of developmental on-farm research.

Peter Gubbels and Patrick Sikana provide cases from Burkina Faso and Zambia where changes in policies and practices have occurred within two very different kinds of institutions, the first a grassroots NGO and the second a national agricultural research unit. As these contributions show, both NGOs and government agencies are capable of becoming strategic, flexible, people-centred institutions, provided there is a commitment to change and the wherewithal to do it.

The future role of extension is the subject of papers by Niels Röling and Parmesh Shah. Röling argues that the new challenges of a farmer-first approach to agricultural development requires a radical reorientation of extension systems and philosophy. If extension services are to be transformed from supply-led, technology-driven agencies to organizations that are demand-led, client-driven and performance-based, then a new profession of extension is required. Shah's paper (Part III) presents one of a growing number of cases of village-based extension systems found in various parts of the world. Village extension volunteers in Gujarat, India, offer services, such as soil and water conservation planning, as part of extension services run by and paid for by local people to meet their own needs.

Andrew Campbell provides a very different case of demand-led research and extension support: the Landcare programme in Australia. Today, Landcare represents what is arguably the largest and most effective locally-driven resource management programme in the world. With new professional challenges for agricultural research, extension and development workers, the need for fundamental changes in curricula and teaching styles in educational institutions become essential ingredients for success. In the final paper of Part III, Richard Bawden offers the case of Hawkesbury Agricultural College (the University of Western Sydney) as an example of one institution that has managed to shift from a conservative, top-down, *teaching* institution to a flexible *learning* organization committed to a people-centred, systems approach to agricultural science.

Towards a learning paradigm: new professionalism and institutions for a sustainable agriculture

JULES N. PRETTY and ROBERT CHAMBERS

The context of change

Recent years have seen the growing strength of a new world view in agriculture. The transfer of technology approach for agricultural research and extension has long served industrial and green revolution agriculture, but has increasingly been recognized to be inappropriate for many of the conditions of complex, diverse and risk-prone agriculture. In the transfer-of-technology paradigm, research decisions are made by scientists and technology is developed on research stations, and then handed to extension to pass on to farmers. But the dominant positivist framework has missed local complexity; determinist causality has failed to account for the adaptive performances of farmers; technologies successful in one context have been applied irrespective of context, with widespread failure; and professionals and institutions have engaged in self-deception as a defence against having to learn the lessons of failure.

A new and complementary paradigm for agricultural research, development and extension is emerging both from a recognition of the failures of such approaches and from advances in other domains. A wide range of disciplines and fields of investigation are now providing insights for an emerging learning paradigm. The components of this new paradigm imply the need for new learning approaches, participatory methods, institutional settings and professionalism itself.

New learning approaches and environments

The central concept of the new paradigm is that it enshrines new ways of learning about the world. Learning and teaching, though, are not the same thing. Learning does not necessarily result from teaching. Teaching is the normal mode in curricula; it underpins the transfer of technology model of research; and it is central to many organizational structures (Ison, 1990; Bawden, Part III). Universities and other agricultural institutions reinforce the teaching paradigm by giving the impression that they are custodians of knowledge which can be dispensed or given (usually by lecture) to a recipient (a student). But teaching can impede learning. Professionals who are to work with local complexity, diversity and uncertainty need to engage in sensitive learning about the particular conditions of rapid change. Where teaching does not include a focus on self-development and enhancing the ability to learn, 'teaching threatens sustainable agriculture' (Ison, 1990).

There is little experience of institutional reform that has put learning approaches at the core. A move from a teaching to a learning style has profound implications. The focus is then less on what we learn, and more on how we learn. Institutions will need to provide creative learning environments, conditions in which learning can take place through experience, through open and equal interactions and through personal exploration and experimentation. The pedagogic goals become self-strengthening for people and groups through self-learning and self-teaching. Russell and Ison (1991) have indicated that a central component of new research and development will be that 'the role and action of the researcher is very much a part of the interactions being studied'.

New participatory approaches and methods

In recent years, there has been a blossoming of participatory approaches in government and non-government research, extension and planning institutions (Cornwall *et al.*, Part II). This great diversity is a sign of strength. It implies that each variation is to some extent dependent on contexts and

183

problem situations specific to locations and institutions. Common principles underpin most of them (Pretty, 1994a; Checkland, 1989). These are:

- *A defined methodology and systemic learning process* – the focus is on cumulative learning by all the participants and, given the nature of these approaches as systems of inquiry, their use has to be participative.
- *Multiple perspectives* – a central objective is to seek diversity, rather than characterise complexity in terms of average values. Different individuals and groups make different evaluations of situations, which lead to different actions. All views of activity or purpose are heavy with interpretation and prejudice, and this implies that there are multiple possible descriptions of any real-world activity.
- *Group inquiry process* – all involve the recognition that the complexity of the world will only be revealed through group inquiry. This implies three possible mixes of investigators, namely those from different disciplines, from different sectors and from different background (e.g. outsider professionals and insider local people).
- *Context specific* – the approaches are flexible enough to be adapted to suit each new set of conditions and actors, and so there are multiple variants.
- *Facilitating experts and stakeholders* – the approaches are concerned with the transformation of existing activities to try to bring about changes which people in the situation regard as improvements. The role of the 'expert' is best thought of as helping people in their situation carry out their own study and so achieve a desired outcome.
- *Leading to sustained action* – the inquiry process leads to debate about change, and debate changes the perceptions of actors and their readiness to contemplate action. Action is agreed, and implementable changes will therefore represent an accommodation between different conflicting views. The analysis both defines changes which would bring about improvement and seeks to motivate people to take action to implement the defined changes. This action includes local institution building or strengthening, so increasing the capacity of people to initiate action on their own.

These new approaches and methods imply shifts of initiative, responsibility and action downwards in hierarchies, and especially to farmers and rural people themselves. Earlier extractive investigations are superseded by investigation and analysis more by farmers themselves (Chambers 1992a; Cornwall, *et al.*, Part II).

New institutional settings

Many agricultural institutions, whether universities, research organizations, or extension agencies are characterized by restrictive bureaucracy. They have centralized hierarchical authority, specialized disciplinary departments and standardized procedures. Personal promotion and institutional survival depend less on external achievement, such as farmers adopting the products of research, and more on internal criteria, such as

Table 1: Comparison between old and new institutional settings

	From the Old Institutional Setting	To the New Institutional Setting
Mode of decision-making	Centralized and standardized	Decentralized and adapted to context
Mode of planning and delivery of technologies or services	Static design, fixed packages, supply-push	Evolving design, wide choice, demand-pull
Response to external change	Collect more data before acting	Act immediately and monitor consequences
Mode of field learning	Field learning by 'rural development tourism' and questionnaire surveys; error concealed or ignored	Learning by dialogue and participatory inquiry and methods; error embraced
How those in institutions learn (especially at the top)	Self-deceiving; misleading feedback from peripheries give falsely favourable impressions of impact	Learning through feedback and feedforward; adaptive and iterative processes
Linkages and alliances	Institutions work in isolation	Institutions linked formally and informally to each other

performance according to professional norms. Such institutions are sustained by modes of learning which present misleading feedback from the peripheries, giving falsely favourable impressions of the impact of their packages and programmes.

Institutions that respond better to open learning environments and participatory methods must be decentralized, with multidisciplinarity, flexible teams, and outputs responding to the demands of farmers. In these conditions, personal promotion and institutional survival should depend more on external achievement. The new institutions will be learning organizations, with realistic and rapid feedback flows for adaptive responses to change. Multiple realities will be understood through multiple linkages and alliances, with continuous dialogue between different actors (Table 1).

Old and new professionalism

The new roles of farmers, the new participatory approaches and methods and the new learning environments, all imply new roles for agricultural scientists and extensionists. Scientists must continue their normal science, in laboratories and on research stations. In addition, they will have to learn

Table 2: Changing professionalism

	From the old professionalism	*To the new professionalism*
Assumptions about reality	Assumption of singular, tangible reality	Assumption of multiple realities that are socially constructed
Scientific method	Scientific method is reductionist and positivist; complex world split into independent variables and cause-effect relationships; researchers' categories and perceptions are central	Scientific method holistic and constructivist; local categories and perceptions are central; subject-object and method-data distinctions are blurred
Strategy and context of inquiry	Investigators know what they want; pre-specified research plan or design. Information is extracted from respondents or derived from controlled experiments; context is independent and controlled	Investigators do not know where research will lead; it is an open-ended learning process. Understanding and focus emerges through interaction; context of inquiry is fundamental
Who sets priorities?	Professionals set priorities	Local people and professionals set priorities together
Relationship between all actors in the process	Professionals control and motivate clients from a distance; they tend not to trust people (farmers, rural people etc.) who are simply the object of inquiry	Professionals enable and empower in close dialogue; they attempt to build trust through joint analyses and negotiation; understanding arises through this engagement.
Mode of working	Single disciplinary – working alone	Multidisciplinary – working in groups
Technology or services	Rejected technology or service assumed to be fault of local people or local conditions. Careers are inwards and upwards – as practitioners get better, they become promoted and take on more administration	Rejected technology or service is a failed technology or service. Careers include outward and downward movement – professionals stay in touch with action at all levels

from and with farmers, and so serve diverse and complex conditions and farming systems. The new roles for outsider professionals include convenor for groups; catalyst and consultant to stimulate, support and advise; facilitator of farmers' own analysis; searcher and supplier for materials and practices for farmers to try; and tour operator to enable farmers to learn from one another (Chambers, 1992a; 1993). These new roles require a new professionalism with new concepts, values, methods and behaviour (Table 2).

Although to characterize an old and a new professionalism is to risk a polarized caricature between the bad and the good, the contrasts stand out. Typically, old professionals are single-disciplinary, work largely or only on research stations, are insensitive to diversity of context and are concerned with generating and transferring technologies. The new professionals, by contrast, are either multidisciplinary or work closely with other disciplines, are not intimidated by the complexities of close dialogue with farmers and rural people, and are continually aware of the context of inquiry and development.

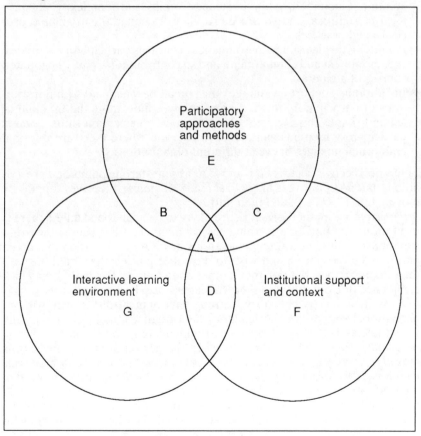

Figure 1:   *Conceptual framework for* Beyond Farmer First

A vision for sustainable agriculture

This vision for the future, in which the new professionalism becomes the norm in new institutional structures and partnerships, has been achieved in certain places. There are, for example, an increasing number of environmental and economic successes in complex, diverse and risk-prone areas, where agricultural and economic regeneration has occurred. Local groups, supported by new professionals working in enabling institutions, have increased yields, reduced environmental impacts, built capacities and resilience and reduced dependencies. For this vision, evidence suggests there are three essential areas to tackle. These are new methodologies for participatory analysis and sharing; new learning environments for professionals and rural people to develop capacities; and new institutional environments, including improved linkages within and between institutions. These three areas for action are shown in Figure 1 as intersecting circles.

The following assumptions underlie this conceptual framework:

- Participatory approaches and methods support local innovation and adaptation, accommodate and augment diversity and complexity, enhance local capabilities, and so are more likely to generate sustainable processes and practices;
- An interactive learning environment encourages participatory attitudes, excites interest and commitment, and so contributes to jointly negotiated courses of action;
- Institutional support encourages the spread between and within institutions of participatory methods, and so gives innovators the freedom to act and share. This includes where a whole organization shifts towards participatory methods and management, and where there are informal and formal linkages between different organisations.

In this perspective, sectors G, F and E represent starting points and preconditions, but no initiative is likely to spread well unless it receives support by moving into D, C or B, and then into A.

Participatory methods, as in E, are likely to be abandoned unless there is institutional support or a learning environment. This has been a recurrent experience with field training workshops in PRA. Those who have taken part may be convinced, and wish to introduce participatory methods into their organizations, but find they cannot do this alone. Partly they may lack confidence or clout, but also their colleagues may be sceptical or hostile.

A creative and participatory learning environment on its own, without institutional support or participatory field methods, as in G, is typically vulnerable and short-lived. Such environments tend to rely on one person or a small group, and so disappear when the person or group moves or is moved out. Where there is institutional support for participatory modes, as in F, it is liable to remain only rhetoric and intent unless expressed through a participatory learning environment and/or the use of participatory field methods. Examples are known where a director has been convinced of the value of participatory methods but staff, wedded to top-down methods of investigation, have resisted reform; and where, in consequence, nothing much has changed.

Box 1: A success from Kenya: The Soil and Water Conservation Branch

In 1974, the National Soil Conservation Programme was established in the Ministry of Agriculture. During the first ten years, emphasis was placed on the construction of mechanical protection works, mainly various forms of terracing. The extension services targeted those individual farmers who were willing and able to accept technical assistance. During the 1980s, it became increasingly apparent that this individual approach to extension was not supporting sufficient soil and water conservation measures. Erosion was outstripping conservation, despite the financial incentives and subsidies.

As a result, in 1987 the Ministry adopted the catchment approach. This concentrates resources and efforts within a specified area for a limited period of time. A team with extension officers from different ministries works together for a week in a catchment area using Participatory Rural Appraisal methods for the catchment planning. They work with local people to analyse local ecological and social conditions, produce inventories of local knowledge and practices and develop an action plan. This is discussed at an open meeting, or *baraza*, where farmers are able to comment and express their needs. A catchment committee of local people is elected, and this local organization co-ordinates soil and water conservation within the catchment area.

This group approach to extension planning has increased the credibility of extension staff as they are seen to be listening and learning from local people. It does not make use of direct subsidies. Instead, it has mobilized communities around a productive interest. It has changed attitudes in both local and outside people. The approach has resulted in significant environmental and economic regeneration, with sustained increases in agricultural yields, resource conservation and strength of local groups.

Sources: MALDM, 1988–93; Pretty et al., 1994

In sector A, support within institutions exists at the top, and authority is more decentralized. Linkages are encouraged with other institutions, whether NGO, government or local organizations. The learning environment focuses on problem-solving, and is interactive and field-based. Responsibility is more personal than procedural, relying more on discretion and judgment and less on rules and manuals. Behaviour and attitudes are democratic, stressing listening and facilitation, not didactic teaching. Local groups and organizations are supported, encouraged to conduct their own experiments and extension and to make demands on the system. Examples of these conditions, or conditions close to them, can now be found in many countries and contexts (e.g. Box 1; Farrington and Bebbington, Part III).

The role of governments and state institutions

There is growing acceptance that participatory approaches can contribute to the development of technologies by and for resource-poor farmers, and to community management of natural resources. But government organizations are limited in their ability to conduct systems-based participatory agricultural research and development. This is accounted for by several well-known factors.

At the macroeconomic level, tight limits are set by debt burdens, structural adjustment, low revenue and budget deficits. At the institutional level, inflexible management generates misleadingly favourable feedback based on centrally determined criteria. Government field agencies, with the deadlines of financial years, often concentrate on physical construction to meet targets to the neglect of community and farmer participation. In consequence, attempts to scale up successes frequently founder. At the individual level, agricultural researchers are deterred from working with farmers by reward systems based on scientific papers derived from on-station research, and by sheer lack of physical and financial resources, such as transport and travel allowances.

Many problems, as well as strengths, were brought to light by ISNAR's study of nine NARSs that had been conducting on-farm client-oriented research for at least five years. The study found that the hardest part of on-farm research to institutionalize was getting feedback from farmers to affect research priorities (Merrill-Sands *et al.*, 1991). As Merrill-Sands and Collion (1992) have stated: 'This finding is particularly disturbing given that we were looking at relatively mature FSR efforts that had had time to train researchers in FSR methods'.

Extension also thoroughly embodies the teaching, positivist paradigm. Extension means extending knowledge from a centre of learning to those presumed to be in need of that knowledge. Researchers have the prestigious role of being the source of new technologies, whilst farmers are

---

Box 2: Erroneous assumptions in conventional agricultural research and extension

- Real knowledge is the sole domain of the researcher;
- The farmer is a passive and malleable recipient of information;
- The initiative for disseminating information rests exclusively with the communicator;
- Increased production is the main criterion for farming improvement;
- Farmers' information needs are technical research results rather than in the area of management of their livelihood systems.

Sources: Chambers et al., *1989; Ison, 1990; Moris; 1990; Röling, Part III*

190

passive recipients. The erroneous assumptions underpinning much extension and transfer-of-technology are shown in Box 2.

In group-based approaches, extension becomes facilitation, through using and developing farmers' knowledge, teaching observational skills and using adult education methods to develop joint decision making skills (Röling, Part III). Russell and Ison (1991) have suggested that: 'It is time to abandon the term extension altogether because of what it has come to mean in practice and the network of faulty assumptions which are at its core'.

Government Successes

Despite these constraints, there are a growing number of successful innovations in national systems. A selection includes:

- Working groups, interdisciplinary research teams and joint treks in Nepal (Chand and Gurung, 1991; Mathema and Galt, 1989); ·
- Catchment approach to soil and water conservation, Ministry of Agriculture, Kenya (Kiara et al., 1990; Pretty et al., 1994; MALDM, 1988–93);
- Adaptive Research Planning Teams and village research groups, Ministry of Agriculture, Zambia (Sikana, Part III; Drinkwater, Part II);
- Farmer groups for technology research and extension in the Ministry of Agriculture, Botswana (Heinrich et al., 1991; Norman et al., 1989);
- Innovator workshops in Bangladesh (Abedin and Haque, 1989);
- Farmer and community groups for Landcare, Australia (Campbell, 1994; Part III);
- Policy analysis network of universities in Nepal, coordinated by Winrock International (Gill, 1993);
- Participatory research teams, Tamil Nadu Agricultural University, India (TNAU/IIED, 1992);
- Farmer groups for technology adaptation and extension, Narendra Deva University of Agriculture and Technology, India (Maurya, 1989).

These cases were successes because progress was made in several areas. There were incentives for change, and a recognition that past approaches had failed. There were enabling management structures, with support from senior staff giving the space to innovators who, in turn, were often charismatic individuals able to promote and achieve change. Smaller, autonomous groups within the larger bureaucracies innovated, and then became a model for the rest. Participatory methods were used not just for information gathering, but to establish new dialogues, change behaviour and empower local people.

Many successes reflect the growing experience of farmer-to-farmer extension and peer-training. Professionals play the role of bringing interested groups together and facilitating the process of information exchange. During the visits, participants are stimulated by the discussions and observations, and many will be provoked into trying the technologies for themselves. For farmers 'seeing is believing', and the best educators of farmers are other farmers themselves (Jintrawet et al., 1985). Such farmer-

191

to-farmer extension has resulted in the spread of contour hedgerows in the Philippines (Fujisaka, 1989a and b); new rice rotations in NE Thailand (Jintrawet et al., 1985); management innovations for irrigation systems in Nepal (Pradan and Yoder, 1989); agroforestry in Kenya (Huby, 1990); velvet beans for green manuring in Honduras (Bunch, 1990); and watershed protection measures in India and Kenya (Mascarenhas et al., 1991; Shah, Part II; MALDM, 1988–93).

Replicability and new problems

An important question is to what extent these successes are replicable. The most pressing problems arise from the approaches themselves. Feedback and learning from farmers' experiences are essential for improvement of technologies and for sustained dialogue between scientists and farmers, but these have proved difficult to sustain on a large scale. In Botswana, feedback has been effective, but on a small scale, from farmer groups in one region (Heinrich et al., 1991). In Nepal, field staff could not devote sufficient time to supervision or collection of feedback, because of the large number of on-farm activities (Chand and Gurung, 1991). New reward systems are needed for agricultural scientists to reduce emphasis on controlled on-station experimentation and the publication of conventional scientific papers.

Successful local groups can also be seen as a threat to state institutions, or political patronage and hijacking can occur when successes are seen as vehicles for achieving other aims. In Australia, there are now more than 1000 local groups, comprising at least a quarter of all farmers in the country. With a growing influence over agricultural policy and funding, there is a very real danger of a backlash from central authorities (Campbell, 1994; Part III).

The national policy environment has a major bearing. For wider impact, attention has also to be paid to factors which impede the spread of locally-led successes, such as macro-economic policies (subsidies for inputs; food pricing policies; food-for-work schemes); regulatory policies (lack of land title for local people); financial constraints; and the desire by politicians to maintain political control of actions at all levels.

Given these problems, and the scale of the challenges and opportunity, it is evident that governments cannot and should not try to go it alone. There is then a compelling case for partnerships and alliances with NGOs, local groups and international organizations.

Non-governmental organizations

The scale, scope and influence of NGOs concerned with development has grown enormously in recent years (Korten, 1990; Edwards and Hulme, 1992; Fowler, 1992; Farrington et al., 1993; Farrington and Bebbington, Part III). In the South, there are perhaps some 10–20,000 development NGOs, and in the OECD countries a further 4,000. Their activities are now very diverse. In some of the poorest areas and countries, they perform many of the service roles elsewhere carried out by government. Activities include not only relief, welfare, community development and agricultural research and extension, but also advocacy and lobbying, development education, legal reform, training, alliance building and national and international networking. These varied functions and roles mean they are critical actors in their own right, as well as potential partners for government and international institutions.

A number of strengths of NGOs contribute to their relative success. They have:

- The flexibility to choose the subject area and sources of information;
- The freedom to develop their own incentives for professionals;
- The capacity to struggle to get things right, and so more ability at the local level to question, change and learn;
- The strength to support community-level initiatives, and help to organize federations and caucuses;
- The ability to work on longer time horizons, as they are less affected by the time and target-bound 'project' culture.

Like state organizations, NGOs have undertaken a wide range of agricultural activities. In some countries or parts of countries, the coverage by farmers' groups and NGOs in extension, training and input supply is more extensive than that provided by the public sector.

Scaling up the impact of NGOs

NGOs which operate on a very large scale are the exception. Most NGOs are quite small, though quite often conspicuous. They can appear to be doing a lot, but the observer is easily misled. Coverage by NGOs as a whole is usually patchy and small compared with that of government field organisations. Three types of strategy have been identified by Edwards and Hulme (1992) for widening the impact of NGOs:

- *Additive*: NGOs increase their size and expand operations;
- *Multiplicative*: NGOs achieve impact through deliberate influence, networking, policy and legal reform, or training;
- *Diffusive*: NGOs achieve impact through informal and spontaneous spread of ideas, approaches and methods.

The additive strategy is widespread as donors' interest and support has fostered organizational expansion. But it has dangers. Some of the comparative advantage of NGOs is liable to be lost when they expand. Close relationships with farmers, the capacity to experiment and the ability to be flexible to local contexts may all be weakened. Korten's (1990) description of the growth of the International Planned Parenthood Federation as an evolution to 'an expensive and lethargic international bureaucracy' may be an extreme case, but the dangers of size are real.

The multiplicative strategy can take many forms. Intermediary NGOs have provided stimulus, resources and technical assistance for the formation and functioning of community-based organisations. NGOs in these cases can act as intermediaries, channelling financial and technical resources from other agencies to community-based organizations, instead of using those resources themselves (Mitlin and Satterthwaite, 1992).

The diffusive strategy entails developing and spreading ideas, approaches and methods which others pick up, and which have a capacity to spread on their own. Examples include various forms of self-help savings and credit, such as that of the Grameen Bank, the very ideas of which may encourage others to try similar approaches, and the approaches and methods of Participatory Rural Appraisal (Mascarenhas *et al.*, 1991; Chambers, 1992d).

NGO – government partnerships

Some NGOs choose to work alone, as when, in their opinion, there is little of relevance in the public sector programmes for their clientele. Increasingly though, there is a case for collaborative partnerships between NGOs and the public sector. The size of human capital and resources locked up in government institutions usually represents a huge underutilized potential. As Roche (1991) has argued: 'NGOs need to identify how best they might support but not substitute for what exists'. There is also a case for working with, not necessarily for, governments in long-term partnership. Since the pace of reform is usually slow and subject to reverses, the chances of achieving an impact on government policy and practice are enhanced when NGOs are prepared to work closely in a constructive dialogue.

Many types of relationships have developed between NGOs and governments in agriculture. These include:

- Support for marginalized regional administrations;
- Training of government and NGO staff and farmers in participatory methods;
- Development of alliances during training courses, leading to increased job satisfaction on the part of government staff;
- Research dissemination: it is uncommon for NGOs to generate technology which government disseminates, but quite common for NGOs and NARSs to conduct research jointly (Farrington and Bebbington, Part III). In this mode the NGOs generally operate in a more obviously, and often on-farm, 'adaptive' mode than the NARSs.
- Consortia of government, NGO and farmers' organisations for joint planning and coordination.

These new state–society relations have significant implications (Curtis, 1991). There are benefits from synergism, from greater efficiency of resource use and from NGOs and farmer organizations becoming more accountable. There are also costs and dangers. The state's capabilities may be weakened in two ways: through NGOs substituting for government activities; and through a brain drain to NGOs, as increasingly NGOs are able to attract skilled people away from the public sector, even though this may enrich NGOs with professionals who understand government bureaucracies.

This raises questions about the dividing line between what the state can and should provide, and what can and should be provided by organizations outside government; of how to negotiate appropriate deals between government and NGOs; and of the allocation of resources to achieve an optimal balance between incentives, personal rewards and the costs faced by different parties.

International agricultural research and the CGIAR

The CGIAR Institutions

The international research centres of the CGIAR have a professional influence out of all proportion to their size and budgets. In 1988, the Centres' expenditure of US$250 million was some 6 per cent of the global expenditure on agricultural research (Ravnborg, 1992). Nevertheless, agricultural scientists worldwide see the Centres as embodying and setting the standards of professional excellence. Through their training of national scientists, international networking of research programmes, publications, and prestige, the Centres spread and sustain the dominant concepts, values, methods and behaviour of agricultural science. Still basking in the afterglow of the green revolution, they still in the mid-1990s predominantly accept and propagate the transfer-of-technology paradigm.

Recently, the CGIAR system has responded to the increasing priority attached to the management of natural resources and sustainability in agriculture. The shortcomings of commodity-based research have been increasingly recognized and much discussion has focused on an ecoregional approach to research. In a 1993 report (TAC, 1993), a second green revolution is seen to be needed to double food supplies in the next 25–40 years. The new approach seeks to achieve this by better and more equal collaboration with NARSs, and by co-operation between Centres.

But this revolution can only be achieved through decentralization, farmer participation and through scientists coming closer to farmers. This is well represented by some professionals in some institutions (Fujisaka, Part III). Yet there are still three major challenges which are basic for a revolution in sustainable agriculture.

The first challenge is the development and dissemination of methods for analysis conducted by farmers themselves. The assumption has been that farming systems research has to be done by professionals. Yet recent experiences with participatory methods indicate that farmers have a far greater ability than agricultural or other professionals have supposed to conduct their own appraisal, analysis, experimentation, monitoring and evaluation.

The second is approaches and methods for changing the values of scientists. A striking finding of recent experience with participatory methods is how powerfully inhibiting is the normally dominant behaviour of professionals with farmers – lecturing, criticising, advising, interrupting, 'holding the stick' and 'wagging the finger'. The astonishing time it has taken to realize the analytical capabilities of farmers can be attributed to this almost

195

universal tendency of outsiders. The need, then, is for experiential training approaches to enable scientists to make the changes.

The third challenge relates to the view that traditional production systems provide limited opportunities for intensification since they use only small amounts of external resources (TAC, 1988). A very small proportion of the system's total budget is spent on technologies that focus on regenerative agriculture. This imbalance undervalues low-external input farming, and overlooks the striking potential for intensification through resource-conserving technologies and enterprises to diversify farming systems (Pretty, 1994b; Cheatle and Njoroge, 1993; Reijntjes *et al.*, 1992; Altieri, 1987).

Opportunities for alliances with NARSs, NGOs and farmers' groups

To support the development and dissemination of participatory approaches and methods within and outside the CG system, there is a need to form new alliances and to strengthen those that already exist. Groups of professionals in some Centres have already been conducting participatory research in partnership with other organizations. These include or have included:

- Post-harvest potato technology research with Peruvian farmers, from CIP (Rhoades and Booth, 1982);
- Bean research with Bolivian, Colombian and Rwandan farmers and NGOs, from CIAT (Ashby *et al.*, 1989; Bebbington and Farrington, 1992; Sperling, 1989);
- Aquaculture systems research and development with Malawian and Filipino farmers, from ICLARM (Lightfoot and Noble, 1992);
- Upland conservation research and development in the Philippines and elsewhere, from IRRI (Fujisaka, Part III);
- Pigeonpea research with women farmers in Andhra Pradesh (Pimbert, 1991) and pearl millet research in Rajasthan (Eva Weltzien Rattunde, pers. comm.), from ICRISAT;
- Soil and water conservation research with Indian government agencies, NGOs and farmers, from ICRISAT (Kerr and Sanghi, 1992);
- Countrywide network for potato research in Philippines, UPWARD at CIP (UPWARD, 1990);
- Continent-wide network for farmer participatory research for alley farming and agroforestry, Alley Farming Network for Tropical Africa (AFNETA), supported by IITA, ILCA and ICRAF (AFNETA, 1993; Atta-Krah, Part III).

These programmes are, however, not yet the norm. Those individuals who have succeeded in developing and using participatory approaches have tended to be isolated and marginalized within their institutions. At least until recently, they have been more recognized and respected in the outside world than by their colleagues. The central question remains whether the CGIAR system as a whole, and the IARCs individually, will embrace participatory approaches and methods, as mainstream professional activities, or whether these will remain on the fringe.

Local institutions

Types of local institution

Local groups and other institutions have been relatively neglected in agricultural research, extension and development. This is another symptom of agricultural development that focuses on technology rather than on the organisational and institutional setting. Yet all the positive experiences in Sector A of the conceptual model (Figure 1) have built upon existing institutions or helped to develop new ones. Local institutions can have many positive effects. Although local institutions are fundamental for a sustainable agriculture, they function in a wide range of ways (Box 3). Five types of local group are directly relevant to the new agenda for agricultural research and development:

- *Community development groups*, such as for hill resource management in India (Poffenberger, 1990) and agricultural development in Nepal (Rahman, 1984);
- *Farmer experimental and village research groups*, such as in Zambia (Sikana; Drinkwater, Part II), Botswana (Heinrich *et al.*, 1991), Ecuador and Colombia (Ashby, *et al*, 1989; Bebbington, 1991a and b);
- *Farmer-to-farmer extension groups*, such as for soil regeneration in Honduras (Bunch, 1990) and for irrigation management in Nepal (Pradan and Yoder, 1989);
- *Natural resource management groups*, such as for local forests, for irrigation tank management in India (CWR, 1990–91; Mosse, 1992), for soil and water conservation in Kenya (MALDM, 1988–92), for irrigation in the Philippines (Bagadion and Korten, 1991), and for land rehabilitation in Australia (Campbell, Part III);

Box 3:   Functions of local institutions

- Organize labour resources for production;
- Mobilize material resources to help produce more (credit, savings, marketing);
- Assist some groups to gain new access to productive resources;
- Secure sustainability in natural resource use;
- Provide social infrastructure at village level;
- Influence policy institutions that affect them;
- Improve access of rural population to information;
- Improve flow of information to government and NGOs;
- Improve social cohesion;
- Provide a framework for co-operative action;
- Help organize people to use their own knowledge and research to advocate their own rights;
- Mediate access to resources for a select group of people.

Sources: Uphoff, 1992a, b; Cernea, 1991a, b; Curtis, 1991; Norton, 1992

- *Credit management groups*, such as in MYRADA groups in India (Fernandez and Mascarenhas, 1993), Grameen Bank groups in Bangladesh and Small Farmer Development Programme groups in Nepal (Conroy and Litvinoff, 1989; Rahman, 1984).

Strategies for supporting local institutions

Local groups do have some shortcomings. Some community level institutions establish and legitimize unequal access to natural resources, as with water allocation in Tamil Nadu during times of scarcity (Mosse, 1992), and in the common field system in medieval Britain (Pretty, 1990). Also, if only one institution is present in the community, with powers to refuse membership, then, as with farmers' clubs in Malawi, the poor are liable to be excluded (Kydd, 1989). External interventions can also create problems. They are liable to warp and weaken local institutions. There are dangers that the state will suffocate local initiative and responsibility, or capture and harness local initiatives and resources for other purposes. Local politicians may also seek to take over local successes or gain reflected glory from them.

Problems also arise during the evolution of groups. Groups are sometimes more effective in their early years. As they grow in size, confidence and prominence, their power and position can bring them into new conflicts. The original leaders may not build up secondary leadership, creating an internal vacuum. A diversity of local institutions can also lead to factionalism and conflict unless attention is paid to articulation between groups and federation to higher level bodies.

These problems have been largely overcome by external organizations using the following strategies:

- Where there has been little spontaneous local organization, external agents can play a positive role in change, often by concentrating first on rural context rather than content. They may mobilize resources and act as a broker between interest groups, as in a Tamil Nadu case (Mosse, 1992); or they may create demand for local institutions by beginning with awareness and articulation of local needs and interests, as in Ecuador and Bolivia, where land tenure and marketing were addressed before research activities (Bebbington, 1991; Part III).
- Responsible leadership is crucial. It is encouraged where groups select their own members and make their own rules, as with MYRADA credit groups (Fernandez, 1992), and in Sri Lanka irrigation groups (Uphoff, Part III). Good leaders need adequate rewards to guard against unofficial or corrupt practices.
- Training, where it is involved, is to help people gain new problem-solving skills. This is more useful than technical training. Local people can then take on the roles of researcher and extensionist, and by so doing increase effectiveness by farmer-to-farmer training and extension.
- Perhaps the most important strategy is to find ways of helping local institutions to come together and federate, with small groups at the base represented by wider and stronger institutions at higher levels (Bebbington, Part III).

Educational and learning organizations

Universities and their agricultural faculties are often the most conservative of agricultural organizations. They remain in the conceptual strait-jacket of positivism and modernization, arising partly out of the functional demarcation of research and teaching, and the focus on teaching rather than learning (Pearson and Ison, 1990). Most have developed structures that reflect the proliferation of disciplines which have emerged over the past thirty years. The problem is that an innovative field is usually accommodated by adding on a new department (Gibbon, 1992). Such new ideas have hardly ever stimulated radical rethinking or restructuring. This is because the structure of agricultural universities and faculties creates biases hugely in favour of the teaching paradigm (Box 4).

The most fundamental need is to enable universities to evolve into communities of participatory learners. Academics must become involved in learning, learning about learning, facilitating the development of learners and exploring new ways of understanding their own and others' realities. Radical change is required. The education system does not need patching and repairing; it needs transformation.

The strategic implications for learning are threefold (Ison, 1990). The first is greater learning autonomy for students. The aim is to enhance, not stifle, their responsibility, leadership and creativity. This requires the development of flexible, learner-centred curricula. The second is more focus on applying concepts to real problem situations. This requires working to reach agreement in identifying the existence and nature of the problem,

---

Box 4: The biased structures of agricultural universities and faculties

- They are frequently organized along authoritarian rather than participatory management lines;
- Management positions are often held on the basis of seniority rather than management skills;
- Creative and eccentric innovation is rarely tolerated;
- Institutional rewards, particularly senior authorship of papers, promotes individual and isolated research – making many institutions lonely places;
- Organizations become introspective and resistant to new ideas, processes and changing environmental circumstances;
- Staff development, if it exists, is frequently in the form of refresher training, where content (new faces) is the primary input, rather than a balance between content and the development of new management or learning skills;
- Explicit or implicit status divisions become set in stone, e.g. researcher versus extensionist, natural versus social scientist.

Source: Ison, 1990

with the participation of all concerned, including the student learner. And the last is devolving more responsibility and power to students. The aim is to enable them to learn how to understand realities better. This requires assessment procedures which encourage them to pursue independent inquiry, rather than just pass examinations. As a result, it is necessary to:

> Think about things in a quite different way – for what we *do* in the world reflects what we *know* about it, and what we *know* depends on how we go about *knowing*, or in other words when thinking about change we should start by thinking about thinking (Bawden and Macadam, 1988, quoted in Ison, 1990).

The change suggested here is very rare in universities, an exception being the former Hawkesbury Agricultural College in Australia (Bawden, Part III). It is more common in small colleges and in training institutions linked less to the mass production of graduates, and more to the development of capable professionals (Lynton and Pareek, 1990; Lynton, 1960); and in some adult education institutions (Rogers, 1985). An unresolved question is how these agricultural education institutions can be reformed.

One example of how educational institutions can take on a new role for sustainable agriculture comes from Honduras. Since 1988, scientists at a small agricultural college in El Zamorano have been working to build the capacity of small farmers to control pests without pesticides (Bentley, Part II; Bentley and Melara, 1991). This is done through short courses with farmers. Farmers' knowledge is already profound, but there are aspects of pest control they do not know about. For example, they can describe social wasps, but do not know that solitary parasitic wasps exist; they know that pesticides are toxic, but equate smell with toxic strength and so have no means of perceiving chronic toxicity. The successful new learning is based on the collaboration between farmers and scientists, and now small-scale farmers help to set scientists' formal research agendas. Such collaboration results in the development of better technologies than either University staff or farmers alone could invent. As Bentley and Melara (1991) put it: 'we depend on farmers to help tell us what to study and to work with us carrying out the experiments in their fields, fine-tuning the technologies to their conditions'.

Institutional and policy implications for the new professionalism

Some of the practical implications for support and spread for the new agricultural professionalism are well known and have been described elsewhere (Merrill-Sands *et al.*, 1991; Chambers, *et al.*, 1989). The personal and institutional changes envisaged must be supported by the adoption of new incentives, structures and linkages. Some of these can be taken on by individual institutions; others will require more co-ordinated action at policy level:

- *Shifting resources*: scientists, extensionists, teachers and trainers need the physical and financial means to travel and stay in villages often enough and long enough for good participatory interactions. Support is needed for field training experiences, and opportunities to share ideas and innovations, within regions, countries and globally.

- *More recognition and new rewards*: far from being marginal in institutions, those who work as new professionals in a participatory mode deserve recognition as pioneers. This is occurring with the rise in international, donor and government interest in participatory approaches, but requires backing also from theory, books, prestigious journals, academic and international prizes and awards and sustained funding by governments, foundations and donor agencies.

- *Changing personal behaviour and attitudes*: personal behaviour and attitudes remain the great blind spot of agricultural research and extension. The quality and sensitivity of personal interactions are critical. In training for participatory methods, it has been found that listening, learning and low-key facilitation are more important than the methods. Methodologically, a major frontier for institutional change is how first to enable individuals to change, for personal change will often have to precede as well as accompany changes in the cultures of organizations.

- *Supportive leadership*: consistent and strong support from the upper levels of organizations can provide space and security for innovation, even when a whole organization does not change. Familiarisation of senior managers and administrators with the new professionalism has to be one part of a strategy for spread.

- *Creating alliances, support and sharing*: even with strong leadership, whole institutions will rarely change at once. In PRA, sharing experience through inviting participants in field training workshops from a range of organizations has proved effective. Friendships develop, and mutual support can take place afterwards. The crucial time is often shortly after returning from a training to the parent organization. Professionals then often need support in order effectively to share their experience with colleagues.

- *Training, trainers and dissemination*: demand for training in new participatory methods far exceeds the supply of good trainers. The strategic use of trainers and training opportunities therefore matters. Key factors include selecting participants for field workshops who are likely to be able to spread the participatory approaches and methods, and themselves become trainers later; inviting at least two from the same organization so that they can provide mutual support on their return; ensuring that sharing and critical self-awareness are built into participatory approaches from the start; and support and dissemination through producing and sending materials to targeted individuals. These materials can include slide packs, reports on applications of methods and on innovations; local networking; and notes on 'how-to-do-it' for methods of learning, rather than manuals and cookbooks which are liable to inhibit self-learning.

- *Policy and practice:* the history of agricultural policy shows a common pattern. Technical prescriptions are derived from controlled and uniform settings, and applied widely with little regard for diverse local needs and conditions. Differences in receiving environments and livelihoods then often make the technologies unworkable and unacceptable. Policies actively encourage dependency on external inputs, even when they are financially costly, environmentally damaging and economically inefficient. When technologies are rejected, policies shift to seeking success through the manipulation of social, economic and ecological environments and through enforcement. For sustainable agriculture to succeed, these mistakes must not be repeated. Instead, policy and practice need a new, enabling orientation. With this, conditions would be created for sustainable development based more on locally available resources and local skills and knowledge. Agricultural policies must focus in a more practical manner on enabling people and professionals to make the most of available social and biological resources.

Conclusions

The new agricultural professionalism places responsibility on the individual as well as on institutions. Each person can contribute to or constrain its spread. Each person can, through critical self-awareness and embracing error, learn and improve, so that the new professionalism grows and gets better.

The intention to adopt new values and practices are prerequisites for change, and cannot be assumed. But even when they exist, both institutions and individuals face difficulties. In institutions, standardization and speed stand out as recurrent dangers, pursued in the interests of wider and more rapid application. As Sumberg (1991) has observed:

It would appear absolutely essential to avoid the temptation of a rapid institutionalization of farmer-participatory research. It was this . . . that eventually limited the overall impact of farming systems research.

It would be ironic if approaches developed to deal with diversity and complexity became institutionalized in such a way that whatever positive contribution they might have been able to make is effectively marginalized.

For individuals, too, there are problems, especially for those trapped in conventional organizations. In outlining the new professionalism, we do not wish to discourage those for whom, in their current institutional context, there may seem so little room for manoeuvre that it is out of reach. There are many paths, and many small steps that can be taken towards it. Nor should the new professionalism be seen as an alternative, completely to replace the old. The old and the new have mutual strengths. For the new to succeed, both drive and restraint must be exercised so that its spread can be sustained and self-improving. Learning how to evolve and spread the new professionalism must itself be a slow and sensitive learning process.

From research to innovation: getting the most from interaction with NGOs

JOHN FARRINGTON and ANTHONY J. BEBBINGTON

Introduction

Public-sector research institutes in many developing countries need to break out of a prevailing narrow view of research which, whether on-station or on-farm, follows the conventional cycle of diagnosis, screening, testing, wider verification and dissemination. Greater benefits to users, and higher job satisfaction among researchers, will result if more attention is paid to inter-institutional linkage strategies in which researchers are given the mandate and skills to identify technologies suitable for local conditions from a wide range of sources and test them collaboratively with local organizations, reserving only the more intractable issues for specialized testing in a conventional research mode.

Drawing on a large body of new empirical material from Africa, Asia and South America (Farrington et al., 1993; Farrington and Lewis (eds), 1993; Wellard and Copestake (eds), 1993; Bebbington et al., (eds), 1993), this paper examines the strengths and weaknesses of both NGOs and public sector research and extension services in developing technologies for low-income farmers, for women and for the landless in difficult areas, and the scope for closer interaction between them.

This study draws attention in particular to the tension between those casting NGOs in predominantly 'service delivery' roles and those (including many of the more reflective NGOs themselves) who see NGOs' most valuable contribution in influencing the wider policies or strategies of development, in developing approaches towards livelihood enhancement for the poor which GOs might emulate in helping to identify clients' needs and generating 'demand pull' on government services to meet them and in the design and monitoring of projects, rather than merely in their implementation.

Features of the NGOs studied

Our concern is mainly with the stronger of the South-based NGOs that provide services either directly to the rural poor or to grassroots membership organizations. The path chosen through various criteria for selection of case study NGOs is indicated by the solid line in Figure 1. Most of the NGOs considered pursue livelihood enhancement in a participatory fashion and in the context of wider value-driven objectives, including group formation and conscientization. However, a wide range of NGO philosophies and approaches exists, including those which are somewhat 'top-down' and those which have become narrowly tied to government contracts for service delivery. There is evidence that approaches from across

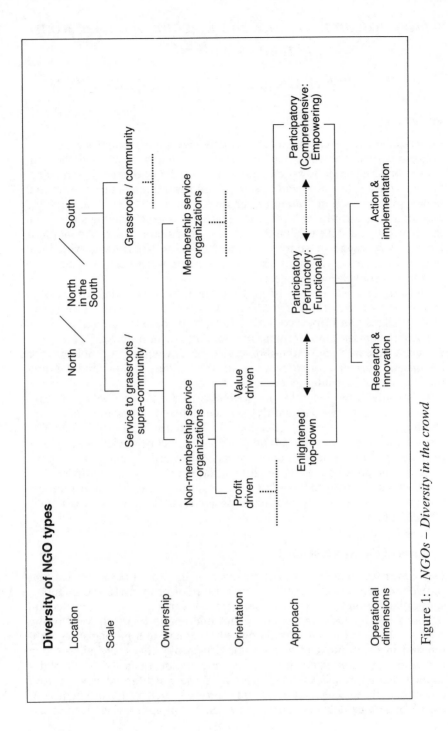

Figure 1: *NGOs – Diversity in the crowd*

the spectrum have succeeded in the limited objective of achieving technology adoption. Our particular interest in the more empowering approaches has been in their objective of setting up local institutions and mechanisms capable of sustaining processes of innovation – either within communities themselves, or through a capacity for 'demand-pull' on government services. In addition, the potential of these approaches, within and beyond the context of agriculture, for generating institutional pluralism and so strengthening (broadly-defined) democratic processes has not gone unnoticed (Clark, 1991).

The origins of NGOs vary widely, and are likely to have a strong bearing on the type and extent of potential NGO–GO collaboration. Some were formed in opposition to governments which discriminated against the rural poor. This opposition has covered a range of forms. For instance, Ghandian NGOs in India lie at the less confrontational end of the spectrum, in contrast with, say, those NGOs in the Philippines that have campaigned for land reform. Others arose as a reaction to government support for, or indifference to, prevailing patterns of corruption, patronage or authoritarianism.

Many NGOs were formed by left-leaning professionals, formerly employed in universities or in the public sector. Their intellectual calibre has generally been high, but they were often socially and ethnically distinct from the rural poor. In the early stages of their formation, almost all NGOs were characterized by small size, institutional flexibility, horizontal structure and short lines of communication. Many have found these characteristics conducive to a quick response to clients' needs and to changing circumstances and a work ethic conducive to generating sustainable processes and impacts, and so have sought to retain them well beyond the initial establishment period. But the smallness and the political origins and orientation of NGOs are also their 'Achilles' heel' since:

- NGO projects rarely address wider-scale structural factors that underlie rural poverty;
- NGOs have limited capacities for agricultural technology development and dissemination, and limited awareness of how to create effective demand-pull on government research services;
- The activities of different NGOs remain unco-ordinated, and information exchange is poor, especially among small NGOs where transaction costs are high.

These strengths and weaknesses of NGOs, and their implications for NGO–GO relations, are discussed in more detail below, and illustrated by examples from Africa, Asia and Latin America.

Successes and failures of NGO technology development

Public sector agricultural technology development is conventionally analysed by stage, i.e. from basic agricultural technology development through strategic, applied and adaptive, with some consideration of agricultural technology development-dissemination linkages. Application of this approach to NGOs would not be particularly illuminating, since practically all

NGO agricultural technology development is problem or 'issue'-based and NGOs tend to draw on several stages simultaneously in an 'action-oriented' mode.

Here we consider five main areas in which NGOs have been innovative and relatively successful:

Diagnostic and farming systems agricultural technology development methods

Conventional public sector approaches to agricultural technology development have difficulty in coping with the wide range of agroecological and socioeconomic conditions characteristic of the complex, diverse and risk-prone areas in which many of the rural poor live (Chambers *et al.*, 1989; Richards, 1985). In such areas, agricultural technology development must not merely be on-farm and farmer-managed, but participatory in order to draw on local knowledge and to meet farmers' needs, opportunities, constraints and aspirations. The approaches introduced in GOs have frequently been expensive and time consuming, and often not participatory (Biggs, 1989a). Some NGOs, on the other hand, have been innovative in developing more parsimonious approaches. For instance:

• In Kenya, the Diagnosis and Design methodology practised and diffused by ICRAF partly grew out of the development of methods by CARE and Mazingira in the early 1980s to elicit rapid farmer assessment of tree species (Buck, 1993);
• In Chile, NGOs were responsible for the elaboration of farming systems perspectives, and their subsequent teaching to other institutions (Aguirre and Namdar-Irani, 1992; Sotomayor, 1991);
• In India, MYRADA has been instrumental in developing participatory rapid appraisal methods and training for both other NGOs and government staff in their implementation (Fernandez and Mascarenhas, 1993).

NGOs have also introduced systems approaches to agricultural technology development which go beyond conventional farming systems research. First, several have used food systems perspectives. For instance,

• In Chile, AGRARIA is experimenting with means of commercializing small farmer grain, which a government department is now considering scaling up (Aguirre and Namdar-Irani, 1992);
• In Bangladesh, the Mennonite Central Committee conducted the varietal, processing and market research on which around 1000 ha of soya production by farmers is now based (Buckland and Graham, 1990);
• In the Gambia, production of sesame introduced by Catholic Relief Services at its peak reached 8000 ha owing in part to the simultaneous introduction of oil extraction technology (Gilbert, 1990).

NGOs have also been instrumental in introducing a social organizational and management dimension into the testing and subsequent adoption of certain technologies, which government services typically find difficult to introduce. For instance:

• In India, Action for World Solidarity and a consortium of GROs in Andhra Pradesh devised a strategy for integrated pest management of a caterpillar (*Amsacta* sp.) on castor together with government research institutes, and then helped to organize farmers to take certain action simultaneously in order to achieve maximum impact (Satish *et al.*, 1993);

- In the Gambia, and Ethiopia, NGOs have helped farmers to organize local informal seed production in ways designed to avoid undesirable cross-pollination (Henderson and Singh, 1990);
- In Bangladesh, NGOs have helped to organise landless labourers to acquire and operate 'lumpy' irrigation technology (Mustafa *et al.*, 1993), and have organized groups (mainly of women) to interact both among themselves and with government services in chicken and duck rearing (Khan *et al.*, 1993; Nahas, 1993).

Innovations in technologies and management practices

While funding constraints make long-term agricultural technology development difficult for NGOs, several have done work which has had far-reaching implications. For instance:

- In India, the Bharatiya Agro-Industries Foundation pioneered research into frozen semen technology in India, and, through its 500 field programmes in six states, has been responsible for producing around 10 per cent of the country's cross-bred dairy herd;
- Similarly, the Southern Mindanao Baptist Rural Life Centre (Philippines) has identified integrated methods of managing hill slopes using Sloping Agricultural Land Technologies (Watson and Laquihon, 1993).

Most NGO research efforts are, however, at the adaptive end of the spectrum. For instance:

- In India, PRADAN has scaled down technologies developed by government institutes for mushroom and raw silk production, and for leather processing and, in the case of the latter, has devised integrated schemes of credit and marketing (Vasimalai, 1993);
- Under the Farmer Innovation and Technology Testing programme in the Gambia, eight NGOs collaborated with the Department of Agricultural Research in 1989 for on-farm testing and feedback on a number of new crop varieties (Gilbert, 1990);
- In East and Southern Africa, NGOs have been testing new crop varieties in Zambia (Copestake, 1990) and in Zimbabwe (Ndiweni *et al.*, 1991), and have been adapting tree management practices in Zimbabwe (Ndiweni *et al.*, 1991) and Kenya (Mung'ala and Arum, 1991).

Dissemination methods

In general NGOs have sought to develop participatory dissemination methods. For instance:

- In Thailand, the Appropriate Technology Association developed farmer-to-farmer methods of disseminating rice-fish farming technologies which have subsequently been adapted by the Department of Agriculture (Sollows *et al.*, 1991);

• In Ecuador, CESA has developed systems for farmer-managed seed multiplication and distribution (CESA, 1991).

Training activities and methods

A number of NGOs train both members of other NGOs and of GOs in participatory methods, (Fernandez and Mascarenhas, 1993; Chakraborty *et al.*, 1993; Berdegué, 1990). A recently emerging role for NGOs is that of intermediary. For instance:

• In Gujarat, India, the Aga Khan Rural Support Project (AKRSP) identi-fied village training needs through discussions with farmer groups (Shah, Parts II and III). Government staff were brought in to observe, particip-ate in and, finally, adopt the methodology;
• In a different context, the International Institute for Rural Reconstruc-tion in the Philippines brought together resource people from NGOs and GOs at a one-week workshop, the objective of which was to produce a completed 'Agroforestry Resources Training Manual'. The manual is now widely used (Gonsalves and Miclat-Teves, 1993).

Promoting farmer organizations

For many NGOs, to strengthen participation means to work in strengthen-ing peasant organizations and in popular education, enhancing the rural poor's capacities for self-management and negotiation with government, external institutions and dominant interest groups (Farrington and Beb-bington, 1991).

NGOs have therefore emphasized project methodologies and actions that contribute to strengthening the co-ordination among individual pro-ducers, and subsequently among communities. Seed and input distri-bution systems, small-scale irrigation and work with farmer groups in on-farm trials have thus become priority areas of action. In many cases such a combination of productive and organizational initiatives can increase the impact of the project and strengthen the organization simultaneously (Uphoff; Shah, Part III). The ultimate aim is to establish financially and administratively self-sustaining organizations, and, although NGOs' con-tributions to the formation of farmer organizations have not always matched their rhetoric, most experience in linking agricultural develop-ment projects with organizational strengthening has been gained in the NGO sector.

The abilities and experiences of NGOs in each of these areas suggest contributions NGOs could make to wider public sector programmes. But it is important to recognize that NGOs also suffer from a variety of limita-tions. Careful examination of the above examples reveals numerous NGO weaknesses:

• Their small size and limited resources limit NGO activity to the applied end of the agricultural technology development spectrum;

208

- Funding patterns tend to be short-term and pressure from funding agencies is towards 'action' and 'results', thus hampering work on issues requiring long-term R&D;
- Small size, combined with poor co-ordination among NGOs, makes it difficult for effective two-way links to be established between them and government research services.

Potential public sector contributions to enhance NGO effectiveness and set the context for NGO-GO links

The weaknesses outlined above suggest three general ways in which government initiatives could enhance NGO effectiveness:

Public sector commitment towards the needs of the rural poor

Whilst NGOs may grow in size and number to fill 'gaps' left by government, they will not be able to substitute for *all* the services that might normally be expected from government in *all* of the areas. Their efforts are likely to be more focused and defective where government makes a clear policy commitment to remove economic distortions against the rural sector and provides the physical infrastructure (roads; telecommunications) and human capital formation (de Janvry *et al.*, 1989) which NGOs cannot provide in more than a piecemeal fashion. Policies of this kind are also a prerequisite to the establishment of inter-institutional links between NGOs and GOs.

Easing access to quality resources and information controlled by the public sector

NGOs often express the need to access the skills, facilities, genetic material and specialist knowledge of government services and, also, to have an opportunity to influence government policies and strategies at the design stage. Large NGOs acting in consortium have occasionally persuaded government to cater to their needs (e.g. Sethna and Shah, 1993), but simply to garner information on government plans, let alone influence them, is generally beyond the resources of smaller NGOs. To address such obstacles, NGO desks have been created in some Philippine line departments in order to elicit NGOs' views on draft plans and to cater to NGO enquiries (Ganapin, 1993). At the opposite extreme, the views of the rural poor – no matter how well articulated by NGOs – are unlikely to be heard by governments whose resource allocation decisions are driven by crisis management or patronage (Healey and Robinson, 1992).

Fostering greater grassroots influence over NGOs

A recurrent and widely voiced criticism is that NGOs' rhetoric on participation exceeds reality. NGOs are self-appointed, rather than elected bodies, and control institutional resources from within.

The 'non-representativeness' of NGOs offers those governments – particularly the nominally democratic – the excuse of not working with any whose views they find uncomfortable. NGOs can attempt to safeguard against this in two ways: first, by stimulating transparent participation by the rural poor in decisions on strategy and resource-allocation; second, by instituting more thorough-going processes of internal monitoring and evaluation, involving in-depth consultation with their clients.

Governments also have a contribution to make here: they might best enhance NGO accountability to the rural poor indirectly, particularly by supporting broad-based educational programmes in rural areas – perhaps the most important single factor facilitating increased assertiveness and forms of self-organization among the rural poor.

Obstacles to closer links, within and beyond the public sector

The current NARS setting

Attention to NGOs as potential actors in national agricultural research and extension systems (NARSs) is timely in view of:

- Increasing acceptance that public sector research is only one of the multiple sources of innovation that generate technologies or management practices used by farmers. Others include farmers' own experimentation (often incorporating ideas and materials obtained through personal contacts), the private commercial sector, special projects (often donor-funded) of various kinds and NGOs (Biggs, 1989b);
- Increasing recognition that GOs in many countries face intractable problems in the organization and management of agricultural research, such as highly centralized structures and rigid budgeting. Consequently, field work and regular contacts with farmers are disrupted; equipment and facilities are under-maintained; remuneration is inadequate to retain the more capable staff; and little scope exists for devising career structures and reward systems to encourage researchers' responsiveness to clients' needs (Pretty and Chambers, Part III);
- The low motivation and performance resulting from these difficulties mean that research is poorly prioritized, weakly monitored and inadequately linked to clients' needs (Merrill-Sands and Kaimowitz, 1990).

In order to counteract some of these weaknesses, GO scientists should be allocating a large part of their time to the management of links with field-based agencies (such as NGOs) in order to identify farmers' requirements, field test candidate technologies locally and obtain feedback and with a multiplicity of development agencies (including the private commercial sector, international public sector and GOs in neighbouring countries) in order to draw down from them technologies and ideas likely to be locally relevant (Gilbert and Matlon, 1992). In what follows, we explore the prospects of developing such links more fully.

Wider obstacles

Even where the broad conditions for NGOs and GOs to work together are in place – i.e. broader relations between NGOs and the State are non-antagonistic, and GOs and NGOs share a common vision of the future of the rural poor, and of strategies necessary to achieve that future – several potential barriers to closer links remain to be overcome, including:

- The levels of resources currently being channelled into NGOs, their strong grassroots contacts and the high moral ground they occupy may all be sources of friction between GOs and NGOs. GOs are often aggrieved by NGO 'headhunting' of their staff. Rates of staff attrition are so high in some that they threaten their very existence;
- Formal links between NGOs and GOs need to grow out of long-standing informal contacts. Each side has been less aware – and often suspicious – of the other's motives and capabilities where such informal contact is lacking;
- Inadequate exchange of information and coordination among NGOs themselves. These lead to duplication of effort (and of failures – Kohl, 1991), and to competition among them for clients. Whilst NGO *information* networks abound, their record of setting up *co-ordinating* mechanisms beyond areas of immediate concern (in specific campaigns) is poor. National NGO apex organizations tend to be weak and too distant from field issues to have credible impact.

What can NGOs, research services and funding agencies do?

In many countries the potential exists for mutually beneficial links between NGOs and public sector research and extension services. However, two forewarnings are essential: first, the prospects will vary widely among countries, according to the wider context of NGO-State relations and according to how far NGOs and Government share a common view of the future of the rural poor, and of strategies for achieving that future. Second, within countries there is a wide diversity of NGO types, and their relations with government will lie along a spectrum from outright hostility to willing collaboration. Linkages can be promoted by the following actions:

- Efforts by GOs to keep a small percentage of their budgets 'unallocated' to allow for rapid response to NGO requests as they arise. Needs and opportunities for potentially productive interaction often occur unexpectedly: they cannot always be held over to the next financial year. Alternatively, a percentage of staff time might be kept unallocated, and NGOs use their resources to contract in GO staff (e.g. Hanvey *et al.*, 1992);
- GO and NGO staff can jointly participate in training courses (ideally led by a joint team) in the 'learning-by-doing', 'action-oriented' methods favoured by NGOs such as participatory rural appraisal. The relevance of these methods to individual GO staff will vary, but their capacity to consolidate farmer-oriented perspectives is important;
- Efforts need to be made by NGOs to interact more fully with each other. Interaction may be based on technologies, agriculture sub-sectors or geographical areas. It may begin with exchanges of information and joint meetings, perhaps extending in some cases to fully collaborative projects. Most countries are characterized by a large number of NGOs of

varying size, and, for certain tasks (e.g. dissemination and obtaining feedback) GOs may find it easier to work through effective NGO networks. Continuing attention is therefore needed to the difficult problem of area-based, or thematically-based co-ordinating mechanisms. However, for other tasks (e.g. identification of local opportunities and constraints requiring research) GOs' efforts will have to be location-specific so that interaction with individual NGOs and farmers will be more appropriate;

- Collaborative field trials quickly allow each side to work out in what tasks it will be most cost effective. Existing cases in which respective GO and NGO roles have been worked out in field testing and feedback include those in Ecuador (Cardoso et al., 1991), and the Bolivian lowlands (Thieve et al., 1988), but examples are few and progress is not always smooth, as the Gambia's Farmer Innovation and Technology Testing programme indicates (Gilbert, 1990; Cromwell and Wiggins, 1993);
- Efforts have been made by GOs to institutionalize the presence not only of NGOs, but of other 'intermediate users' of GO technology, such as the private commercial sector and development projects of various kinds, in annual planning meetings and other fora (Botanic, 1991; Vales, 1991);
- An area in which GOs can gain advantage from NGOs' work – but only if they liaise cross-sectoral – lies in NGOs' capacity to address issues beyond the farm-gate. Some, for instance, have been concerned with processing and marketing (Buckland and Graham, 1990; Aguirre and Namdar-Irani, 1992). Others have been concerned with the interaction between farming and wider resource management issues, often involving common property resources such as trees (Sethna and Shah, 1993) or water (Mustafa et al., 1993).

The conclusion that progress towards realizing the potential of strengthened NGO-GO links is likely to require careful effort on both sides over a long period is unexceptional. It would, after all, be surprising if the institutions – and interactions among them – necessary to respond in detail to the technological and management needs of highly diverse farming systems were themselves anything other than complex. Strong potential for promoting progress in this area lies with funding agencies. Some of the more imaginative, but small-scale, financing agencies (e.g. Ford Foundation; IDRC) have supported NGO–GO interaction in ways which allow for the diversity of NGOs, recognize their potential as 'brokers' between farmers and research services and do so in ways sensitive to NGOs' fears of being 'co-opted' into government programmes. The funding agenda of some of the larger donors, on the other hand, remains dominated by perceptions that NGOs should occupy service delivery roles, effectively substituting for activities and interventions that conventionally lie in the domain of government. Whilst some NGOs may feel comfortable with this, many of the more innovative ones will not.

Funding for closer linkages, from whatever source, will have to be tailored to the diverse qualities that NGOs bring to analysis of small farmers' conditions, and to the development and dissemination of technologies, if valuable potential is not to be lost.

Conclusions

Providing that NGOs and the State share a common view on the future of the rural poor, and on strategies to realise that future, each side can strengthen the other through a series of functional complementarities, each of which is important in its own right. It is concluded, however, that for public sector organizations, the most significant advantages to be gained from close interaction with NGOs lie in broader shifts of three kinds:

- First, enhanced client-orientation, and an awareness that users' needs can best be served by 'problem' or 'issue'-oriented approaches to technology development and dissemination;
- Second, a recognition that a multiplicity of agencies and individuals innovate and that a valid and increasingly necessary role for researchers is to stimulate and facilitate such innovation, possibly at the expense of reducing some on-farm or on-station research. This would make researchers effective 'brokers', capable of identifying needs for technological change, of efficiently screening available sources for appropriate ideas, of liaising with a wide range of institutions in testing these ideas and obtaining feedback (Gilbert and Matlon, 1992);
- Third, a series of changes to institutional mandates, management procedures and reward systems to facilitate the introduction and consolidation of wider perspectives of this kind.

Viewed in this context, whilst macro-economic pressures to reduce the size of the public sector are bound to remain threatening, they might also, if handled skilfully, mark the beginnings of an opportunity for GOs to intensify dialogue with NGOs in order to explore new ways of enhancing the effectiveness of their own work.

Local organization for supporting people-based agricultural research and extension: lessons from Gal Oya, Sri Lanka

NORMAN UPHOFF

The Gal Oya case

In 1980, the Agrarian Research and Training Institute (ARTI) in Sri Lanka, with assistance from the Cornell Rural Development Committee, began working with the Irrigation Department in the Gal Oya irrigation scheme with small-holder farmers (average holding 0.75 hectares). This was, at the time, the largest and perhaps the most run-down scheme in the country. The Irrigation Department's senior deputy director for water management said that 'if we can make progress in Gal Oya, we can make progress anywhere in Sri Lanka.' The district's senior administrator tried to encourage the young community organisers to introduce water-user associations by saying that if they could get even 10 or 15 of the farmers to work together, this would be an accomplishment. The assignment was to organize 10 to 15 *thousand* farmers.

The programme started in an extremely water-short season, when the main reservoir was only one-quarter full. The organizers, who had been recruited, trained and deployed by ARTI to live and work in the communities, wanted to do whatever they could to improve water management under the circumstances. The programme proceeded with the proviso that all plans must be the farmers' own, with nothing imposed from outside.

Over the next four years, some dramatic and lasting changes were made in the efficiency and equity of water use in Gal Oya. In aggregate terms, water use in the wet and dry seasons was reduced by about half. While some of this improvement in water use efficiency can be credited to physical rehabilitation of the system, most was achieved through farmers' self-help co-operative efforts within the first two years, before most of the system had been physically renovated. Reinforcing the quantitative improvements were qualitative ones. For instance, the farmer chairman for one of the most water-constrained subsystems, which included both Sinhalese and Tamil households (the two principal ethnic groups), stated that they used to have murders over water in his area, but now, by working together through their farmer organizations, they rarely had conflicts any more.

The results of this programme often seemed too good to be true, but the farmer associations have maintained themselves and have even progressed institutionally, despite many difficulties, including ethnic conflict, budget cutbacks, massive turnovers and attrition in the cadre of organizers, bureaucratic interference and unkept promises (Uphoff, 1992b). The most salient aspects of the strategy used in Gal Oya, inductively formulated, for establishing farmer organizations are described below. Some of these elements are relevant for building local organizational capacities elsewhere in order to bolster participatory agricultural research and extension programmes.

Means for strengthening local organization for agricultural development

Use of catalysts

Ideally, when seeking farmer participation in agricultural research and extension efforts, one can deal with rural people who are already organized and used to working together. Where rural people are not organized or not able to communicate or act through some acknowledged collective channels, however, creation of such channels can be stimulated and nurtured by 'catalysts' who have been appropriately recruited, trained and deployed. These are variously called organizers, animators, promoters, or motivators.

Catalysts are different from extension agents, who take a known technology to rural communities and enlist their co-operation. Along with promoting new structural arrangements, catalysts seek to change prevailing psychological and normative orientations, forge new social relations and encourage new ways of thinking and evaluating, as part of the process of organizational development.

Starting with informal organization

After reviewing prior experience with farmer organizations in Sri Lanka, it was concluded that the usual approach to establishing rural organizations – calling a meeting, passing a constitution, electing officers, etc. – did not yield sustainable local capabilities. Therefore, rather than proceed in a 'supply-side' manner, it was decided to try a 'demand-led' approach.

Organizers worked with farmers first individually and then in small groups, eventually bringing together all the farmers who cultivated along a single field channel (10 to 20). Groups began meeting on an informal basis, focusing on problem identification and solutions. Ad hoc committees and acting representatives took initiatives on behalf of the group to carry out actions agreed by consensus. When the group felt a need to have an organization, officers were chosen and the group would be recognized externally. This sequence – work first and organize later – brought forth better (more tested and more altruistic) leadership and built more solid support among members.

Whether farmer organizations should *remain* informal is a different matter. The programme tried to help groups evolve from informal to formal status, at their own pace. A related question is whether farmer organizations should have legal status and powers. Farmers will at some point demand this if they lack it. But legal standing and authority should not be conferred until it is sought and in some way 'earned', not simply given. Formal authority with legal backing is more easily abused than social authority which grows out of consensus and mutual obligations. Organizations established by legislation or legal instruments are likely to be and remain hollow shells, belonging more to the agency that created them than to their members.

Mobilizing a new kind of leadership

While 'leadership' is essential for this process to succeed, 'leaders', at least of the usual type, are often adverse influences. In our programme, the term widely used by FAO and government agencies, farmer-leader (FL), was replaced by the more democratic one, farmer-representative (FR). The latter is understood to be more accountable to the rural community than is the former, in part because representatives can and should be rotated. It is difficult for a 'leader' to be succeeded by another, since this takes away exalted status. Outsiders can strike deals with 'leaders', but 'representatives' are expected to facilitate reaching agreements that everyone can live with.

215

Two strategies were developed in the Gal Oya programme to encourage the emergence of leadership that was accountable and altruistic:

- FRs were chosen by their groups not by election but by consensus. This process can be manipulated by powerful local leaders and, in some situations, may not work. But when the representative must be acceptable to *all* members, factional leaders are less likely to come forward. Because groups had started working informally, everyone knew who within their group was serious about improving irrigation performance. Those who had taken the lead in giving generous, effective, voluntary leadership were the obvious choices.

  Once chosen, FRs felt accountable to every member because all had assented to their selection. Farmer-representatives had no reason to discriminate against any member since all had openly supported them. At the same time, all members felt some obligation to comply with their FRs' requests because all had publicly consented to these persons being given responsibility to improve irrigation.

- The terms of reference for the FR role were prepared not by the programme but by each group before it selected someone for this role. The organizer working with the group would get its members to spend some time discussing what they expected from a farmer-representative.

  Members articulated very high expectations: the FR should have enough time for the job, listen well, not be partisan, not lose his/her temper, not get drunk, etc. Simply stating these criteria, which could be rejected if there was no consensus on them, implicitly narrowed the pool of potential representatives to those who best satisfied the desired characteristics. Without pointing a critical finger at anyone, persons who did not meet these criteria would be passed over.

  A further consequence was to inform whoever was chosen by consensus about what the group expected. The selection process was thus a kind of non-formal training programme for representatives, made all the more effective because it was given by and among peers. Since FRs were not paid, there was no strong financial incentive to occupy this position. This created a certain moral obligation for members to co-operate, since FRs were not doing their job for personal benefit. Representatives reported that their authority (which was *de facto*) was enhanced by their voluntary status.

Within four years the Gal Oya programme covered a 25,000-acre area and involved almost 13,000 farmers. Representatives had no formal or legal authority, just the support and co-operation of district officials. The groups' performance, however, generated great informal, and so social, authority. At some point, once the utility and legitimacy of these groups and the role of farmer-representatives had been established in people's minds, legal recognition added further to their effectiveness.

Importance of small groups at the base, grouped into a federation

This process of leadership selection was possible because of the structure established, which evolved inductively with farmers. The process was quite

216

literally 'bottom-up', starting at the field channel level. Each field channel would be helped to organize itself, first informally, then more formally, each with its own representative chosen by consensus. Having base-level groups of 10–20 members, meant that everyone knew each other. This has been found to be important for effective rural organization (Coward, 1977, 1980; Esman and Uphoff, 1984; Uphoff, 1986; Bebbington, Part III.) It is possible to create and maintain a greater sense of solidarity and mutual responsibility in small groups, in part because 'free riding' is then more difficult.

Studies of rural development experience have found that more successful efforts correlate with multi-tiered patterns of rural organization. These have small base-level groups which give the benefits of solidarity and are then aggregated or federated within higher-level associations that offer the benefits of scale (Esman and Uphoff, 1983).

At Gal Oya, field channel representatives came together to form a Distributary Channel Organisation covering all the field channel areas served by the distributary channel. This organization in turn sent farmer-representatives to an Area Council which met periodically. The councils sent a few representatives each to sit with district-level officials on a Project Management Committee. Communication upwards and downwards, from the field to the project level, was thereby provided for. If lower-level organizations lagged in their performance, they could be encouraged by higher bodies, and *vice versa*. Today, building on the Gal Oya experience, there are Project Management Committees for all major irrigation schemes. Farmer-representatives constitute a majority on these committees, which now have a farmer chairperson as a matter of government policy.

One benefit of such a structure was to reinforce the selection of desirable leadership. The system of indirect representation initially appeared to be less democratic than direct election of representatives at all levels. But with all representatives coming 'from below' and chosen by their peers, more genuine farmers got into responsible positions, not merchants, school principals and others who could have infiltrated the programme at higher levels if there had been a system of direct election. Although the time that farmer-representatives had to devote to their responsibilities was substantial, many fine people were willing to accept this role if asked to do so by their peers, and if the task was rotated.

Adoption of a problem-solving approach

The programme was conceived and carried out in a 'learning process' mode (Korten 1980). During programme implementation, the need to follow a regular process of identifying critical problems and dealing with them on a systematic basis was stressed. This was never done as thoroughly or as consistently as hoped, but it resulted in a continuing orientation towards action. The farmer groups, the organizers and our management group at ARTI were encouraged to work, as explicitly as they had time for, through the following six steps:

(1) Identify several priority *problems* to be dealt with, either existing or anticipated; attention is directed to those problems that are judged to be both important for programmatic progress and solvable or ameliorable;

(2) Gather appropriate and adequate *information* concerning each of the priority problems and possible courses of action to deal with each;

(3) Formulate *strategies* for solving each priority problem and decide on which are the most promising;

(4) Devise *plans* for implementing each strategy, assigning responsibility for who does what, when, how, etc.;

(5) Undertake plan *implementation* as best the group and its members can;

(6) Conduct periodic *evaluation* of the progress made with each problem.

Once a problem is solved or has solved itself, it can be taken off the list and a new one added. Otherwise, if the problem persists, the group should retrace its steps. First, it may need to assess whether the plan was implemented; if not, this should be done (repeat 5). Then, if the plan did not succeed, a new one should be devised (repeat 4). Next, if the strategy in retrospect seems faulty, it should be reformulated (repeat 3). Finally, if the information base was inadequate, it should be improved (repeat 2). Alternatively, if the problem has changed or the situation was not well enough understood, the group should engage in renewed problem identification and prioritization (repeat 1).

This process was supplemented by encouraging organisers, farmers, officials, administrators and supervisors within the programme to maintain an attitude of self-criticism and to 'embrace error' (Korten, 1980). Catalysts were told that there is no disgrace in making mistakes, only in *not* identifying them, learning from them and avoiding repeating them. This is critically important, as a philosophy and as an operational principle, for effective local organization.

Starting with one or a few important tasks, but expanding as members wish

It is a truism that people sustain their participation only in things which they perceive benefit them. The corollary of this is that organizations should undertake only one or a few activities of direct and tangible benefit. This has led to a recommendation that organizations be and remain single-functional (e.g. Tendler, 1976). However, a quantitative analysis of local organizations' performance with a sample of 150 cases from across the Third World (Esman and Uphoff, 1984) found the relationship between the overall calibre of performance and the number of functions performed was the opposite of what was predicted (i.e. the correlation was positive rather than negative, though not very high). This reflects the 'natural history' of organizations. Those undertaking many tasks and doing them poorly cease to function, while organizations effectively performing single tasks are likely to take on more responsibilities as they gain experience and competence.

As shown in Gal Oya, organizations do best if they start with a focus on something very important to members, such as improving water management. This builds membership attachment to the organization, as well as its

218

managerial capability. As the organization becomes stronger, it can and should evolve, taking on more functions, but only those which members want it to perform. It was found that farmer organizations, once established, used their capabilities to deal with many other needs: crop protection, production credit, bulk input purchases, savings schemes, mortgage release, employment generation, settlement of domestic disputes, land consolidation, reducing drunkenness, etc.

Both those who advocate a narrow focus of activity and those who see merit in multi-functional organization are, or can be, correct if the time dimension is considered. It is good to start with a narrow focus, but supporting organizations should be prepared to assist with multiple tasks when and as members see a need for moving beyond their initial concentration of effort. Programmes supporting local organizations engaged in agricultural research and/or extension should be prepared to work with those groups in matters like domestic water supply, replacing lax schoolteachers or reassessing taxes.

The principle is that the organizations belong to their members, not to the sponsoring programme. Prudent advice may be given, about not expanding too rapidly, or not undertaking tasks in which the group seems likely to fail. Such suggestions can be offered in a collegial way, with decisions left to the groups themselves, since they are the ones who will have to live with the consequences, for better or for worse. It should be anticipated that the organizational capacities being created will not be static and should evolve according to the needs, wishes and competencies of the members. While there is now often appreciation that sustainable development should be community-based, it should also be 'community-paced' to use the words of Dr Joe Riverson, director of the World Vision NGO in Ghana.

Provision for horizontal diffusion of innovation

As farmer organizations get involved in agricultural research and extension and in other means for improving their situation, it is important that horizontal, farmer-to-farmer channels of communication and learning be established. Visits of farmer-representatives between irrigation systems in Sri Lanka proved very beneficial, getting away from the otherwise 'vertical' orientation of communication and learning.

Attention to normative dimensions

In programme design, there is much attention given to structures and processes but little to norms. Indeed, the latter are regarded often as something to be avoided by professionals, as something outside the scope of development planning. Experience with establishing and maintaining farmer organizations in Sri Lanka, on the other hand, showed the importance of getting people to move away from predominantly selfish, individual and material orientations (though these cannot be and need not be entirely eliminated) and of reinforcing more generous and co-operative orientations to make them the dominant ones (Uphoff, 1992a).

Getting rural people to take more responsibility for agricultural experimentation and improvement is often more dependent on having officials – extension agents, bank staff, research technicians, irrigation engineers and others – accept more interactive and accountable relationships with rural people than on persuading farmers to participate. The latter decisions are greatly influenced by farmers' perceptions of how willing and able bureaucrats and technocrats are to listen to and appreciate what less educated and lower-status people have to offer.

In Gal Oya, having discovered the importance of getting engineers and officials to change their thinking and behaviour toward farmers, it became apparent that this was not simply a precondition for farmers to become involved. Rather it is part of a process for increasing participation in rural development. Bureaucratic reorientation is best promoted by demonstrations of farmers' knowledge and capability, winning respect for farmers from their social 'betters'. An iterative process was observed in Gal Oya, where displays of initiative and intelligence by farmers gained some respect from officials, and this in turn encouraged farmers to show more capability, which again increased the respect accorded them by officials (Uphoff, 1992a).

These are some of the elements and methods for building a local organizational base under people-centred agricultural research and extension efforts. Rural people need to become themselves more empowered, with accountable leadership and able to deal collectively with persons from outside their communities, if we are to have effective and equitable farmer-extensionist-researcher partnerships.

Farmers' federations and food systems: organizations for enhancing rural livelihoods

ANTHONY J. BEBBINGTON

Federations and the farm: the limits of farmer-to-farmer extension

Responding to the challenges of enhancing rural livelihoods is beyond the capacities of most formal research and extension organizations as they are currently organized, as their focus is on production technology and 'messages'. In contrast, some farmers' federations concentrate on processing technologies, local institutional development and skill formation. The experiences of farmers' federations in Andean America suggest a range of lessons regarding research and extension and local organizations.

In the central province of Chimborazo in the highlands of Ecuador a long history of everyday resistance on feudal estates spilled over into a more strategic and organized struggle for land in the 1950s and 1960s. One of the fruits of this peasant activity has been the steady formation of indigenous people's (Indian) farmer federations, of which there are now over thirty in the province.

These federations link together base organizations, generally at a parish or county level, uniting up to forty organizations. Much of their activity has revolved around literacy training, in which issues of social and cultural rights and the revalidation of ethnic identities were addressed as part of educational programmes. Much effort was expended in strengthening the internal management and negotiating capacities of base organizations, by forming leaders and providing basic training in land and community legislation, accounting and administration. In this they generally worked with the support of the local church and NGOs.

This politico-cultural action was combined with attempts to negotiate better public services for communities. Some such negotiation was direct with the state: the federations essentially absorbing administrative costs and facilitating member community access to public resources. Over time, federations began to negotiate funds, and began to deliver services to their members on the federations' own account (Bebbington, 1992). Agricultural development projects grounded in farmer-to-farmer extension activities were central to these project activities. These constitute the federations' own attempt to identify a regional resource management strategy, and had to respond to a situation of demographic increase on fragile sloping lands ranging from 3200 metres to over 4000 metres above sea level. Agriculture on these slopes is rainfed, with periods of summer drought; climatic risks are high and topsoils are easily disturbed.

Although some federations initially aimed to promote native technologies, the increasing inability of traditional practices to respond to heightened pressures on production in this environment, led federations to choose to promote knowledge about modern agricultural technologies among their members (new varieties, fertilizers, pesticides). The reasoning behind this strategy was largely that out-migration is the principal cause of cultural erosion and weakened social ties in communities, and that therefore the main concern of local R & E intervention ought to be to reduce migration by increasing farm incomes. The federations provided technical assistance and subsidized inputs to members, largely following the administrative models of public sector rural development and agricultural extension programmes. Their coverage and distribution of inputs was impressive in comparison with formal R & E services. Federations have thus moved towards the incorporation of modern technologies, the technologies of the 'cultural other' (as opposed to indigenous technologies), as part of a programme aimed at sustaining other intrinsically Indian practices (Bebbington, 1992).

Yet the strategy appears to have been economically and ecologically unsustainable. With currency devaluations, the cost of agrochemicals at the farm gate has risen dramatically. At the same time, in this particularly eroded environment, soil loss on unterraced slopes means the returns from the use of fertilizers have fallen, and will continue to do so until such erosion problems are addressed. Finally, farm units are very small, and for

221

most families yield increases from applying fertilizers do not generate sufficient income to reverse migration pressures. Federations, and farmers, are thus faced with a situation in which neither traditional nor agrochemical technologies provide a viable basis for local livelihood strategies.

This in turn has implications for the organizational sustainability of the federations as vehicles for local R & E. Initially, the delivery of subsidized inputs and free technical assistance enhanced the legitimacy of the federations among their members. Over time, however, it became apparent that the income impact of this assistance at a family level was negligible: most federations could not attend the needs of all families, and service delivery was often concentrated among favoured communities. With member communities showing decreasing interest in the federations, the federations weakened. At the same time, the federations are unable to continue funding the strategy of delivering subsidies to their members, which makes their *raison d'être* seem increasingly tenuous.

These weaknesses have led to some splintering within the popular organizations in this region of the highlands. Member organizations of the federations break away to negotiate their own projects. This loss of interest undermines the co-ordination of activities among local groups. Obviously, this weakens the possibility of co-ordinated participation of Indian populations in regional and agricultural development strategies. For these federations to be a vehicle of locally managed agricultural research and extension they will need to respond to a range of economic, as well as institutional challenges.

Federations and food systems

The challenge to Chimborazo's federations is, in some respects, no different to that of formal research and extension services. They too have had little success in making significant impacts on rural livelihoods; they too are financially dependent on other paymasters; and their legitimacy is questioned, far more so, at the grassroots.

In responding to this challenge, they have much to learn from other federations who have moved further along the food system into processing and marketing activities. As a consequence, they have begun to institutionalize vertical linkages *within* the food system in two senses:

- *Vertical economic linkages*: linking farm production to marketing and processing activities within the region, and indeed to markets outside the region;
- *Vertical technology development linkages*: linking research and extension activities, and farmers' own choice and adaptation of technical practices, to information on the demands and nature of final product markets.

As a consequence of these activities the federations have assumed critical roles in local livelihood development, and in integrating local and non-local knowledge and information systems. At a more basic level, they have also generated income and jobs, two of the criteria of any technology development institution.

Lessons from the federations

The successes of some farmers' federations in improving family income, in helping introduce economically significant technological innovations and in sustaining their para-technician extension system have doubtless been due to a series of especially favourable circumstances. Among these are:

- Occupation of agroecological zones that fortuitously favour the production of high value goods for niche markets;
- Geographic isolation reducing both the intensity of competition from other traders and the likelihood of commercial capital taking over the processing activities;
- Sustained donor and technical support from other institutions.

It is not my intention to imply that such experiences are easily replicable across the Andes (or elsewhere). Nonetheless, the experiences of farmer federations suggest a range of lessons, or points for reflection, regarding research and extension practices.

Implications for R & E and farmers' federations

Research and extension

- An R & E system needs to make a difference, and generally an economic difference, in order to gain legitimacy with farmers;
- In order to make a difference, R & E systems will benefit from taking non-agricultural or off-farm income sources into consideration. This not only opens the possibility of generating rural incomes, but in some cases, new jobs;
- It is highly questionable whether agriculture is the place to start if one is to address the felt needs of the rural poor. In very impoverished areas, extension programmes seem little more than means of distributing small subsidies to farmers. They become social welfare programmes with little impact;
- Federations have shown particular concern to combine R & E with general educational activities at the grassroots, reflecting a belief that the two ought to be more closely linked (and results suggest some support for this idea);
- A food systems perspective, bringing on- and off-farm elements of rural livelihoods under the same strategy, and linking production, R & E, processing and marketing seems far more likely to meet these challenges. This involves decentralization and providing local institutions with support to develop their capacity to 'draw down' resources as needed;
- A food systems perspective can link R & E with poverty alleviation and regional development, but any poverty alleviation programme must be based on the retention of regional surplus and promotion of greater demand for rural labour.

Farmers' federations:

- When given financial and training support, federations can establish formalized farmer-to-farmer extension and give as much, and often more support than do public sector services. However, they are not intrinsically any more able to achieve a significant impact on rural poverty than are state services;

- Federations can internalize a food systems approach, make non-local, market and technical, information available to farmers and extensionists, and adapt extension advice and farmer practice to the demands of richer markets;
- Federations are mechanisms that, when strong, can draw down resources in ways individual farmers would not be able to do;
- Federations are institutional mechanisms that favour the retention of regional surplus and its reinvestment in activities (such as R & E, job creation) that have a broad impact, benefitting significant numbers of poor people;
- The strength of federations is directly related to their human capital resources, *and* to the social distribution of these resources. They can only remain strong if their members receive ample administrative and technical training and support.

Institutional biases: who sets the research and extension agenda in Amazonia?

JORGE UQUILLAS

Multiple actors, multiple interests

In Ecuador, the research and extension agenda is set from above, responding to political considerations and the economic interests of pressure groups. In the Ecuadorian Amazon these economic and political contests are particularly intense. This paper identifies the range of interest groups involved, from the state to local-level, contrasting the different perceptions of agricultural development. Participatory approaches to agricultural development must take cognizance of the political dynamics of different interest groups and ensure that local voices are heard. This is a difficult task, requiring local-level institutional capacity strengthening leading to political leverage at a national level.

Institutional biases

Research and extension agendas in the Ecuadorian Amazon are influenced by a range of institutional actors. Effecting shifts from a 'top-down' approach to agricultural development that concentrates on high-input and commercial agriculture means tackling the institutional biases of the more powerful groups. Currently, such groups actively undermine rural people's knowledge and indigenous people's interests. Understanding the economic

and political rationale for the research and extension strategies of different
actors is key to exploring avenues for change. At present, there are four
main interest groups (and dozens of sub-groups) competing with one
another.

State interests

State policies in Ecuador have promoted human occupation, rapid resource extraction and conversion of forests to pastures in Amazonia. Consequently, the National Agricultural Research Institute (INIAP) has
devoted the largest proportion of its resources to research on pastures and
forages for cattle production. INIAP engages farmers in agricultural research through the work of technology transfer and validation research
teams. In the Amazon, however, there is no such programme. Furthermore, public extension efforts are affected not only by the transfer-of-
technology bias, but also by the lack of involvement of social scientists.

Formal agricultural training obtained through the vocational high
schools and universities concentrates exclusively on modern science and
technology and is mostly theoretical. Questions about the social construction and articulation of indigenous and scientific knowledge are absent
from the agriculture curriculum. In this training, modern technology is
given an aura of prestige, while rural people's knowledge and practices are
considered deficient, rudimentary and vague.

International interests

The research agenda of INIAP responds not only to the state's interests,
but to financing opportunities, which in turn represent donor priorities.
The International Development Research Center (IDRC) of Canada has
sponsored much of INIAP's research on pastures and forages. Donor support has enabled the Tropical Pastures Programme of the International
Centre for Tropical Agriculture (CIAT) and the Inter-American Institute
for Cooperation in Agriculture (IICA) to provide technical assistance and
resources to INIAP. The international centres, through their promotion of
improved varieties and resource-intensive methods, have contributed to
the enthronement of modern agricultural science and the devaluation of
traditional knowledge. Local practices are seen as something to be avoided
or supplanted.

Non-governmental organizations' interests

NGOs have had little direct involvement in setting the research agenda in
Amazonia. Some NGOs are involved in supporting Indian organizations,
however. For instance, the Federation of Native Communes of Ecuadorian
Amazonia (FCUNAE), with assistance from a local NGO (COM-
UNIDEC), using a group-participatory approach, has worked with local
people to increase their standards of living through the design and implementation of forest management and sustainable use plans (Thrupp *et al.*,
Part II). Specific objectives include the regularization of Indian lands, social organization, resource management and, significantly, the rescue of

indigenous forest management practices, such as shifting cultivation and itinerant horticulture.

Non-indigenous versus indigenous interests

Non-indigenous interests dominate the research and extension agenda. Thus, little work has focused on local agricultural systems or traditional agroforestry systems. Indigenous people have interests that go beyond individual crops and domesticated animals. The recovery and revalorization of indigenous resource utilization, particularly traditional forest management practices, are a corollary of their struggle for land. For some Indian organizations it has become one of the means of asserting their identity and resisting the dominant society.

Defining goals at the local level

The problem of addressing different needs

Discussions about national economic development, and the sustainability of production systems, are usually carried out in academic institutions or at the top levels of government, usually in the major urban centres. Local people are concerned about bread and butter issues, often in remote rural areas. In some extreme cases, rural people, such as small ethnic groups of Amazonia are concerned about their very cultural and physical survival. For colonists and members of larger indigenous groups, the concern is to provide adequate food, shelter, health and education. Research and extension has to keep in mind both levels: the more abstract one that considers national policies and models of economic development and the more tangible and complex one that addresses local people's needs and priorities.

From the national standpoint, it might be convenient to work on the development and diffusion of a monocrop that has high export potential or to concentrate efforts on technologies that reduce human pressure on the natural forest. However, from the standpoint of rural people, the priority is to work on improving what already exists, to increase crop and animal production without depleting the resource base, to raise farm income levels, to increase food security while reducing risk and uncertainty and to expand the range of choices available. In addition, local differences have to be considered. The needs of indigenous people are not always the same as those of colonists. A balanced approach to development must try to satisfy at least part of each set of needs.

The problem of contradicting national goals

When local needs are in contradiction with national goals, grassroots organizations and NGOs – independent of public institutions – are forced to play a greater role in agricultural development. The clearest example of this sort of contradiction is found in Peru and Bolivia, where coca production and consumption are part of the indigenous tradition, while the national goal has been to eradicate or sharply reduce coca plantations. In

226

Ecuador, indigenous forest management practices in Amazonia have had to give way to policies that promote the expansion of agriculture by converting forest to pastures. As a consequence, indigenous organizations, often with NGOs' support, have stepped in to reaffirm the value of traditional technologies and to point out the limitations of government policy.

The potential for 'ground up' development

Despite conflicting national goals and local needs, there is potential for 'ground up' development. National goals are being revised and the concepts of environmental protection, the preservation of biological diversity and the search for sustainable production systems have been incorporated into the vocabulary of public policy-makers. In addition, appropriate approaches to farmer-based agricultural development are being developed. Farmers, researchers and extensionists have at their disposal many tools to help them work in a collaborative, participatory fashion. There is a growing harmony between national and local goals in terms of obtaining food security, the creation of sustainable farming systems and the production of surpluses in order to exchange them for other goods. Development 'by decree', from above, has not functioned well. Therefore, the road for 'ground up', people-centred development is open.

Will farmer participatory research survive in the International Agricultural Research Centres?

SAM FUJISAKA

Four Stages of Research at IRRI

There have been four distinct stages to research in the Consultative Group of International Agricultural Research Centres (CGIAR) since the 1960s (Rhoades, 1988). These historical trends are illustrated in detail with the example of the International Rice Research Institute (IRRI).

Stage 1: breeding for yield increases

As the first research centre of what was to become the CGIAR system and as a source of the 'Green Revolution', IRRI provided improved germplasm – high-yielding semi-dwarf rices – in order to increase global food output in the face of high population growth. Plant breeders, geneticists, physiologists and pathologists contributed to the effort.

In terms of results, IR8 yielded 8.2 t/ha in the dry season on experimental fields and was released for use by other breeders in 1966. By 1968, IR8 was grown on ten million hectares and rice yields began to rise in the tropics. By 1969, some 30 varieties, with IRRI origins and with greater resistance to insects and diseases, had been released by national programmes. Twenty years later, in 1989, more than 900 varieties with IRRI parentage were released in 38 countries. Up to the present, IRRI has also collected more than 85,000 germplasm accessions (IRRI, 1991).

During this stage, farmers were considered recipients and, along with consumers, beneficiaries of breeding research.

Stage 2: cropping and farming systems research

As rice breeding gains were consolidated, concerns about the impacts and on-farm relevance of new technologies led to the inclusion of agronomists and agricultural economists in IRRI's research efforts. Farming systems research represented an expansion of concerns to include gender issues, livestock, including rice-fish, and the rainfed lowland environment. IRRI had a visiting anthropologist in the early 1980s and many of her efforts were directed to establishing the role of anthropologists in interdisciplinary teams developing improved food technology (IRRI, 1982).

Farmer participation in cropping systems research was generally in the form of researcher-designed and farmer-managed cropping pattern trials. Participation of farmers ranged from their labour contributions in trials conducted on their fields to the inclusion of farmer feedback in both *ex ante* and *ex post* technology evaluations. Cropping pattern trials by IRRI researchers largely ceased by 1991 in favour of more farmer participatory research (Fujisaka, 1989a, 1991).

Stage 3: research by rice environment: a farmer-first stage

During the mid-1980s, IRRI researchers and the CG system became increasingly concerned with sustainability and equity issues. A 'matrix' structure was implemented in 1990 in which research divisions (e.g. agronomy, physiology, agroecology, entomology) formed one axis and the irrigated, rainfed lowland, upland, deep-water and tidal wetland (and cross-ecosystems) rice environments formed another. Research was conducted within defined projects and programmes, with members of many projects forming into multidisciplinary teams.

The issue of equity was addressed because research resources were then specifically allocated to the unfavourable rice agroecosystems in which many of Asia's poor producers and consumers live. Sustainability was addressed in terms of both long term sustainability of the resource base (e.g. research on land management in the uplands) and in terms of sustaining past yield gains made in irrigated environments (Pingali, 1991). For IRRI, on-farm multidisciplinary team research (with an agricultural anthropologist on the team) marked this stage.

Farmer-to-farmer training, farmer participatory research, farmer experiments and consideration of farmer practice and technical knowledge were components of research at this stage. Some examples of such research include:

- *Farmer technology adaptation and adoption.* After farmer-to-farmer training, farmers at an upland site in the Philippines adapted and

228

adopted contour hedgerows over a period of four years. They developed hedgerow establishment methods that required less labour, eliminated grasses that were too competitive with crops, stopped planting trees that were initially intended to produce green manures and planted species that might provide cash returns. The systems they developed controlled soil erosion equally effectively. Farmer technology adaptations are being fed back into the on-farm research at the site (Fujisaka, 1989b).

- *Research to transfer a farmer technology.* Farmers in Tupi, South Cotabato, Philippines, grow rice and maize in an upland environment characterized by favourable soils and slope, but risky rainfall. Rice production features two innovations. First, use of both stable yielding traditional upland and higher yielding, but disease susceptible, modern lowland rice varieties and second, development and refinement of implements and management practices for land preparation, seeding, weed control and for reducing turn-around time between crops. Costs, benefits and reasons underlying alternative farmer-developed strategies were examined. As a result, the farmers' *panudling*, a five-tined furrow opener and inter-row cultivator, combined with broadcast seeding, are being farmer-to-farmer introduced and tested in other upland rice areas (Fujisaka, forthcoming).

- *Rejecting cropping systems research.* Cropping systems research was conducted to improve productivity in the same area. Farmers rejected introduced patterns. Cost-benefit analyses and examinations of farmers' perceptions of cropping patterns and choices were conducted. These indicated that an approach that starts with understanding farmers' systems in order to conduct research on the weak points of such systems, together with evaluation of farmer technology and adaptation, may be more effective than researcher-designed, farmer-implemented cropping pattern trials (Fujisaka, 1991a).

- *Farmers' dry-seeded rice.* A variety of traditional rainfed, lowland dry-seeded rice systems were examined in Myanmar, Indonesia and India. Farmers' practices were well matched to field environments and included ways to address not only weeds, but also poor soil physical properties, water deficit and excess and poor plant stand. Farmers' dry-seeding systems did not necessarily reduce labour, but could increase cropping intensity, result in stable yields using low material inputs or distribute labour demands where some fields are dry seeded and others transplanted. Because of difficult and uncertain environmental conditions, IRRI's research on direct dry-seeding now builds upon farmer practice.

- *Farmers' rejection of a recommendation.* Since 1982, the Philippines recommended that rice farmers apply one-half to two-thirds of their nitrogen (N) fertilizer 'basally' to drained fields prior to final harrowing and transplanting, and the rest at panicle initiation. Interviews with more than 200 farmers in three irrigated areas during 1990 and 1991 revealed that few applied N in this manner. Farmers continually adjust practices to fit their field conditions and, overall, these practices agree with research suggesting that yields do not increase with basal-N applications, and that N is optimally applied at mid-tillering and panicle initiation.

229

Table 1: Four research stages* at IRRI and respective farmer participation

Stage Concerns	Participants and Farmer Participation
Germplasm improvement	• Increase rice yields through new varieties • Breeders, geneticists, pathologists • Farmers receive varieties and germplasm collected from farmers
Cropping/farming systems	• Increase productivity of rice-based systems • Add agronomists, economists and others • Researcher-designed and farmer-managed trials, farmer *ex post* feedback on technologies
Environmental	• Address issues of sustainability of production in favourable environments and sustainability of less favourable rice agroecosystems; work in less favourable environments to address equity concerns • Add agroecosystems analysis, modelling, GIS • On-farm inter-disciplinary research teams • Substantial farmer participation in farmer-to-farmer training, farmer participatory experiments and farmer experiments, especially in knowledge-intensive technologies
Upstream and Institutional	• Need to focus on strategic and basic research; national programmes conduct applied or adaptive research; collaborative work via consortia with strong national programmes; possible eco-regional directions • Biotechnology, modelling, GIS, policy • Less emphasis on on-farm farmer participatory research; farmer participation possibly in resource management, IPM and in developing non-yield germplasm improvements.

* With thanks to Rhoades (1988).

This led to a critical reappraisal of the research from which the basal-N recommendation was derived and a reinforcement of the need to understand farmer practices inconsistent with recommendations.

• *Farmers' traditional rices.* There is increased interest in eliciting and applying farmer technical knowledge associated with rice germplasm. That is, to conserve and better utilize rice biodiversity, farmer technical knowledge is being collected along with the rice seed. International programmes for upland rice have shifted their strategy from *Indica* to *Japonica*-based breeding, while farmers' cultivars and knowledge are now considered a major resource for national programmes. Many traditional (*Japonica*) cultivars selected by farmers to suit local conditions can provide needed parent materials, while farmers' criteria are increasingly being included as breeding targets (Fujisaka *et al.*, 1992b).

Stage 4: the emerging scenario at IRRI

A fourth stage is emerging at IRRI, driven by the CG system and its Technical Advisory Committee (TAC). Key concepts in the emerging rhetoric of the international centres are 'upstream' and 'strategic' research to be conducted by IRRI; a wider definition of National Agricultural Research Systems (NARSs) to include universities, NGOs and others (these are collectively now known as 'stakeholders'); stakeholders as equal collaborators in research; and, at the same time, a move towards 'ecoregional', rather than commodity-based, research.

In response to these shifts in 'mandate', the current scenario at IRRI is to emphasise such supposedly strategic and more basic approaches as biotechnology, geographic information systems (GIS) and modelling. IRRI would attempt to work with strong national programmes via collaborative arrangements (i.e. via consortia of partners, rather than IRRI-led networks). The scenario assumes that national programmes will conduct the necessary more applied and adaptive research, including on-farm and farmer-participatory research. As a result, such research conducted directly by IRRI researchers is tacitly discouraged.

Finally, IRRI and other centres are responding to a recommendation by the TAC to shift to the conduct of ecoregional, rather than commodity-oriented research. For IRRI, the shift would require much greater collaboration with other CG centres (e.g., with CIMMYT on the rice-wheat system, ICRISAT on tropical legumes in rice systems and ICRAF on trees in upland rice systems). The shift could also push IRRI's return to more basic rice germplasm improvement, as other centres and national programmes are given the responsibility to conduct more of the needed on-farm, systems and farmer participatory research.

The current situation at other CG Centres: more farmer participation?

Researchers at the Maize and Wheat Improvement Centre (CIMMYT), the International Centre for Research in Agroforestry (ICRAF), the West Africa Rice Development Association (WARDA) and the International Potato Centre (CIP) responded to a request sent to all CG centres to briefly discuss farmer participatory methods used at their centres. This is a review of their activities.

CIMMYT

Farmer participatory methods at CIMMYT evolved from on-farm and farming systems research and are effective in initially narrowing alternative interventions to those with the greatest potential for adoption. Research includes farmer participatory experiments to elicit assessments of green manure relay cropping in maize, farmer-to-farmer extension methods in southern Mexico and farmer adaptation of wheat production technologies to widely varying environments. Participatory diagnosis has been used in CIMMYT-IRRI-NARS research on rice-wheat systems in South Asia. As is also the case at IRRI, on-farm researchers recognize the utility of early farmer germplasm assessment in the process of germplasm improvement. Scientists predict that farmer participatory methods will become more important over the next ten years, especially in crop management research, research on natural resource conservation and management and germplasm improvement activities aimed at non-yield and other non-conventional characteristics (Larry Harrington, personal communication).

ICRAF

ICRAF scientists say that farmer participatory methods have a critical role to play in all stages of the research process (i.e. in diagnosis, design, testing and evaluation). A major challenge is making participatory research more 'rigorous' in order to improve the accuracy, precision and predictive power of results and to thereby strengthen credibility among colleagues and donors. In evaluation, for example, researchers are using methods from social psychology and consumer marketing research to elicit farmers' criteria for evaluating tree species. Overall, researchers are optimistic that incorporating farmers' perspectives into research will *increase* in importance in the CG system, even if the term FSR does not (Steve Franzel, personal communication).

WARDA

WARDA researchers are equally optimistic: farmer participatory approaches were adopted in the face of earlier non-adoption of 'improved' technologies and such research will continue to be important. The highest pay-offs will be in modifying research to address client objectives from the outset. Current returns have been high where on-farm technology testing has allowed non-existent or weak extension services to be by-passed. WARDA researchers feel that such impacts will be lasting, that everyone is committed and that opposition to such approaches is no longer apparent in Africa (Peter Matlon, personal communication).

CIP

In the late 1970s, CIP compared the narrow technology-focused approach to farmer participatory methods via a special FSR project. The mainstream FSR approach developed a large team and complex research agendas, used over 80 per cent of the budget and learned lessons from poor research designs and false assumptions about farmer technology. The participatory approach emphasised interdisciplinary co-operation of social and biological scientists and the close involvement of technology users in the process – from problem definition to evaluation of technology options. It spent less than 20 per cent of the budget and identified a potato storage technique known to

232

Table 2: CGIAR Centres: year founded, percentage of total funds and participatory research activities

Centre	Year founded	% of total CG funds (1990)	Activities
ICRISAT	1972	13.3	– Mainly commodity research on sorghum, millet, chickpea, pigeonpea, groundnut; economists, no anthropologists; evaluation of end-user systems at technology evaluation stage
IRRI	1960	12.5	– Rice and rice systems; anthropologists; farmer participation in on farm-research, IPM
CIAT	1967	11.7	– Lowland tropical agriculture: rice, beans, cassava, farmer forages. Anthropologists and farmer participation in Latin America and Africa
CIMMYT	1966	11.4	– Maize, wheat, barley, triticale; agricultural economists and others doing on-farm work with farmers
IITA	1967	9.5	– Crop improvement, land management in humid, sub-humid tropics; maize, cassava, cowpea, plantain, soybean, rice, yam; alley farming (Atta-Krah, Part III); economists do on-farm work with farmers
ILCA	1974	8.5	– Livestock, sub-Saharan Africa; FSR involves farmers; anthropologists
ICARDA	1975	7.9	– FSR in north Africa and west Asia
CIP	1970	7.1	– Potato and root crops; started 'farmer-back-to-farmer'; reduced agricultural anthropology since 1970s-80s
ILRAD	1973	5.7	– Livestock diseases in sub-saharan Africa
IFPRI	1975	3.8	– Economists in Washington, DC working on policy
IBPGR	1974	2.9	– Conservation of genetic resources
ISNAR	1980	2.9	– Social sciences in the Hague; strengthen NARS
WARDA	1970	2.6	– Rice improvement in west Africa
AVRDC	1971		– Vegetables in Asia
ICLARM	1977		– Fisheries and aquaculture; now building a social sciences programme
ICRAF	1977		– Agroforestry; diagnosis and design
IIMI	1984		– Better management of irrigation systems; trying PRA
INIBAP	1984		– Bananas and plantains; plans to develop regional on-farm teams

both science and farmers, and successfully supported its diffusion as a means to improve the quality of seed potatoes. As a result, CIP's narrower FSR programme wilted, while the participatory approach received the blessing of the institution (Gordon Prain, personal communication).

Despite the positive prognoses about the future of farmer participatory research given by a number of scientists in the CG system, such 'downstream' research is threatened in many centres under the present funding and policy climate of the CGIAR. Currently, there is an infatuation with biotechnology as a top-down cure-all, and several donors have pushed for more 'strategic' and less adaptive research at the international level. Thus, pressure against participatory approaches is coming from both scientists wanting to expand the role of biotechnology and from management looking at which way donor winds are blowing. As an answer, participatory approaches need to achieve tangible successes which can be directly related to the involvement of local people. Those active in participatory approaches within the CG need to seek close links with NGOs to help ensure that both technical and political/policy issues can be addressed.

Table 2 lists centres, their founding dates, the percentage of the CGIAR core budget each receives and my additional impressions regarding what is going on at each centre in terms of farmer participatory research.

The future of farmer participatory research in the CGIAR

Farmer participation in agricultural research from the initial stages onwards continues to be needed and appears to have the greatest likelihood of being continued at the CG centres in crop management research, especially where technologies are knowledge intensive (such as integrated pest management or adaptation of wheat to new environments); in research on natural resource conservation and management and in germplasm improvement activities aimed at non-yield and other non-conventional characteristics. But the likelihood of these approaches continuing to be of importance at the CG centres will depend on tangible successes directly stemming from the participation of farmers and other 'users'.

Shrinking budgets have led many to conclude that the various players in agricultural research need to act according to their respective comparative advantage. On the one hand, for IARCs in places where the NARSs are relatively weak (e.g. parts of Africa), this appears to mean *increases* in farmer participatory research conducted by CG centre researchers (Atta-Krah, Part III). On the other, and as a result of recommendations by the CG system and TAC, IRRI may be exiting from a stage of substantial on-farm and farmer participatory research in favour of such activities as plant breeding and biotechnology to improve the basic rice germplasm, agronomy to address a possible yield decline in irrigated rice, modelling to quantify the behaviour of rice ecosystems and GIS to characterize agro-ecological zones and define extrapolation domains.

For IRRI, these changes need to be accompanied by increased and better collaboration with strong national research programmes and with other IARCs. But which, if any, national programmes have a comparative advantage in working with farmers? Our experience with NARS (most often government departments of agriculture) has revealed a general reluctance to involve farmers until technologies are 'proven'. That is, many of IRRI's partners have preferred to set up more 'top down' demonstrations after lengthy on-station testing, rather than involving farmers as research partners from the onset of research (Fujisaka and Garrity, 1991). In sum, the challenge is that if IRRI is to move 'upstream', some way must be found to increase the efforts of national rice research institutes – including universities and NGOs – to incorporate farmers in agricultural problem solving.

Linking researchers and farmers through developmental on-farm research

A.N. ATTA-KRAH

The on-farm research framework

The International Agricultural Research Centres (IARCs) need to extend their technology development research programmes to the point where technologies have been proved to be acceptable by farmers. Farmer Participatory Research (FPR) skills and tools can be used for this assessment. A framework within which this can be done is the developmental on-farm research process, one version of which is now being implemented through the Alley Farming Network for Tropical Africa (AFNETA), a jointly supported network of the International Institute for Tropical Agriculture (IITA), the International Livestock Centre for Africa (ILCA), and the International Centre for Research in Agroforestry (ICRAF).

On-farm research has been described as the crucial link between the research and transfer (extension) arms of technology development. Two distinct types of on-farm research – experimental on-farm research (EOFR) and developmental on-farm research (DOFR) – have also been identified and described (Atta-Krah and Francis, 1987; Atta-Krah, 1990). EOFR is that form of on-farm experimentation which involves validation or comparison of different technologies or components of technologies, on the basis of standard experimental designs, research controls and statistical analysis. Such trials are expected to provide quantitative data on the technical, biological and to a lesser extent, economic parameters of the systems under study, and require a high level of researcher control. The farmers' input in such trials is often highly structured in order to obtain comparable (and analysable) data from a number of trials (Sumberg and Okali, 1989). This situation may limit the farmers' ability to experiment with and manipulate the system under study.

DOFR, on the other hand, is much less tightly controlled and structured. It is concerned with the introduction of new technologies or systems to the farmer community, and involves the assessment of their relevance, workability and acceptability by farmers, within a framework of research–development interaction. DOFR enables researchers to study how farmers react to an introduced technology, and how they might adapt and adopt the system to meet their local needs and resource patterns (Gubbels; Sikana, Part III). The elements of this developmental research approach are as follows:

- *Community focus.* The research begins with few individual farmers, but moves gradually to involve more and more farmers, and culminates in a community-based or village-based pilot project.
- *Research/development collaboration.* It requires collaboration between research and development institutions. The research approach draws heavily from extension methodologies for making farmer contacts and for the development of farmer – and researcher – awareness. Continuous contact with farmers at the grassroots level is also required. This calls for the involvement of development or extension personnel as a critical requirement in this activity. It is during this phase that research and development can operate together to introduce and test the performance of the technology in the farm environment, and to link the research process with the eventual extension of the technology.
- *Farmer involvement.* In DOFR, the definition of 'farmer involvement' changes from that of the farmers having to take actions in accordance with treatment specifications as defined by researchers, to that of the farmers using their own experience and knowledge to shape experiments with a particular technology and make modifications in management as they deem appropriate. In other words, this process approaches a state of full farmer control and responsibility in the management of the system in question. Appropriate research tools and methods are used to promote farmer participation and encourage farmer initiatives and experimentation. It is important the farmers continue to treat the trial farms as their own, rather than as 'research plots'.
- *Hard data requirement.* The fact that there is full farmer control and limited researcher interference, and the involvement of farmers on a community basis makes it unrealistic to expect 'high quality hard data' on the system's biological and technical components. Furthermore, the specific objectives of these developmental trials make such data of only secondary importance. Conventional hard data collection and conventional statistical analyses, therefore, are of limited relevance in this work.
- *Socioeconomic and anthropological analyses.* Since the process culminates in a local-level pilot project, socioeconomic and anthropological issues operating within the community come to bear on the system and these give an opportunity for the assessment of adoption potential within a real-life situation. The process requires an adequate understanding of the socioeconomic environment, as well as continuous monitoring, analysis and interpretation of farmer reactions and emerging sociocultural concerns relevant to the adoption and adaptation of the system. FPR methods are useful for these research activities. The need for an interdisciplinary team is clearly obvious in this type of activity, and the contribution of socioeconomics and anthropology are crucial.

AFNETA: alley farming and on-farm research

The technology of alley farming was developed at IITA through research initiated in 1976 to find an alternative to traditional shifting agriculture. The underlying rationale of alley farming as a sustainable farming system is based on its potential for restoring and maintaining soil fertility. With increasing intensity of land use and shortening fallow periods, shifting cultivation is becoming less able to ensure fertility maintenance and sustainability of cropping. With proper management, and under the right conditions, alley farming is expected to maintain soil fertility and improve yields.

The Alley Farming Network for Tropical Africa (AFNETA) was established in 1989 with the goal of making a significant contribution towards the development of sustainable cropping systems, based on alley farming and general agroforestry principles, for different agroecological zones in sub-Saharan Africa. Today, it promotes and co-ordinates alley farming research and development within the National Agricultural Research Systems (NARSs) in over 20 countries in the region.

Phase I of AFNETA's work (1990–92) sought to establish basic trials for the assessment of biophysical feasibility of alley farming in the various regions, as well as obtain early indications on the workability of the system through on-farm trials. Much of the research conducted during this first phase was EOFR, with only a limited amount of a developmental nature. Hence, NARS research scientists designed and managed the on-farm experiments, while farmers contributed their land and some defined management input, but few original ideas or initiatives. While this strategy was useful for standardizing experimental designs and establishing research controls, it proved far less successful at enhancing or assessing the actual rate of adoption and adaptation of the technologies by the farmers.

Recognition of these limitations led AFNETA to incorporate farmer participatory elements into its research activities and shift its focus towards DOFR. Thus, AFNETA Phase II (1993-present) concentrates on the joint assessment of alley farming and agroforestry systems and on the social acceptability of those systems to farmers. Biophysical and socioeconomic feasibility studies are carried out to understand the agricultural priorities of small-holders and to engage them in a constructive dialogue about the adoptability and adaptability of alley farming and related technologies. This new research direction requires collaboration between the IARCs, the NARSs and development organizations, such as NGOs.

AFNETA's on-farm research (OFR) work is usually preceded by Participatory Rural Appraisals (PRAs) to assess, conceptualize, design and evaluate their viability in social and economic, as well as technical terms. The new projects are investigating the adoption potential of alley farming and other agroforestry options, as well as traditional systems for the whole farm. This whole farm perspective enables researchers, development workers and farmers to evaluate these technologies and to address issues, such as labour constraints and competing resource management priorities, in their research designs.

At present, the AFNETA country research teams are engaged in three types of on-farm research. The first, Developmental OFR, is the principal

237

focus. Experimental OFR and Case Studies (CSs), with relevant linkages to DOFR, are also conducted on a more limited scale.

CS trials involve the detailed study of the management system, and costs and benefits of the system or technology, in relation to the farmer's overall production. Thus, it requires thorough data collection and analyses of inputs and outputs associated with the system under selected farmer management situations. CSs enable the research team to gather specific quantitative data to assess the biological (e.g. maize production), social (e.g., labour requirements of women) and economic (e.g. farm income) impacts of alley farming and alternative technologies.

Using this approach, OFR on alley farming is currently being designed and conducted by interdisciplinary teams of NARS researchers, government extensionists, NGO workers and farmers in Bénin, Côte d'Ivoire, Ghana, Kenya, Togo and Uganda, with plans for more countries to follow.

The potential for FPR can best be realized if the concept is seen in its broadest sense. This should range from situations in which realistic farmer participation is infused into existing research structures, to situations in which farmers themselves are doing their own research. Mechanisms for monitoring, evaluation and impact assessment are required to demonstrate the capabilities and potentials of the farmer participatory approach.

There is the need for more emphasis on farmers' role in on-farm research and clear demonstrations of what can be achieved, beyond the rhetoric of 'participation' or 'experimentation'. International and national research institutions and other research and development organizations all have a stake in further developing and promoting the concept of FPR. As the AFNETA example illustrates, this task can only be executed successfully within a spirit of partnership and inter-institutional collaboration.

Populist pipedream or practical paradigm?
Farmer-driven research and the Projet Agro-Forestier in Burkina Faso

PETER GUBBELS

Projet Agro-Forestier: changing course

The well documented crisis of conventional agriculture in West Africa has generated growing interest in the potential of farmer-driven research and extension. However, due to constraints faced by public sector institutions in West Africa, this experience remains confined to the work of a few NGOs. One of the most notable examples is the Projet Agro-Forestier (PAF) in Burkina Faso, which is supported by Oxfam (UK).

PAF started in 1979 with a remit to address perceived widespread environmental degradation in the drought-prone region of Yatenga. Initially, the Programme's approach was to adapt micro-plots and half-moon techniques of micro-water catchment for growing trees. From 1979–80, PAF did on-farm experiments on those techniques with interested farmers' groups.

While PAF conducted its more formal on-farm experiments, participating farmers undertook a parallel series of informal experiments of their own. After observing that the micro-catchments trapped much run off water, several farmers planted upland rice in the basins designed for tree seedlings. Sorghum was introduced by accident through the manure. Both of these crops did very well. During subsequent evaluation sessions, participating farmers expressed far greater interest in growing food crops than trees. Furthermore, the mortality rate of tree seedlings during the dry season was massive. Villagers barely could find enough drinking water, let alone water for trees.

PAF agreed to shift its focus to food crops in accordance with farmers wishes. Moreover, as farmers realized the potential benefits of conservation, they asked to shift their experiments from group plots to their own land. In 1981, PAF reoriented its research approach to concentrate on helping farmers design experiments to improve existing indigenous conservation techniques. After two years of joint experimentation, an improved version of the indigenous rock bund *diguette* proved successful for soil and water conservation.

Impacts

Informal evaluations undertaken between 1981–86 indicated an average increase of 40 per cent in sorghum yields on treated versus untreated land (Kabore, 1992). Yield differentials were highest in low rainfall years, when water retention is greatest. Thus rock bunds decrease the risk of crop failure in dry years. Between 1983–91, PAF instituted a farmer-to-farmer extension programme and trained 4542 peasant farmers from 406 villages in the rock bund technique. More than 8000 ha were treated (Ouedrago, 1992). Rock bunds are now found throughout Yatenga, even where they have not been promoted. The rapid rate of adoption, with little subsidy (except for tools and transport), indicates the farmers' enthusiasm. In interviews, many farmers cite higher yields and increased food security as the primary benefits.

A cost-benefit analysis of PAF recently undertaken by the World Bank calculated the internal rate of return to investment, using conservative assumptions, at 37 per cent. The World Bank study concluded that 'the return to PAF is at worst quite respectable and at best extraordinary' (Younger and Bonkoungou, 1989: 16).

A practical paradigm?

The description of the PAF experience appears to confirm many of the principles of a farmer-first approach. In a complex, diverse and risk-prone region experiencing apparently severe environmental degradation, substantial out-migration and chronic drought, PAF's achievement suggests that, with appropriate technology, the production potential can be raised significantly. Indeed, with rock bunds and *zai* tillage and composting, farmers have reclaimed substantial areas of abandoned, eroded land.

The technology development process was built upon a combination of indigenous and external technical knowledges. Both traditional techniques and modern approaches, when applied in isolation, had proved inadequate. But results were achieved when modern science (experimental methods, the use of the water level) and indigenous knowledge (stone barriers across the slope, farmer involvement in experiments) were combined in a complementary manner.

PAF has developed technologies that are capable of generating substantial increases in food production, are ecologically sustainable and are low-cost and low-risk, requiring low external inputs. The impact of farmer influence on the research process is striking. PAF began with a transfer-of-technology approach and a predetermined agenda (agroforestry), but PAF's flexibility in redirecting the content and approach of research in response to farmers' feedback was the key to success.

PAF's approach in refining and improving indigenous technologies points to the potential of a collaborative process of technology development. The effectiveness of rock bunds in controlling erosion generated conditions that made other innovations feasible (e.g. agroforestry).

Economic analysis indicates that PAF's approach has been cost-effective, in striking contrast to the total failure of expensive state SWC programmes. PAF's modestly scaled research and development work was low-cost and efficient, largely because farmer participation in designing, testing and evaluating technologies under a variety of local conditions ensured relevance. Another factor was PAF's integration of research with extension by promoting farmer-to-farmer extension.

In support of the claim that the farmer-first is a practical paradigm, PAF shows how effective feedback mechanisms, flexibility, client-responsiveness, building on indigenous knowledge and farmer participation can succeed, at low cost, in a situation where top-down, centre-outward, expensive approaches directed by highly qualified technicians have repeatedly failed. By developing ecologically sustainable, low risk, productivity enhancing technologies with farmers, PAF provides a striking example of how marginal areas may have untapped potential for agricultural growth and that investment in farmer-first research and extension can generate acceptable rates of return.

A populist pipedream?

The PAF experience, however, also indicates the drawbacks of a populist focus. Evidence indicates that even low-cost, ecologically sustainable technologies tend to benefit the strong over the weak. A majority of farm families have not adopted SWC technologies. PAF has achieved striking success in SWC technology, but has not demonstrated an ability to develop technologies to suit a range of socioeconomic groups (particularly women) with diverse livelihood strategies and needs. Even for SWC adopters, non-technical factors, contributing to poverty and hunger, remain to be addressed.

The analysis suggests that PAF's policies and practice are inadequately informed by a realistic assessment of power relationships inherent in the technology development process. Particularly, PAF's practice appears to be marked by misconceptions about the nature of poverty, participation and intervention. Lack of clarity in use and definition of these concepts, and insufficient rigour in identifying constraints may contribute to confused or inconsistent policy objectives.

An analysis of PAF's impact on women graphically illustrates that there can be no significant technical or social change, no development, without costs. Treating 'farmers', 'households' and 'communities' as undifferentiated and harmonious entities does not permit analysis of what those costs are likely to be, and who is likely to bear them. Nor does it help reflection on how to provide a greater choice of solutions for diverse socioeconomic problems and livelihood systems.

Such an assessment is not intended to detract from PAF's significant achievements, as PAF's experience makes a strong case for the potential of peasant and NGO agency. Rather, it is to illustrate the very real constraints in West Africa, to caution against treating the combination of farmer-first approaches and NGOs as a panacea for all situations where conventional research and extension have failed and to avoid an unjustifiably voluntaristic view of what is possible merely by changing the methods of technology development.

Some constraints are internal. Achieving 'role reversals' and 'putting farmers first' is striking, resonant rhetoric, but not easy to put into practice. It requires deciding *which* category of farmers should come first. *Not* deciding inevitably means that local elites come first. Indeed, to achieve goals such as promoting self-reliance, peasant organization and community environmental management, outside intervention is often not able to avoid working with rural power structures and may have to compromise on equity issues.

Mutually reinforcing mentalities of outsiders and village leaders obviate against role reversals. Project staff easily slip back into transfer-of-technology mode (TOT) behaviour. A less recognized, but more difficult, problem is that villagers themselves, often for rational reasons, may resist accepting role reversals. Participation cannot be considered a costless resource, either for NGOs or villagers.

PAF's experience also demonstrates the difficulty of a 'supply-side' populist approach (Richards, 1990) to strengthening local capacity and self-reliance. Most initiatives for technology development originated from PAF. Partly, this is due to institutional pressures within PAF to achieve quick and tangible results and its strong problem-solving focus. Partly, it is due to villagers perceiving PAF as a new type of patron within traditional client-patron relationships that often are an integral part of local coping strategies.

The scepticism of some scientists about the validity of PAF's experiments suggests that there has been little impact in empowering farmers to influence research policy. PAF appears to have had more success in influencing extension. By initiating an annual process of technical agency-peasant-NGO joint planning, PAF has enabled village leaders to have a voice for providing feedback and influencing decisions. However, as project staff readily admit, this does not constitute 'empowerment' of farmers *vis-à-vis* research and extension institutions, or a shift in power relations within broader society.

The mode of state control in West Africa places great constraints on the emergence of strong peasant organizations. Even in a country like Burkina Faso, where policies are relatively less discriminatory against peasant interests, the margins of operation for reaching and organizing the poor and building local capacity are narrow. Nonetheless, the PAF example shows that, within this generally restrictive structural context, there is room to improve the influence that peasant leaders can exert by creating institutional frameworks for public debate and accountability at the local level.

Beyond Farmer First?

The PAF experience reveals inherent limitations of farmer-first intervention strategies and rationale. The primary aim is to promote participatory methods that build upon rural people's knowledge and innovative capacity. However, as the PAF case suggests, innovative methods and the involvement of NGOs in technology development, while important, cannot solve these problems alone.

More importantly, changes in public sector research organization, management, priorities and policy are required. Development of more effective ways to harness local knowledge through farmer participation and NGOs is not sufficient to overcome the fact that the majority of farmers are not well-served by national agricultural research systems.

The issue, therefore, is not so much the institutionalization of farmer-first thinking into mainstream research and extension, it is how to bring about reforms so that research and extension institutions will define their goals and commitments to develop a public sector capability for poverty-focused, ecologically-oriented research. Such a capability, as the PAF example illustrates, will require a mix of TOT and farmer-first approaches.

In this regard, farmer-first shows itself to be essentially a prescriptive policy strategy which advocates what *ought* to happen. Although it offers a compelling critique of conventional research and extension and argues persuasively that combining modern and peasant science will generate more cost-effective and relevant technology development, farmer-first fails to offer an adequate theory of explanation, specifying the necessary and sufficient conditions in which a truly farmer-first approach could emerge.

Such a theory must consider sociocultural dimensions of knowledge creation, innovation, transmission and use within rural societies and communication approaches that allow dialogue between 'modern' and peasant rationalities and 'languages' of science (Part I). An adequate theory must also enable analysis of the social, institutional, economic and political structures (at both the macro- and micro-level) within which the technology development process is embedded. This requires a politically differentiated view of technology development which considers the inherent conflicts between the state and groups within civil society, between socioeconomic groups and between genders. It follows that interventions to identify appropriate technological responses to agricultural problems of various client groups in complex, diverse and risk-prone areas must be situated within a broader social and political strategy.

The purpose of analysing PAF's experience was not to conclude with prescriptions about how to better assist people in Yatenga in addressing their formidable problems. There are no quick and easy answers. Future action will necessarily be a product of negotiation between the various actors. Future outcomes will be continue to be mediated by context specific internal and external constraints and unforeseen events.

Farmer-first approaches will take different paths in different contexts. PAF's outcomes were based on a coincidence of factors: Oxfam's flexibility, PAF's exceptional leadership, happy accidents (sorghum seeds in the compost), the capacities and characteristics of Yatenga villagers, openings created by revolutionary political and policy changes and motivated personalities within technical agencies. PAF illustrates that human agency and the variability of the sociohistorical, agroecological and political economic context within West Africa will lead to different farmer-first strategies and institutional responses to peasant science.

Such analysis provides reason for both optimism and scepticism. The optimism arises from the possibility that underlying forces will slowly act on research and extension (perhaps through NGOs) to incorporate the practical aspects of the farmer-first paradigm. The scepticism arises from the likelihood that farmer-first research will be 'supply led', providing a coping mechanism for helping peasants adapt to agrarian crisis, rather than an opportunity to explore viable strategies for broader change. The danger inherent in a supply-led, populist approach to technology development, particularly when funded through NGOs, is that it can divert attention and resources away from reforms required to develop a viable, public sector, poverty-focused research capability.

Alternatives to current research and extension systems: village research groups in Zambia

PATRICK SIKANA

Village research groups

In 1988–89, the Adaptive Research Planning Team in Northern Province, Zambia (ARPT-NP) initiated village-level participatory research groups (VRGs) to run concurrently with its on-farm trial programme. A number of practical considerations necessitated this approach. The main objectives were to clarify farmers' understanding of the purpose of on-farm research and to dispel scientists' misconceptions about the nature of farmer experimentation. These would be accomplished by providing a forum for farmers to describe problems to researchers and extensionists and to facilitate discussions regarding viable solutions. It was envisaged that the VRGs would enable farmers and researchers jointly to design their research programme, as well as provide a forum for on-going appraisal of field trials.

Despite these well-intended objectives, the VRGs were not very successful. The main problem was the way the research groups were formed and constituted. One VRG was formed in each ARPT target area. Each VRG was made up of ARPT and extension officials, as well as a number of local representatives drawn from different villages. The over-representation of outsider authorities had an adverse effect on local autonomy and local initiative, and the VRGs soon became known locally as 'ARPT Committees'. Furthermore, ARPT played an active role in choosing the local representatives of the VRGs. Only the most powerful and eloquent individuals (resource-rich male farmers) were chosen, which resulted in the reinforcement of existing social hierarchies.

A new approach

In 1990, an internal appraisal study proposed a number of recommendations to make the VRGs more effective. Today, the new VRGs are modelled on existing local institutions which use the village as the basis of social organization. They are comprised exclusively of local people. The informal VRGs are encouraged to diagnose farming problems in their fields, hold meetings to discuss these problems and, if necessary, design experiments to solve them. The groups are supported by a resident research assistant, who is a member of the local village community. Complex problems that cannot be solved by the VRGs are channelled to farming systems research scientists based at national agricultural research stations, who will undertake research at the farmers' request. One of the principal aims is to strengthen local initiative by backing the changes and innovations that farmers are already making, instead of imposing completely new technological packages which do not take into consideration their resource constraints. In this way, farmer involvement is demand-led and institutionalized within the FSR routine.

Many challenges still remain in the refinement of this new approach, including ensuring the active involvement of sufficient numbers of women farmers and fostering a new confidence in the value of local capacities and knowledge. Outside intervention in these initial stages is essential. Once farmers' confidence to articulate their knowledge and priorities is restored, the decision-making process at the local-level needs to be strengthened and institutionalized so that it becomes part of the local political culture. The ultimate objective is to make these local initiatives part of a self-generating process resulting in demand-led agrarian change.

Facilitating sustainable agriculture: turning policy models upside down

NIELS RÖLING

When the paradigm fails

Over the last 25 years, we had become satisfied that technology transfer was the basis for non-coercive change in agriculture. First, we generalized from the thousands of empirical studies on adoption and diffusion to try and understand the basic processes underpinning innovation in agriculture (Rogers, 1983). Next, we formulated a linear model of technology transfer from generation by scientific research, and transfer by extension to use by farmers. Finally, we elaborated a systems approach to knowledge management so as to enhance the mutual articulation of institutions involved in the science–practice continuum (Röling and Engel, 1991).

Over time, these efforts began to gel into a consistent paradigm for deciding about investment in agricultural extension and research, institutional design and staff training, and for supporting day-to-day management. What is more, this achievement culminated in a simple and apparently indestructible management system, the Training and Visit (T&V) system of extension delivery. Millions of dollars are invested every year in T&V, supposedly enhancing the mutual linkages between research, extension and farmers, and so transforming the science-practice continuum into a super highway.

The whole situation appeared highly satisfactory . . . until the experiences with efforts to introduce more sustainable forms of agriculture made us aware of painful inconsistencies between the technology transfer paradigm and actual practice. Thus, the paradigm, once thought to be all-encompassing, was shown to have only limited applicability.

245

From technology transfer to facilitation

Technology transfer focuses on technology generation by scientists, and passing on to farmers via extension. Farmers are basically considered as passive receivers of expertize from outside. Adoption is usually only possible under three conditions: if technology transfer focuses on farmers who are helped through other sources (such as special projects) to acquire credit and inputs; if technology transfer focuses on rich farmers; or if the technology transferred is carefully targeted to the conditions of designated farmers, which requires collaboration between research and extension, and farmer influence on technology development.

Needless to say, a focus on richer farmers is the usual option. The fact that technologies are developed by research institutes implies that the products are usually blanket recommendations, comprising routine, calendar-based applications. For example, in the Netherlands, broad recommendations by research and extension services usually only cover individual crops and practices, leaving the farmer to adapt and integrate them into the complex system. Even the 'study clubs' which flourish in Dutch horticulture usually only deal with one crop. There is no study club which helps farmers with complex system management.

Compared with conventional, modern, industrial agriculture, more sustainable agriculture is more complex, requiring the management of a greater ecological and economic diversity. Sustainable agriculture is information-intensive instead of physical input-intensive. Information is critical in the management of highly complex systems for taking timely and multi-faceted decisions in accordance with season, climate, crop needs, pest and disease prevention, etc. Sustainable agriculture relies, above all, on the management of natural processes, such as rotation, crop combinations, the characteristics of cultivars, natural predation and so on. General principles must be carefully applied in locality-specific systems through active experimentation by local people. System management relies on careful observation and monitoring. Farmers must know what they see and be able to anticipate outcomes on the basis of observation. This requires a great deal of knowledge about local conditions, seasonality and natural processes. Decision-making is usually complex and must take many factors into consideration.

In technology transfer, the focus of the intervention is on transfer via various extension methods, such as farm visits, demonstrations, group training sessions, articles in farm journals and other forms of access to outside expertize. In the T&V system, transfer has been developed into a highly regulated and controllable management system, whereby extension workers are provided small chunks of calendar-based knowledge every month to pass on to farmers whom they visit every two weeks.

Of course, technology development and transfer is also applicable to enhancing sustainable agriculture. The development of resistant cultivars, working out beneficial rotations, developing nitrogen-fixing qualities in plant species and developing biological controls are all essential components. But facilitating sustainable agriculture differs in some very important respects. Technical information alone is insufficient; a great deal of

246

information needs to be provided about the nature of the policy and the context which it creates for agricultural production. In the Netherlands, policy information is now as important as research and market information. Farmers are keenly interested in policy; they assess the extent to which it will be able to affect their lives, will be actually implemented, can be circumvented and is to be taken seriously. Government has privatized technical agricultural extension, but still has a special office in each province to explain its agricultural policies to the public.

Making things visible also becomes vitally important (Bentley, Part II). In Indonesia farmers are urged to keep simple insect zoos made of a piece of netting, some bamboo stick and a rice plant in a container. Thus, the nature of predation by natural enemies on pests was made very visible indeed (Winarto, Part II). In the Netherlands, making things visible has become a national pastime. For instance, experiments are under way with mineral bookkeeping, a prelude to exact registration of the amounts of N, P, K that go into a farm and leave it, itself a condition for focused training and sanction of emissions.

A crucial element in sustainable agriculture is thus continuous observation and feedback from the physical environment, leading to the development over time of a body of local data, knowledge and wisdom which grows and becomes more finely tuned and responsive with each passing season. To tackle broader environmental issues, entire communities not just individual farmers, must become involved in monitoring the condition

Box 1: Contrasting paradigms in extension science		
Item	Transfer of technology	Facilitation
Criterion variable	Adoption, knowledge utilisation	Ownership of problem, quality of decision-making, convergence
Model of farmer	Individual adopter client, target	Independent, strategic actor, capable of expertise (indigenous knowledge), knowledge generation and exchange, local group process
Relevant disciplines	Communication, diffusion, information processing, social psychology	Policy science, sociology, convergence models, group dynamics, networks
Relevant applied sciences	Marketing, advertising, applied communication	Adult learning and education soft systems methodology (Checkland, 1981; 1989)
Philosophical foundations	Science is the basis of truth	Consensus is the basis of truth. Reality is socially constructed

of natural resources, an area of environmental education which is rapidly growing in Australia under the name 'Land Literacy' (Campbell, Part III).

The most important aspect of supporting sustainable agriculture is facilitation. The central issue is, after all, that farmers take charge of managing local agroecosystems in a manner consistent with the public good. Thus, an important aspect of intervention is to create a shared perspective on the problem and help developing decision-making capacity to deal with it. This is perhaps the most distinguishing characteristic of facilitation.

A system for supporting sustainable agriculture will be highly decentralized, with facilitators in the field, who have considerable 'people skills', in addition to technical understanding. They need to be supported by a network of specialists and local experiment stations. But such attempts to introduce decentralized, 'bottom-up' approaches must be complemented by strong 'top-down' commitment and a very clear, shared view of the mission of the organization, permeating its culture at all levels. The emergence of facilitation as a professional practice has major consequences for extension science (Box 1).

Village-managed extension systems in India: implications for policy and practice

PARMESH SHAH

Village institutions and extension volunteers

The Aga Khan Rural Support Programme (AKRSP) has worked with village communities in Gujarat, India, since 1985. A major thrust of the work has been to support the emergence of strong village institutions that can design, plan, implement and monitor their own participatory watershed management programmes and run their own extension system.

Following an exploratory investigation of the potentials for watershed development in the village area, using a range of Participatory Rural Appraisal and Planning techniques (Shah, Part II), a village institution (VI) is formed. VIs must represent the range of groups and interests in the village and be committed to taking on the tasks of appraisal, planning, implementation, conflict resolution, group action, extension, monitoring and evaluation.

The VI nominates a group of three extension volunteers (EVs) on the basis of their experience and interest in watershed development. The EVs are provided basic training in PRA techniques, simple technical skills for soil and water conservation management, as well as project preparation, accounting and monitoring procedures. The group of EVs then manage the extension process at the village level on behalf of the VI, with the teams dividing up responsibilities between soil and water conservation activities, dryland farming, credit and other commercial activities. Each EV is compensated by the VI in some way. This is left to the VI to decide, but most have opted for a performance related payment which is highly competitive compared to prevailing rural wage rates. The money is derived from revolving funds held by the VI; these are increasing as projects result in higher incomes and improved agricultural returns.

Knowledge about the success of village based EVs has spread rapidly, and EVs have been invited by other villages to assist them in conducting PRA exercises and developing village institutions for watershed management of their own. This has reduced the dependence on AKRSP staff for project initiation and training considerably, as the process is increasingly run by villagers themselves. AKRSP now hopes to assist the formation of a federated support institution of VIs and their EVs, which can take over AKRSP's support functions, provide training for new groups and develop a more effective interface with local and other external research, extension and technical institutions. It is hoped that a federated group of VIs will develop a lobbying and advocacy capacity of its own, so that a demand-pull on government and other development services can evolve.

The AKRSP experience has shown that external support institutions can play a useful role in catalysing local level development. But it requires a fundamental rethink of conventional project programming procedures. Instead of leaping into project formulation from the start, the process must start with a slow and patient building up of village-level capacity through skills training and institutional support. This phase may last several years and must precede formal project planning. The disbursement of project funds will thus differ. Initial investment in human resource development may be quite expensive in terms of staff support, but will require very limited project hardware. As local capacities increase and cost recovery procedures are put in place by village institutions taking over responsibility for operations, the support institution's costs will decrease, until the point where they can effectively withdraw.

Implications for policy and practice

Participatory watershed programmes, such as AKRSP's, will require major reversals of the existing policies of research and extension, organizational procedures, resource allocations, evaluation procedures and, most importantly, the attitudes of professionals. Experience indicates that these reversals are possible in public systems and bureaucracies and are not necessarily happening only in NGO supported projects.

Design of implementing institutions. Implementing organizations need to be redesigned as learning and enabling institutions in order to support local initiatives and institutions effectively. In participatory programmes, professionals act as facilitators and trainers in the initial phases. This requires a willingness and ability to learn from and work with people. Since these skills are not very common in most external technical professionals they have to be acquired through practical experience, initially without the pressure of achieving physical 'targets'.

249

Operating procedures of support institutions. Institutions have to adopt flexible procedures. Participatory fieldwork by staff members needs to be encouraged. The staff performance evaluation procedures have to be radically different from conventional programmes. The emphasis is on what the staff have *learnt* and what *processes* have been initiated in the communities.

Using para-professionals for scaling-up. The village institutions should be encouraged to carry out the implementation of the programme through their para-professionals and should be actively involved in scaling-up the programme in other areas. Extension agents at the local level should be accountable to the village institutions and their client groups should decide their compensation packages. This means a reduction in the size of extension bureaucracies and an increase in the enterprise component in extension. Extension then primarily becomes a function of the village institutions or their federations. Over a period of time, these para-professionals develop relationships with research stations and form collaborative partnerships with these institutions to carry out on-farm research.

Extension process and technology adaptation. Subsequently, the extension process also involves the interaction of the village volunteers with the research and extension wings of the support institutions. Extension wings of the external support institutions would play the role of information *providers* and facilitate the interaction of the research wing with the village institution extension agents.

Research management. Most present research institutions have made efforts to undertake farm research, but have failed because of professional attitudes and lack of sustained experimentation and facilitation at the local level. The villagers do not own these experiments, and collaborate mainly because of financial incentives in terms of supply of seeds. Moreover, these experiments do not link into the existing networks of village experimenters.

Access to village institutions and their functionaries increases the capacity of the research institutions to do effective research and get rapid feedback on the performance of new technologies and practices introduced. This also helps in evolving location-specific technologies by building upon local innovations and experiments.

Training. Training is one of the most critical inputs for the creation of local cadres for extension and management of the village institutions. Most training must be through field exercises and on-the-job learning, not in the classroom. Trainers first have to spend substantial time in the field, learn about the problems and, above all, develop skills of active listening, facilitation and participatory methods for group work. They also have to work on developing the skills of farmers as trainers. The availability of good trainers is likely to be a bottleneck in the spread of participatory programmes.

Programme and project design and management. The conventional project cycle framework has to be modified to include learning, capacity strengthening and development of human resources at the initial stages in the programme. This is followed by participatory planning, implementation and evaluation. The time-frame for the human resources development need not be more than two years. This leads to plans being prepared by the village institutions and supported by the project. Physical and financial targets are drawn up in detail at this stage, and conventional tools of appraisal and economic analysis are used in conjunction with analysis of institutional development. Project cycles need to be longer and the technical and management objectives of the project evolved after the initial phase of capacity building and assessment of institutional and local capacities. The performance assessment procedures and the criteria for assessment also need to change, and innovations and learning have to become important indicators for performance assessment.

Evaluation indicators. Evaluation indicators for economic and technical performance are well worked out, and used in a number of projects. However, the performance of projects is rarely evaluated for local capacity and institution strengthening. New approaches and indicators have to be developed to measure institutional performance and the institutional capacity to perform the functions for management and maintenance of the projects. Methodologies to combine economic and institutional evaluations also have to be devised.

Financial implications. There are compelling economic reasons why participatory approaches are more attractive than more conventional approaches. However, economic evaluations have to be done over a longer period, and the survival and maintenance of soil and water conservation structures and resultant benefits must be taken into account when making any comparisons of economic returns. What is clear is that the cost of watershed programmes can be considerably reduced and contributions from villagers can be increased, thus resulting in higher benefits to the community per unit of investment.

Decentralization and democracy. AKRSP has learned from its work in Gujarat that if local people see the possibility of implementing their own plans and taking key decisions regarding their implementation, then they will participate actively in the appraisal and planning process. This can lead to the development of viable local institutions and a greater willingness of local people to collaborate with external support organizations. The experience has also shown that local people's participation in the decision-making of formal institutions like *Panchayats* and fora like the *Gram Sabha* is also more effective and can lead to changes in the attitude of the bureaucracy and the political environment.

In some instances, AKRSP has witnessed changes in the leadership pattern in favour of functional leaders (EVs and active members of the village institution, who are leaders by virtue of their performance) over traditional

251

leaders (who are there by virtue of lineage, patronage, muscle power and social hierarchy). This could have long-term implications for improving governance and enhancing local democracy.

Community first – Landcare in Australia

ANDREW CAMPBELL

The imperatives of sustainability

In Australia, a grass-roots revolution called 'Landcare' has turned land conservation extension on its head. More than one thousand voluntary community Landcare groups are working to develop more sustainable systems of land use. They are supported by a national ten-year funding programme, which was initiated in 1989 when the major farmers' union and the peak conservation lobby jointly approached the Prime Minister, proposing, with compelling political potency, that scientists and public officials must share the challenge (and the dollars) of sustainable agriculture with the Australian community.

Whether viewed according to ecological, social or economic criteria, most Australian farming systems are presently unsustainable. Natural resources have been (and in many areas are still being) depleted and degraded, most agricultural sectors are in financial difficulties and rural communities are under severe stress in a period of sharp decline. Landcare blends elements of community and environmental and production issues (increasingly moving into social concerns), in a tremendous diversity of environments.

Responding to the imperatives of sustainability, Landcare is challenging traditional thinking in agricultural research and extension. Taking sustainability seriously means broadening the focus from the farm and farmers to much larger arenas in space and time, involving many more stakeholders than the traditional troika of farmers, research and extension.

Involvement of farmer groups in soil conservation is not new, but the breadth of issues being tackled by Landcare groups, the impetus for groups forming, the degree of group autonomy and the momentum and ownership of the Landcare programme is quite distinct from past group approaches, which were essentially driven by state government agencies and focused more narrowly on reducing soil erosion.

What is a Landcare group?

One of the features of the Australia Landcare movement is its extraordinary diversity. So one cannot describe a 'typical' Landcare group, except in broad terms as a group of (usually rural) people who have come together voluntarily to co-operatively tackle environmental issues and develop more sustainable systems of land management. Common activities of Landcare groups include: field days and farm walks; demonstration projects – usually land degradation rehabilitation works; flights over a group area and/or tours to Landcare groups in other regions; development of a catchment or district plan which identifies land degradation problems, discusses the challenges of achieving sustainability in the local context and sets out a co-ordinated approach of implementation; facilitating the development of individual property plans within the context of the catchment plan – employing consultants, running workshops, short courses, coordinating incentives and resources such as aerial photos; active involvement in natural resource monitoring programmes, often in conjunction with schools, state agencies and scientists; development or purchase of land conservation equipment for hire to members and other land users; research and development trials with state agencies, universities, agribusiness, CSIRO; and production of educational pamphlets, videos and manuals.

It is still too early to measure many of the impacts of Landcare. But it is not too soon to be asking who is involved in Landcare and what they are getting out of their involvement. Roughly one in four farmers are involved in Landcare or rely on Landcare groups for information, and in some areas in southern Australia Landcare membership is over seventy per cent of the farming community. This is a significant penetration of Landcare into rural communities over a period when many people could have been expected to be pre-occupied with pressing short-term financial difficulties.

People involved in Landcare are learning a lot about their own property, about the land in their district and about issues they may have rarely considered in the past. Group leaders in particular have gained great satisfaction from seeing other people get involved, from influencing others through their interaction in the group and from group projects. Landcare groups have already created a climate of opinion more favourable to the adoption of improved land management practices in their districts and some groups have achieved notable successes in land management improvements particularly suited to group action, such as controlling rabbits, weeds, goats and wind erosion, and planning and implementing coordinated drainage schemes, watercourse revegetation and wildlife corridor networks.

Landcare and associated land literacy activities, by involving committed people closest to the land, are evolving new land use systems and new relationships between people and land, which build upon human resources instead of discounting them or seeing them as part of the problem.

Land literacy

For most of human history the ability to read and interpret the signs of nature has been crucial for survival. But humans have become progressively more insulated from the immediate need to be able to read and understand nature in order to eat, be clothed or find shelter. Such skills still reside within some indigenous communities and are being re-learned and rediscovered by people seeking more sustainable forms of land management.

253

The personal and direct involvement of people in gathering and interpreting information about the health of the land around them as an everyday activity seems to be inextricably linked with an accompanying ethic – of land stewardship, of respect for and humility towards nature. Such an ethic both underpins and is invigorated by contact with, and understanding of, the natural world. Understanding comes with direct involvement in gathering and recording information about vital signs such as water quality, the extent and status of indicator species, problems such as soil salinity and erosion and so on. A land ethic alone may be insufficient to guarantee sustainability, but it is a good start. Sustainability is a pipedream without a land ethic as a foundation stone.

Many of the most important land degradation problems in Australia are complex, insidious and not startlingly obvious. Or, when they do become obvious, it is often too late to do much more than take graphic photographs and contemplate the horrendous cost (and often ecological ineffectiveness) of rehabilitation. For land degradation, it is wise to assume that prevention is always cheaper and more effective than cure. But it is difficult to get people excited about prevention, if they cannot see or appreciate the problem.

Complementing the activities of Landcare groups is an extensive, and still rapidly growing, array of innovative environmental monitoring, research and education programmes under the banner of 'land literacy'. These programmes aim to help people to learn to read and listen to the land in which they live in order to reach a much deeper understanding of the land and human impact upon it.

Land resource assessment and monitoring land condition does not have to mean highly specialized survey teams using complex instruments with unpronounceable names producing beautiful maps which then reside in map files, vertiplans and computers in government offices, never to be seen by the people who actually live on and manage the land. There are much more exciting and useful ways to generate and use information about the condition of natural resources, ways which can improve the management of those resources.

Some of the land literacy activities occurring in Australia include: farmer fly-overs, enabling farmers to see their catchments and farms from the air at times when land degradation trends are most visible, often with a profound impact on their perceptions; making the invisible, visible – publications which better assist land users to recognize emerging problems, for example soil salinity and soil structure assessment kits and farm monitoring handbooks; and community action research, exemplified by 'Saltwatch', 'Drainwatch' and 'Watertable Watch'.

Saltwatch began in Victoria in 1987 and is now taking place in five States. By 1992, more than 900 schools and 50 Landcare groups were involved in gathering and analysing tens of thousands of water samples from creeks, rivers, lakes, reservoirs, irrigation channels and bores in Victoria, South Australia, New South Wales, Queensland and the Australian Capital Territory. Each school or community analyses its data and sends it to a central agency for processing, receiving in return a computer-generated overlay map of water quality in the district – which might be placed in the school, the store, the hall or the pub, ensuring that the whole community 'owns' the problem. Data is stored on school computers, as well as in government agencies, and groups are encouraged to look at trends over time within their catchment. The composite maps are used for interpretation, discussion and planning further action such as excursions, revegetation or creek fencing projects, or displays for local shows and festivals.

Drainwatch successfully involved 2500 farmers and their families in collecting water samples from the underground drains flowing from 6000 irrigation farms in Victoria, South Australia and New South Wales in November 1990, and school children assisted with testing samples for their salt content. Streamwatch involves schools within the Sydney Water Board area, in investigating water quality using nine basic tests, which are used to generate a water quality index, so that water quality can be compared across a networks of schools and water catchments. Schools are provided with water testing equipment, and training for teachers in use of the kits and in computer networking. 'Ribbons of Blue' in Western Australia involves students in gathering and managing information on water turbidity, pH, temperature, sediment, biological oxygen demand, nitrogen, phosphorous and conductivity. It also pioneered the involvement of local government as sponsors and recipients of survey information and reclamation suggestions.

Watertable Watch is a great example of making the invisible, visible. In irrigation areas where rising groundwater is a major, but insidious problem, auger holes are dug and lined with plastic pipe, into which is placed a light rod with a float at the bottom and a flag at the top. The rod is painted red at the bottom, orange in the middle and green at the top. As watertables rise, first the orange part of the rod, then the red appears, signalling danger to irrigators – once again, making the invisible, visible.

The 'canary in a coal mine' principle is also being used in land literacy programmes. For example, frogs' thin skins make them extremely sensitive to environmental insults of all kinds and frogs are thus very good biological indicators of catchment conditions. 'Frog watch' is now involving students from Victoria, New South Wales and South Australia in recording details of the presence or absence of frogs (using a field guide and audio tape of frog calls to become familiar with local species) and investigating local environmental conditions. Seeing things from the frog's perspective makes people far more sensitive to the presence of poisons and destruction of habitats. The South Australian 'Wormwatch' programme provides a kit with illustrations of worm species and information about their life cycle and crucial role in soil structure and fertility, and asks rural and urban students to find, identify, count and record the worms in their localities. This information is used by national scientists in research on earthworms and sustainable agriculture.

In these programmes, land users are collecting and monitoring information which was largely the province of specialists five years ago. Many Landcare groups and individuals are now familiar with technology such as piezometers, Geographic Information Systems (GIS), neutron moisture probes, aerial magnetometric surveys and electromagnetic detection of potentially saline areas. The major value of these land literacy programmes is the speed and effectiveness with which they transmit local environmental knowledge through communities, teach people to observe and monitor the health of the land around them and democratize technology, giving local communities ownership of technical information and local responsibility for local issues, and enabling them to formulate much more acute questions for scientists and regulators. Community groups and schools can gather more data from more sampling points than is conceivable for government agencies paying professional staff, and a demand is generated for the analyses and interpretations of this data. People involved in gathering information are more interested in finding what it means and taking it seriously. They feel ownership of this information, commitment to dealing with its implications and are less overawed by the language and the aura of science and bureaucracy.

Farm and catchment planning

One of the most common activities for Landcare groups is property and catchment planning. Most land degradation problems which concern groups cross property boundaries and are thus more suited to catchment-based approaches. Preparing a catchment plan, as a framework for individual property plans, is a valuable strategic activity for Landcare groups. Various planning processes are evolving in different circumstances, but common ingredients include the following:

- A base map of the district is prepared, often using an enlarged aerial photograph (although sometimes on a GIS as well), and group members receive base maps for their own properties at a larger scale;
- The group, with the aid of a facilitator or consultant, drives and/or walks around their district, developing a common understanding of its characteristics – soils, landforms, hydrogeology, native flora and fauna, wetlands and so on, and agreeing on a common local language for describing the different types of land – the natural land units;
- Group members use their local knowledge and the information generated in the group to analyse and map the land units on their own properties. This information is aggregated to compile a land unit map for the catchment;
- The group discusses land management issues and potential elements of more sustainable systems, both at the farm scale and at the catchment scale, where issues such as protection of remnant vegetation and wetlands, wildlife habitat, drainage, management of pest plants and animals and catchment hydrogeology are examined by the group as a whole to develop a coordinated approach.

Developing an Australian agriculture

The context in which land users are seeking and applying information is critical for research and extension. The congruence of the quest for sustainability, the emergence of property and catchment planning and the

256

explosion in community participation through Landcare groups represents a watershed in the development of an *Australian* agriculture.

Landcare groups have precipitated the emergence of new roles within the agricultural knowledge and information system, which are distinctly different from the roles associated with the traditional labels of extensionist, researcher and farmer. In addition to technical advice, Landcare groups need assistance with *process* – how to go about co-operatively planning and setting directions, how to delegate, tackle apathy and creatively resolve conflict in order to make the best use of the human resources available. These are not traditional tools in the extension agent's kitbag. The two roles which have evolved to meet this need are facilitation and co-ordination.

Well over one hundred nationally funded facilitators and co-ordinators are working with Landcare groups. Facilitators usually are based in government agencies, working with up to twenty groups over large areas, concentrating on the groups just getting started, or troubleshooting to assist established groups with particular problems. Essentially the aim of the facilitator is to foster community synergy, helping to develop a shared sense of direction among all the relevant actors. Facilitation is much more a matter of skilled listening, asking the right questions of the right people at the right time, than it is delivery of technical information or packages.

Co-ordinators tend to work part-time with a single group, of which (particularly in southern Australia) they are often a former leader. Thus co-ordinators tend to be local residents, using their own car and phone, who get paid for up to 20 hours per week when group activities become too much for voluntary inputs. Coordinators assist group leaders to organize meetings, they take an active role in planning and managing group projects, keep less active group members interested and provide a link between group members and sources of technical, administrative and financial assistance.

The challenge of developing more sustainable systems of land use and management is fundamentally different from the task of increasing the adoption of an agricultural innovation. The time frames, geographical scale and technical uncertainties implicit in ecological sustainability; and the political, economic and social complexities of changing land use systems, mean that new social and institutional competencies and modes of action need to be developed.

In response to Landcare, extension and research is being required to change to mission-centred, rather than problem-focused approaches; it is having to learn new skills to work effectively at a community, rather than a paddock level; and it is having to concentrate far more on process: who is involved at what level? Who asks the questions and who listens? And who owns the process, rather than on its traditional concerns of tasks and outputs? The social and economic aspirations of many Landcare groups, and their focus on the community and catchment level, necessarily limit the applicability of the traditional technology transfer approaches to a narrow portion of their spectrum of concerns.

Landcare in Australia is an example of a community-based response to the challenge of sustainability during a period of severe resource constraints. The key ingredients of Landcare are its lack of structure, the primacy of land users in determining group directions and activities, the integration of conservation and production issues, the involvement of people other than farmers in groups and the extent to which groups assume responsibility for their own problems and resources. Landcare group activity often involves, and is complemented by, innovative approaches to monitoring land status (land literacy) and by participatory approaches to planning better systems of land management at farm and catchment scales.

'Community First' thinking means a change in focus: from transferring information to asking the right questions; from presenting to skilled listening and interpretation of feedback; from starting with research outputs to building upon the diverse knowledge and inputs of many stakeholders. Facilitating community synergy, assisting communities to work together to assume responsibilities for defining and tackling their own problems, can inform research and extension approaches at both the individual farm level and at the institutional level.

Creating learning systems: a metaphor for institutional reform for development

RICHARD BAWDEN

Learning how to learn

The increasing application of learning approaches to a wide range of human endeavours is releasing all kinds of creative responses to problematic institutional situations. Nowhere is this more welcome than in the practice of rural development. For far too long, the heart of development practice has been characterized by an irony which saps the energies and motivations of even the most enthusiastic practitioner: those very institutions that are established to facilitate societal change at one moment, invariably become its next major constraint.

The challenge for development is not to reject institutionalization, but to create a different kind of institutional organization which has the capacity to retain its abilities to facilitate, as well as respond to, change; one which is able to co-evolve in its relationships with the dynamic and complex environments in which it exists. As learning is the only process by which such a co-evolving relationship can be established and subsequently sustained, it is important that a learning approach to institutional and organizational development be explored.

This is the story of Hawkesbury College (the University of Western Sydney) and one attempt in Australia to bring a critical and systemic learning approach to the process of institutional reform as the key to responsible rural development. The aim of such an approach is to create learning systems which are able to retain their abilities to be influenced by, as well as to continue to have a positive influence on, the circumstances which surround them: to create learning systems which create learning organizations through the synthesis of different ways of learning.

A context for institutional reform

The radical reform of educational or development institutions requires that we create flexible learning organizations. But even when we set out to institutionalize new laws, norms, rituals, shared beliefs and so on, the processes that we use invariably remain grounded in old norms and beliefs. This somewhat self-denying paradox is a prime example of a phenomenon of organizational development described as 'single loop learning' (Argyris and Schön, 1978):

> There is a single feed-back loop which connects detected outcomes of action to organisational strategies and assumptions which are modified so as to keep organisational performance within the range set by organisational norms. The norms themselves . . . remain unchanged.

If the prevailing norms are to be transcended in the name of genuine innovation and profound institutional reform, then there will need to be 'new sorts of inquiry which resolve incompatible organizational norms by setting new priorities and weightings of norms, or by restructuring the norms themselves' – the double loop learning concept (Argyris and Schön, 1978).

It is useful to imagine that organizations can themselves learn, and that accordingly, organizational development can proceed through both single and double loop learning strategies. This metaphor of the learning organization is useful for examining institutional reform and it can be further enriched through the use of another metaphor – the organization as a learning or inquiring system. It is this enriched systems metaphor that provides the context for the work that has been under way at Hawkesbury for the past dozen years or so.

What started out as an exercise in curriculum reform to incorporate new ways of learning about systems approaches to agriculture, has transformed itself into a pervasive process for creating learning systems for development – including its own! In this regard, the Hawkesbury experience is a deliberate exception to the observation of Simon (1967) that 'we do not in our colleges today, make use of *any* learning principles in a considered, systematic way. We do not design the college as a learning environment.'

The essence of learning systems

Learning organizations are collectives or communities of individuals who share experiences and understanding through co-operative learning and genuine participation in those events which affect them. For any organization or community to learn, individuals must not only themselves be active learners, but they must also be committed to sharing that learning in ways which allow consensual understanding or meaning to be reached. Here then is the essence of the participative process through which 'people-centred development' is made possible through 'social learning concepts and methods' (Korten, 1984).

Here too lies the clue to the systems nature of the argument – the learning organization can be transformed into that of the learning or action researching system (Bawden, 1990). The nature of this sort of systems thinking needs to be carefully described for it relates not to the conventional idea of a group of individuals comprising a social system, but to a collaborative process of systemic learning; an 'ecology of mind' to use Bateson's (1972) graphic phrase. In this manner there is, as Checkland (1984) would describe it, 'a shift in systemicity from reality to the process of inquiry into reality' – from knowledge systems to systems of knowing or inquiring systems.

A model of learning which draws on a number of different intellectual traditions, is developed below. It represents a moment in the 'history of ideas' which has been flowing both with and from Hawkesbury's recent 'history of events' (Bawden, 1992a). Central to its logic is the notion that learning is the exploration of difference which must include differences in the learning process itself.

Of learning and differences

A useful point of entry into the theoretical framework which is informing the Hawkesbury learning systems approach is that of a 'cycle' of learning activities developed by David Kolb. The context for this lies in his definition of experiential learning as: 'the creation of knowledge through the transformation of experience' (Kolb, 1984). This process of transformation is conceptualized as a cycle comprising four different, though inter-related, activities. These see individuals systematically, if iteratively, finding out about situations in both 'concrete' and 'abstract worlds' and taking actions in those 'worlds' too (Checkland, 1981).

Whilst these concepts refer to the psychology of learning of individuals, learning is essentially a social act (Habermas, 1972). As part of the finding-out activities the learner frequently turns to accessing social knowledge, engaging in 'conversations' with written and/or spoken ideas, theories or philosophies. Similarly, the learner may engage in activities with others to learn some new and relevant practice. Three different forms of learning – propositional, practical and experiential – can therefore be recognized (Reason and Heron, 1986).

Habermas (1972) adds a vital perspective to these distinctions in proposing that people create knowledge for three fundamentally different motivations which reflect – a technical interest for prediction and control (human/nature interaction), a practical interest for understanding (human communicative interaction), and an emancipatory interest (social relations of power, domination and alienation). As this model allows us insights into learning about how and why we come to know for knowing, know for doing and know for being, it also allows us to explore different levels of learning (Bateson, 1972). As part of our exploration of learning, it is necessary to learn about how we come to learn. Engagement at this second level of learning allows us to change the process of the first level of learning.

This multi-dimensional model of learning, positing different stages, styles, forms, levels, epistemological states and interest constitutions, suggests a complexity of the process which severely tests the adequacy of the simplistic concept of learning as a cyclical process. An alternative is to present the process as a dynamic system involving all of the above aspects related to each other in a densely interconnected and recursive – that is, always reciprocal and dynamic – manner. This notion of the inquiring or learning system must also embrace the concept of recursiveness between the different levels of learning (of seeing, interpreting and acting), as well as between different epistemic states, with each representing profoundly different assumptions about the nature of knowledge.

What we see in the world is thus both a function and an outcome of the way we interpret the world and *vice versa*. We can go further and include our actions within this schema: what we do in this world is a function and a outcome of the way we both see and interpret the world and *vice versa*. It is through individuals becoming conscious of the potential for learning about learning as the basis for learning how to learn differently, that reform can be institutionalized. So far the discussion has concentrated on the learner as an individual; it is now important to explore how individuals can collaborate as learning collectives – as institutions which learn.

Collaborative learning: consensus for action

The picture that has begun to emerge is of individual learners attempting to reconcile their abstract thoughts and theories, along with their imaginings and expectations, with their ordinary everyday experiences, through their own learning system. This notion must now be expanded to present learning systems in relation to groups of co-operating individuals sharing in this process as social beings. Here we have learning individuals conversing with each other as they collaborate to reach a common understanding in order to find agreement about what needs to be done in their shared everyday worlds of events and ideas. It is these critical conversations between learning people seeking to find some mutual understanding – some consensus about actions to be taken – that Habermas (1984) refers to as communicative action.

In this context of communicative action, three vital aspects of development through institutional reform suggest themselves from the experiences at Hawkesbury:

- Consensus for action, arises through conversations amongst those participants in events (current or projected) who are attempting to share common understanding about the practical circumstances in which they find (or could find) themselves;

261

- Consensus for action is difficult precisely because it is a function of the quality of those conversations, which itself is a function of the abilities of individuals to share their different experiences, different ways of understanding and different dispositions for action;
- Consensus for action must embrace exploration of learning differences in such a way that they can be creatively used both to maintain internal coherence within the collaborative learning system, as well as to develop and maintain appreciative relationships between the system and other systems in the environment.

From these perspectives, dynamic learning systems are characterized by what might be referred to as coherence through difference. Communities or organizations facing problematic situations will only retain their coherence if they are conscious of, and competent at dealing with, the differences between the individuals that comprise the group with respect to a host of issues surrounding the situation. Not the least of these issues is the very significant differences that can exist between such individuals in the way by which they might go about their learning.

Differences exist in the way different individuals experience their everyday worlds. They also exist in the ways by which meaning is constructed from these experiences. Individuals differ in the way they value particular knowledge and knowledge created in particular ways. Individuals hold particular epistemological stances – even though they might not know that they do! And each individual has particular notions about the nature of the world (ontology), about what is beautiful and ugly (aesthetics), about what is good and evil (morals), about how things make sense (logic) and about what is right and what is wrong (ethics).

If the various domains within the learning systems of individuals are the source of significant differences in style, form, states and so on, then the possibilities for difference when two or more individuals come together to seek consensual action for changes to shared events, must be many-fold more!

The challenge that faces creators of learning systems is to institutionalize ways of creating learning systems; to facilitate organized communicative actions which will encourage learners to explore both their own indigenous ways of knowing, as well as those of others, in ways that provide fresh insights into pervasive problems, such that the learning organization is now reconceptualized as the institutionalized learning system.

Institutionalized learning systems

The need to develop ways of thinking and acting systemically (or systemic learning) has been a central focus of the Hawkesbury approach (Bawden *et al.*, 1984). Systems methodologies can be used as vehicles for helping facilitate systems thinking by all involved with any complex and dynamic inquiry (Bawden, 1990). This is the reason for the adoption by the Hawkesbury faculty of action research as the predominant mode of inquiry – albeit with many variations, depending on the nature of the issues under investigation, as well as the particular predilections and competencies of the various individual researchers.

Experience at Hawkesbury has revealed that it is not an easy task to encourage students, or any other 'client' learners for that matter, to adopt systemic methodologies, and this in spite of the fact that there is often general agreement that conventional ways of scientific inquiry are quite inappropriate, given the complexity and messiness of the particular situation at hand. Salner (1986) provides a most useful insight here in concluding that:

> Systems learning requires a certain way of thinking that is independent of the content of systems concepts.. (and) requires something more than presenting information and encouraging student problem solving. For general systems learning, with its emphasis on structures rather than on content, epistemic competence may be the most critical competence of all . . . student development is most likely to occur when mild pressure in the environment toward movement is consistently present so that the student cannot conveniently escape the kinds of confrontations that produce growth.

Here then is the key to institutional reform as the basis for sustainable development praxis: the judicious combination of a gently provoking practice with a comprehensive and multi-dimensional and systemic model of learning. This is the design framework for institutions as critical learning systems. The ultimate goal for those who make up institutional learning systems is to learn how to learn systemically!

Afterword

Robert Chambers

Much can be done in broadening and extending the concepts, principles, methodologies and strategies presented in this book. Academic research has its place in analysing and understanding what is happening, but the most important contributions now will come from those who engage in practice and who find things to do and ways to do them that work. Many of these will be farmers. Others will be new professionals.

Three priorities stand out. All three have been opened up by contributors to this book. And all three run counter to convention and offer new fields of action.

The first is methods for observation, experimentation and analysis by farmers themselves. Farmers have already taken part in the development of new methods and approaches. One of the greatest contributions scientists and extensionists can now make is to interact with farmers to develop more methods and approaches that farmers can themselves use and share; and then to disseminate these to other farmers and facilitators.

The second lies in the approaches and methods for changing the behaviour, attitudes and beliefs of scientists, extensionists, teachers and trainers, in the field, in headquarters, and in universities, colleges and training institutes. Trainers and facilitators in Participatory Rural Appraisal have found that brief but intensive field experiences can enable scientists to 'flip', to see things the other way round, and to put first the newly perceived priorities of farmers. The frontier here is to develop and spread more approaches and methods for such personal and professional change.

The third is complementary strategies for institutional change. Recent studies have shed light on comparative experience, and have shown the need for action research to learn more (Merrill-Sands, *et al.*, 1991; Farrington and Bebbington, 1993). Questions include how universities, colleges and training institutes can shift from teaching which embodies and imprints the transfer-of-technology mode, to become places where people learn to learn and learn to help others learn; how large top-down bureaucracies can transform themselves to promote, reward and meet diverse demands from below; how organizations can themselves become more participatory and adaptable, learning to learn; and how such learning organizations can share and spread their new ways.

The last word is that there is no last word. The concerns of *Farmers First* with performance and of *Beyond Farmer First* with process both point to change, adaptation and innovation as vital. In moving away from reductionism, linear thinking and standard solutions, in favour of more inclusive holism, open systems thinking and methodological pluralism, they promise to serve better the growing population of vulnerable resource-poor farm families. The new sensitivity to context, the new awareness of behaviour and the new repertoire of methods present agricultural scientists and extensionists with challenges and opportunities which imply deep and long-term change. Meeting those challenges and exploiting those opportunities presents an agenda for the 1990s and for the twenty-first century.

This book opens up the issues, presents evidence of what is being accomplished, and supports those who work for change. Who now will take up the challenge? Academic researchers? Teachers and trainers? Extensionists? National and international scientists? NGO fieldworkers? Or farmers – poor or rich, women or men? Perhaps the answer is that all have a part to play; and that most of the transforming initiatives will be through creative alliances which invent, share and spread new approaches, methods and behaviour. This book points to what needs to be done. For all who can act, there is no need to wait.

The 'Beyond Farmer First' Researcher:
A play in two acts

LORI-ANN THRUPP and JORGE UQUILLAS

Near the end of the IIED/IDS *Beyond Farmer First* Workshop in October 1992, Lori-Ann Thrupp and Jorge Uquillas performed a short play about the difficulties of operationalizing a *Beyond Farmer First* approach in the field and in a conventional agricultural research institution. The play raised much laughter and provoked many participants to nod their heads in agreement, for while there is more than a hint of irony in it, there is also a great deal of truth.

Act I: The Beyond Farmer First Researcher and The Campesino

The *Beyond Farmer First Researcher* (with no disciplinary identity) and the *Campesino* meet in a remote rural village in Latin America. The Researcher is part of an interdisciplinary team from an external support organization which is planning to initiate a farmer participatory research activity in the village. The Campesino is an 'average' peasant farmer. This is their first encounter.

RESEARCHER: Hello, my name is Sharing Interactiva. I work with a dynamic non-government organisation called INPABEFFA, which is the acronym for Interactive Non-Positivist Participatory Beyond Farmer First Associates. I'm very pleased to meet you! What is your name?

CAMPESINO: *Hola, me llamo* Jorge Camposeios – My name is George Dryfields. I live in Macondo. [They shake hands]

RESEARCHER: We've come to construct a creative interface with you and the community in order to engage in an interactive discourse regarding your adaptable indigenous knowledge, to appreciate and examine livelihood strategies, and to sensitively disaggregate differentiated social actors and confront conflictual relationships in order to facilitate a process by which you as agents in this agroecosystem become empowered to engage in analysis, resolve conflicts and legitimize your worldviews, as part of the contextual process of sustainable development.

CAMPESINO: [Looks puzzled] I'm sorry, but I don't understand what you're saying.

RESEARCHER: Excuse me . . . I'll try to use more direct semantics and linguistic clarity: we're very interested in learning from the 'insiders' in your community about your unique epistemologies and cosmovisions, while providing you access to ideas, methods and processes that may create an enabling environment in which the local knowledge base can be dynamized, appreciated by outsiders and validated for effective change.

CAMPESINO: I'm sorry again, Señora, but your words are foreign . . . What are you trying to tell me? You sound like a missionary.

RESEARCHER: Let me explain: we'd like to participate with people in your community and facilitate methods so you can identify and analyse your *own* problems, opportunities and needs, and establish your *own* priorities and action plans for sustainable alternatives and improved livelihoods.

CAMPESINO: 'Participate' . . . 'participar' . . . 'Facilitate' . . . 'facilitar' . . . I hear something maybe interesting . . . But tell me, what are you offering? Do you have money or seeds or fertilizers?

RESEARCHER: No, we don't have money. We instead have some very unique analytical frameworks, very innovative, post-positivist, post-populist methodologies, along with long-term commitment and skills for fostering participatory dialogue and self-critical awareness, for creating interactive and empowering processes!!!

CAMPESINO: [Starts to stand up and walk away] Listen, Señora, a lot of gringos and technical guys from the government come around here using big words and asking questions. They always have big promises, but things never work. We seem to get along better organizing our own ways . . . We don't have much time . . . [Starts to leave]

RESEARCHER: Wait! Wait! Please! Could I just ask a few questions, and maybe talk with your wife and family so we can get to know each other and I can explain?

CAMPESINO: [Hesitates] OK, OK . . . Come to my farm. I'll introduce you to my family and show you our farm and crops and we can start talking together . . .

Act II: The Beyond Farmer First Researcher and The Deputy Director

The *Beyond Farmer First Researcher*, whom we saw in Act I, meets with her supervisor, the *Deputy Director* of the Standard National Agricultural Research Institute. The Researcher has been developing a project using a participatory farmer-first approach and has submitted a progress report and proposal to the Deputy Director requesting additional support to begin Phase II. The Deputy Director has several concerns about the initiative.

DEP DIR: I have reviewed your findings and I have considered your proposal for continuing a project using this farmer participatory approach. I must say that I am somewhat perplexed. Let me start with several questions [spoken in rapid succession]: *One*, where is your quantitative analysis? *Two*, have you used regression models to substantiate the findings and significant correlations? *Three*, what is your sample frame? Where is your control plot? *Four*, where is the cost-benefit analysis that shows the rate of return of investment in this project? *Five*, can you apply this methodology in another area and obtain comparable data? *Six*, the report describes achieving success for improving farmers' livelihoods and sustainability of agricultural ecosystems . . . Do you have measures for these concepts? What criteria of evaluation are used? *Seven*, the report also stresses participation of women in the research. I know this gender issue is important, but do you have *evidence* that women are contributing a significant percentage of labour to the gross agricultural income in this region? *Eight*, the proposal also discusses work with marginalized people in marginal areas. How do you intend to justify this when our institutional mandate is to work in areas where there is strong potential for high-yield production and income generation?

These are a few questions to start . . . I have additional queries and comments, of course . . .

RESEARCHER: Well, sir, I can attempt to answer each of these questions, but first let me explain some basic background information and the premises of this work. As I described briefly in the report, this project is based on a unique methodological and philosophical approach. It can be complementary to conventional methodologies used in this and other R&D institutions, but it is distinct in many ways. This work starts with the principle that the transfer-of-technology mode of research and extension has limitations and has not served the interests of resource-poor farmers in many areas. It argues that an alternative mode or *paradigm* of research and extension is needed to enable peasant farmers living in complex, diverse, risk-prone environments to be fully involved in and control the development process . . .

DEP DIR: [Interrupts the Researcher] . . . Well, you know that your colleagues here do not generally *agree* with these ideas. Moreover, these new modes are contrary to the models and methods that we learned in our advanced institutions of professional training . . . [Points to the many diplomas and certificates hanging on the wall behind him].

268

RESEARCHER: I know that, sir, but you see there has been a transformation in paradigms. Farmer-first methods have been tried and used successfully in many parts of the world. Such methodologies are at the 'cutting-edge' of research in the agricultural sciences. They have been shown to generate processes of innovation and technology adaptation that meet the livelihood needs of poor farmers in a sustainable way. Our initial experiences here in this country have also shown great potential . . .

DEP DIR: Let me ask you another serious question: How do you expect to *publish* your results in the *Journal of Agricultural Economics* or *Crop Science*? Do you expect to earn your unit points with these findings?

RESEARCHER: Well, sir . . . perhaps other journals might . . . [Voice fades]

DEP DIR: Hmm, I'm not sure I understand your approach. You will have to present this proposal to the Board of Directors. And, frankly, I am not optimistic. This sounds *too* esoteric, *too* soft, *too* idealistic, *too* . . . suspicious. Maybe they use these participatory approaches in places like England or India, but we have different standards and different priorities here in this country. Given present international economic conditions, we must stress agro-exports and agribusiness productivity . . .

APPENDIX II

Sources of information on agricultural development which are available free or at low cost to Third World readers

It is not always easy to obtain up-to-date information on agricultural development. Academic journals are often very expensive and sometimes slow to catch up with innovations and trends in the field. Many good books on the subject are over-priced and hard to acquire. However, there are a number of institutions that provide relevant information either free-of-charge or at low cost to Third World readers.

AFSR/E – The Association for Farming Systems Research-Extension is a global association made up of individuals and networks involved in farming systems research and development. The association produces the *Journal for Farming Systems Research-Extension*, the *AFSR/E Newsletter*, regional journals and holds conferences and workshops regularly. Clive Lightfoot

269

at ICLARM, PO Box 1501, Makati, Metro Manilla 1299, The Phillipines is charged with developing networking contacts.

CDC – Clearinghouse on Development Communication, 1815 North Fort Myer Drive, Suite 600, Arlington, VA 22209, USA, publishes *Development Communication Report*, which is available free of charge to readers in the South. The report covers applications of communication approaches to development problems.

CIDE/WRI – The Centre for International Development and the Environment at the World Resources Institute, 1709 New York Avenue, NW, Washington DC 20006, USA produces a range of publications on sustainable agriculture and community development approaches, including reports of its *From the Ground Up* programme in Africa.

CIRAN – Centre for International Research and Advisory Networks, PO Box 90734, 2509 LS The Hague, The Netherlands, produces the *Indigenous Knowledge and Development Monitor*. The monitor is a publication for people who are interested in all aspects of indigenous knowledge and development. It is produced in collaboration with the **Centre for Indigenous Knowledge for Agricultural Development (CIKARD)**, 318 Curtiss Hall, Iowa State University, Ames, Iowa, 50011, USA, the **Leiden Ethnosystems and Development Programme (LEAD)**, Institute of Cultural and Social Studies, University of Leiden, PO Box 9555, 2300 RB, Leiden, The Netherlands and various national and regional Indigenous Knowledge Resource Centres in Nigeria, The Phillipines, Ghana, Kenya, Indonesia, Sri Lanka and Mexico (contactable through CIKARD).

CTA – Technical Centre for Agricultural and Rural Cooperation, Postbus 380, 6700 Wageningen, The Netherlands was established to improve access to information on agricultural development for ACP (Africa, Carribean and Pacific) countries. ACP nationals may request free subscriptions to the magazine, *Spore*, and free access to *Question-Answer* and *Document Delivery Services*.

FAO – Food and Agriculture Organisation of the United Nations, via delle Terme di Caracella, 00100, Rome, Italy. FAO's Office for External Relations publishes *DEEP – Development Education Exchange Papers*, a regular bulletin intended to promote the exchange of ideas between FAO and NGOs working in agricultural and rural development. It is produced in English, French and Spanish. Other publications on agriculture, forestry, and rural development are also available.

FARMI – Farm and Resource Management Institute, Visayas State College of Agriculture, 6521-A Baybay, Leyte, Phillipines publishes *On-farm Research Notes*, which reports on PRA and on-farm trial work being carried out in the Phillipines.

FTP – Forests, Trees and People Newsletter is a quarterly publication produced in English, French and Spanish and distributed to people interested in community forestry activities. It forms part of the FTP programme's networking activities which are jointly run by the Community Forestry Unit, FAO, Rome, Italy, IRDC, Uppsala (below), SILVA at 21 rue Paul Bert, 941300 Nogent-sur-Mame, France and regional programmes in Cameroon, Ecuador and Thailand.

Honey Bee is a global network for documenting, testing and exchanging information about indigenous ecological and technological innovations. The *Honey Bee* newsletter is published in five languages and the network extends to 57 countries. Network membership for those in the South is based on exchange of material. The main contact point is Anil Gupta, Indian Institute of Management, Ahmedabad 380015, India.

IDS – Institute of Development Studies at the University of Sussex, Brighton, BN1 9RE, UK produces *Discussion Papers* series and the *IDS Bulletin*. Topics cover a broad range of development issues.

IIED – International Institute for Environment and Development, 3 Endsleigh Street, London WC1 HODD, UK. The Sustainable Agriculture Programme produces an informal journal, *RRA Notes*, which is available free to those who apply. There is a small charge for back issues. A French series, *Rélais MARP*, has recently been launched to provide practical information on participatory appraisal in West Africa. The programme also produces a range of training materials, including training guides, videos, slide and picture packs, source books and workshop reports. The *Gatekeeper Series* provides short briefing papers on policy issues, while the *Research Series* covers recent research related to sustainable agriculture. Both series are free to Third World readers. The Drylands Programme produces a quarterly bulletin, *Haramata*, along with *Issues Papers* in English and French that deal with natural resource management issues in dryland areas, largely in Africa. This bulletin is free to those working for Southern organizations. The Human Settlements Programme produces the journal *Environment and Urbanisation* which covers a range of community development issues in urban settings, including agriculture.

ILEIA – Information Centre for Low External Input Agriculture, PO Box 64, 3830 AB Leusden, The Netherlands produces the quarterly *ILEIA Newsletter* on a range of issues relating to sustainable agriculture and participatory technology development (PTD). Individuals and organizations in the South may request free subscriptions from ILEIA.

IRDC – International Rural Development Centre, Swedish University of Agricultural Sciences, Box 7005, S-75007, Uppsala, Sweden, publish a series of issues papers targetted at policy makers and implementors of rural development.

IT – Intermediate Technology Publications produces several quarterly journals including *Appropriate Technology* and *Waterlines*. They also run a *Books by Post* scheme, which increases access to a catalogue of recommended books on appropriate technology and development issues. More information can be obtained from IT Publications, 103–105 Southampton Row, London WC1B 4HH, UK.

MYRADA – Mysore Relief and Development Agency, 2, Service Road, Domlur Layout, Bangalore, 560 071, India. MYRADA's *Participatory and Learning Methods (PALM)* series is a useful collection of papers, videos and training materials focussing on participatory methods for learning and analysis.

ODI – Overseas Development Institute, Regent's College, Inner Circle, Regent's Park, London NW1 4NS, UK produces a newsletter for the *Agricultural Administration (Research and Extension) Network*, which covers a range of methodological and institutional issues relating to participatory agricultural research and extension. Other ODI networks cover Social Forestry, Pastoral Development and Irrigation Management. Newsletters are available at low subscription rates or free on application.

Oxfam – 274 Banbury Road, Oxford, OX2 7DZ UK produces a journal *Development in Practice* which examines methodological, institutional and development policy issues. *Baobab*, produced by the Arid Lands Information Network, Casier Postal 3, Dakar, Senegal is designed for field practioners working in dryland areas and is produced in both English and French.

Panos – Panos/London, 9 White Lion Street, London N1 9PD, UK produces *Panoscope* six times per year, aimed at stimulating debate on a wide range of development issues. Panos Briefings are intended for journalists reporting on environment and development issues. These publications are available free to Southern organisations on application.

PPP – Popular Participation Programme at the Development Studies Unit, Department of Social Anthropology, Stockholm University, S-10691, Stockholm, Sweden produce a discussion paper series.

Rodale Institute publishes *International Ag-Sieve* newsletter, a summary of news about regenerative agriculture, six times a year. Subscriptions are available from Rodale Institute, 611 Siegfriedale Road, Kutztown, PA 19530, USA. *Entre Nous* is published in French by Rodale International, BP A237, Thiès, Senegal and focuses on regenerative agriculture in West Africa.

TVE – the Television Trust for the Environment, at Postbus 7, 3700 AA Zeist, The Netherlands, distributes the video, *Participatory Research with Women Farmers*, produced by ICRISAT in India. It is available in French, Spanish and English, and is free of charge for organizations in developing countries.

World Neighbors, 5116 Portland Avenue, Oklahoma City, OK 73112, USA publishes *World Neighbors in Action*, a newsletter with practical new ideas for agricultural development. It is free to applicants from the South.

List of participants and contributors
(authors of papers included in this book are identified with a star – *)

Alsop, Ruth
The Ford Foundation ▪ 55 Lodi Estate ▪ New Delhi ▪ INDIA

Atta-Krah, Kwesi (A.N.)*
AFRENA-East Africa ▪ International Centre for Research in Agroforestry ▪ United Nations Avenue ▪ Nairobi ▪ KENYA

Barrow, Edmund
African Wildlife Foundation ▪ P.O. Box 48177 ▪ Nairobi ▪ KENYA

*Bawden, Richard**
Faculty of Agriculture and Rural Development ▪ University of Western Sydney ▪ Hawkesbury NSW 2753 ▪ AUSTRALIA

*Bebbington, Anthony J.**
Overseas Development Institute ▪ Regent's College ▪ Inner Circle, Regent's Park ▪ London NW1 4NS ▪ UNITED KINGDOM

*Bentley, Jeffrey**
Escuela Agricola Panamericana ▪ El Zamorano ▪ A. Postal 93 ▪ Tegucigalpa ▪ HONDURAS

Blauert, Jutta
Institute of Latin American Studies ▪ University of London ▪ 31 Tavistock Square ▪ London WC1H 9HA ▪ UNITED KINGDOM

Blowfield, Mick
Natural Resources Institute ▪ Central Avenue ▪ Chatham Maritime ▪ Kent ME4 4TB ▪ UNITED KINGDOM

Brokensha, David
Tanrhocal House ▪ 86 Newland ▪ Sherborne ▪ Dorset DT9 3DT ▪ UNITED KINGDOM

*Cabarle, Bruce**
Center for International Development and Environment ▪ World Resources Institute ▪ 1709 New York Avenue, NW ▪ Washington, DC 20006 ▪ USA

Caldas, Tadeu
ECOTROPIC ▪ Parracombe ▪ Chapel Lane ▪ Forest Row ▪ East Sussex, RH18 5BU ▪ UNITED KINGDOM

*Campbell, Andrew**
MAKS ▪ Department of Communication and Innovation Studies ▪ Agricultural University ▪ Hollandseweg 1 ▪ 6706 KN Wageningen ▪ THE NETHERLANDS

Carloni, Alice
Investment Centre ▪ Food and Agriculture Organisation of the United Nations ▪ via delle Terme di Caracalla 00100 Rome ▪ ITALY

273

Chambers, Robert*
Institute of Development Studies ▪ University of Sussex ▪ Brighton BN1 9RE ▪ UNITED KINGDOM

Cornwall, Andrea*
Department of Social Anthropology ▪ School of Oriental and African Studies ▪ Thornhaugh Street, Russell Square ▪ London NR4 0XG ▪ UNITED KINGDOM

de Boef, Walter
Programme Coordinator ▪ CPRO-DLO ▪ Local Management and Use of Biodiversity ▪ Centre for Genetic Resources ▪ P.O. Box 16 ▪ NL 6700 AA Wageningen ▪ THE NETHERLANDS

Devavaram, John
Society for Peoples Education and Economic Change ▪ 14, Jeyaraja Illam Opp. Kasirajan Hospital ▪ Tirupalai, Madurai ▪ INDIA 625 014

Diop, Amadou
CRAR-Senegal ▪ Rodale International File ▪ P.O. Box – A 237 ▪ Thies ▪ SENEGAL

Drinkwater, Michael*
Kabwe Research Station ▪ PO Box 80908 ▪ Kabwe ▪ ZAMBIA

Fairhead, James*
Department of Social Anthropology ▪ School of Oriental and African Studies ▪ Thornhaugh Street, Russell Square ▪ London WC1E OXG ▪ UNITED KINGDOM

Farrington, John*
Overseas Development Institute ▪ Regent's College ▪ Inner Circle ▪ Regent's Park ▪ London NW1 4NS ▪ UNITED KINGDOM

Fre, Zeremariam
Pastoralist and Environmental Network for the Horn of Africa ▪ Panther House, Room 201, West Block ▪ 38 Mount Pleasant ▪ London WClX OAP ▪ UNITED KINGDOM

Fujisaka, Sam*
International Rice Research Institute ▪ P.O. Box 933 ▪ Manila ▪ PHILIPPINES

Gacitúa, Miguel Diaz
El Fondo de Solidaridad e Inversion Social ▪ Calle Ahumada 48 ▪ Piso 11 ▪ Santiago ▪ CHILE

Gibbon, David
School of Development Studies ▪ University of East Anglia ▪ Norwich ▪ Norfolk NR4 7TJ ▪ UNITED KINGDOM

Go, Alicia
Visayas State College of Agriculture ▪ Baybay ▪ Leyte 6521-A ▪ PHILIPPINES

Go, Samuel
Visayas State College of Agriculture ▪ Baybay ▪ Leyte 6521-A ▪ PHILIPPINES

Gubbels, Peter*
Project Coordinator ▪ Voisins Mondiaux ▪ 01 BP ▪ Ouagadougou 01 ▪ BURKINA FASO

274

*Guijt, Irene**
Sustainable Agriculture Programme ▪ International Institute for Environment and Development ▪ 3 Endsleigh Street ▪ London WC1H ODD ▪ UNITED KINGDOM

*Jiggins, Janice**
De Dellen 4 ▪ 6673 MD Andelst ▪ THE NETHERLANDS

Jodha, N.S.
Mountain Farming Systems Programme ▪ International Centre for Integrated Mountain Development ▪ P.O. Box 3226 ▪ Kathmandu ▪ NEPAL
World Bank ▪ 1818 H Street, NW ▪ Washington, DC 20433 ▪ USA

*Leach, Melissa**
Institute of Development Studies ▪ University of Sussex ▪ Brighton ▪ Brighton BN1 9RE ▪ UNITED KINGDOM

*Long, Norman**
School of Social Sciences ▪ University of Bath ▪ Claverton Down ▪ Bath BA2 7AY ▪ UNITED KINGDOM

Lundberg, Jan Olof
Senior Research Officer ▪ SAREC ▪ PO Box 16140 ▪ S-103 23 Stockholm ▪ SWEDEN

*Marsden, David**
Centre for Development Studies ▪ University College of Swansea ▪ Singleton Park ▪ Swansea SA2 8PP ▪ WALES

*Matose, Frank**
Forest Research Centre ▪ Forestry Commission ▪ Box HG 139, Harare ▪ ZIMBABWE

Mazonde, Isaac
NIR ▪ University of Botswana ▪ Post Bag 0022 ▪ Gaborone ▪ BOTSWANA

*Millar, David**
Tamale Archdiocesan Agricultural Programme ▪ PO Box 42 ▪ Tamale-N./R. ▪ GHANA

Moris, Jon
Department of Sociology, Social Work and Anthropology ▪ Utah State University ▪ Logan, Utah 84322–0730 ▪ USA

*Mukamuri, Billy**
ISSS ▪ Tampereen Yliopiston ▪ Box 607 ▪ 33101 TRE ▪ FINLAND

Norrish, Patricia
AERDD ▪ University of Reading ▪ 3 Earley Gate, Whiteknights Road ▪ Reading RG6 2AL ▪ UNITED KINGDOM

Ocan, Charles
Centre for Basic Research ▪ P.O. Box 9863 ▪ Kampala ▪ UGANDA

Okali, Christine
School of Development Studies ▪ University of East Anglia ▪ Norwich NR4 7TJ ▪ UNITED KINGDOM

Partap, Tej
Mountain Farming Systems Programme ▪ International Centre for Integrated Mountain Development ▪ P.O. Box 3226 ▪ Kathmandu ▪ NEPAL

Pimbert, Michel
Biological Diversity ▪ Conservation Policy Division ▪ WWF International ▪ CH-1196 Gland ▪ SWITZERLAND

Pottier, Johan*
Department of Social Anthropology ▪ School of Oriental and African Studies ▪ Thornhaugh Street, Russell Square ▪ London WC1E OXG ▪ UNITED KINGDOM

Pretty, Jules N.*
Sustainable Agriculture Programme ▪ International Institute for Environment and Development ▪ 3 Endsleigh Street ▪ London WC1H ODD ▪ UNITED KINGDOM

Reddy, K.C.
Alabama A&M University ▪ Normal ▪ Alabama 35762 ▪ USA

Richards, Paul*
Department of Technology and Agriculture ▪ Agricultural University ▪ Newark Canal 11 ▪ 6709 KA Wageningen ▪ THE NETHERLANDS
Department of Anthropology ▪ University College London ▪ Gower Street ▪ London WC1E 6BT ▪ UNITED KINGDOM

Röling, Niels*
Department of Communication and Innovation Studies ▪ Agricultural University ▪ Hollandseweg 1 ▪ 6706 KN Wageningen ▪ THE NETHERLANDS

Salas, Maria A.*
Universitat Hohenheim (430) ▪ Institut für Agrarsoziologie ▪ 7000 Stuttgart 20 ▪ GERMANY

Sanghi, N.K.
Zonal Coordinator ▪ Central Research Institute for Dryland Agriculture Complex ▪ Santosh Nagar ▪ Hyderabad ▪ INDIA – 500 059

Schoonmaker Freudenberger, Karen*
637 N. Blackhawk Avenue ▪ Madison, Wisconsin 53705 ▪ USA

Scoones, Ian*
Sustainable Agriculture Programme ▪ International Institute for Environment and Development ▪ 3 Endsleigh Street ▪ London WC1H ODD ▪ UNITED KINGDOM

Shah, Parmesh*
Institute of Development Studies ▪ University of Sussex ▪ Brighton ▪ Brighton BN1 9RE ▪ UNITED KINGDOM

Sikana, Patrick*
Adaptive Research Planning Team ▪ Misamfu Research Station ▪ PO Box 410055 ▪ Kasama ▪ ZAMBIA

Sotomayor, Octavio
Grupo de Investigaciones Agrarias ▪ Ricardo Matte Perez 0342 ▪ Providencia ▪ Santiago ▪ CHILE

*Stolzenbach, Arthur**
Department of Communication and Innovation Studies ▪ Agricultural University ▪ Hollandseweg 1 ▪ 6706 KN Wageningen ▪ THE NETHERLANDS

Sumberg, J.E.
School of Development Studies ▪ University of East Anglia ▪ Norwich NR4 7TJ ▪ UNITED KINGDOM

*Thompson, John**
Sustainable Agriculture Programme ▪ International Institute for Environment and Development ▪ 3 Endsleigh Street ▪ London WC1H ODD ▪ UNITED KINGDOM

*Thrupp, Lori-Ann**
Center for International Development and Environment ▪ World Resources Institute ▪ 1709 New York Avenue, NW ▪ Washington, DC 20006 ▪ USA

Tillmann, Hermann
Gomaringerstr. 6 ▪ 7413 Gom-Stockach ▪ GERMANY

*Uphoff, Norman**
Cornell International Institute for Food, Agriculture and Development ▪ Box 14, Kennedy Hall ▪ Cornell University ▪ Ithaca, NY 14853 ▪ USA

*Uquillas, Jorge**
FUNDAGRO ▪ Moreno Bellido No. 127 y Amazonas ▪ P.O. Box 17–16-219 ▪ Quito ▪ ECUADOR
World Bank ▪ 1818 H Street, NW ▪ Washington, DC 20433 ▪ USA

*Villarreal, Magdalena**
Department of Sociology of Rural Development ▪ Wageningen Agricultural University ▪ P.O. Box 8130 ▪ 6700 EW Wageningen ▪ THE NETHERLANDS

*Waters-Bayer, Ann**
Institute for Low External Input Agriculture ▪ ETC Foundation ▪ Kastanjelaan 5 ▪ PO Box 64 ▪ 3830 AB Leusden ▪ THE NETHERLANDS

*Welbourn, Alice**
c/o Sustainable Agriculture Programme ▪ International Institute for Environment and Development ▪ 3 Endsleigh Street ▪ London WC1H ODD ▪ UNITED KINGDOM

*Winarto, Yunita**
Jl. Pesang-grahan 61 ▪ Ciputat 15412 ▪ Jakarta Selatan ▪ INDONESIA

Wright, Sue
Department of Community Studies ▪ University of Sussex ▪ Brighton BN1 9QN ▪ UNITED KINGDOM

*Zazueta, Aaron**
Center for International Development and Environment ▪ World Resources Institute ▪ 1709 New York Avenue, NW ▪ Washington, DC 20006 ▪ USA

Zinyama, Lovemore
Department of Geography ▪ University of Zimbabwe ▪ Box MP167 ▪ Harare ▪ ZIMBABWE

References

Abedin, Z. and Haque, H. 1989. Innovator workshops in Bangladesh. In: Chambers, R., Pacey, A. and Thrupp, L. (eds.) 1989. *Farmer First: Farmer Innovation and Agricultural Research.* Intermediate Technology Publications Ltd., London.

AFNETA. 1993. *Workshop Report: Interim Research Committee Meeting in Research Planning and Methodological Development for Phase II of the Alley Farming Network for Tropical Africa (AFNETA) Research.* AFNETA/International Institute for Tropical Agriculture (IITA), Ibadan.

Aguirre, F. and Namdar-Irani, M. 1992. Complementarities and tensions in AGRARIA-State relations in agricultural development: a trajectory. *Agricultural Research and Extension Network Paper No. 32.* Overseas Development Institute (ODI), London.

Allen, T.J. and Cohen, S.I. 1969. Information flow in research and development laboratories. *Administratives Science Quarterly,* 14: 12–19.

Altieri, M.A. 1987. *Agroecology: The Scientific Basis of Alternative Agriculture.* Westview Press, Boulder and Intermediate Technology Publications, London.

Amanor, K. 1990. Analytical abstracts on farmer participatory research. *Agricultural Administration Unit Occasional Paper, 10.* ODI, London.

Arce, A. and Long, N. 1987. The dynamics of knowledge interfaces between Mexican agricultural bureaucrats and peasants: a case study from Jalisco. *Boletin de Estudios Lationamericanos y del Caribe,* 43: 5–30.

Argyris, C. and Schön, D. 1978. *Organizational Learning.* Jossey Bass Publisher, San Francisco.

Ashby, J.A. 1990. *Evaluating Technology with Farmers.* International Centre for Tropical Agriculture (CIAT), Cali, Colombia.

Ashby, J.A., Quiros, C. and Rivera, Y. 1989. Experiences with group techniques in Colombia. In: Chambers *et al.* (eds.) *Farmer First: Farmer Innovation and Agricultural Research.* Intermediate Technology Publications Ltd., London.

Atta-Krah, A.N. and Francis, P.A. 1987. The role of on-farm trials in the evaluation of composite technologies: alley farming in Southern Nigeria. *Agricultural Systems* 23: 133–152.

Atta-Krah, A.N. 1990. From research plots to farmer adoption: a strategy for on-farm alley farming research. *AFNETA Technology Transfer Symposium, 1–3 August, 1989,* IITA, Ibadan.

Bagadion, B.U. and Korten, F.F. 1991. Developing irrigators' organisations: a learning process approach. In: Cernea, M.M. (ed.) *Putting People First.* Oxford University Press, Oxford. 2nd Edition.

Barsky, O. 1990. *Politicas Agrarias en America Latina.* Educational Corporation for Development (CEDECO), Santiago.

Bateson, G. 1972. *Steps to an Ecology of Mind.* Balentine, New York.

Bawden, R.J. 1988. *Experiential Learning and Strategic Change.* Mimeo, Hawkesbury College, Australia.

Bawden, R.J. 1990. Of agricultural systems and systems agriculture. In: Jones, J. (ed.) *Systems Theory Applied to Agriculture and the Food Chain.* Elsevier, New York.

Bawden, R.J. 1992a. Systems approaches to agricultural development: the Hawkesbury experience. *Agricultural Systems.*

Bawden, R.J. 1992b. Of systemics and farming systems research: a critique. In: Raman, K. and Balaguru, T. *Farming Systems Research in India: Strategies for Implementation.* NAARM, Hyderabad.

Bawden, R.J., Macadam, R., Packam, R. and Valentine, I. 1984. Systems thinking and practices in the education of agriculturalists. *Agricultural Systems* 13: 205–25.

Beal, G.M., Dissanayake, W. and Konoshima, S. (eds.) 1986. *Knowledge Generation, Exchange and Utilisation.* Westview Press, Boulder, Colorado.

Bebbington, A.J. 1991a. Farmer organisations in Ecuador: contributions to 'Farmer First' research and development. Sustainable Agriculture Programme *Gatekeeper Series* SA26. International Institute for Environment and Development (IIED), London.

Bebbington, A.J. 1991b. Indigenous agricultural knowledge systems, human interest and critical analysis: reflections on farmer organizations in Ecuador. *Agriculture and Human Values* 18(12): 14–24.

Bebbington, A.J. 1992. Searching for an indigenous agricultural development: Indian organizations and NGOs in the Central Andes of Ecuador. *Working Paper 45,* Centre of Latin American Studies, Cambridge University.

Bebbington, A.J. and Farrington, J. 1992. The scope for NGO-government interactions in agricultural technology development: an international overview. *Agricultural Administration (Research and Extension) Network Paper* 33. ODI, London.

Bebbington, A.J., Thiele, G., Davies, P., Prager, M., and Riveros, H. (eds.) 1993. *Non-Governmental Organizations and the State in Latin America.* Routledge, London.

Bellman, B. 1984. *The Language of Secrecy: Symbols and Metaphors in Poro Ritual.* Rutgers University Press, New Brunswick.

Bentley, J.W. 1992. The epistemology of plant protection: Honduran campesino knowledge of pests and natural enemies and the implication for control strategies. Proceedings of the *CTA/NRI Seminar on Crop Protection for Resource-Poor Farmers, Isle of Thorns, University of Sussex, 4–8 November, 1991.* Natural Resources Institute, Chatham, UK.

Bentley, J.W. and Melara, W. 1991. Experimenting with Honduran farmer-experimenters. *ODI Agricultural Administration (R & E) Network Newsletter* 24: 31–48. ODI, London.

Berdegué, J. 1990. NGOs and farmers organisations in research and extension in Chile. *Agricultural Research and Extension Network Paper No. 19.* ODI, London.

Bernstein, R.J. 1976. *The Restructuring of Social and Political Theory.* Basil Blackwell, Oxford.

Bernstein, R.J. 1983. *Beyond Objectivism and Relativism: Science, Hermeneutics, and Praxis.* The University of Pennsylvania Press, Philadelphia.

Bhaskar, R. (1979). *Reclaiming Reality.* Verso, London.

Biggs, S. 1980. Informal R&D. *Ceres* 13(4): 23–26.

Biggs, S. 1989a. Resource-poor farmer participation in research: a synthesis of experiences from nine national agricultural research systems. *OFCOR Comparative Study Paper 3.* International Service for National Agricultural Research, The Hague.

Biggs, S. 1989b. A multiple source of innovation model of agricultural research and technology promotion. *Agricultural Research and Extension Network Paper No. 6.* ODI, London.

Biggs, S. and Clay, E. 1981. Sources of innovation in agricultural technology. *World Development* 9(4): 321–6.

Bledsoe, C. 1984. The political use of Sande ideology and symbolism. *American Ethnologist:* 455–472.

Boal, A. 1979. *Theatre of the Oppressed.* Pluto Press, London.

Bojanic, A. 1991. La transferencia de tecnología en Bolivia: la marcha para llegar al modelo de usuarios intermedios. Paper presented at *Taller regional para América del Sur: Generación y Transferencia de Tecnología Agropecuaria; el papel de las ONGs y el Sector Público. 2nd-7th December.* Santa Cruz, Bolivia.

279

Borlaug, N. 1992. Small-scale agriculture in Africa: the myths and realities. *Feeding the Future* (Newsletter of the Sasakawa Africa Association) 4: 2.

Bourdieu, P. 1977. *Outline of a Theory of Practice.* Cambridge University Press, Cambridge.

Box, L. 1987. Experimenting cultivators: a methodology for adaptive agricultural research. *ODI Agricultural Administration (Research and Extension) Network Discussion Paper* 23. ODI, London.

Box, L. 1989. Knowledge, networks and cultivators: cassava in the Dominican Republic. In: Long, N. (ed.) *Encounters at the Interface: A Perspective on Social Discontinuities in Rural Development. Wageningen Studies in Sociology* 27. Wageningen Agricultural University, The Netherlands.

Bradley, P. and Dewees, P. 1993. Indigenous woodlands, agricultural production and household economy in the communal areas. In: Bradley, P. and McNamara, K. (eds.) *Living with Trees: Policies for Forestry Management in Zimbabwe.* World Bank Technical Paper, 210. World Bank, Washington DC.

Brokensha, D., Warren, D. and Werner, O. 1980. *Indigenous Knowledge Systems and Development.* University Press of America, Maryland.

Brown, L. 1982. *Innovation Diffusion.* Methuen, London.

Buck, L. 1993. Development of participatory approaches for promoting agroforestry: collaboration between the Mazingira Institute, ICRAF, CARE-Kenya, KEFRI and the Forestry Department (1980–91). In: Wellard, K. and Copestake, J.G. (eds.) *Non-Governmental Organizations and the State in Africa.* Routledge, London.

Buckland, J. and Graham, P. 1990. The Mennonite Central Committee's experience in agricultural research and extension in Bangladesh. *Agricultural Administration (Research and Extension) Network Paper* 17. ODI, London.

Bunch, R. 1985. *Two Ears of Corn: A Guide to People-Centred Agricultural Improvement.* World Neighbours, Oklahoma.

Bunch, R. 1987. Small farmer research: the key element of permanent agricultural improvement. Paper presented to IDS Workshop *Farmers and Agricultural Research: Complementary Methods.* University of Sussex, UK.

Bunch, R. 1989. Encouraging farmers' experiments. In: Chambers, R., Pacey, A. and Thrupp, L-A (eds.) *Farmer First: Farmer Innovation and Agricultural Research: Complementary Methods.* Intermediate Technology Publications Ltd., London.

Bunch, R. 1990. Low input soil restoration in Honduras: the Cantarranas Farmer-to-Farmer Extension Programme. Sustainable Agriculture Programme *Gatekeeper Series,* SA 23. IIED, London.

Burnham, P. 1973. The explanatory value of the concept of adaptation in studies of culture change. In: Renfrew, C. (ed.) *The Explanation of Culture Change.* Duckworth, London.

Byerlee, D. 1987. Maintaining the momentum in post-Green revolution agriculture: a micro-level perspective from Asia. *Michigan State University International Development Paper* No. 10.

Cabieses, F. 1982. Historia de la ciencia y de la tecnología en el Perú. *Historia del Perú: Procesos e Instituciones.* Vol.X: 127–277. Juan Mejía Baca, Lima.

Campbell, A. 1994. Community first: Landcare in Australia. Sustainable Agriculture Programme *Gatekeeper* Series, SA42. IIED, London.

Cardoso, V.H., Caso, C. and Vivar, M. 1991. A public sector on-farm research programme's informal relationships with NGOs: the PIP's growing interest in collaboration. Paper presented at *Taller regional para América del Sur: Generación y Transferencia de Tecnología Agropecuaria; el papel de las ONGs y el Sector Público,* 2–7 December. Santa Cruz, Bolivia.

Carney, J. 1991. Indigenous soil and water management in Senegambian rice farming systems. *Agriculture and Human Values* 8 (1/2): 37–48.

Carruthers, I. and Chambers, R. 1981. Rapid Rural Appraisal: rationale and repertoire. *IDS Discussion Paper* 155. University of Sussex, UK.

Cernea, M.M. (ed.) 1991. *Putting People First. Sociological Variables in Rural Development* (2nd Edition). World Bank, Washington DC.

Cernea, M.M. 1991. Social actors of participatory afforestation strategies. In: Cernea, M. M. (ed.) *Putting People First*. 2nd Edition. World Bank, Washington DC.

CESA 1991. La relacion de CESA con el estado en la generación y transferencia de la tecnologia agropecuaria. Paper presented at *Taller regional para América del Sur: Generación y Transferencia de Tecnología Agropecuaria; el papel de las ONGs y el Sector Público*. 2nd–7th December. Santa Cruz, Bolivia.

Chakraborty, S., Mandal, B., Das, C. and Satish, S. 1993. Ramakrishna Mission: research, extension and training in a farming systems context. In: Farrington, J. and Lewis, D. (eds.) *Non-Governmental Organizations and the State in Asia*. Routledge, London.

Chambers, R. 1974. *Managing Rural Development. Ideas and Experiences from East Africa*. Scandinavian Institute for African Studies, Uppsala.

Chambers, R. 1983. *Rural Development: Putting the Last First*. Longmans, London.

Chambers, R. 1988. Sustainable livelihoods, environment and development: putting poor rural people first. *IDS Discussion Paper 240*. University of Sussex, UK.

Chambers, R. 1991. Farmers' practices, professionals and participation: challenges for soil and water management. Paper for the *Workshop on Farmers' Practices and Soil and Water Conservation Programmes. ICRISAT Centre, Hyderabad, India.*

Chambers, R. 1992a. Rural Appraisal: rapid, relaxed and participatory. *IDS Discussion Paper 311*. Institute of Development Studies, University of Sussex, UK.

Chambers, R. 1992b. Participatory Rural Appraisals: past, present and future. *Forests, Trees and People Newsletter* 15/16. FAO.

Chambers, R. 1992c. Methods for analysis by farmers: the professional challenge. Paper presented at the *12th Annual AFSR/E Symposium, Michigan State University, East Lansing, 14–18 September.*

Chambers, R. 1992d Spreading and self-improving: a strategy for scaling-up. In: Edwards, M. and Hulme, D. (eds.) *Making a Difference? NGOs and Development in a Changing World*. Earthscan Publications Ltd, London.

Chambers, R. 1993. *Challenging the Professions: Frontiers for Rural Development*. Intermediate Technology Publications, London.

Chambers, R. and Ghildyal, B. 1985. Agricultural research for resource poor farmers – the farmer first and last model. *Agricultural Administration* 20: 1–30.

Chambers, R., Pacey, A. and Thrupp, L-A. 1989. *Farmer First: Farmer Innovation and Agricultural Research*. Intermediate Technology Publications, London.

Chand, S.P. and Gurung, B.D. 1991. Informal research with farmers: the practice and prospects in the hills of Nepal. *Journal of Farming Systems Research-Extension* 2(2): 69–79.

Cheatle, R.J. and Njoroge, S.N.J. 1993. Smallholder adoption of some land husbandry practices in Kenya. In: Hudson, N. and Cheatle, R.J. (eds.) *Working with Farmers for Better Land Husbandry*. Intermediate Technology Publications, London.

Checkland, P.B. 1981. *Systems Thinking, Systems Practice*. John Wiley, Chichester.

Checkland, P.B. 1984. Systems thinking in management: the development of soft systems methodology and its implications for social sciences. In: Ulrich, H. and Probst, G. *Self Organization and Management of Social Systems*. Springer, Berlin.

Checkland, P.B. 1989. Soft systems methodology. *Human Systems Management,* 8: 273–289.

CIP 1984. *Potatoes for the Developing World*. CIP, Lima.

Clark, J. 1991. *Democratising Development: The Role of Voluntary Organizations*. Earthscan Publications Ltd, London.

Clegg, S.R. 1989. *Frameworks of Power*. Sage Publications, London.

Cleveland, D.A. 1990. Development alternatives and the African food crisis. In: Huss-Ashmore, R. and Katz, S.H. (eds.) *African Food Systems in Crisis. Part Two: Contending with Change*. Gordon and Breach, New York.

Clifford, J. 1988. *The Predicament of Culture. Twentieth-Century Enthnography, Literature and Art*. Harvard University Press, Cambridge.

Collinson, M. 1981. A low cost approach to understanding small farmers. *Agricultural Administration*, 8(6): 433–450.

Collinson, M. 1982. Farming system research in eastern Africa: the experience of CIMMYT and some national agricultural research services, 1976–1981. *MSU International Development Paper* 3. Michigan State University, East Lansing.

Collinson, M. 1987. Farming systems research: procedures for technology development. *Experimental Agriculture* 23: 365–86.

Conroy, C. and Litvinoff, M. 1989. *The Greening of Aid*. Earthscan Publications Ltd., London.

Conway, G. 1985. Agroecosystem analysis. *Agricultural Administration*, 20: 31–55.

Conway, G. 1987. Rapid Rural Appraisal and agroecosystem analysis: a case from northern Pakistan. In: *Proceedings of the 1985 International Conference on Rapid Rural Appraisal*. Rural Systems Research and Farming Systems Research Projects, University of Khon Kaen, Thailand.

Conway, G., Sajise, P. and Knowland, W. 1989. Lake Buhi: resolving conflicts in a Philippines development project. *Ambio* 18(2): 128–135.

Copestake, J.G. 1990. The scope for collaboration between government and private voluntary organisations in agricultural technology development: the case of Zambia. *Agricultural Research and Extension Network Paper* 20. ODI, London.

Copperbelt Province ARPT 1992. *Research Results: 1991/92 Season*. Mpongwe, Zambia.

Cornwall, A., Chakavanda, M., Makumbirofa, S., Shumba, G. and Mawere, A. 1989. The use of community theatre in project evaluation: an experimental example from Zimbabwe. *RRA Notes* 6: 30–37. IIED, London.

Cotlear, D. 1989. The effect of education on farm productivity. *Journal of Development Planning* 19: 73–99.

Coward, E.W. 1977. Irrigation management alternatives: themes from indigenous irrigation systems. *Agricultural Administration* 4(3): 233–257.

Coward, E.W. 1980. Management themes in community irrigation systems. In: Coward, E.W. (ed.) *Irrigation and Agricultural Development in Asia: Perspectives from the Social Sciences*. Cornell University Press, Ithaca, New York.

Cromwell, E.A. and Wiggins, S. (1992). *Sowing Beyond the State: NGOs and Seed Supply in Developing Countries*. ODI, London.

Cross, N. and Barker, R. (eds.) 1991. *At the Desert's Edge: Oral Histories from the Sahel*. Panos/SOS-Sahel.

Curtis, D. 1991. *Beyond Government: Organisations for Common Benefit*. Macmillan Education Ltd. London.

CWR. 1990–91. *Alternative Approaches for Tank Rehabilitation and Management – A Proposed Experiment*. Annual Reports 1988–89, 1989–90. Centre for Water Resources, Anna University, Madras.

Davies, J., Easterby-Smith, M., Mann, S. and Tanton, M. (eds.) 1989. *The Challenge to Western Management Development: International Alternatives*. Routledge, London.

De Janvry, A. and Sadoulet, E. 1988. *Investment Strategies to Combat Rural Poverty: A Proposal for Latin America*. Mimeo, Department of Agricultural and Resource Economics, University of California, Berkeley.

De Janvry, A., Marsh, R., Runtsen, D., Sadoulet, E. and Zabin, C. 1989. Impacto de la crisis en la economía campesina de América Latina y el Caribe. In: Jordan, F.

(ed.) *La Economía Campesina: Crisis, Reactivación, Políticas.* Instituto Interamericano de Cooperación para la Agricultura, San José.

Derrida, J. 1978. 'Genesis and structure' and phenomenology. In: *Writing and Difference.* (Trans. A. Bass). Routledge and Kegan Paul, London.

Devavaram, J., Nalini, M., Vima Inathan, J., Sukkar, A., Kristian, M., Mayandi, A.P. and Karunanidhi, M. 1991. PRA for rural resource management. *RRA Notes* 13, 102–111. IIED, London.

De Vries, P. 1992. *Unruly Clients: A Study of How Bureaucrats Try and Fail to Transform Gatekeepers, Communists and Preachers into Ideal Beneficiaries.* Doctoral thesis, Wageningen Agricultural University, The Netherlands.

Dissanayake, W. 1986. Communication models in knowledge generation, dissemination and utilization activities. In: Beal, G.M., Dissanayake, W. and Konoshima, S. (eds.) *Knowledge Generation, Exchange, and Utilization.* Westview Press, Boulder, Colorado.

Dougnac, M. 1986. Dry season cropping – two years of experimental work under residual moisture conditions on dambos in Luapula Province. *Proceedings of the National Workshop on Dambos*, 22–24 April. Nanga, Zambia.

Drèze, J. and Sen, S. 1989. *Hunger and Public Action.* Clarendon Press, Oxford.

Drinkwater, M.J. 1992a. Visible actors and visible researchers: critical hermeneutics in an actor-oriented perspective. *Sociologia Ruralis XXXII*, 4: 367–88.

Drinkwater, M.J. 1992b. Methodology evolution within ARPT: the use of farmer research groups and RRA informal surveys within Central and Copperbelt Provinces. Revised version of the paper presented at the *Methodology Review Session of the ARPT Biannual Review Meeting*, 13–16 April, Mongu, Zambia.

Drinkwater, M.J., and McEwan, M.A. 1992. Household food security and environmental sustainability in farming systems research: developing sustainable livelihoods. Paper presented at the *ARPT Biannual Review Meeting, Mongu, 13–16 April.* Zambia.

DSE/INP. 1989. *Ecología, Agricultura y Autonomía Campesina en los Andes.* DSE/INP, Feldafing-Lima-Hohenheim.

Dunkel, F. 1985. *Rwanda Local Crop Storage / FSM II. Report of a Visit.* Typescript.

Earls, J. 1991. *Ecología y Agronomía en los Andes.* Hisbol, La Paz.

Edwards, M. and Hulme, D. 1992. *Making a Difference? NGOs and Development in a Changing World.* Earthscan Publications Ltd. London.

Eicher, C. and Staatz, J. (eds.) 1984. *Agricultural Development in the Third World.* Johns Hopkins Press, Baltimore.

Esman, M.J. and Uphoff, N. 1983. Comparative analysis of Asian experience with local organization and rural development. In: Uphoff, N. (ed.) *Rural Development and Local Organization in Asia,* Vol. III. Macmillan, New Delhi.

Esman, M.J. and Uphoff, N. 1984. *Local Organizations: Intermediaries in Rural Development.* Cornell University Press, Ithaca, New York and London.

Fabian, J. 1990. *Power and Performance: Ethnographic Explorations Through Proverbial Wisdom and Theatren Shaba, Zaire.* University of Wisconsin Press, Madison.

Fabian, J. 1991. Dilemmas of critical anthropology. In: P. Nencel and P. Pels (eds.) *Constructing Knowledge: Authority and Critique in Social Sciences.* Sage Publications, London.

Fairhead, J. 1990. *Fields of Struggle: Towards a Social History of Farming Knowledge and Practice in a Bwisha Community, Kivu, Zaire.* Doctoral thesis, School of Oriental and African Studies, University of London.

Fairhead, J. 1992. Indigenous technical knowledge and natural resources management in sub-Saharan Africa: a critical overview. Paper presented at *Social Science Research Council Project on African Agriculture Conference, Dakar, Senegal, January 1992.*

Fairhead, J. 1993. Representing knowledge: the 'new farmer' in research. In: Pottier, J. (ed.) *Practising Development: Social Science Perspectives.* Routledge, London.

Fals-Borda, O. and Rahman, A. (eds) 1991. *Action and Knowledge: Breaking the Monopoly with Participatory Action Research.* Apex, New York.

FARM-Africa/IIED 1991. *Farmer Participatory Research in N. Omo, Ethiopia.* IIED, London.

Farrington, J. (ed.) 1988. Farmer participatory research. *Experimental Agriculture* 24(3).

Farrington, J. and Martin, A. 1988. Farmer participation in agricultural research: a review of concepts and practices. *Agricultural Administration Unit Occasional Paper 9.* ODI, London.

Farrington, J. and Bebbington, A. 1991. Institutionalization of farming systems development: are there lessons from NGO-government links? Paper for *FAO Expert Consultation on the Institutionalization of Farming Systems Development, October 1991.* Rome.

Farrington, J. and Lewis, D. (eds.) 1993 *Non-Governmental Organizations and the State in Asia.* Routledge, London.

Farrington, J., Bebbington, A., Wellard, K. and Lewis, D.J. (eds.) 1993. *Reluctant Partners? Non-Governmental Organizations, the State and Sustainable Agricultural Development.* Routledge, London.

Fay, B. 1975. *Social Theory and Political Practice.* George Allen and Unwin, London.

Feierman, S. 1990. *Peasant Intellectuals: Anthropology and History in Tanzania.* University of Wisconsin Press, Madison, WI.

Fernandez, A. and Mascarenhas, J. 1993. Mysore Relief and Development Agency (MYRADA): participatory rural appraisal and participatory learning methods. In: Farrington, A. and Lewis, D.J. (eds.) *Non-Government Organizations and the State in Asia. Rethinking Roles in Sustainable Agricultural Development.* Routledge, London.

Feyeraband, P. 1975. *Against Method: Outline of Anarchistic Theory of Knowledge.* Verso, London.

Figueroa, A. and Bolliger, F. 1985. *Productividad y Aprendizaje en el Medio Ambiente Rural. Informe Comparativo.* Rio de Janeiro. ECIEL.

Foucault, M. 1971. The order of discourse. In R. Young (ed.) *Untying the Text: A Post-Structuralist Reader.* Routledge and Kegan Paul, London.

Foucault, M. 1973. *The Order of Things: An Archaeology of the Human Sciences.* Vintage Books, New York.

Fowler, A. 1992. Prioritizing institutional development: a new role for NGO centres for study and development. Sustainable Agriculture Programme *Gatekeeper Series* SA35. IIED, London.

Fre, Z. 1993. Ethno-veterinary knowledge among pastoralists in Eastern Sudan and Eritrea: implications for animal health, participatory extension and future policy. Sustainable Agriculture Programme Research Series, 1(2): 1–23. IIED, London.

Freire, P. 1972. *Pedagogy of the Oppressed.* Penguin, Harmondsworth, UK.

Fresco, L. 1986. *Cassava and Shifting Cultivation: A Systems Approach to Agricultural Technology Development.* Royal Tropical Institute, Amsterdam.

Fujisaka, S. 1989a. Participation by farmers, researchers and extension workers in soil conservation. Sustainable Agriculture Programme *Gatekeeper Series* SA16. IIED, London.

Fujisaka, S. 1989b. A method for farmer-participatory research and technology transfer: upland soil conservation in the Philippines. *Experimental Agriculture* 25: 423–433.

Fujisaka, S. 1991a. Improving productivity of an upland rice and maize system: farmer cropping choices or researcher CP trapezoids? *Experimental Agriculture* 27: 253–261.

Fujisaka, S. (forthcoming) Taking farmer knowledge and technology seriously: seeding and weeding upland rice in the Philippines. In: Warren, M., Brokensha, D. and Slikkerveer, L.J. (eds.) *Indigenous Knowledge Systems: The Cultural Dimension of Development*. London.

Fujisaka, S. and Garrity, D.P. 1991. Farmers and scientists: a joint effort. In: Moldenhauer, W.C., Hudson, N.W., Sheng, T.C. and San-Wei Lee (eds.). *Development of Conservation Farming on Hillslopes*. Soil and Water Conservation Society, Ankeny, Iowa.

Fujisaka, S., Elliot, P., Jayson, E. and Dapusala, A. 1992b. Where there has been no 'green revolution': farmers' upland rices and related knowledge in Mindanao, Philippines. Paper presented at the *International Symposium on Indigenous Technical Knowledge and Sustainable Development, 20–26 Sept 1992*. International Institute of Rural Reconstruction, Silang, Philippines.

Funtowicz, S.O. and Ravetz, J.R. 1990. *Global Environmental Issues and the Emergence of Second Order Science*. D.G. Telecommunications, Information Industries and Innovation, Commission of the European Communities, Luxembourg.

Ganapin, D. 1993. The Philippines Debt-for-Nature swap programme. In: Farrington, J. and Lewis, D.J. (eds.) *Non-Governmental Organizations and the State in Asia*. Routledge, London.

Gartner, J. 1990. Extension education: top(s) down, bottom(s) up and other things. In: Jones, J. (ed.) *Systems Theory Applied to Agriculture and the Food Chain*. Elsevier, New York.

Gatter, P. 1993. Anthropology in farming systems research: a participant observer in Zambia. In: Pottier, J. (ed.) *Practising Development: Social Science Perspectives*. Routledge, London.

Gaventa, J. and Lewis, H. 1991. Participatory education and grassroots development: the case of rural Appalachia. Sustainable Agriculture Programme *Gatekeeper Series* SA25. IIED, London.

Geertz, C. 1983. *Local Knowledge: Further Essays in Interpretive Anthropology*. Basic Books, New York.

Gibbon, D. 1992. The future of farming systems research in developing countries. In: Raman, K.V. and Balaguru, T. (eds.) *Farming Systems Research in India: Strategies for Implementation*. NAARM, Rajendranagar, Hyderabad.

Giddens, A. 1979. *Central Problems in Social Theory*. Macmillan, London.

Giddens, A. 1984. *The Constitution of Society: Outline of the Theory of Structuration*. Polity Press, Cambridge.

Giddens, A. 1987. *Social Theory and Modern Society*. Basil Blackwell Ltd., Oxford.

Gilbert, E. 1990. Non-governmental organisations and agricultural research: the experience of the Gambia. *Agricultural Research and Extension Network Paper* 12. ODI, London.

Gilbert, E., Norman, D. and Winch, F. 1980. Farming systems research: a critical appraisal. *MSU Occasional Paper* No. 6. Michigan State University, East Lansing.

Gilbert, E. and Matlon, P. 1992. The small west African NARS – an endangered species? Draft paper prepared for the *ISNAR workshop on Small National Agricultural Research Systems at the University of Mauritius, April 28th – May 1st, 1992.*

Gill, G.J. 1991. But how does it compare with the real data? *RRA Notes* 14. IIED, London.

Gill G.J. 1993. OK, the data's lousy, but it's all we've got (being a critique of conventional methods). Sustainable Agriculture Programme *Gatekeeper Series* SA38. IIED, London.

Goldman, A. 1991. Tradition and change in postharvest pest management in Kenya. *Agriculture and Human Values* 8(1 & 2): 99–113.

Gonsalves, J. and Miclat-Teves, A. 1993. The International Institute for Rural Reconstruction: developing an agroforestry kit. In: Farrington, J. and Lewis, D.J. (eds.) *Non-Governmental Organizations and the State in Asia.* Routledge, London.

Goodman, N. 1978. *Ways of Worldmaking.* Harvester, Hassocks.

Gordon, C. (ed.) 1980. *Power/Knowledge: Selected Interviews and Other Writings 1972–1977 by Michel Foucault.* Random House, New York.

Granovetter, M. 1983. The strength of weak ties: a network theory revisited. In: Collins, R. (ed.) *Sociological Theory.* Jossey-Bass, San Francisco.

Grillo, E. *et al.* 1991. *Cultura Andina Agrocéntrica.* PRATEC, Lima.

Guba, E. (ed.) 1990. *The Paradigm Dialogue.* Sage Publications, Beverly Hills, CA.

Gubbels, P. 1990. *Peasant Farmer Agricultural Self-Development: the World Neighbors Experience in West Africa.* World Neighbors, Oklahoma City.

Guijt, I. and Pretty, J.N. (eds.) 1992. *Participatory Rural Appraisal for Farmer Participatory Research in Punjab, Pakistan.* Pakistan-Swiss Potato Development Project, PARC, Islamabad, and IIED, London.

Gupta, A. 1989. Scientists' view of farmers' practices in India: barriers to effective interaction In: Chambers, R., Pacey, A. and Thrupp, L.-A. (eds.) *Farmer First: Farmer Innovation and Agricultural Research.* Intermediate Technology Publications Ltd., London.

Gypmantasiri, P. *et al.* 1980. *An Interdisciplinary Perspective of Cropping Systems in the Chiang Mai Valley: Key Questions for Research.* Faculty of Agriculture, University of Chiang Mai, Thailand.

Habermas, J. 1972. *Knowledge and Human Interests.* Heinemann, London.

Habermas, J. 1984. *The Theory of Communicative Action: Reason and the Rationalization of Society*, Vol. I. Translated by T. McCarthy. Beacon Press, Boston.

Habermas, J. 1987. *The Theory of Communicative Action: Critique of Functionalist Reason*, Vol.II. Translated by T. McCarthy. Beacon Press, Boston.

Habermas, J. 1992. *Communication and the Evolution of Society.* Translated by T. McCarthy. Beacon Press, Boston.

Hacking, I. 1983. *Representing and Intervening: Introductory Topics in the Philosophy of Natural Science.* Cambridge University Press, Cambridge.

Hacking, I. 1990. *The Taming of Chance.* Cambridge University Press, Cambridge.

Hägerstand, T. 1968. *Innovation Diffusion as a Spatial Process.* University of Chicago Press, Chicago.

Hanvey, D.A.R., Watkin, E.M., Bakarr, M. and Hassan-King, A. 1992. *Environmental Management Programmes at Sierra Rutile Ltd.* Draft mimeo.

Harvey, D. 1989. *The Condition of Postmodernity.* Basil Blackwell Ltd., Oxford.

Harding, F. 1987. Theatre for development. In: *African Futures: Proceedings of the 25th Conference of the Centre of African Studies, Edinburgh.* Centre for African Studies, University of Edinburgh.

Healey, J. and Robinson, M. 1992. *Democracy, Governance and Economic Policy: Sub-Saharan Africa in Comparative Perspective.* ODI, London.

Heinrich, G. Worman, F. and Koketso, C. 1991. Integrating FPR with conventional on-farm research programs: an example from Botswana. *Journal for Farming Systems Research-Extension* 2: 1–15.

Henderson, P. and Singh, R. 1990. NGO-government collaboration in seed supply: case studies from The Gambia and from Ethiopia. *Agricultural Research and Extension Network Paper* 14. ODI, London.

Hesse, M. 1978. Theory and value in the social sciences. In: Hookway, C. and Pettit, P. (eds.) *Action and Interpretation.* Cambridge University Press, Cambridge.

Hiemstra, W., Reijntjes, C. and van der Werf, E. (eds.) 1992. *Let Farmers Judge: Experiences in Assessing the Sustainability of Agriculture.* Intermediate Technology Publications, London.

286

Hildebrand, P.E. 1981. Combining disciplines in Rapid Rural Appraisal. *Agricultural Administration* 8: 423–432.

Hobart, M. 1993. Introduction. In M. Hobart, (ed.) *The Growth of Ignorance: A Critique of Development*. Routledge, London.

Hope, A., Timmel, S. and Hodzi, C. 1984. *Training for Transformation*. Mambo Press, Gweru, Zimbabwe.

Howes, M. and Chambers, R. 1979. Indigenous technical knowledge: analysis, implications and issues. Rural Development: whose knowledge counts? *IDS Bulletin* 10(2): 5–11.

Huby, M. 1990. *Where You Can't See the Wood for the Trees*. Kenya Woodfuel Development Programme Series. The Beijer Institute, Stockholm.

Huizer, G. 1979. Research-through-action: experiences with peasant organisations. In: G. Huizer and B. Mannheim (eds.). *The Politics of Anthropology: from Colonialism and Sexism towards a View from Below*. Mouton, The Hague.

IDS. 1979. Rural development: whose knowledge counts? *IDS Bulletin* 10(2). Institute of Development Studies, University of Sussex.

IIED. 1988-present. *RRA Notes*. Sustainable Agriculture Programme, International Institute for Environment and Development, London.

Illich, I. 1972. *Deschooling Society*. Penguin, Harmondsworth.

IRRI. 1982. *The Role of Anthropologists and Other Social Scientists in Interdisciplinary Teams Developing Improved Food Production Technology*. International Rice Research Institute (IRRI), Los Banos, Laguna, Philippines.

IRRI 1991. *IRRI 1990–1991: A Continuing Adventure in Rice Research*. IRRI, Los Banos, Laguna, Philippines.

Ison, R. 1990. Teaching threatens sustainable agriculture. Sustainable Agriculture Programme *Gatekeeper Series* SA21. IIED, London.

Jintrawet, A., Smutkupt, S., Wongsamun, C., Katawetin, R., and Kerdsuk, V. 1985. *Extension Activities for Peanuts after Rice in Ban Sum Jan, N.E. Thailand: A Case Study in Farmer-to-Farmer Extension Methodology*. Khon Kaen University, Khon Kaen.

Jodha, N. and Partep, T. 1993. Folk agronomy in the Himalayas: implications for agricultural research and extension. Sustainable Agriculture Programme *Research Series*, 1(3): 15–37. IIED, London.

Jonfa, E., Tebeje, H., Dessalegn, T., Halala, H. and Cornwall, A. 1992. Participatory modelling in North Omo, Ethiopia: investigating the perceptions of different groups through models. Sustainable Agriculture Programme *RRA Notes* 14: 24–26. IIED, London.

Kabore, R. 1992. *Evaluation du Projet Agro-Forestier: Volet Agriculture-Elevage*. Unpublished OXFAM Impact Study.

Kaimowitz, D. 1991. El papel de las ONG en el sistema Latinoamericanode generacion y transferencia agropecuaria. In: Bebbington, A., Davies, P., Prager, M., Thiele, J. and Wadsworth, J. (eds.) *Memorias del Taller: Generacion y Transferencia de Tecnologia Agropecuaria: el Papel de las ONG y el Sector Publico*.

Khan, M., Lewis, D.J., Alia Sabri, A. and Shahabuddin, Md. 1993. Proshika's livestock and social forestry programmes. In: Farrington, J. and Lewis, D.J. (eds.) *Non-Governmental Organizations and the State in Asia*. Routledge, London.

Khon Kaen University 1987. *Rapid Rural Appraisal: Proceedings of the 1985 International Conference*. Khon Kaen University, Rural Systems Research and Farming Systems Research Projects, Khon Kaen, Thailand.

Kiara, J.K., Segerros, M., Pretty, J.N. and McCracken, J. 1990. *Rapid Catchment Analysis in Murang'a District, Kenya*. Ministry of Agriculture, Nairobi, Kenya.

Klein, E. 1992. El empleo rural no agricola en America Latina. Paper presented at conference on *La Sociedad Rural Latinoamericana hacia el Siglo XXI.* CEPLAES, Quito, 15–17 de julio, 1992, CEPLAES, Quito.

Knorr-Cetina, K. 1981. *The Manufacture of Knowledge: An Essay on the Constructivist and Contextual Nature of Science.* Pergamon Press, Oxford.

Kohl, B. 1991. Protected horticultural systems in the Bolivian Andes: a case study of NGOs and inappropriate technology. *Agricultural Research and Extension Network Paper 29.* ODI, London.

Kokwe, M. 1991. The role of dambos in agricultural research in Zambia. *Wetlands in Drylands: The Agroecology of Savanna Systems in Africa, Part 3E.* IIED, London.

Kolb, D. 1984. *Experiential Learning: Experience as the Source of Learning and Development.* Prentice Hall, New Jersey.

Korten, D.C. 1980. Community organisation and rural development — a learning process approach. *Public Administration Review,* 40(5): 480–511.

Korten, D.C. 1984. People centred development: toward a framework. In: Korten, D.C. and Klauss (eds.) *People Centred Development: Contributions Toward Theory and Planning Frameworks.* Kumarian Press, West Hartford, CT.

Korten, D.C. (ed.) 1987. *Community Management: Asian Experience and Perspectives.* Kumarian Press, West Hartford, CT.

Korten, D.C. 1990. *Getting to the 21st Century: Voluntary Action and the Global Agenda.* Kumarian Press, West Hartford, CT.

Kronenburg, J.B.M. 1986. *Empowerment of the Poor, a Comparative Analysis of Two Development Endeavours in Kenya.* Royal Tropical Institute, Amsterdam.

Kuhn, T. 1962. *The Structure of Scientific Revolutions.* Chicago University Press, Chicago.

Kydd, J. 1989. Maize research in Malawi: lessons from failure. *Journal of International Development* 1: 112–144.

Lamb, E. 1985. Record of the methodologies used and results realized by the component *An Inventory of Bean Varieties Produced in Rwanda.* LCS/FSM GRENARWA II project on bean and sorghum storage in Rwanda. Mimeo.

LaSalle, J. and Gauld, I.D. 1991. Parasitic hymenoptera and the biodiversity crisis. *Insect Parasitoids. 4th European Workshop – Perugia 3–5 April, 1991. REDIA 74 Appendice.*

Latour, B. 1986. The powers of association. In: Law, J. (ed.). *Power, Action and Belief: A New Sociology of Knowledge?* Routledge and Kegan Paul, London, Boston and Henley.

Latour, B. 1987. *Science in Action.* Open University Press, Milton Keynes.

Leach, M. 1992. Women's crops in women's spaces: gender relations in Mende rice farming. In: Croll, E. and Parkin, D. (eds.) *Bush Base, Forest Farm.* Routledge, London.

Leach, M. 1991. Locating gendered experience: an anthropologist's view from a Sierra-Leonean village. *IDS Bulletin,* 22(1): 44–50.

Leeuwis, C. 1991. From electronic to social interfaces. In: Kuiper, D. and Röling, N. (eds) *Edited Proceedings of the European Seminar on Knowledge Management and Information Technology.* Wageningen Agricultural University, The Netherlands.

Leeuwis, C. and Arkesteyn, M. 1991. Planned technology development and local initiative. *Sociologia Ruralis,* XXXI, (2/3): 140–161.

Lightfoot, C. and Noble, R. 1992. Sustainability and on-farm experiments: ways to exploit participatory and systems concepts. Paper for *12th Annual Farming Systems Symposium,* 13–18 Sept. Michigan State University, East Lansing.

Lightfoot, C., de Guia, O. and Ocado, F. 1988. A participatory method for system problem research: rehabilitating marginal uplands in the Philippines. *Experimental Agriculture* 24: 301–309.

Lightfoot, C., Dalsgaard, P., Bimbao, M. and Fermin, F. 1992. Farmer participatory procedures for managing and monitoring sustainable farming systems. Paper presented at the *Second Asian Farming Systems Symposium*, BMICH, Colombo, Sri Lanka.

Lincoln, Y.S. 1990. The making of a constructionist. In E. Guba (ed) *The Paradigm Dialogue*. Sage Publications, Beverly Hills, CA.

Lincoln, Y.S. and Guba, E.G. 1985. *Naturalistic Inquiry*. Sage Publications, Newbury Park, CA.

Lionberger, H. 1960. *Adoption of New Ideas and Practices*. Iowa State University Press, Ames, IA.

Long, N. 1972. Kinship and associational networks among transporters in rural Peru: the problem of the 'local' as against the 'cosmopolitan' entrepreneur. Paper presented to *Seminar on Kinship and Social Networks, Institute of Latin American Studies, London University*. Shortened version in Long, N. and Roberts, B. 1984. *Miners, Peasants and Entrepreneurs*, Cambridge University Press, Cambridge.

Long, N. 1984. Creating space for change: a perspective on the sociology of development. *Inaugural Lecture*, Wageningen Agricultural University. Shortened version appears in *Sociologia Ruralis*, XXIV (3/4) 168–184.

Long, N. (ed.) 1989. *Encounters at the Interface: A Perspective on Social Discontinuities in Rural Development. Wageningen Studies in Sociology 27*. Wageningen Agricultural University, The Netherlands.

Long, N. and Roberts, B. 1984. *Miners, Peasants and Entrepreneurs*. Cambridge University Press, Cambridge.

Long, N. and Villarreal, M. 1989. The changing life-world of women in a Mexican ejido: the case of beekeepers of Ayuquila and the issues of intervention. In Long, N. (ed.) *Encounters at the Interface: A Perspective on Social Discontinuities in Rural Development. Wageningse Sociologische Studies 27*. Landbouwuniversiteit: Wageningen Agricultural University, The Netherlands.

Long, N. and Van der Ploeg, J. 1989. Demythologizing planned intervention: an actor perspective. *Sociologica Ruralis* XXIX (3/4): 227–49.

Long, N. and Van der Ploeg, J. 1991. Reflections on the actor-oriented approach to social development research: towards a new concept of structure. Paper prepared for the *Workshop on Relevance, Realism and Choice in Social Development Research. University of Hull, 10–12 January, 1991*.

Long, N. and Long, A. (eds.) 1992. *Battlefields of Knowledge: The Interlocking of Theory and Practice in Social Research and Development*. Routledge, London.

Lynton, R.P. 1960. *The Tide of Learning. The Aloka Experience*. Routledge and Kegan Paul, London.

Lynton R.P. and Pareek U. 1990. *Training for Development*. 2nd Edition. Kumarian Press, West Hartford, Connecticut.

MALDM/MOA 1988–present. *Reports of Catchment Approach Planning and Rapid Catchment Analysis*. Soil and Water Conservation Branch, Ministry of Agriculture, Livestock Development and Marketing, Nairobi, Kenya.

Marglin, F. and Marglin, S. (eds.) 1990. *Dominating Knowledge: Development Culture and Resistance*. Clarendon Press, Oxford.

Mascarenhas, J., Shah, P., Joseph, S., Jayakaran, R., Devavaram, J., Ramachandran, V., Fernandez, A., Chambers, R. and Pretty, J. (eds.) 1991. Participatory Rural Appraisal: Proceedings of the February 1991 Bangalore PRA Trainers Workshop. *RRA Notes 13*. Sustainable Agriculture Programme, IIED, London.

Mathema, S.B. and Galt, D. 1989. Appraisal by group trek. In: Chambers, R., Pacey, A. and Thrupp, L-A. (eds.) *Farmer First: Farmer Innovation and Agricultural Research*. Intermediate Technology Publications, London.

Maurya, D.M. 1989. The innovative approach of Indian farmers. In: Chambers, R., Pacey, A. and Thrupp, L-A. (eds.) *Farmer First: Farmer Innovation and Agricultural Research.* Intermediate Technology Publications, London.

Mavro, A. 1991. *Development Theatre: A Way to Listen.* SOS-Sahel, London.

McCarthy, T. 1984. *The Critical Theory of Jürgen Habermas.* Polity Press, Cambridge.

McGregor, J. 1991. *Woodland Resources: Ecology, Policy and Ideology. An Historical Case Study of Woodland Use in Shurugwi Communal Area, Zimbabwe.* Doctoral thesis, Loughborough University of Technology.

Merrill-Sands, D. and Collion, M-H. 1992. Making the farmers' voice count: issues and opportunities for promoting farmer-responsive research. Paper for *12th Annual Farming Systems Symposium*, 13–18 Sept. Michigan State University, East Lansing.

Merrill-Sands, D. and Kaimowitz, D. 1990. *The Technology Triangle: Linking Farmers, Technology Transfer Agents, and Agricultural Researchers.* ISNAR, The Hague.

Merrill-Sands, D., Biggs, S., Bingen, R.J., Ewell, P., McAllister, J. and Poats, S. 1991. Institutional considerations in strengthening on-farm client-oriented research in National Agricultural Research Systems: lessons from a nine-country study. *Experimental Agriculture* 27: 343–373.

Messerschmidt, D. 1991. Some advantages of having an outsider on the team. *RRA Notes* 12: 4–7. IIED, London.

Messerschmidt, D. 1992. *Rapid Appraisal for Community Forestry. The RA Process and Rapid Diagnostic Tools.* Institute of Forestry, Pokhara, Nepal.

Milardo, R.M. (ed.) 1988. *Families and Social Networks.* Sage Publications, London.

MINAGRI (Ministère de l'Agriculture, de l'Elevage et des Forêts) 1985. *OPROVIA – Project GRENARWA II: Programme de recherche.* Typescript.

Mitlin, D. and Satterthwaite, D. 1992. Supporting community level initiatives. In: Edwards, M. and Hulme, D. (eds.) *Making a Difference? NGOs and Development in a Changing World.* Earthscan Publications Ltd, London.

Moock, J. and Rhoades, R. (eds.) 1992. *Diversity, Farmer Knowledge and Sustainability.* Cornell University Press, Ithaca, New York.

Moore, B, Jr. 1987. *Injustice: The Social Basis of Obedience and Revolt.* M.E. Sharpe, White Plains, NY.

Moore, S.F. 1973. Law and social change: the semi-autonomous social field as an appropriate subject of study. *Law Society Review,* Summer: 719–746.

Moris, J. 1991. Extension alternatives in tropical Africa. *AAU Occasional Paper* No.7. ODI, London.

Mosse, D. 1992. Community management and rehabilitation of tank irrigation systems in Tamil Nadu: a research agenda. Paper for *GAPP Conference on Participatory Development*, July 9–10, London.

Mukamuri, B. 1992. *Concept and Context of Social Forestry Projects in Zimbabwe.* MSc thesis, University of Tampere, Finland.

Mung'ala, P. and Arum, G. 1991. Institutional aspects of environmental research and extension in Kenya: the Department of Forestry and Kenya energy and environment organisations. *Agricultural Research and Extension Network Paper* 23. ODI, London.

Murra, J. 1983. *La Organización Económica del Estado Inca.* Siglo XXI/IEP, Mexico City.

Mustafa, S., Rahmann, S. and Sattar, G. 1993. Bangladesh Rural Advancement Committee (BRAC): backyard poultry and landless irrigators programmes. In: Farrington, J. and Lewis, D.J. (eds.) *Non-Governmental Organizations and the State in Asia.* Routledge, London.

Nahas, F. 1993. Friends in Village Development, Bangladesh (FIVDB): improved duck-rearing practices. In: Farrington, J. and Lewis, D.J. (eds.) *Non-Governmental Organizations and the State in Asia.* Routledge, London.

Ndiweni, M., MacGarry, B., Chaguma, A. and Gumbo, D. 1991. Involving farmers in rural technologies: case studies in Zimbabwean NGOs. *Agricultural Research and Extension Network Paper* 23. ODI, London.

Nitsch, U. 1991. Computers and the nature of farm management. In: Kuiper D. and Röling, N.G. (eds.) *The Edited Proceedings of the European Seminar on Knowledge Management and Information Technology.* Agricultural University, Department of Extension Science, Wageningen, The Netherlands.

Norman, D., Baker, D., Heinrich, G., Jonas, C., Maskiara, S. and Worman, F. 1989. Farmer groups for technology development: experience in Botswana. In: Chambers, R., Pacey, A. and Thrupp, L.-A. (eds.) *Farmer First: Farmer Innovation and Agricultural Research.* Intermediate Technology Publications, London.

Norton, A. 1992. Analysis and action in local institutional development. Paper for *GAPP Conference on Participatory Development*, July 9–10, 1992, London.

Ouedraogo S. 1992. *Evaluation du Projet Agro-Forestier: Volet Information Generale.* Unpublished OXFAM Impact Study.

Pearson, C.J. and Ison, R.L. 1990. University education for multiple goal agriculture in Australia. *Agricultural Systems.*

Peters, D.U. 1951. Land usage in Serenje District. *The Rhodes Livingstone Papers* 19. Institute for African Studies, University of Zambia, Lusaka.

Pimbert, M. 1991. *Participatory Research with Women Farmers.* 30 min. VHS-PAL Video. ICRISAT Information Series. International Centre for Research in the Semi-Arid Tropics, Hyderabad, India.

Pingali, P. 1991. Technological prospects for reversing the declining trend in Asia's rice productivity. Paper presented to the *Conference on Agricultural Technology: Current Policy Issues for the International Community and the World Bank, 21–23 October 1991*, Arlie House, Virginia.

Poffenberger, M. 1990. *Joint Management of Forest Lands. Experiences from South Asia.* The Ford Foundation, New Delhi.

Poffenberger, M., McGean, B., Khare, A. and Campbell, J. (eds.). 1992. *Community Forest Economy and Use Patterns: Participatory Rural Appraisal (PRA) Methods in South Gujarat, India* Volumes 1 and 2. Joint Forest Management Support Program, Ford Foundation, New Delhi.

Pottier, J. 1989. Three is a crowd: knowledge, ignorance and power in the context of urban agriculture in Rwanda. *Africa* 54 (4): 461–477.

Pottier, J. 1993. Taking stock: food marketing reform in Rwanda, 1982–1989. *African Affairs*, January issue.

Pradan, N.C. and Yoder, R. 1989. *Improving Irrigation Management Through Farmer to Farmer Training: Examples from Nepal.* International Irrigation Management Institute Working Paper 12, Kathmandu.

PRATEC/UNSCH. 1990. *Curso de Formación en Agricultura Campesina Andina.* Mimeo, Ayacucho.

Pretty, J.N. 1990. Sustainable agriculture in the Middle Ages: the English Manor. *Agricultural History Review* 38: 1–20.

Pretty, J.N. 1994a. Alternative systems of inquiry for a sustainable agriculture. *IDS Bulletin,* 25(2): 19–30.

Pretty, J.N. 1994b. *Regenerating Agriculture: Policies and Practice for Sustainable Growth and Self-Reliance.* Earthscan Publications Ltd., London.

Pretty, J.N., Thompson, J. and Kiara, J. 1994. Agricultural regeneration in Kenya: the catchment approach to soil and water conservation. *Ambio* (forthcoming).

Pretty, J.N. and Shah, P. 1992. *Soil and Water Conservation and Watershed Development: Overview of Successes and Failures.* Mimeo, IIED, London.

Prigogine, I. and Stengers, I. (1985: orig.1984). *Order Out of Chaos: Man's New Dialogue with Nature.* Flamingo, London.

Quine, W. 1953. Two dogmas of empiricism. In: Quine, W. (ed.) *From a Logical Point of View*. Harvard University Press, Cambridge, MA.

Rahman, M.A. (ed.) 1984. *Grass-Roots Participation and Self-Reliance*. Oxford and IBH Publication Co., New Delhi.

Rajchman, J. and West, C. (eds.) 1985. *Post-Analytic Philosophy*. Columbia University Press, New York.

Rap, E. 1992. *A Collaborative Mode of Participation in Adaptive Research*. Unpublished report on field work, Kabwe, Zambia.

Ravines, R. (ed.) 1978. *Tecnología Andina*. IEP/ITINTEC, Lima.

Ravnborg, H.M. 1992. The CGIAR system in transition. Implications for the poor, sustainability and the national research systems. *Agricultural Administration (Research and Extension) Network Paper* 31. ODI, London.

Reason, P. and Heron, J. 1986. Research with people: the paradigm of cooperative experiential inquiry. *People-Centred Review* 1: 457.

Reed, M.I. 1989. *The Sociology of Management*. Harvester Wheatsheaf, Hemel Hempstead.

Reij, C. 1991. Indigenous soil and water conservation in Africa. Sustainable Agriculture Programme *Gatekeeper Series* SA27. IIED, London.

Reijntjes, C., Haverkort, B. and Waters-Bayer, A. 1992. *Farming for the Future: An Introduction to Low-External-Input and Sustainable Agriculture*. The Information Centre for Low-External-Input and Sustainable Agriculture (ILEIA). Macmillan Press Ltd., London.

Rhoades, R.E. 1982. *The Art of the Informal Agricultural Survey*. International Potato Centre, Lima, Peru.

Rhoades, R.E. 1983. Technicista versus campesinista: praxis and theory of farmer involvement in agricultural research: a post-harvest example from the Andes. Paper presented at *ICRISAT/SAFGRAD/IRAT Conference, Burkina Faso*.

Rhoades, R.E. 1984. *Breaking New Ground. Agricultural Anthropology*. CIP, Lima.

Rhoades, R.E. 1988. Changing perceptions of farmers and the expanding challenges of international agricultural research: 1960–1990. *Paper presented at the Conference on Farmers and Food Systems 26–30 Sept 1988, Lima, Peru*.

Rhoades, R.E. 1990. *The Coming Revolution in Methods for Rural Development Research*. Users' Perspective Network (UPWARD), International Potato Centre (CIP), Manila.

Rhoades, R.E. and Booth, R. 1982. Farmer-back-to-farmer: a model for generating acceptable agricultural technology. *Agricultural Administration* 11: 127–137.

Rhoades, R.E., Horton, D. and Booth, R. 1987. *Anthropologist, Biological Scientist and Economist: The Three Musketeers or the Three Stooges of Farming Systems Research?* CIP, Lima.

Rhoades, R.E. and Bebbington, A. 1988. *Farmers Who Experiment: An Untapped Resource for Agricultural Development*. CIP, Lima, Peru.

Richards, P. 1985. *Indigenous Agricultural Revolution: Ecology and Food Production in West Africa*. Hutchinson, London and Westview Press, Boulder.

Richards, P. 1986. *Coping with Hunger: Hazard and Experiment in an African Rice-Farming System*. Allen and Unwin, London.

Richards, P. 1987. *On the South Side of the Garden of Eden: Creativity and Innovation in Sub-Saharan Africa*. Department of Anthropology, University College, London.

Richards, P. 1989. Agriculture as a performance. In: Chambers, R., Pacey, A. and Thrupp, L-A. (eds.) *Farmer First: Farmer Innovation and Agricultural Research*. Intermediate Technology Publications, London.

Richards, P. 1990. Local strategies for coping with hunger: northern Nigeria and central Sierra Leone compared. *African Affairs* 89: 265–275.

Roche, C. 1991. ACORD's experience in local planning in Mali and Burkina Faso. *RRA Notes* 11, 33–41. IIED, London.

Rogers A. 1985. *Teaching Adults*. Open University Press, Milton Keynes.

Rogers, E.M. 1962. (Third edition 1983) *Diffusion of Innovation*. The Free Press, Glencoe, UK.

Rogers, E.M. and Shoemaker, F.F. 1971. *Communication of Innovations: A Cross-Cultural Approach*. Free Press, New York.

Röling, N.G. and Engel, P.G.H. 1991. The development of the concept of Agricultural Knowledge and Information Systems (AKIS): implications for extension. In: Rivera, W. and Gustafson, D. (eds.) *Agricultural Extension: Worldwide Institutional Evolution and Forces for Change*. Elsevier Science Publishers, Amsterdam.

Rorty, R. 1980. *Philosophy and the Mirror of Nature*. Basil Blackwell, Oxford.

Rorty, R. 1982. *Consequences of Pragmatism*. University of Minnesota Press, Minneapolis.

Rorty, R. 1989. *Contingency, Irony and Solidarity*. Cambridge University Press, Cambridge.

Russell, D.B. and Ison, R.L. 1991. The research-development relationship in rangelands: an opportunity for contextual science. Plenary paper for *4th International Rangelands Congress*, Montpellier, France, 22–26 April 1991.

Sachs, W. 1992. *The Development Dictionary: A Guide to Knowledge as Power*. Zed Press, London.

Salas, M.A. 1987. *Los Mates de Cochas*. Mosca Azul, Lima.

Salas, M.A. 1988. Minka – eine peruanische Bauernzeitung im Wandel. In: Albrecht, *et al. Landwirtschaftliche Beratung* Bd.2: 113–134. GTZ-CTA-BMZ, Rossdorf, Germany.

Salas, M.A. 1991. The categories of space and time and the production of potatoes in the Mantaro Valley, Peru. In: Dupré, G. (ed.) *Savoirs Paysans et Development*. ORSTOM, Paris.

Salner, M. 1986. Adult cognitive and epistemological development. *Systems Research* 3: 225–232.

Sayer, A. 1992. (2nd Edition) *Method in Social Science: A Realist Approach*. Routledge, London.

Schön, D.A. 1983. *The Reflective Practitioner: How Professionals Think in Action*. Avebury, Aldershot, UK and Basic Books, New York.

Schoonmaker Freudenberger, M. and Schoonmaker Freudenberger, K. 1993. Fields, Fallow and Flexibility: natural resource management in Ndam Mor Fademba, Senegal. Drylands Paper 5. IIED, London.

Scott, J. 1985. *Weapons of the Weak. Everyday Forms of Peasant Resistance*. Yale University Press, New Haven, CT.

Scott, J. 1990. *Domination and the Arts of Resistance: Hidden Transcripts*. Yale University Press, New Haven, CT.

Sen, A. 1983. *Poverty and Famines: An Essay on Entitlement and Deprivation*. Clarendon Press, Oxford.

Sethna, A. and Shah, A. 1993. The Aga Khan Rural Support Project (AKRSP): influencing wasteland development policy. In: Farrington, J. and Lewis, D.J. (eds.) *Non-Governmental Organizations and the State in Asia*. Routledge, London.

Seur, H. 1992. *Sowing the Good Seed: The Interweaving of Agricultural Change, Gender Relations and Religion in Serenje District, Zambia*. Doctoral thesis, Wageningen Agricultural University, The Netherlands.

Shah P. 1993. Participatory watershed management programmes in India: reversing our roles and revising our theories. *Sustainable Agriculture Programme Research Series* 1(3): 38–67. IIED, London.

Shaner, W., Philipp, P. and Schmehl, W. 1982. *Farming Systems Research and Development: Guidelines for Developing Countries*. Westview Press, Boulder, CO.

Sharpe, B. 1990. Nutrition and the commercialisation of agriculture in Northern Province. In: Wood, A.P., Kean, S.A., Milimo, J.T. and Warren, D.M. (eds.) *The Dynamics of Agricultural Policy and Reform in Zambia*. Iowa State University Press, Ames, IA.

Simon, H. 1967. The job of a college president. *Educational Record* 58: 68–78.

Sollows, J., Jonjuabsong, L. and Hwa-Kham, A. 1991. NGO-government interaction in rice-fish farming and other aspects of sustainable agricultural development in Thailand. *Agricultural Research and Extension Network Paper* 28. ODI, London.

Sotomayor, O. 1991. GIA and the new Chilean public sector: the dilemmas of successful NGO influence over the state. *Agricultural Administration (Research and Extension) Network Paper* 30. ODI, London.

Sperling, L. 1989. *Farmer Participation and the Development of Bean Varieties in Rwanda*. Mimeo, CIAT, Butare.

Sumberg, J.E. 1991. NGOs and Agriculture at the Margin: Research, Participation and Sustainability in West Africa *Agricultural Administration (Research and Extension) Network Paper* 27. ODI, London.

Sumberg, J.E. and Okali, C. 1989. Farmers, on-farm research and new technology. In: Chambers, R., Pacey, A. and Thrupp, L-A. (eds.) *Farmer First: Farmer Innovation and Agricultural Research*. Intermediate Technology Publications Ltd., London.

Sutherland, A.J. and Drinkwater, M.J. 1990. Food security: a farming systems perspective. Paper presented at the *Planning Division/ARPT Seminar on Adaptive Research Data, Planning and Policy, Siavonga, 13–16 November*, ARPT, Siavonga, Zambia.

Swift, J. 1979. Notes on traditional knowledge, modern knowledge and rural development. *IDS Bulletin* 10(2): 41–43.

Swift, J. 1989. Why are rural people vulnerable to famine? *IDS Bulletin* 20(2): 8–15.

TAC. 1988. *Sustainable Agricultural Production: Implications for International Agricultural Research*. Technical Assistance Committee (TAC) Secretariat of the Consultative Group on International Agricultural Research. FAO, Rome.

TAC. 1993. *The Ecoregional Approach to Research in the CGIAR: Report of the TAC/Center Directors Working Group*. TAC Secretariat of the Consultative Group on International Agricultural Research, March 1993. FAO, Rome.

Taylor, C. 1992. *Milk, Honey and Money: Changing Concepts in Rwandan Healing*. Smithsonian Institute, Washington and London.

Tendler, J. 1976. *Inter-Country Evaluation of Small Farmer Organizations in Ecuador and Honduras*. Program Evaluation Study. United States Agency for International Development (USAID), Washington DC.

Thiele G., Davies, P. and Farrington, J. 1988. Strength in diversity: innovation in agricultural technology development in Eastern Bolivia. *Agricultural Administration (R&E) Network Paper* 1. ODI, London.

Thomas-Slater, B., Kabutha, C. and Ford, R. 1991. Traditional village institutions in environmental management. *From the Ground Up Case Study Series* 1. The Center for International Development and Environment, World Resources Institute, Washington, DC, and the African Centre for Technology Studies, Nairobi.

Thompson, J. 1991. Combining local knowledge and expert assistance in natural resource management. *From the Ground Up Case Study Series* 2. The Center for International Development and Environment, World Resources Institute, Washington, DC, and the African Centre for Technology Studies, Nairobi.

Thrupp, L-A. 1989. Legitimizing local knowledge: from displacement to empowerment for Third World people. *Agriculture and Human Values* 3: 13–25.

TNAU/IIED, 1992. *Participatory Rural Appraisal for Agricultural Research at Aruppukottai, Tamil Nadu.* Department of Agricultural Economics, Centre for Agricultural and Rural Development Studies, Tamil Nadu Agricultural University, Coimbatore and IIED, London.

Uphoff, N. 1986. *Local Institutional Development: An Analytical Sourcebook, with Cases.* Kumarian Press, West Hartford, CT.

Uphoff, N. 1992a. Local institutions and participation for sustainable development. *IIED Gatekeeper Series* SA31. Sustainable Agriculture Programme, IIED, London.

Uphoff, N. 1992b. *Learning from Gal Oya: Possibilities for Participatory Development and Post-Newtonian Social Science.* Cornell University Press, Ithaca, NY.

UPWARD 1990. *Proceedings of the Inaugural Planning Workshop on the User's Perspective With Agricultural Research and Development, Los Banos, Philippines.*

van den Berg, H. 1989. *La Tierra no da así no Más. Los Ritos Agrícolas en la Religión de los Aymaras-Cristianos.* CEDLA, Amsterdam.

van der Ploeg, J.D. 1986. The agricultural labour process and commoditization. In: Long, N. *et al. The Commoditization Debate: Labour Process, Strategy and Social Network.* Wageningen Agricultural University, The Netherlands.

van der Ploeg, J.D. 1989. Knowledge systems, metaphor and interface: the case of potatoes in the Peruvian highlands. In: Long, N. (ed.) *Encounters at the Interface: a Perspective of Social Discontinuities in Rural Development. Wageningse Sociologishce Studies, 27.* Wageningen Agricultural University, The Netherlands.

van der Ploeg, J.D. 1993. Potatoes and knowledge. In: Hobart, M. (ed.) *An Anthropological Critique of Development: The Growth of Ignorance.* Routledge, London and New York.

van der Ploeg, J.D. and Bolhuis, E.E. 1985. *Boerenarbeid en Stijlen van landbouwbeoefening Proefschrift.* RU Leiden, The Netherlands.

Vasimalai, M. 1993. Professional Assistance for Development Action (PRADAN): an NGO de-mystifies and scales down technology. In: Farrington, J. and Lewis, D.J. (eds.) *Non-Governmental Organizations and the State in Asia.* Routledge, London.

Velez, R. 1991. Primeras experiencias con un nuevo modelo de transferencia de tecnología. Paper presented at *Taller regional para América del Sur: Generación y Transferencia de Tecnología Agropecuaria; el papel de las ONGs y el Sector Público.* 2–7 December. Santa Cruz, Bolivia.

Villarreal, M. 1990. *A Struggle Over Images: Issues on Power, Gender and Intervention in a Mexican Village.* MSc. Thesis. Wageningen Agricultural University, The Netherlands.

Villarreal, M. 1992. The poverty of practice: power, gender and intervention from an actor-oriented perspective. In: Long, N. and Long, A. (eds.) *Battlefields of Knowledge: The Interlocking of Theory and Practice in Social Research and Development.* Routledge, London.

Vitebsky, P. 1993. 'Shamanism' as local knowledge in a cosmopolitan world. Unpublished paper presented to the *Association of Social Anthropologists' Decennial Conference*, 26–31 July, Oxford, 26–31 July.

Voss, J. 1992. Conserving and increasing on-farm genetic diversity: farmer management of varietal bean mixtures in Central Africa. In: Moock, J. and Rhoades, R. (eds.) *Diversity, Farmer Knowledge and Sustainability.* Cornell University Press, Ithaca.

Warren, D. 1991. Using indigenous knowledge in agricultural development. *Discussion Paper* 127. World Bank, Washington, DC.

Waters-Bayer, A. 1988a. Dairying by settled Fulani agropastoralists in central Nigeria. *Farming Systems and Resource Economics in the Tropics* 4. Wissenschaftsverlag Vauk, Kiel.

Waters-Bayer, A. 1988b. Soybean daddawa: an innovation by Nigerian women. *ILEIA Newsletter* 4(3): 8–9.

Watson, H.R. and Laquihon, W.A. 1993. The Mindanao Baptist Rural Life Centre's Sloping Agricultural Land Technology (SALT) research and extension in the Philippines. In: Farrington, J. and Lewis, D.J. (eds.) *Non-Governmental Organizations and the State in Asia*. Routledge, London.

Watts, M. and Carney, J. 1990. Manufacturing dissent: work, gender and the politics of meaning in a peasant society. *Africa* 60 (2): 207–241.

Welbourn, A. 1991. RRA and the analysis of difference. *RRA Notes* 14. IIED, London.

Wellard, K. and Copestake, J.G. (eds.) 1993. *Non-Governmental Organizations and the State in Africa*. Routledge, London.

Wilson, E.O. (ed.) 1988. *Biodiversity*. National Academy Press, Washington DC.

Young, K. and Evans, A. 1989. *Gender Issues in Household Labour Allocation: The Transformation of a Farming System in Northern Province, Zambia*. Report prepared for ODA's Economic and Social Research Committee, London.

Younger, S.D. and Bonkoungou, E. 1989. Burkina Faso: The Projet Agro-Forestier: a case study of agricultural research and extension. In: World Bank. *Successful Development in Africa: Case Studies of Projects, Programs and Policies*. Economic Development Institute, Washington DC.

Index

'actors' 3, 6, 48, 112, 173–4
adaptive change 33, 34, 155
Adaptive Research Planning Teams
    (ARPTs) 36–8, 80, 133–6, 244
Aga Khan Rural Support Programme
    (AKRSP) 118–24, 248–52
'agency' 48
Agrarian Research and Training
    Institute (ARTI) 213–20
agricultural research and extension *see*
    research and extension
agroforestry 20, 237
alley farming 237
Alley Farming Network for Tropical
    Africa (AFNETA) 237
Amazonia 224–7
Andes 48, 57, 90, 92, 171, 220
    knowledge & culture of 26, 57–8,
        60–4, 66–8
    see also Latin America
Australia 11, 192, 200, 248, 252–8

beans 36–7, 38, 62, 83–7, 159
beekeepers, women 45–6
beliefs 26, 134, 149
    mythology 60, 63, 68
    religion 71, 162–4
    rituals 61, 63, 65, 68, 86, 161–4
Beyond Farmer First (and Beyond
    Farmer First) 1–4, 7, 8, 17, 21–3,
    34, 187, 188–9, 242–3
bias 72, 78, 109, 115, 128–9, 173–4, 199,
    224–5
Bolivia 226
Botswana 192
bottom-up approach 19, 175, 217, 227,
    248
bureaucracy 44, 184, 193, 194, 220, 251
Burkino Faso 238–43

cassava 36, 38, 46, 81, 160, 161
catalysts 18, 22, 31, 115, 116, 118, 187,
    214–15
    see also facilitators
catchment planning 256
cattle 225

CGIAR *see* Consultative Group for
    International Agricultural
    Research
change 1, 2, 112–13, 242
Chivi-Zvishavane project 70–1, 73–4
CIMMYT *see* Maize and Wheat
    Improvement Centre
CIP *see* International Potato Centre
clusters and cluster types 134, 136, 137,
    138
coca 226
cocoyam 160
collaboration 106–7, 119, 147–50, 172,
    194, 200, 236–7, 250, 261–2
colonialism 69
communication 68–9, 74, 101, 112, 133,
    153–4, 163, 174, 217
    see also dialogue
community workers (CW) 72, 73,
    74
complementarity 32–3, 77, 87
COMUNIDEC 171, 172, 173, 174
conflict 21, 74, 121, 214
    co-operative 134, 138
    creative 3, 111, 115
    system 134, 138
conservation 54, 71, 239, 252
Consultative Group for International
    Agricultural Research
    (CGIAR) 10, 19, 59, 195, 227,
    233–4
context *see* socio-political context
co-ordinator 257
cosmology 58, 61, 62, 66, 69
Costa Rica 170, 175

dairying 144–6
decentralization 9, 53, 185, 189, 195,
    223, 248, 251
DELTA (Development Education
    Leadership Teams in Action)
    110–11, 114, 115
democracy 9, 53, 189, 251–2
development 18, 33, 53–4, 72, 206
Development Education Programme
    (DEP) 51–2

297

India 117–24, 142, 248–52
indigenous/local knowledge 18–19,
    55–8, 60–1, 70, 75, 81–2, 125, 127,
    165–6
    see also Andes, knowledge of;
        indigenous technical knowledge;
        rural people's knowledge
indigenous management 52–5, 70–1
indigenous technical knowledge
    (ITK) 18–19, 25, 101, 105,
    165
Indonesia 150–4, 247
information *see* knowledge
INIAP *see* National Agricultural
    Research Institute
insects 149–52, 200, 247
'insiders' 3, 6, 22–3, 101
Institute of Development Studies
    (IDS) 2
institutions
    changing 4, 9, 11–12, 181–5, 242, 259,
        261–3, 265
    educational 11, 199–200, 249, 258–60,
        261
    links 9, 188, 196, 203, 236, 237
    local/village 53, 118–24, 197–8, 205,
        244
    support 117–18, 122, 188–9, 249, 250
integrated pest management
    (IPM) 150–4
interactions/interfaces/intersection 6,
    20–1, 31, 43–4, 57, 103, 115, 125,
    164
    social systems 20–1, 27–8, 43–7
    govt/official-local/village 44–6, 48,
        72–3
intercropping 19, 20, 36, 150, 160
interdisciplinarity 41, 114, 134, 228,
    236, 238
interest groups 114, 173, 224–5
International Agricultural Research
    Centres (IARC) 9, 59, 196
International Centre for Research in
    Agroforestry (ICRAF) 232
International Potato Centre (CIP)
    58–9, 232, 234
International Rice Research Institute
    (IRRI) 227–31, 234–5
investment 122–4, 145, 239, 251
IPM *see* integrated pest management
irrigation 58, 213–14, 255
    see also water management

Kenya 51–2, 110, 189
Kissi people (Guinea) 78
knowledge 3, 15–16, 35, 46–7, 55–6, 106
    conflict 57, 64–6
    context 19, 24–8, 36–9, 42–3, 46–7,
        49–50, 57, 70, 77–9, 101, 169, 243
    creation/generation 42–3, 49, 59, 99,
        101, 124–5, 255–6
    cultural 18, 57, 61
    differences 3, 25, 47, 55, 57, 64–6, 71,
        75–9, 101, 112, 148
    exchange 21, 68, 153–4
    gaps and ignorance 48, 78, 101, 102,
        149
    nature of 3, 19, 21, 24, 25, 34–6, 40,
        42–3, 49–50, 54–7, 100
    secret 78–9, 83–5, 87
    tacit 155
    transmission/dissemination 26–8,
        42–3, 49, 153–4, 243
    use 47, 58, 129–33, 243
    see also Andes, knowledge of;
        indigenous/local knowledge;
        indigenous technical knowledge;
        rural people's knowledge
Kouranko people (Guinea) 76–7, 78,
    79

land literacy 248, 253–4
Landcare 11, 252–8
language 24, 54, 86, 87, 146
Latin America 90, 170–7, 220
    see also Andes
leaders/leadership 70–3, 153, 174, 198,
    201, 215–17, 251–3, 257
learning 134, 165, 183, 188–9, 199,
    258–63, 265
    experiential 116, 143, 260
    experimental 157
    mutual 32, 107, 115, 185, 187
    process 116, 159, 184, 217–18
    see also education; training
lifeworlds 39, 44, 46
livelihood strategies 83, 89, 91–2, 108,
    124, 126, 132, 135, 222
local knowledge *see* indigenous
    knowledge; rural people's
    knowledge

maize 36, 37, 38, 138–9, 229
Maize and Wheat Improvement Centre
    (CIMMYT) 231–2